# True Patent Value

## Defining Quality in Patents and Patent Portfolios

LARRY M. GOLDSTEIN

Published by True Value Press

ISBN-10: 0-9895541-0-4

ISBN-13: 978-0-9895541-0-7

*This book is dedicated to all those people who had a dream, overcame self-doubts, and did their best to make the dream true.*

"Had we but world enough, and time,
This coyness...were no crime...
[But] though we cannot make our sun
Stand still, yet we will make him run."

— English poet and politician Andrew Marvell (1621–1678), "To His Coy Mistress"

*Carpe diem, quam minimum credula postero.*
"Seize the day, putting as little trust as possible in the future."

— Roman poet Horace (65–8 BCE), Odes 1.11

"And if not now, when?"

— *Ethics of the Fathers*, Chapter 1, Verse 14

# Summary Table of Contents

# Detailed Table of Contents

## PART I — FUNDAMENTAL CONCEPTS

## Part II — Examples of Good Patents and Good Patent Portfolios

## PART III — SUMMARY

## Appendix, Bibliography, and Indexes

# Acknowledgments

Acknowledgments: Thank you to the following people for having reviewed all or portions of the book: Jonathan A. Barney (Founder and CEO of PatentRatings, LLC, Newport Beach, California), Michael L. Craner (President of MediaComm Innovations, Philadelphia), Dr. Benjamin Fechner (German patent attorney, Munich), Brian N. Kearsey (Founder of the W-CDMA patent pool, London), Joseph Kessler (Managing Director at FIG LLC, Intellectual Property Finance Group, Tel Aviv), John C. Paul (Partner at Finnegan, Henderson, Farabow, Garrett & Dunner, Washington, D.C.), Grant K. Rowan (Partner at WilmerHale, Washington, D.C.), Richard N. Weiner (Corporate and Securities attorney, Philadelphia), and Gal Zuckerman (Engineer and entrepreneur, Tel Aviv).

I would also like to note several people who took a chance on me, in one way or another, including John Sarallo, Jacob Katz, Menachem Kenan, Eli Jacobi, Brian Kearsey, Bill McCall, Andrew Ramer, and Joseph Kessler. Thank you, my friends.

And to my wife, Jessica, who took the biggest chance of all.

# Preface

"And further, my child, be forewarned: of the making of books there is no end, and much study is a weariness of the flesh". (Ecclesiastes, 12:12)

## Why another book about patents?

I am a patent lawyer, registered to practice before the United States Patent and Trademark Office, with a background in physics and communication technology. For the past few years, I have focused on patent commerce, analyzing thousands of patents for purchase or sale. I have worked on behalf of dozens of clients, and they always ask me the same question:

*"How do I know if my patent's any good?"*

In cases involving more than one patent, the question may be asked a little differently, such as: "How do I know if my patent portfolio's any good?" But in all the years that I have been analyzing patents, no one has ever asked me:

*"How do I know if I have a crummy, lousy, worthless patent?"*

Patent owners are hopeful they have something of value. They are averse to considering the possibility they may have junk. But patent "value" is very hard to determine. Patents are not buildings or machinery that can be touched, tested, tweaked, or repaired. Patents are abstract, intangible, and subject to a multitude of invisible conditions and considerations.

I am writing this book to try to help you answer the essential question, "Is my patent any good?"

A secondary question — "*How* good is my patent?" — is a question of *financial or quantitative* value. This secondary question is not the main focus of this book, although the many examples we consider here will provide insights about this question as well

## Who will find this book useful?

This book is intended for people who want or need to understand patent value. That includes, in particular:

1. Patent Attorneys and Patent Agents: You are writing a patent, and you want guidelines to understand whether this particular patent is good and, more generally, the overall concept of "patent value". The book is intended to give you a concentration of real cases in which specific actions created (or failed to create) valuable patents.
2. Engineers and Entrepreneurs: You are reviewing an application drafted for you by a patent attorney or patent agent. You want to know before filing if the application would result in a good patent (assuming the patent office allows it), or perhaps you want tips on what you can do to improve the value of the patent. If you are interested in selling or licensing-out the patent, then you will also want to understand the patent's financial value.

3. Corporate Executives, Members on Boards of Directors, Patent Brokers (and others engaged in patent commerce): You own a patent and you want to do something with it, but you need to understand its value before deciding what to do. This group includes also patent brokers advising such executives or directors.
4. Investment Bankers, Investment Advisors, Equity Analysts, and Corporate Brokers: You or your company does not own patents, but you are analyzing a company's patents as an equity analyst, as a potential investor in the company, or as a corporate broker, trying to figure out if the patents in question are any good, and how they might impact the value of the company.

If you see yourself in any of these scenarios, then this book is for you. *However, depending on who you are, you may wish to read only specific parts of the book*, and skip the rest (more on this below).

## What does this book cover?

When we ask if a patent is "good", we are really asking if it has high quality from an objective point of view. A patent is objectively good if:

1. It has "good claims", meaning that the claims are well written, and
2. The claims have "good support" in the written description.

To say that a patent is "good" means that the people who

wrote the patent did a good job — both the description of the invention and the claims are as good as they can be.

However, to say that a patent is "good" does *not mean* that the patent is "valuable". For a patent to be not just "good" but also "valuable" requires, in addition:

1. There is significant infringement by outside parties of the patent's claims, and
2. No events have happened, external to the patent, which reduce or destroy the patent's value. A patent may have been very valuable at one point, but external events can destroy its value.

Preface Chart 1 illustrates these concepts, with four concentric circles.

**Preface Chart 1: The Hierarchy of Patent Value**

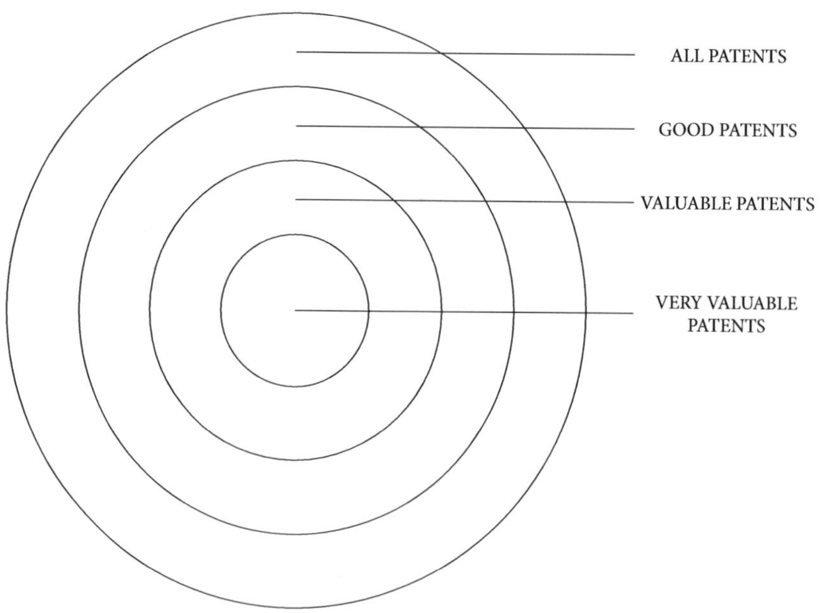

As shown in Preface Chart 1, a "good patent" (meaning a high-quality patent) may or may not be valuable, but high quality is a prerequisite to value. In other words, if a patent is *not* high-quality (meaning it is not a good patent), it cannot have value.[1]

The concentric circles represent different concepts:

- The largest circle, "All Patents", is the world of existing patents, including patents that are both "good" and those that are not good.
- The next circle, "Good Patents", includes only patents with good descriptions and good claims, meaning that the patents have been written as well as possible for the subject matter.
- The next circle, "Valuable Patents," includes the "good patents" which are also infringed and whose value has not been destroyed by external events. Not all "good patents" are also "valuable patents", but the circles are concentric because only a "good patent" may be a "valuable patent". *The circle "Valuable Patents" is the focus of this book. All of the case studies, the lessons learned, and the principles discussed are intended to define patents which are both "good" and "valuable". These are the patents with "true value".*
- The smallest circle, "Very Valuable Patents", includes those "valuable patents" which have passed through

---

1 There may be cases where people are uncertain about the quality of the patent, but will still value it very highly due to the broad scope of the claims. This might be the case, for example, with patent US 5,133,079, which is discussed in one of the case studies in Chapter 5. The main idea remains, however — a patent that *is known* to have low quality is not a valuable patent.

full market and financial analyses and have been found to be not just "valuable", but "very valuable". This book discusses market and financial analysis, but only in passing. The purpose of this book rather is to define the patent's internal quality and value, which form the basis of market and financial analysis.

This book is, in essence, an explanation of the concepts just noted. Discussions include: "What is a good patent claim?"; "What is good support for the claims?"; "What is broad scope of claim coverage?"; "What are external events that destroy patent value?"

In the end, the claims of the patent will determine its value. Giles S. Rich, formerly the Chief Judge of what was then the sole appellate court in the United States for patent decisions of lower federal courts, famously wrote in 1990: "The name of the game is the claim."[2]

Identification of a "good patent" for inclusion in this book involved a two-step process.

1. The patent demonstrates some measure of validation by a person or party *other than the patent owner*. If there is no such validation, then the patent may or may not be "good" or "valuable", but it is not a candidate for inclusion in this book.
2. After identifying validated patents, I selected, based on years of reviewing thousands of patents, a few "good

---

2 Giles S. Rich, *The Extent of the Protection and Interpretation of Claims-American Perspectives*, 21 Int'l Rev. Indus. Prop. & Copyright L., 497, 499 (1990). Judge Rich meant that the scope of protection afforded by the patent can only be as broad as what the patent owner claims it to be. For this reason, this book focuses on a patent's claims, which is where the patent's value ultimately resides.

patents" which I felt best illustrate what you need to know about this subject.

What are the measures of validation used to identify "good patents?" I use five measures, which I call "gateways to validation":

1. Court Victory: The patent won a victory in court, which means that court litigation resulted in a multi-million dollar verdict for the patent's owner, or a multi-million settlement.
2. ITC Victory: The patent won a victory in an administrative proceeding such as that of the United States International Trade Commission ("ITC"), and the ITC issued an injunction preventing the infringer from importing the infringing product into the United States.
3. Sale: The patent was sold for a substantial amount of money.
4. Essential to a Technical Standard: The patent was accepted as a member of a patent pool with a wide market.
5. Seminal Patent: Patents which by their subject, their priority date,[3] and extremely heavy "forward citations" received, are groundbreaking or "seminal" patents.

These gateways do not, in themselves, determine that a patent is "valuable", but they do suggest that "value" might

[3] The "priority date" of a patent is the date on which the patent is considered to have been filed. If the patent does not rely on any earlier filing, then the "priority date" is simply the date the patent was first filed. If the patent specifically states that it relies on an earlier filing, then the priority date is the date of the earlier filing.

be found in this patent. "Value" may be wholly financial, in that money flows to the patent owner in (1) court victory, (3) sale of the patent, or (4) licensing revenue from a patent pool. "Value" might also be not financial primarily, but rather a competitive advantage, such as (2) an injunction against a competitor (issued by the ITC), or (5) a seminal patent (which creates a competitive advantage).

Some patents pass more than one gateway, as for example (1) court victory and (2) injunction, or (1) court victory and (5) seminal. The more gateways passed, the more likely the patent is to be a "good patent", the more likely it is to have "true value", and the more likely it is to be "very valuable" as illustrated in Preface Chart 1 above.

Not every patent that passes a gateway is a patent suitable to show what is meant by a "good patent." I reviewed many candidates that have passed one or more gateways, then selected several well-suited to illustrate the concept of a good patent.

The book is organized into three main parts:

*Part 1 — Basic Information About Patents:* Introduction to patent concepts (Chapter 1) and basic concepts of patent evaluation (Chapter 2).

*Part 2 — Case Histories that Illustrate Good Patents:* In-depth analysis of patents, organized by the five gateways cited above:

- Victory in court (Chapter 3), Victory at the ITC (Chapter 4), Sale (Chapter 5), Participation in a patent pool for a technical standard (Chapter 6), and "Seminal" or breakthrough patents (Chapter 7). Each of Chapters 3 — 7 is structured in the same way: an introduction to the topic followed by discussion of at least one claim in each of several patents, and concluding with a summarizing section called "Lessons Learned."

- Chapter 7 includes, in addition to reviews of individual patents, discussions of good "patent portfolios". A patent portfolio is a group of patents owned by one company or other entity. Understanding of what constitutes a "good patent portfolio" is important for everyone interested in patents, and particularly for the last two groups of interested parties listed above — corporate executives, corporate Directors, and patent brokers on the one hand; investment bankers, investment advisors, equity analysts, and corporate brokers, on the other hand.

*Part 3 — Conclusion:* A summary of lessons learned in Question & Answer format, and a Glossary of acronyms and key terms used in the book. Chapter 8 and the Glossary will be useful to everyone reading this book.

## What should you read?

If you have the time and interest to read the entire book, that would be best. However, if you are pressed for time, or if you want to focus on topics of particular interest to you, focus on the material in Preface Table 1 below, and skip the rest.

**Preface Table 1: Reading Recommendations**

| Who You Are | What to Read, in Which Order | Why |
|---|---|---|
| Patent Attorney or Agent | Chapters 8, then 3–7. Glossary as needed. | Chapter 8 is the Summary. Chapters 3–7 are case studies. |
| Engineer or Entrepreneur | Chapters 1–2, then 8, then "Lessons Learned" in 3–7. Glossary as needed. | Chapters 1–2 are the basis. Chapter 8 is the summary. In Chapters 3–7, you can use mainly the Lessons Learned. |
| Corporate Executives, Corporate Directors, Patent Brokers (and others engaged in patent commerce) | Chapters 1–2, then 8. Glossary as needed. If you need to understand patent portfolios, Chapter 7 also. | Chapters 1–2 are the basis. Chapter 8 is the summary. Chapter 7 discusses portfolio analysis, if you need that. |
| Investment Bankers, Investment Advisors, Equity Analysts, and Corporate Brokers | Chapters 1–2, then 8, then 7, Glossary as needed. | Chapters 1–2 are the basis. Chapter 8 is the summary. Chapter 7 is critical for understanding patent portfolios. |

# Chapter Summaries

## CHAPTER 1: An Introduction to Patents

This chapter introduces patents to people who do not have significant background in patent law. It provides a summarized view of some key points related to either (1) obtaining a patent from the patent office, or (2) revising a patent after it has issued in what is called a "reexamination proceeding".

## CHAPTER 2: Evaluating Patents

This chapter has three main topics.

First, there are many different ways to evaluate a patent, but all these ways may be organized into two main categories, which are "fundamental" evaluation and "financial" evaluation. The focus of this book is fundamental analysis, which considers the technology protection achieved by the patent. and which serves as the basis of financial value. The second broad evaluation category is quantitative or financial evaluation of patents, which answers the question, "How much money can you make in licensing or litigation?" This second category, financial evaluation, is mentioned at several points, but it is not the focus of this book.

Second, there are two kinds of fundamental analysis.

One kind is what I call "expert fundamental analysis" ("EFA" for short), which is analysis performed by an expert human evaluator reviewing the claims, the written description, and the prosecution history of the patent. The other kind is what I call "proxy fundamental analysis" ("PFA" for short), which is the use of pre-defined factors in an automated manner to attach a quality score to the patent. Both types of fundamental analysis are important, and both are explained, but the focus of this book is on expert fundamental analysis. In actual practice, analysis of a patent portfolio will probably include proxy fundamental analysis for all or most of the patents in the portfolio, and also expert fundamental analysis for the relatively few patents deemed worthy of a human evaluation.

Third, several key concepts are explained, particularly Point of Novelty (or "PON" for short), which is the specific innovation in a patent claim that is new and that creates value. In a formal sense, nothing in a patent is really "new", since everything in the world is either pre-existing or is based on pre-existing pieces. However, a Point of Novelty is the introduction of some structural component or procedural step into an environment that people did not consider prior to the introduction — in that sense, it is the specific component or step that is the Point of Novelty, and therefore the reason for which the patent was granted by the patent office.

## CHAPTER 3: Court Cases With Good Patents

This chapter has two main topics.

First, there is a very brief discussion of some basic information about patent litigation.

Second, four cases are presented in which patent litigation

led to multi-million dollar verdicts or large settlements. Why did these patents achieve these results? What makes these patents "good?"

## CHAPTER 4: ITC Cases with Good Patents

This chapter has three main topics.

First, litigation may occur either in court, or at an administrative body such as the United States International Trade Commission ("ITC"). There are differences between court litigation and ITC litigation. Some of these differences are explained.

Second, two cases are presented in which patent owners won ITC litigations. Why did the companies win? What made the patents "good"?

Third, five additional cases of ITC litigation are presented, but only in brief. Each additional case is focused on a single lesson to be learned from the case.

## CHAPTER 5: Sales of Good Patents

This chapter has two main topics.

First, there is a brief discussion of why patents seem to be attracting so much attention in today's market.

Second, patents may be sold individually, or as part of a patent portfolio. Two cases are presented, the first being the sale of an individual patent, and the second being an example of a patent sold as part of a large portfolio. Each case focuses solely on an individual patent, and not on a patent as part of a patent portfolio. (Patent portfolios are discussed in Chapter 7.)

## CHAPTER 6: "Essential" Patents in Pools

This chapter has three main topics.

First, the concept of a "patent pool" is explained. Standards bodies — usually public organizations — create technical standards that allow products to work together. Patents cover technology in a standard. If a standard cannot be implemented without infringing a particular patent, then that patent is considered "essential" to a standard. To get into a pool, a patent must pass the review of a technical and legal expert, who certifies that the patent is indeed "essential" to a technical standard and thus admissible to the pool. The pool is organized and administered by private bodies known as "patent pool administrators," which administer aggregations of essential patents admitted into the pool. The concept of "patent essentiality" is explained.

Second, a case is presented of a patent that was found essential and hence admitted into a patent pool. The case presented relates to a patent found essential to the electronic audiovisual standard MPEG-2.

Third, three cases are presented of patents that were found essential and admitted into the patent pool for the cellular technology known as third generation Wideband CDMA ("W-CDMA"). The cases are preceded by a brief discussion of basic information related to power control in a cellular system — this brief discussion will help you understand the three cases.

## CHAPTER 7: Seminal Patents

This chapter has two main topics.

First, the concepts of "forward non-self citations" and "seminal patents" are explained.

Second, three cases are presented of patents that have hundreds of forward non-self citations. Each case includes lessons about what are good patents, and additional lessons about what are good patent portfolios.

## CHAPTER 8: Summary

When all is said and done, what can we say about patent "value"? What are the criteria by which a patent's true value is determined? Lessons learned are summarized in this chapter. The chapter is presented in a Q&A format. This chapter is not a mere copying of the lessons from the prior chapters, but rather summarizes such lessons by topic. The following topics are presented:

- What is a good patent?
- What are valuable claims?
- What is good support for claims?
- What are external events that destroy patent value?
- What is a good patent portfolio?
- Final thoughts

## Afterword

Comments on the role of patents in business and technology.

## Glossary (Including Acronyms)

Approximately 80 terms used in this book are listed and defined. The Glossary should be read with Chapter 8.

## Appendix

The Appendix is patent US 5,133,079, discussed in Chapter 5. It is presented so that you may understand the specific sections of a patent, and how a patent is structured.

# Part I

# Fundamental Concepts

## Chapter 1

# An Introduction to Patents

This chapter gives you an understanding of some basic concepts of patents. No prior knowledge, technical or legal, is needed.

I. Patents — Basic Concepts:
   (1) Types of Intellectual Property
   (2) Utility and non-utility patents[4]
   (3) Patent territoriality
   (4) The two basic fields of technology: ICT and BCP[5]
   (5) Relevant parts of a utility patent
   (6) Relevant sections of the United States patent statute[6]

---

4 There are several kinds of patents, explained further in the text. This book deals only with what are called "utility patents", which protect the structure and/or operation of an invention, but not its design.

5 Patent professionals divide the world of patents into two very general kinds of technologies. One general kind of technology is called "ICT", an acronym for "information & communication technologies". The second general kind of technology is "BCP", an acronym for "biotechnology, chemical, and pharmaceutical". These concepts are further developed below.

6 This book is focused on U.S. patents. Patents in other jurisdictions, including various locations in Asia, Canada, and various locations in Europe, are also mentioned, particularly in Chapter 7. However, the geographic focus of this book is on U.S. patents. *Nevertheless the definition of a "good patent" and the principles of high-quality patents discussed in this book apply to **every** country that has utility patents.* There are some differences in local patent

(7) Structure of a patent claim
(8) Independent and dependent patent claims
(9) Patent claim formats you should know
II. Patents — Procedures at the Patent Office:
(1) Getting a patent
(2) Reexamination

## I. Patents — Basic Concepts:

### *(1) Types of Intellectual Property*

Patents make up one kind of "intellectual property". There are other kinds of intellectual property — trademarks, service marks, copyrights, trade names, trade secrets, etc. — that are not of interest to us here. Many kinds of questions can arise with conflicts of intellectual property, or ways of coordinating different kinds of intellectual property, to help the company or owner of the patent. For example, one of the classic questions in the field is, "Should we file for a patent, which will cause us to reveal the technology, or should we maintain the technology as a trade secret?" That may be an interesting question, but it is not a question relevant to this book, which focuses on the question of patent quality.[7]

---

statutes and judicial decisions that will impact the strength of particular patents in particular countries, but the basic principles of good patents do not change from country to country.

[7] Probably the most famous trade secret in the United States, mentioned time and again, is the secret formula for Coca Cola. The Coca Cola company might have patented this formula, which would have given the company a monopoly on the formula during the life of the patent, but that patent would have expired long ago. Coca Cola definitely made the correct decision by maintaining a trade secret rather than patenting the secret formula, but each company will make its own decision about the best way to protect its confidential information.

Intellectual property and other intangible assets make up the great majority of corporate value in the United States today, as depicted in Chart 1–1 below.

**Chart 1–1: Tangible versus Intangible Assets**[8]

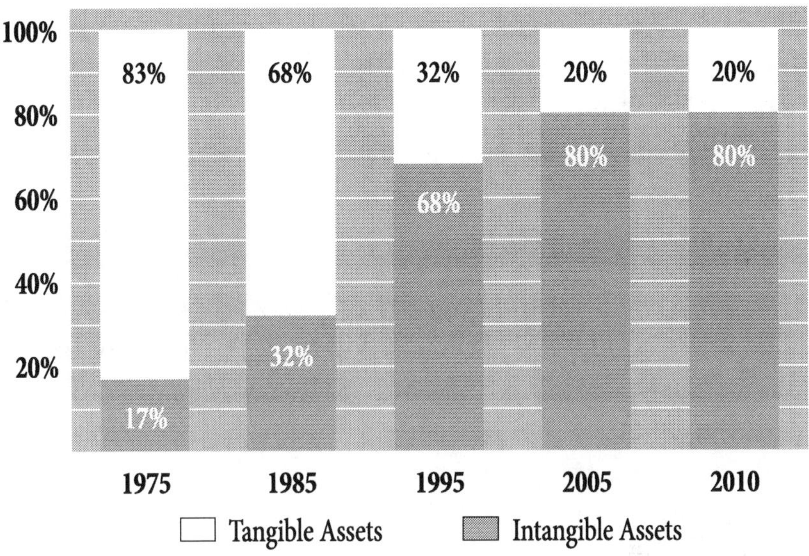


*Source: Ocean Tomo*

---

8 This chart was copied from the web site of Ocean Tomo, an Intellectual Capital Merchant Bank and the initiator of the public auction for patents. The chart's original name is "Components of S&P 500 Market Value", but I have renamed it to highlight the relative decline of tangible assets and the relative rise of intangible assets. Ocean Tomo explains that "intangible assets" are calculated as total market capitalization minus the book value of physical and financial assets. The term "intangible assets" generally includes both intellectual property of all types — patents, trademarks, copyrights, etc. — plus other intangibles such as goodwill and brand recognition. I will not attempt to assign a value to patents among various types of "intangible assets" listed in Chart 1–1, but there is little doubt that patents comprise a significant portion of the total value of those assets. This chart is available at http://www.oceantomo.com/productsandservices/investments/intangible-market-value. All Internet references are current as of May 22, 2013, unless stated otherwise.

## *(2) Utility and Non-Utility Patents*

The patent category of interest here is the "utility patent". Such patents protect the structure of an invention, or the way the invention works, or both. There are other patent categories, but they are not relevant here.[9] Nor are we interested in patent applications that have not yet become patents. Applications have potential value, but determining value prior to patent issuance is extremely difficult, since claims may be amended or entirely disallowed before issuance.

## *(3) Patent Territoriality*

Patents are "territorial", which means that they are valid only in the country of issuance. For example, a patent in the United States cannot be enforced in Germany, and vice versa. This book focuses on U.S. patents.[10]

## *(4) Two Basic Fields of Technology: ICT and BCP*

Patents can cover basically any kind of technology known

---

9 There are "design patents, which cover the way a product looks or feels. Design patents are mentioned, but only in passing. There are "plant patents", which patent certain kinds of new plants. These are not discussed at all in this book.

10 Patents in other countries may also be valuable. For example, important patent litigation often occurs in the district courts of Düsseldorf, Germany, or in the High Court of Justice in London, England. Also, in large-scale patent wars, particularly in the cellular industry, multiple lawsuits in Asia, Europe, and the U.S., are not uncommon. The importance of other jurisdictions, such as Japan, the People's Republic of China, and the Republic of Korea, is rising. Still, the U.S. remains the largest market for technology goods, and the location with the highest damage awards for patent infringement. Future editions of this book may include analysis of European and Asian patents, but the current edition focuses on U.S. patents.

to humankind. However, the great majority of technologies fall into one of two broad categories: ICT, short for "information & communication technologies", and BCP, short for "biotechnology, chemical, and pharmaceutical". These acronyms encompass well-known distinctions between two fundamentally different kinds of technologies. Some of the differences are summarized in Table 1–1 below.

**Table 1–1: ICT versus BCP Technologies**

| Characteristic | ICT | BCP | Notes |
|---|---|---|---|
| **Full name** | Information & communication technologies | Biotechnology, chemical, and pharmaceutical | |
| **Basic science** | Physics | Biology, Chemistry | |
| **System feature** | Networked | Non-networked | A critical difference |
| **Technical Standards** | Created by quasi-public bodies or voluntary forums | Usually no technical standard; usually created by one entity; requires government approval. | The joint nature of ICT, versus the solo nature for BCP, is a critical difference between these two areas. |
| **Patent commerce** | Licensing, cross-licensing, and sale | Licensing and cross-licensing. Sale is not common. | "Cross-licensing", when it occurs, often includes multiple R&D or manufacturing companies. |
| **Patent claim transition** | "comprising" only | "comprising" or "consisting" | Explained below |

This book focuses on ICT, not on BCP, for two reasons:

First, there are substantial differences in the natures of these technology areas, and in the impacts of patents. A chief characteristic of ICT is that, typically, many companies contribute to a working system. In the cellular world, for example, one company may make a cell phone, another may make a base station, and a third may make the network controller. The scenario is far more complicated, however, in that multiple companies may make hardware or software components for the phone, the base station, and the network controller. There may be hundreds or even thousands of patents involved in the provision of a single service to a single cellular telephone.

This complexity is called "system networking" or the "network economy." In ICT, generally the technology required to make a system work is not owned by one entity, but is rather "fragmented" among dozens to hundreds of entities. ICT industries, such as "cellular" or "cable television" or "the Internet", are generally considered to be "networked industries" subject to the problem of fragmentation of patent ownership among many different companies.[11] For this reason, in ICT industries much more than in BCP, patents must be sold, bought, licensed, or otherwise acquired in whole or for specific purposes, to provide meaningful products and services

---

[11] The concept of the "network economy" is discussed in my prior book, Larry M. Goldstein and Brian N. Kearsey, *Technology Patent Licensing: An International Reference on 21st Century Patent Licensing, Patent Pools and Patent Platforms*, (Aspatore Books, a division of Thomson Reuters, Boston, Massachusetts, 2004), at pp.23–26. On fragmentation of patent ownership in a network economy, see Ilkka Rahnasto, *Intellectual Property Rights, External Effects and Anti-Trust Law: Leveraging IPRs in the Communications Industry*, (Oxford University Press, 2003), at pp.21 and 174–181.

to customers. The inter-dependency of thousands of patents is one factor that creates a need and a demand for evaluation of patents involved in patent commerce.[12]

Second, patents in ICT are created by large companies, small companies, individuals, and diverse combinations of entities. This is part of the reason that ownership of patents is so fragmented in ICT industries. By contrast, in BCP, individuals typically do not file patents for new drugs. Therefore, the variety of people asking the key question of a patent's value — "Is my patent any good?" — is greater in ICT than in BCP industries, although the question is of course important for all technical areas. For these reasons, and in the interest of brevity, this book focuses on ICT patents.

### *(5) Relevant Parts of a Utility Patent*

A utility patent is a grant of a right by the government to the owners of the patents to exclude other people from making, using, or selling the patented invention. Contrary to popular belief, a patent is *not* a "right to practice an invention" but rather a negative right to stop others from practicing the invention. Further, the patent does not provide for automatic exclusion of an infringer — rather, the patent owner must

---

12 I have called the difference between ICT patents and BCP patents "networked" versus "non-networked". Some people follow this nomenclature. However, another way of looking at the difference is to call ICT "complex technologies" and BCP "discrete technologies". For example, in the web site of the Swedish company Avvika AB, there is a clear discussion of the difference between "complex technologies", such as the technologies relevant to a laptop computer, and the "discrete technologies", with the example being a prescription drug. See the web site at www.avvika.com/patentengineering4.html. See also the article, "Patents: a necessary evil", January 5, 2002, at http://news.cnet.com/2009-1001-801896.html.

take affirmative action to prevent infringement, by either threatening to sue or by initiating a lawsuit.

It is commonly said that "a patent is a sword, never a shield." In other words, you may use a patent to stop other people from practicing your invention, but your patent will not stop other people from threatening you with their own patents (unless your threat deters the counter-threat, which does happen often). A patent owner may sell its patent, or license-out the right to use the patent, but the interest conveyed may never be more than what the patent owner originally had — therefore, a patent owner never sells or licenses-out a "right to practice the invention" or a "right to make the product discussed in the invention". Rather, the patent owner licenses-out a promise that the licensee will not be sued for infringing the patent, or the patent owner sells to a buyer the right to stop others from using the patent.[13]

The patented invention is described in the document known as the "issued utility patent." The three general parts of a patent are (1) the "written description" of the invention, which describes in detail how to make and use the invention; (2) the figures (or "drawings"), that show how the invention

---

13 According to this explanation, patents function as tools of aggression, not as tools of defense. In that sense, to say that a patent affords the patentee "protection" is a misnomer — the patent threatens others, but does not really protect the owner from lawsuits that may be filed by other people. Nevertheless, the phrase "patent protection" is used universally to summarize rights provided by the claims in the patent. It is understood that the "protection" comes from being able to threaten and to sue others who might threaten and sue you. The phrase "patent protection" and the word "protection" are used throughout the book — they mean exactly what everyone in the patent industry understands, namely, patents cannot prevent the filing of hostile lawsuits, but they may nevertheless deter such lawsuits by threatening similar legal action against the hostile parties.

is structured and how it operates; and (3) the claims which define the boundaries of the protection afforded by the patent. These three parts together are also sometimes called "the specification".

A patent will now be explained with specific reference to the US 5,133,079, attached at the end of the book as the Appendix. This patent is also the subject of one of the case studies in Chapter 5 of the book.

The "written description" includes a number of sections, some of which are legally required, and others of which are not. Here are sections typically in a written description:

— *Title of Invention*: Required. The title of US 5,133,079, is "Method and Apparatus for Distribution of Movies," which appears at the very beginning of the patent.
— *Inventor(s)*: Required. The inventors are Douglas J. Ballantyne and Michael Mulhall, listed under the title.
— *Assignee*: If there is an assignee, its name may be recorded or not, at the patentee's option. No assignee is listed in US 5,133,079. If there were an assignee of record, it would be listed under the inventors. The fact that no assignee is listed does not mean that the patent has not been assigned, but solely that no assignment was recorded with the patent office at the time the patent was published.
— *Abstract*: Required. The Abstract of US 5,133,079, appearing also on the first page, begins, "A new and useful method for distribution of movies for viewing on a customer's television set."
— *Cross-reference* to other patents or patent applications that establish a priority date for the current document: Required. There is no cross-reference for an

early priority date in US 5,133,079. If there were such a reference, it would appear in Column 1, directly below the title and directly above "Background of the Invention".

— *Field of Invention*: Optional. This is a very short statement of the general area of the patent. This sometimes appears in patents, but other times it does not. If it appears at all, it might be presented as "Field of Technology", or simply "Field". (There is no "Field" in US 5,133,079.)[14]

— *Background of the Invention*: Optional. This section, which is located in Column 1 of US 5,133,079, almost always appears in modern patents, although it often does not appear in patents from the 1960's and earlier.[15]

---

14 For such a short section, the Field of Invention can be surprisingly difficult to write. It should not be overly broad, which could invite an examiner or a court to expand the range of possible prior art applicable against the claims, nor should it be too narrow, which might be used by a court or the ITC to limit the scope of the invention. Because of its problematic nature, the Field of Invention is often left out. Nevertheless, the Field of Invention may be useful to communicate quickly the general area of the patent. Also, some patent practitioners may use the Field of Invention to direct the patent application to particular examination groups within the PTO. See Robert D. Fish, *Strategic Patenting*, (Trafford Publishing, Victoria, British Colombia, Canada, 2007), at pp.207–209.

15 A well-written Background of Invention does *not* describe the invention, but may describe the problem that is solved by the invention, and in that way help explain the nature of the invention. (The invention itself is described only in the Summary of the Invention and the Detailed Description of the Invention, not in the Background section.) If you are writing a patent, I highly recommend that you include the Background of Invention section in your application. Evaluators reviewing a patent for possible commerce will often look at the Background, so a clear statement here can help communicate your invention to interested parties, and in that way increase patent value. People will not pay money to buy or license-in patents they do not understand.

— *Summary of the Invention*, or "Brief Summary": optional. This section, which appears in the middle of Column 1 of US 5,133,079, almost always appears in modern patents.[16]
— *Brief Description of the Drawings*: optional. This section appears in Column 2 of US 5,133,079. Generally, the "Brief Description" is a positive thing to include in a patent, because it usually takes very little time to draft, it may be written in a manner that does not limit the invention, and it helps evaluators understand the invention.
— *Detailed Description of the Invention*: required. This is the key description of the invention. This section will describe each element in each drawing of the patent. In US 5,133,079, this section begins at the bottom of Column 2, and continues through Column 6. The length is not unusual. The "Detailed Description" generally comprises more than 50% of the written part of the patent.

The written description, as defined in the sections above, is supplemented by three additional parts of a patent.

— *Figures*: The inclusion in the patent of "Figures", also called "Drawings", is not required — it is, by law, optional. Nevertheless, in my experience, drawings are *always* included in utility applications. It is generally preferred to have more drawings, with more possible

16 As with Background, the Summary is both optional and recommended. It is optional in that it is not legally required. It is recommended in that it helps enormously in communicating to the reader what the invention is about. In modern patents, the Summary section almost always appears.

embodiments of the invention — more alternative structures, more alternative usages, more alternative combinations, etc. In US 5,133,079, there are seven drawings, where Figures 1A and 1B are described as "flow charts", Figures 2 is a described as a schematic diagram of a method and apparatus, and Figures 3–6 are described as schematic diagrams of various apparatuses.

— *Claims*: at least one claim is required. The claims, as issued by the patent office, set the scope of protection. The claims are of critical importance. In US 5,133,079, there are a total of sixteen claims, which begin at the bottom of Column 6, and continue to the end of the patent in Column 8. Claim #1 is an independent method claim. Claims 2–7 are dependent method claims, all of which depend (directly or indirectly) on claim #1. Claim #8 is an independent apparatus claim, which is one type of structure claim. Claims 9–16 are dependent apparatus claims, all of which depend (directly or indirectly) on claim #8.

— *File History:* The file history is the history of the interaction with the patent office after the application has been filed. All formal reactions of the patent office, called "Office Actions", and all responses of the patent applicant, are part of the file history. When the patent is allowed, a patent examiner will often write a statement of "reasons for allowance", and that, too, will be part of the record. The file history is not physically part of the published patent, but it is nevertheless an integral part of the interpretation of the patent.[17]

### *(6) Relevant Sections of the US Statute*

The U.S. patent statute is located at Title 35 of the United States Code. To answer the key question, "How do I know if my patent's any good?," you need to be familiar with a few sections of this statute:

35 USC sec. 100: This section includes definitions of words and phrases, helpful to understanding the other sections of the law.

35 USC sec. 101:

> Whoever invents or discovers any new and useful
> process,
> machine,
> manufacture, or
> composition of matter,
> or any new and useful improvement thereof,
> may obtain a patent therefor, subject to the conditions and requirements of this title.

Two things are important here. First, a patentable invention must be both "new" and "useful." Second, it must fall into one of the categories of (1) "process" (method); (2) "machine" (a structure); (3) "manufacture" (meaning "an article of manufacture", which is another kind of structure, and is often called

17 As noted, this book focuses on U.S. patents, and for such patents, the file history is often very important. In other countries, such as Germany for example, the file history is not very relevant; indeed, it may have no bearing at all.

"an article");[18] or (4) "composition of matter" (which is relevant for BCP patents, but mainly irrelevant for ICT patents). Finally, any new and useful improvement to any of categories (1) — (4) is also patentable.

There are two basic kinds of inventions: those that are a way of doing things (a "process" in the statute, but commonly called a "method") and the structure by which something is done (called "machine" or "manufacture" in the statute, and often appearing in a claim as "system", "product", "apparatus", or "component"). These types of invention are discussed further below.

35 USC sec. 102: To be patentable, an invention must be "new" — no one has ever invented the exact same thing (method or structure) as the subject of your patent. Technology invented before your patent is called "prior art". If the invention is even a little bit different from the prior art, then your invention is new.

Various sub-sections of section 102 — which I will not quote verbatim because of their complexity and lack of relevance to our main focus — describe situations in which the invention would be considered *not* new. If none of those subsections apply to the invention, then the invention is "new".

35 USC sec. 103(a):

> (a) A patent may not be obtained though the invention is not identically disclosed or described as set forth in section 102..., if the differences between the subject matter sought to be patented and the prior art are such that the

[18] One distinction sometimes made between a "machine" and a "manufacture" is that a "machine" includes no moving parts, whereas a "manufacture" does include moving parts. The key point here is that they both represent structural inventions.

> subject matter as a whole would have been obvious at the time the invention was made to a person having ordinary skill in the art to which said subject matter pertains...

In addition to being "new" under section 102, the invention must be "non-obvious" under section 103(a). Without section 103(a), a patent applicant could obtain a patent on the most modest and least relevant change to current technology. Section 103(a) prevents that.

35 USC sec. 112: Section 112 is especially interesting. While I will not quote it verbatim, here is the essence of its content:

> 112(1): The patent has a clear written description of the invention, stating how to make and use the invention.[19]
>
> 112(2): The specification shall end with claims that describe and in fact define the protected invention.
>
> 112(3): There are "independent" and "dependent" claims, discussed below.
>
> 112(4): Definition of what a "dependent claim" is.
>
> 112(5): Definition of multiple dependent claims, discussed below.
>
> 112(6): Here is the entire paragraph of this sub-section:
>
>> An element in a claim for a combination may be expressed as a means or step for performing a specified

---

19 The U.S. patent statute does not number the sub-sections of section 112. I number these sub-sections as 112(1), 112(2), 112(3), 112(4), 112(5), and 112(6), respectively, and this is the most common way in which these subs-sections are referenced. However, I have also seen the sub-sections specified as 112(a), 112(b), 112(c), 112(d), 112(e), and 112(f), respectively, which is also perfectly acceptable.

> function without the recital of structure, material, or acts in support thereof, and such claim shall be construed to cover the corresponding structure, material, or acts described in the specification and equivalents thereof.

Paragraph 112(6) defines what is known as a "means-plus-function claim". This type of claim warrants a separate discussion, which appears below.

35 USC sec. 271(a): This is the provision for what is called "direct infringement". An infringer is a person who "without authority makes, uses, offers to sell, or sells any patented invention, within the United States or imports into the United States any patented invention during the term of the patent…."

A patent holder may sue, in federal court, anyone who makes, uses, offers to sell, or sells, in violation of a patent claim. The lawsuit may be for damages, or an injunction, or typically both damages and an injunction.

A patent holder may seek an exclusion order at the U.S. International Trade Commission ("ITC") against anyone who imports into the U.S. an infringing product. A suit at the ITC is only for a type of injunction, not for damages.

U5 USC sec. 271(b): This is a provision for what is called "inducement to infringement", which is one of two forms of what is called "indirect infringement". Here is the entire subsection: "Whoever actively induces infringement of a patent shall be liable as an infringer."

35 USC sec. 271(c): This is a provision for what is called "contributory infringement", which is the second form of what is called "indirect infringement". Here it is:

> Whoever offers to sell or sells within the United States or

imports into the United States a component of a patented machine, manufacture, combination or composition, or a material or apparatus for use in practicing a patented process, constituting a material part of the invention, knowing the same to be especially made or especially adapted for use in an infringement of such patent, and not a staple article or commodity of commerce suitable for substantial noninfringing use, shall be liable as a contributory infringer.

A contributory infringer is one who offers to sell in, or sells in, or imports into, the United States a component or other structure that, when used with other structure, is infringing, where the person is "knowing the same to be especially made or especially adapted for use in an infringement of such patent, and not a... [structure] suitable for substantial noninfringing use..."

Although there are several other long and relatively complicated sub-sections of section 271, these three sub-sections, (a), (b), and (c), are the key ones for you to know.

We summarize all of this information as follows:

**Table 1–2: Some Key Provisions of the Patent Statute**

| Section | Essence | Notes |
|---|---|---|
| **35 USC 100** | Words and phrases defined | |
| **35 USC 101** | Says what is patentable. Invention must be "new", "useful", and fit into one of the four categories. | Whatever is not included, is not patentable. It is very easy, generally, to show "usefulness". |

| Section | Essence | Notes |
|---|---|---|
| **35 USC 102** | Defines in detail what is "new" | |
| **35 USC 103(a)** | To be patentable, the invention must be "non-obvious" over prior art | |
| **35 USC 112(1)** | Requires a "written description" of the invention | |
| **35 USC 112(2)** | Requires at least one "claim" | The claims define the scope of protection for the invention |
| **35 USC 112(3)** | Allows "independent" and "dependent" claims | |
| **35 USC 112(4)** | Defines "dependent" claims | |
| **35 USC 112(5)** | Defines "multiple dependent" claims | |
| **35 USC 112(6)** | Allows what are called "means-plus-function claims" | Means-plus-function claims are discussed in Chapter 2 |
| **35 USC 271(a)** | Defines "direct infringement" | |
| **35 USC 271(b)** | Defines "inducement to infringement"* | One form of "indirect infringement" |
| **35 USC 271(c)** | Defines "contribution to infringement"** | The second form of "indirect infringement" |

* Also called "induced infringement"

** Also called "contributory infringement"

Finally, there are two popular misconceptions we should avoid:

First, many people think that a patent must document an enormous breakthrough, a ground-breaking invention. However, ground-breaking patents, like ground-breaking inventions, are extremely rare. The vast majority of patents are small improvements: ways of doing something better, a new approach, a new application of an old approach, a structure that cuts out a component and saves money, etc. All of these contributions are valid and worthy contributions to technology. They may not be breakthrough inventions, but they still merit the grant of patents, and such patents can generate significant value.

Second, many people think of inventions and patents as some kind of creation from nothing, an almost magical process. There is something to this, because many inventions do require some kind of creative spark in which a solution is suddenly discovered to a previously unsolved problem. However, the thought that this solution comes out of thin air is mistaken. All inventions are combinations of items pre-existing in the environment. The combination may be new and patent-worthy, but the pre-existing items are not new. The fact that all human invention comes from pre-existing items does not in any way lessen the accomplishment of the invention, the quality of patent claims, or the value of patents resulting from the invention with pre-existing items.

## *(7) Structure of a Patent Claim*

As explained, the protection afforded by a patent document is determined by the claims which have been allowed by the patent office. People typically ask, "What is the scope of the claims?" That question is addressed in Chapter 2 below.

A claim is composed of three distinguishable pieces. The first piece is what is called "the preamble", which is the introductory part that immediately follows the number. For example, "1. A method for communicating with a computer" could be a preamble.

The second piece is the "transition" or "transition term" or "transitional phrase". There are basically three options for the transition: "comprising", "consisting of," and "consisting essentially of." Other variations are possible, but they are all derivations of these basic three options.

This short phrase, the transition, is surprisingly important. Fortunately, it is also relatively easy to get right. The phrase "comprising" is open-ended, meaning that the claim will definitely include all the elements listed in the claim, but may also include elements or explanations from the written description or from other sources. To be clear, a patent with an open-ended transition will cover all structures (systems, products, devices, machines, or components) and all methods that meet exactly the specific elements listed in the claim, *plus* all structures and methods that include both the specific elements and additional elements not listed in the patent. This transitional phrase, "comprising", may be used for all patents, including both ICT and BCP patents, and in my opinion, it is the *only transition that should ever be seen in ICT patents.*

"Consisting of" means that only the elements listed in the claim are included, and nothing else. In other words, a claim with the transition "consisting of" covers only structures and methods that include the listed elements *and only* the listed elements, but such a claim does not cover structures and methods that include all the listed elements plus an additional element. "Consisting essentially of" means the elements listed in the claim are included, and also possibly "non-material elements", meaning elements that do not impact the points of novelty of the invention. Transitions including the phrase "consisting of" or the phrase "consisting essentially of" should never appear in ICT patents. Two patent lawyers have said to me, on separate occasions, "Any patent agent or attorney who uses 'consisting of' in an ICT patent is guilty of professional malpractice!" I won't express an opinion on the question of malpractice, but the use of the transition "consisting of" in an ICT patent would impact very negatively on the quality of the claims.[20]

The third and final part of a claim is the "claim body", which includes everything that comes after the transition. The claim body is composed of two or more "claim elements", or simply "elements". Everything that comes after the transition is part of one of the claim elements. There are different kinds of claim elements, and they are discussed below under "Claim Format".

## *(8) Independent and Dependent Patent Claims*

A claim is "independent" if it does not depend on any prior claim. By definition, claim #1 in any patent must be an independent claim, because there is no prior claim on which it

20 Other possible transition phrases are ambiguous, or worse. The transition "having" is unclear. The transition "containing" is unclear. The transition "composed of" might seem to be like "comprising", but it is not, and is typically close-ended. There is no reason to use ambiguous transitions. Therefore, if I am reading an ICT patent and I see, for any claim, any transition other than "comprising," I discount the quality of that claim.

can depend. Any other claim in a patent that is listed without making reference by specific claim number to a prior claim is also an independent claim.

Any claim that is not an independent claim must be a dependent claim. In a dependent claim, there will be a specific reference in the preamble to a prior claim. For example, "3. The method of claim 1, further comprising..."

A specific kind of "dependent claim" is one that is called a "multiple dependent claim". This is a dependent claim that can depend on two or more prior claims. For example, let's change the prior example to read, "3. The method of claim 1 or claim 2, further comprising..." In essence, the new example is really two dependent claims, the first of which is the combination of 1 and 3, while the second is the combination of 2 and 3. This format is explicitly allowed by the PTO for U.S. patent applications, but with higher filing fees.

### *(9) Patent Claim Formats You Should Know*

There are about a dozen kinds of patent formats, about half of which are relevant for present purposes. The remainder are not discussed here.

When thinking about claim formats, the main thing to keep in mind is that every invention *has a physical structure* and *does something.*

No patent has a physical structure that achieves nothing, for in that case the "patent" would be useless, and therefore not fulfill a basic requirement of 35 US Code section 101. An application that achieves nothing would never be granted as a patent, or would lack value if granted in error.

Similarly, there is no patent that achieves something without a physical structure. Some people think, in error, that there are such patents, for example "software patents," which create something but lack any physical structure. That thought is wrong. Every such invention must have a physical structure as part of the patent, as discussed in "software patents" below.

In short, every invention and every patent based on an invention has both a structure and a method or process for doing something. A patent might include claims *only* as to structure, or claims *only* as to method, but in all cases, the invention on which the claims are based will include both a structure and a method or process for doing something.

*Format 1 — Structure claims*

There are several kinds of structure claims, but they are easy to keep straight without confusion.

a. The most inclusive kind of structure claim is a "system", which includes various devices, or products, or components, that act together to do something. This type of claim is very "inclusive", because it includes, as claim elements, multiple products working together.
b. The next most inclusive kind of structure claim is a "product" that does something. Actually, you will rarely see the word "product" in claims of this type. Rather, you will see very often the word "apparatus," sometimes "device" or "article" or, less frequently, "machine." All of these words are intended to indicate some kind of structure that functions as a whole, less than a system but more than a component. Further, sometimes one sees the product type listed specifically, such as, "a radio transmitter for transmitting digital data," in which the "product" is "radio transmitter".

If the product type is listed by name, the only consideration relevant to an evaluator of patent quality is this: "Is the specific word that was chosen to represent the 'apparatus' sufficiently broad so as *not to exclude* possible applications?" The example given refers to a "radio transmitter". Would that be restricted to "wireless" transmitters, or would it also include wireline transmitters? A better wording of product type in the claims might be "electronic transmitter", or even "an electrical-mechanical transmitter", rather than "radio" — the former examples would likely include both wireless and wireline transmitters, whereas "radio" might be interpreted to include only wireless transmitters

A "product" is an "inclusive" kind of structure claim in that it includes, either explicitly or by implication, all the components of one product.

c. The least inclusive kind of structure claim is a component of a product, not including either the full product or the full system. For example, an improved processor within a computer is a component of the computer. Typically the structure will be expressed, in the patent claim, as either an "apparatus for doing..." or "a component of a computer for doing...", or by specific name, "a computer processor."

It is very common, and indeed expected, to see multiple types of structure claims in a patent, in which all of the claims may be based on one Point of Novelty. For example, if the Point of Novelty is an improved processor, then the improved processor is a component, a computer with the improved processor is an improved computer, and a system with such an improved computer is a system with improved processing capability. As discussed in Chapter 2 below, a variety of claim types is one sign of a strong patent, so to have multiple structural types, based on one Point of Novelty, is not unusual.

*Format 2 — Method claims*

In the U.S. patent statute at section 101, a new "process" is one of the four categories of patentable invention. In ordinary patent language, this is called a "method claim". A method claim is a new way of doing or using a structure. The structure itself may also be new, in which case perhaps the structure and the method will both be patentable.

The claim elements in method claims are always verbs, and generally in the gerund form, such as in "generat*ing* data; stor*ing* said data in memory cells; and access*ing* said data prior to processing."

*Format 3 — Software claims*

A software claim is a claim that meets two requirements:

(1) It is a way of doing things, embodied in a computer program. This way of doing things is sometimes called an "algorithm".
(2) Either (a) the computer program operates on a computer or other hardware platform as an integral part of the invention, or (b) operation of the computer program creates a tangible effect on outside hardware (such as, for example, opening a valve), or has some other tangible "result".[21]

---

21 This is the U.S. requirement for software patents. The requirement for software patents in other countries may differ. For example, the general rule for patentability of any invention in Europe is that there is a technical

The topic of "software patents" is complicated, controversial, and beyond the scope of this book, except to note that in the United States such patents are definitely allowable if they are correctly written, and in all cases they are subject to particular "validity requirements" as discussed in Chapter 2 below.[22]

*Format 4 — Means-plus-function claims*

Means-plus-function claims are definitely "structure" rather than "method" claims. However, the structure is *not defined in the claim*, but is rather the structure *defined in the written description* that performs the function described in the claim. This is an important point to understand — the structure in a means-plus-function structure claim appears in the written description, and not in the claim itself.

Further, it is more correct to talk about a means-plus-function "claim element" rather than a "means-plus-function claim," since it is the specific element within a claim that appears in this special format. For example, consider this claim: "An apparatus for processing data, comprising: (a) a processor; (b) a memory; and (c) a means for conveying data

---

problem, and the invention as described in the patent makes a technical contribution to solving the technical problem. This general requirement in Europe applies also to European software patents, in which the software must cause the computer to perform a method according to the invention described in the patent. In truth, there is not total clarity in either the U.S. or Europe as to the exact parameters of a "patentable software invention", but the law gives at least a basic guideline to understanding this term.

22 "Software patents" sometimes include what are called "business method claims", which are claims that describe a business method, such as a method for managing a stock portfolio. There is some controversy regarding the validity and scope of "business method claims," but that dispute is beyond the scope of this book.

between the processor and the memory." In this claim, elements (a) and (b) are standard structural elements, whereas (c) is a "means-plus-function element", since element (c) appears in the form, "means for doing..."

The means-plus-function form for a claim element impacts the potential scope of the claim, as discussed in Chapter 2 below.

*Format 5 — Markush group claims*

"Markush structure" is often considered "a generalized formula or description for a related set of chemical compounds". However, despite this formal definition, the use of such claims in patent applications has been extended beyond its original use for chemistry patents, and now appears also in ICT patents. A Markush group claim is a claim, or actually more correctly a claim element, where the element says, "in which the function is conducted from the group of X, Y, and Z", or "said apparatus being selected from the group of X, Y, and Z". An ICT example of a Markush group claim element is: "in which the protocol is selected from the group including GSM, W-CDMA, and WiFi."

The Markush format is permitted, and its use affords coverage of multiple implementations with only one claim. Beware, however, because if prior art covers any one of the implementations, then the entire claim will fall. In the example given, GSM is the oldest of the three wireless air protocols, so if the claim with GSM exists in prior art, the entire claim will fall, even though W-CDMA and WiFi may be new.

Markush group claims often appear in BCP patents, but also, not infrequently, in ICT patents where the patentee wants to cover many possibilities without paying fees for many dependent patents. In ICT patents, this format is generally avoidable if appropriate terms are defined in the written description of the specification. For example, consider the Markush group, "said processor selected from the group including general purpose processors, special purpose processors, single core processors, and multi-core processors." The Markush format could be avoided if the claim used only the term "processor", and if "processor" were defined in the Detailed Description of the Invention to include "general purpose, special purpose, single core, and multi-core processors."

*Format 6 — Jepson claims*

This format is used infrequently in the U.S., but often in Europe. It also appears frequently in U.S. patents that are based on an original European application. The Jepson claim is a structure or method claim where there is a relatively lengthy preamble stating the prior art, plus one or more limitations specifically identified as points of novelty relative to the prior art. The structure is therefore:

> long preamble of prior art => transition "wherein the improvement comprises" or "wherein the improvement is characterized in that" => one or more points of novelty.

This format is not favored in the U.S., because everything in the preamble is considered to be prior art admitted by the applicant, and people typically do not like to admit prior art. By contrast, this format is often used in Europe, in accordance with Rule 43(1)(b) of the European Patent Convention.[23]

---

[23] In Europe, the Jepson claim is often called a "two-part form", in which the first part is the acknowledged prior art in the preamble, and the second part is the invention characterized as an "improvement". However, the effect of

Jepson format, together with its advantages and disadvantages, is discussed further in Chapter 6.

## II. Patents — Procedures at the Patent Office

### *(1) Obtaining a Patent*

Briefly, the inventor or the inventory's proxy files an application, receives a response from the patent office called an "office action" (OA), responds to the OA, continues with the cycle of office actions followed by applicant responses, and eventually receives a "Notice of Allowance" (NOA), typically, but not always, stating the patent examiner's reason for allowance. Although a few applications are allowed in the first response from the patent office, there are usually one or more rounds of negative OAs before allowance.[24] This is the general process for filing an application, then "prosecuting" the application to a final allowance.

During prosecution, matters may arise which can affect the allowed patent, or impact subsequent litigation. For example, every claim must be supported by material in the written

---

this kind of preamble is much different in Europe than in the United States In the U.S, a Jepson-style preamble is considered to be an admission that everything in the preamble is prior art — the patent office will interpret the preamble as prior art for this patent application, whether or not the material in the preamble would actually constitute "prior art" against the described invention. In Europe, quite to the contrary, the elements acknowledged as prior art in a two-part claim form typically have no effect whatever on the scope of the claim. These differences are rooted to a large degree in the history and political institutions of Europe and the U.S.

24 A relatively small minority of applications receive what is called a "first action allowance". I generally tell applicants to expect about two OAs. However, this is an average number only, and I have seen applications with as many as ten office actions.

description. If a claim is not supported, the claim should not be allowed. Even assuming a claim is supported, if the prior art makes the claim either not new, or obvious, the claim will be disallowed by the examiner. If the examiner has missed a relevant piece of prior art that would make the claim either not new or obvious, the claim may later be invalidated at trial. Even if a claim is supported and not invalidated, it might be amended during prosecution at the PTO, in which case, under the *Festo* case discussed in Chapter 2 below, the effective claim scope may be interpreted more narrowly than it would have been absent the amendment. These examples illustrate that both the validity and the scope of patent claims are affected by what happens during prosecution before the PTO.

### *(2) Reexamination by the PTO*

Reexamination is a procedure conducted by the patent office which allows patent claims to be reexamined by a patent examiner in light of new patents or other printed publications presented to the PTO. A reexamination may be initiated by the patent owner, or a third party, or the PTO. The examiner in reexamination may review all the claims against all relevant prior art, including prior art already considered and also new patents or publications. The examiner may cancel claims, or confirm claims. Some claims may be found to be invalid on the basis of the review, but may be narrowed in scope by a patent applicant who submits claim amendments to overcome the recently submitted patents or printed publications.

Reexamination can happen at any time after the patent issues, but it very often happens in connection with patent litigation in court, and in such cases it is frequently initiated by the defendant in litigation. This is a very significant procedure that can impact greatly the validity of any or all of the claims. According to statistics of the PTO, in the thirty-one year period from July 1, 1981, to September 30, 2012, there were 12,569 requests for what is called "ex parte reexamination"[25], resulting in 9,328 ex parte reexamination certificates. Of these 9,328 decisions by the PTO, in 21% of the cases all claims were confirmed (meaning the patent owner won, and the claims became stronger for overcoming additional prior art), in 11% of the cases all claims were cancelled (meaning the patent became officially dead), and in 68% of the cases some or all of the claims survived but only after amendments by the patent

25 There are two kinds of reexamination. In the most common, called "ex parte reexamination", a member of the public may submit the reexamination request, but does not participate in the proceeding. In the second, called "inter partes reexamination", a member of the public may submit the examination request and will participate in the proceedings. The rules regarding the various kinds of reexamination are complicated, and have become more complicated recently by the terms of the Leahy-Smith America Invents Act, signed into law on September 16, 2011. The differences between the two kinds of reexamination are simply irrelevant for present purposes. Of all reexamination decisions in the period 1981–2012, more than 96% were ex parte, and the numbers reported above are for ex parte reexamination. If inter partes reexamination numbers were included, the total numbers would shift slightly against patent validity, with no change to the confirmation rate, a small increase in the cancellation rate, and a small decrease in the amendment rate. These changes are not significant, although they do suggest that defendants tended to be more successful with inter partes reexamination than with ex parte reexamination. All of this relates only to the patent statute prior to the amendments of 2011. It is impossible to know at this time how the amendments to the statute may impact reexamination statistics in the future, but again, that is not relevant, because my only point is that reexamination may have an enormous impact on the validity of patent claims. That was true prior to the new statute in 2011, and it is true also after the new statute.

owner. In this book, we will see several examples where reexamination impacted the value of a patent.[26]

[26] Statistics for the 9,328 ex parte examinations are from a recent PTO report entitled, "Ex Parte Reexamination Filing Data — September 30, 2012", at http://www.uspto.gov/patents/stats/ex_parte_historical_stats_roll_up_EOY2012.pdf. Statistics for the 398 inter partes reexaminations covering the period November 29, 1999, to June 30, 2012, may be found in the report, "Inter Partes Reexamination Filing Data — September 30, 2012", at http://www.uspto.gov/patents/stats/inter_parte_historical_stats_roll_up_EOY2012.pdf.

## Chapter 2

# Evaluating Patents

The purpose of this chapter is to begin to answer three questions:

1. What is a "good patent"?
2. What are the differences between a "good patent", that is, a patent with true value, and a very valuable patent?
3. How are patents evaluated?

These are the core questions of this book. No prior knowledge, technical or legal, is required. Feel free to skip what is already familiar to you.

Here is the organization of Chapter 2:

I. The Eye of the Beholder: Who's Looking?
II. Two Basic Kinds of Patent Analysis: Fundamental and Financial
III. Fundamental Patent Analysis
  (1) Two Basic Types of Fundamental Analysis: EFA and PFA
  (2) Expert Fundamental Analysis — The Three Criteria
    a. Validity
    b. Scope
    c. Discoverability of infringement
  (3) Proxy Fundamental Analysis — Various Factors
IV. Financial Analysis

## I. The Eye of the Beholder: Who's Looking?

The answer to the question, "What is a good patent?", or stated alternatively, "What is a quality patent?", depends on who is asking the question. Patent quality, like artistic beauty, is determined in the eye of the beholder.

If you are an investor in a company, particularly a startup high-tech company, your main concern may be "proof of protection." For you, a "good" portfolio of patents is one that covers the major novelties developed by the company. Clarity of coverage for specific inventions may be key to what you consider "quality".

If you are a technical entrepreneur who seeks to maximize revenues from the patent by licensing-out or sale, you may want a patent broad enough to cover an important area of technology, but also defined enough so that infringement is clear and provable.

If you are a corporate executive in an established company (whatever the company's size), who wants to be left alone to develop and sell products, you might have no interest in licensing-out or selling your patents, because the revenue potential might not be sufficiently interesting. But you will certainly be concerned that you have enough patent coverage, *and especially that the scope of your patents is sufficiently broad* so that you may threaten other people with patent infringement litigation. You would like other people with patents to be afraid to sue you, so that you will be left alone to make and sell your products. As noted, a patent is never a "shield", nor does it give you direct protection. It is only a sword, but the threat of your sword thrust may frighten other people into leaving you alone. So a patent may give you indirect "protection," potentially very effective protection in some cases, but only indirectly. For you, breadth of coverage may be much more important than clarity of coverage, because you want to be able to threaten to sue, not necessarily to sue in reality.

If you are involved in a merger or acquisition ("M&A") transaction, as an executive of an acquired company, as an executive of an acquiring company, as an investor, or as a financial advisor, any of the approaches above might be appropriate. What do you want to achieve in the M&A transaction? Answer that question, and you will be able to figure out what your attitude should be toward the patents of the companies involved in the M&A.

Are you trying to unlock value by borrowing money, where the security on the loan is the patents? Or perhaps you are a bank or lender, lending money secured by potential cash flows from patents? This is called "collateralization" of the patent portfolio. As a lender, you want to make sure that there is enough value in the securitized patents to ensure that a loan will be repaid.

Does any of this really make any difference in looking at patents? Yes, it does, because different people want different things in a patent. They will look primarily for clarity, or primarily for coverage, depending on who they are. They will want different kinds of claims in the patent.

As a general rule, structure claims tend to be clear, because they are defined by the structure described in the claims and in the written description of the invention. A common question with structure claims is: "even assuming infringement, can the infringer design around the patent to create a product that is no longer infringing?" If you intend to sue, having structure claims is particularly valuable if the "design around" option is difficult to implement.

As a general rule, method claims may be less clear than structure claims, primarily because they are not limited to specific structure. That is, a patent with method claims will certainly include at least some discussion of a possible structure supporting a method. In many cases, however, the structure supporting the method *will not be limited* solely to the structure presented in the patent. The reason is that this is a method claim, not a structure claim. If the method claim is properly supported, its scope may be broader than the structure described. Therefore, if you want to threaten people with legal action, but not necessarily sue them, you should have some good method claims in your portfolio. However, method claims, like structure claims, are also subject to design around, in which the question is: "Could an infringer implement a different method while still obtaining the same result?"

What does this all mean? For breadth of coverage and threat of litigation, all good claims are desirable, but broad method claims may be particularly useful. At the same time, for winning lawsuits with very clear infringement, structure claims might be preferable. Does that mean you should write structure claims, and forget about method claims? Absolutely not! One lesson to be learned is that the best patent is one that has a "good claim mix," usually including both method and structure claims.

These results are summarized in Table 2–1 below.

**Table 2–1: Summary Comparison of Method and Structure Claims**

| Characteristic | Method Claims | Structure claims |
|---|---|---|
| **Main Feature** | Breadth of coverage | Clarity of coverage |
| **Usage** | Threaten to sue | Actually sue |
| **Main purpose** | To make others leave you alone | To generate revenues |
| **Who wants these?** | Company executive, entrepreneur | Investor, entrepreneur |

This summary table contains generalizations. Liability can be found in both method claims and structure claims. Chapters 3–7 contain many examples of both successful method claims and successful structure claims. Nevertheless, Table 2–1 expresses the general truth that "patent quality" is related to breadth of coverage, clarity of coverage, and type of patent claim, with significant differences between method claims and structure claims.[27]

As Malackowski and Barney have observed:

> Like beauty, patent quality is often believed to be in the eye of the beholder. If you are a patent owner, the concept of patent quality will be strongly flavored in terms of claim

27 The information presented in Table 2–1 is only a summary, and only general. There are cases where a defendant is found liable for infringing a method but not a corresponding structure, just as there are cases where a defendant is found liable for infringing a structure but not a corresponding method. The information in Table 2–1 is not to be taken as the final word on the difference between *a particular method claim* and *a particular structure claim*. Reviewing the specific claims is always required. Nevertheless, as a general rule, the scope of method claims tends to be broader but potentially less clear than the scope of corresponding structure claims.

> breadth relative to a commercially valuable technology — the broader the claims and the more valuable the underlying technology, the better. If you are a manufacturer or a service provider in a patent-laded technology space, the concept of patent quality takes on stronger overtones of underlying validity concerns (should this patent have been granted?) and clarity and predictability of claim scope interpretation (what are the metes and bounds of this patent? How do I avoid infringing this patent?).[28]

Malackowski and Barney do not discuss claim type, but they do discuss the concerns of various parties. If you are a patent owner suing or threatening to sue, then you want broad claims (whereas clarity is less important). If you are a "manufacturer or service provider" being sued or being threatened with a lawsuit, then you are most concerned with clarity (meaning you want clear claims that you may avoid infringing). In short, breadth of claims tends to favor patent owners, whereas clarity of claims tends to favor defending companies, *assuming, of course, that the defending companies can show no infringement.* I agree with Messrs. Malackowski and Barney, and I add that method claims are often broad, but not as clear, whereas structure claims are often clear, but not as broad.[29] Another way of looking at this is to say that

---

28 James E. Malackowski and Jonathan A. Barney, "What is Patent Quality? A Merchant Banc's Perspective", published in *les Nouvelles*, Journal of the Licensing Executives Society, June, 2008, p. 123, and at http://www.ocean-tomo.com/system/files/What_is_Patent_Quality_lesNouvelles_6.08.pdf, p.1.

29 The statement that method claims tend to be broader but less clear than corresponding structure claims is my own conclusion, but it is supported by a variety of sources. For example, business journalists Charles Duhigg and Steve Lohr, in their article "Innovation a casualty in tech patent wars" the International Herald Tribune, October 9, 2012, page 14, argue that the

structure claims are, by their nature, tied intimately to the structure described in the patent, whereas method claims of course operate on the structure described, but they are not limited to that structure.[30]

There are several general views of "patent quality" which focus on all types of claims, and not specifically on either method or structure claims. Let's look at three such views, as expressed by different people in the article, "Quality is the key to a bright patent future", printed in "Patents in the USA 2008", Intellectual Asset Management Magazine, copyright Global White Page, Ltd., London, 2008), at page 6–11.[31] The three views are:

1. *Only allowable claims should be allowed. If the allowed claims are really valid, then the patent has quality*: Is the patent office allowing only those patents which really should be allowed? If so, the patent is valid, and "validity" is the measure of "quality." This view was expressed by Jon Dudas, former director of the U.S. Patent and Trademark Office, by Las Kellberg and Reza Green of the Danish pharmaceutical company Novo Nordisk, by Sherry Knowles of the pharmaceutical company GlaxoSmithKline, and by Manny Schecter and Marian Underweiser of IBM.

2. *Patents that meet the goals of their owners are high-quality*:

---

proliferation of software patents (which are based on algorithms) and business method patents is stifling innovation due to the broad scope of such patents, combined with their lack of clearly defined boundaries.

30 Means-plus-function claims are, as explained in Chapter 1, tied to the structure described in the specification, but these are *structure claims, not method claims*, despite their unusual format, and they support the general rule that structure claims tend to be more focused than method claims.

31 http://www.oceantomo.com/system/files/IAM_April_May_2008_Barney.pdf.

Are the patents meeting the corporate goals and objectives of the patent owners? This "corporate goal" was noted by Horacio Gutierrez of Microsoft and Carl Horton of General Electric.

3. *Patents that promote the general welfare are high-quality*: Are the patents being allowed meeting the objectives of the public system? This "public measure" of quality was noted by Ms. Knowles of GlaxoSmithKline, who suggested a need for a "strong patent system to provide an adequate return on investment and encourage innovation." This was also the goal noted by Judge Pauline Newman of the U.S. Court of Appeals for the Federal Circuit. I quote from her at length, because her statement is, in my opinion, an excellent summary of the public objective of patents and the public measure of "patent quality." She said:

> Patent quality is measured by the effectiveness of the patent in contributing to the economic incentive to develop and commercialise advances in science and technology, with the resultant public benefit of new products, new industry and new opportunities, all tending to national growth. A patent that is vulnerable because of legal or technical flaws, or a patent that can be readily circumvented, is of diminished quality, no matter how elegant its technical content... Patents provide the broadest, most equitable and most available incentive for technological creativity and industrial commitment. The quality of a patent is measured by how effectively it fulfils that purpose.[32]

---

32 In the paper version of "Patents in the USA 2008", at pp.10–11, and on p. 8 of http://www.oceantomo.com/system/files/IAM_April_May_2008_Barney.pdf.

These three views of patent quality, that is — (1) "Is the patent valid?" (2) "Does the patent meet the goals of the person or company owning the patent?" and (3) "Does the patent encourage technological and commercial innovation?" — are all legitimate views of "patent quality." However, whether you are an inventor, investor, advisor, or company executive, these general views about patent quality, while they may be true, probably do not help you, because they are assumed to be true before serious analysis of the patent begins. In the end, in order to judge the quality of a particular patent in a way that is meaningful for your business, you will need to judge the patent according to specific criteria. The three general views of patent quality complement the methods of evaluations discussed in this book.

## II. Types of Patent Analysis: Fundamental and Financial

There are two very basic kinds of analysis for patents and patent quality: "fundamental" analysis and "financial" analysis. Fundamental analysis is a review of the claims and written description of the invention, according to some judgment criteria and some way of scoring the criteria.

"Financial analysis" covers questions such as:

- Can you make money on this patent?
- How much would it cost to unlock the monetary value in this patent?
- What is the best way to make the money — licensing, litigation, other?

The two basic kinds of analysis are intertwined. Financial analysis techniques are used to determine possible returns on patent commerce. Such techniques are often sophisticated and useful, but if they ignore or distort the results of fundamental analysis (or if no fundamental analysis is performed), then the results of the financial analysis are inadequately supported.

Fundamental analysis is the basis of any quality review of patents. Fundamental analysis alone is not sufficient, however, because it lacks an ultimate purpose. Fundamental analysis must be tied to one of the measures of "quality" discussed above. Does the patent meet the patent owner's business objectives? Can the patent make money? To these questions, fundamental analysis is the first but not the final word.

## III. Fundamental Analysis

### *(1) The Two Basic Types: "Expert" and "Proxy"*

There are two kinds of fundamental analysis, and you must understand both to appreciate how a patent is evaluated. The two kinds of fundamental analysis are what I call (1) "expert fundamental analysis" and (2) "proxy fundamental analysis".[33]

Expert fundamental analysis is where someone with a background in patents and technology, possibly but not necessarily a registered patent lawyer or registered patent agent, analyzes a patent according to some pre-defined criteria. The essence of all "expert fundamental analysis" is that

---

33 These are terms that I have created to explain the difference between a measure based on a review by a person knowledgeable in the technology and in the review of patents, which I call "expert analysis," and automated measures of quality, which I call "proxy analysis." The word "proxy" does not suggest falseness or inferiority, and in fact such analysis has important uses. However, analysis by a qualified legal and technical expert, which I have called "expert fundamental analysis", tends to be the most thorough and accurate kind of analysis.

a person sits down and reads all or parts of a patent to assess its "quality".[34]

"Proxy fundamental analysis," by contrast, is where an algorithm or algorithms are applied to a patent to come up with a "quality score" independent of any human review. Proxy fundamental analysis may be performed by a computer in a wholly automated manner, or by a person adhering strictly to the exact criteria of the algorithms.

Although expert fundamental analysis is more thorough and tends to be more accurate, there are several reasons to use proxy fundamental analysis instead of or in addition to expert fundamental analysis. Here are a few such reasons:

1. Expert fundamental analysis consumes the time of a person knowledgeable in both technology and patents, and is therefore relatively expensive. Even if reviews are short, expert analysis tends to be more expensive and time-consuming than proxy analysis.

2. When thousands of patents must be scored or ranked, expert analysis is simply too time-consuming, and cannot reasonably be achieved. When Google bought 24,000 patent items from Motorola Mobility, did Google perform expert

---

34 A human evaluator may perform various types of analysis. For example, (1) the two-minute review focused on Abstract, Summary, and independent claims; (2) the reasonable review of about fifteen minutes, including additional aspects of the patent and key points in the prosecution history; (3) a lengthy review of about an hour where all aspects of the patent and history are reviewed; and (4) a litigation-ready review in anticipation of licensing, litigation, or sale, which may run into days and tens of thousands of dollars. The two-minute review is the most common, particularly where a large portfolio must be reviewed quickly. However, *all of these reviews* have a human evaluator reading at least part of the patent, and in the end, they are all based on the three general criteria of patent value — Validity, Scope, and Discoverability — discussed later in this chapter.

fundamental analysis on all these items? That is difficult to believe. When a consortium bought 6,000 patent items from Nortel, were all 6,000 subjected to expert fundamental analysis? The former transaction was for $12.5 billion, while the latter was for $4.5 billion. Either transaction could justify the expense of a human review of all the patent items, but time constraints would make this kind of review for all the patents unrealistic. In other words, proxy fundamental analysis may help focus the scope of expert fundamental analysis, particularly for tasks involving the analysis of very large patent portfolios.

3. Apart from financial costs and time constraints, there are simply situations in which expert fundamental analysis is not required. In an M&A takeover of a startup company with patents, expert fundamental analysis might be performed. However, if the acquirer does not intend to sell or license-out the patents, a simpler review might suffice. If a party is charged with infringement of a large portfolio, it is likely that expert fundamental analysis will be performed on all of the "seminal patents" — those that contributed significantly to the creation of a technology. (Seminal patents are discussed in Chapter 7.) However, expert fundamental analysis may not be required for non-seminal patents.

### *(2) Expert Fundamental Analysis - Three Criteria*

a. Validity
b. Scope
c. Discoverability of infringement

A patent evaluator conducts a review in two stages.

The evaluator will first review the basic material in the

patent to understand what the patent is about, and also what the patentee considers to be the patent's "points of novelty." "Points of novelty" are the aspects of the invention, as described in the written description, that are new and patentable, according to the patentee. For this very basic review, the evaluator may look at the Title of the patent, the Summary of Invention, and the independent claims (but probably not the dependent claims).

Second, the evaluator will evaluate the patent on three specific criteria, which are:

(1) *Validity of the claims*: Based on the evaluator's knowledge of the claims, the prior art in the technology, and the current state of the patent law, are the independent claims likely to be valid?

(2) *Scope of the claims*: How broad is the scope of the independent claims? How clear are such claims, so that infringers and infringements may be identified? How easily could an infringer change the design of a product, system or method to avoid infringement?[35]

(3) *Discoverability of infringement*: Even if the claims are valid, and the scope of coverage and infringement is good, would the patent owner be able to discover and prove the infringement? If infringement cannot be discovered or proven, or infringement can be discovered but not proven, then validity and scope are not very meaningful.

I use the acronym "VSD" for the three criteria in a true fundamental analysis, short for **V**alidity, **S**cope, and **D**iscoverability of infringement. These three factors are

35 Changing the product or method to avoid infringement is called "design around" or "work around." These two terms are used interchangeably.

always used to evaluate patents. They are the heart of a patent evaluation by an expert.[36]

### *VALIDITY*

A basic question in patent evaluation, really the first question, is whether the claims are valid or not. Generally, the question is asked only of the independent claims since they are, by definition, the broadest claims in a patent. If the independent claims are valid, it is extremely likely the dependent claims will be valid as well.[37]

For only the Validity criterion, there is a presumption that "Yes, all the claims are valid". This is a correct presumption to make because, after all, a trained technologist working as a patent examiner at the patent office has found the claims to be valid.

---

36 These criteria are typically used to create some kind of score for the patent. For example, each criterion might be judged as a 1, 2, or 3, and the score for the entire patent may be the average of the numbers for the three criteria. Alternatively, different weightings can be given to one or all of the criteria. Conversely, instead of a numeric weighting for a particular criterion, the criterion may be judged on a Yes — No basis: for example, "validity" can be judged as Yes or No, whereas the rest of the evaluation may proceed only if the validity answer is Yes. The scale for scoring may be something different than 1–3. Multiple sub-criteria may be scored instead of only the three main criteria. In the end, regardless of evaluation method, the evaluator will judge in some way whether the patent claims are valid — V for validity, the breadth of claim coverage — S for scope, and the possibility to discover infringement of the patent — D for discovery.

37 If an independent claim is valid, that means, among other things, that it is not invalidated by prior art. Claims that are dependent on the independent claim are always, by definition, narrower than the independent claim on which they depend. Therefore, if prior art does not knock out independent claims, it will not knock out claims that depend on the independent claims.

However, there are at least two situations in which this presumption is overturned, and the patent claims are considered invalid, despite this presumption. These are first, where the claims should not have been allowed, and second, where the claims were properly allowable, but the law has changed in some way to make the claims invalid today.

1. The claims should not have been allowed

A number of possibilities arise:

The most common possibility is that there was a piece of prior art, meaning a patent, patent application, technical article, or other, that made the claims either not new or obvious. The examiner might have missed this piece of prior art. Had the examiner considered this prior art, the claims would not have been allowed. This happens with some frequency. An examiner is a technical expert who examines applications that are within the examiner's area of expertise. However, the examiner is often pressed for time and may not have easy access to some prior art (particularly non-patent material and foreign language patents). In this book, we will see examples where prior art is presented against patents in litigation or in reexamination for the purpose of invalidating claims.

A second possibility is that there was some external event that was not known to the examiner, and in fact could not have been known to the examiner, that invalidates claims that would otherwise be valid. These are what I call in this book, "external events that destroy patent value", and several will be discussed.

A third possibility is that the examiner simply made a mistake. Although U.S. patent examiners generally perform extremely well, mistakes do happen. Examples in this book of patent claims that perhaps might not have been allowed include:

— *Shifting terminology*: A claim uses two phrases for the same idea, or one phrase for two different ideas, in a way that makes understanding of the claim difficult or even impossible.
— *Lack of support in the written description*: Claims rely on what are called "key claim terms", meaning the important words and phrases that define the claim. Sometimes a claim will include a key term not supported in the written description of the invention.
— *Unusual usage of a key term in the claim*: Sometimes a claim uses a key term in a way that is simply non-standard in the industry. Using a standard term in a non-standard way is almost guaranteed to create problems of comprehension and interpretation.

These and other errors might have caused the flawed claim to be rejected at the patent office, but for whatever reason, such claims are sometimes allowed despite the flaw.

2. The law has changed in some way that impacts the validity of the claims.

Claims may be invalidated by changes in law. Such changes may overrule the presumption that patent claims are valid. For example, formerly there was a type of claim called a "signal claim", which was a claim covering an electronic signal bearing information. That type of claim became invalid in 2008 by the case of *In re Nuitjen*.[38]

---

[38] 500 F.3d 1346 (Fed. Cir. 2007), *cert. denied*, 129 S. Ct. 70 (2008).

Conversely, the law may change in some way that strengthens claims, meaning that the change validates formerly invalid claims, or the change in law expands the scope of claims. As an example where claim scope was expanded, in the combined case of *Akamai v. Limelight Networks*, and *McKesson Technologies v. Epic Systems*, the CAFC decided on August 31, 2012, that, contrary to prior judicial doctrine, a patent plaintiff may now prove indirect liability of infringement of a method claim, even where no single person or entity is directly liable due to what is called "divided infringement". This decision is an enormous expansion of possible liability for infringement of method claims that were formerly unenforceable.[39]

A human evaluator, trying to determine if the claims of patent are valid, must take into account changes in law by judicial doctrine or by statute.

### *SCOPE*

"Scope" refers to the ability of patent claims to capture infringers. It includes a number of concepts, such as (1) breadth of technology covered, (2) degree of current patent infringement, (3) expected future infringement, and (4) ability of a defendant to design around a patent claim. Let us discuss these concepts now.

1. *In general, how broad an area of technology is covered by the claims?* Although this might seem clear, very often it is not, due to the patent concepts of (a) direct versus indirect

---

39 692 F.3d 1301 (Fed. Cir. 2012), *writ of cert. requested* in Supreme Court No. 12–960, Supreme Court response expected in the summer of 2013. See http://www.laipla.net/wp-content/uploads/2013/02/Wegner-Top-Ten-02–21–2013.pdf. If the Supremes grant the writ of certiorari, the case is likely to be argued in late 2013 or early 2014, and decided in 2014.

infringement; (b) literal versus "equivalent" infringement; and (c) means-plus-function claims.

(a) *Direct versus Indirect Infringement*: One categorization of infringement distinguishes between "direct" and "indirect" infringement. Direct infringement is exactly what its name implies — the infringer is found to be practicing the method or employing the device that is covered by the patent. Indirect infringement can be of two types: "inducing infringement" and "contributory infringement." "Inducing infringement" generally means encouraging another to infringe, telling another to infringe, or taking some action that results in infringement.[40] "Contributory infringement" is defined in 35 USC sec. 271(c) as offering to sell or selling in the U.S. a component to be used in a patented method, where the component is specially suited for this purpose and has not substantial non-infringing purpose.[41] The distinctions are summarized in Table 2–2 below.

---

40 See Mark A. Lemley, "Inducing Patent Infringement", *University of California Davis Law Review*, Volume 35, pp.225–247 (2005).) See also *DSU Medical Corp. v. JMS Co.*, 471 F.3d 1293 (Fed. Cir. 2006), which makes clear that liability for induced infringement requires that the defendant "knew or should have known his actions would induce infringement", at p.1304.

41 Liability for contributory infringement under section 271(c) requires an intent similar to that for induced infringement under section 271(b). For liability as a contributory infringer, the defendant must know that the component or other item it is selling "is especially made or especially adapted for use in an infringement of such patent, and not a staple article or commodity of commerce suitable for substantial noninfringing use", 35 USC sec. 271(c). See *Aro Mfg. Co. v. Convertible Top Replacement Co.*, 377 U.S. 476 (1964).

**Table 2–2: Direct versus Indirect Infringement**

| Category | Ordinary Infringement | Inducing Infringement | Contributory Infringement |
|---|---|---|---|
| **Type of infringement** | Direct | Indirect | Indirect |
| **Statutory section** | 35 USC sec.271(a) | 35 USC sec.271(b) | 35 USC sec.271(c) |
| **What it is?** | Make, use, offer to sell, or sell | Encourage or tell others to infringe | Supply contributory component |

(b) *Literal Infringement versus "DOE" Infringement*: "Literal infringement" means exactly what its name implies, that is, the infringing party has acted in a way that literally includes all the elements of a structure claim, or all the steps of a method claim. Infringement under the "doctrine of equivalents" ("DOE" for short) is a legal rule that says a party is liable even though it does not literally practice some element or step in the claim, where the party does introduce a substitute element or step in such a way as to perform "substantially the same function" as the claim element, in "substantially the same way" as the claim element, producing "substantially the same result" of the claim element.

There are two problems with DOE infringement.

First, the exact parameters of DOE are not totally clear. The test for DOE infringement — same function, same way, and same result as stated above — does not fully clarify the scope of protection, and thus it is difficult to know how much value DOE adds to a patent. Second, the U.S. Supreme Court determined in the case of *Festo Corp. v Shoketsu Kinzoku*

*Kogyo Kabushiki Co.*[42], that scope of patent claim under the DOE is lost for any claim element that is amended during patent prosecution, unless the patentee can demonstrate that the amendment was not due to demands of patentability. *Festo* therefore added another degree of unclarity, and another limitation, on the DOE.[43]

(c) *Means-plus-function Claims*: Another kind of claim of possibly variable scope is the "means-plus-function" claim. As already explained, this is a structure claim whose structure performs the function stated in the written description. Other structure claims tend to be self-contained, relying on their own terms for definitions of claim elements. By contrast, means-plus-function claims *demand* that supporting structure appear in the written description and/or the figures. If no structure appears in the written description or figures, the means-plus-function claim either will be disallowed by a patent examiner, or will fall during litigation. Therefore, if one evaluates a patent with means-plus-function claims, it is important to understand exactly what kind of structure is required for the claims, and how that structure is presented, if at all, in the rest of the patent.[44]

---

42 535 U.S. 722 (2002)

43 An interesting article on DOE, explaining many of the key concepts, is by Christopher Hughes and Regina Lutz of the New York office of Cadwalader, Wickersham & Taft, "Doctrine of equivalents: prosecution beyond the literal patent claims", printed in *Patents in the USA*, Intellectual Asset Management Magazine, 2008. See http://www.iam-magazine.com/issues/Article.ashx?g=c112a8a4-87b2-4875-ae38-8dfdb05b9827.

44 Some patent practitioners are extremely hostile to means-plus-function claims. For example: "The use of means-plus-function language in the third paragraph [of the example being discussed] is just inexcusable. Means-plus-function limitations are so unnecessarily narrowing that their use is possibly malpractice," *Strategic Patenting, op. cit.*, p.69.

2. *Is there infringement of a patent claim right now? If so, how widespread is the infringement?*

a. Who is infringing? (Technical question)
b. Which products or processes are infringing? (Technical question)
c. How many components, products, processes, or other units are infringing? (Marketing and financial question)
d. How much are sales of the infringement? (Marketing and financial question)

The answers to these questions will impact greatly a patent owner's ability to generate revenue on this patent in the very near future, through licensing or litigation. They are critical questions at the heart of the patent evaluation.

An evaluator performing a true fundamental analysis, such as a patent attorney or patent agent, will try to answer at least the first two questions. The evaluator might or might not attempt some kind of answer to the last two questions, depending on the definition of the evaluator's position, thc nature of the organization in which the evaluator works, and the objectives and means of the client. If *you* are the person doing the evaluation of your own patent — meaning you are asking, "How do I know if my patent has financial value?" — then you need to try to answer all four questions above.

3. *Is there likely to be infringement of the claim in the future? If so, when, and how widespread will the infringement be? Whether or not there is infringement today, what is likely to be the situation in the future?*

If there is infringement today, will it intensify in the future? Why? What additional companies are likely to join the ranks of the infringers? How intensive will infringement is in terms of number of units infringing and dollar sales?

If there is no infringement today, is infringement likely to start in the future? Why will it begin? When will it begin? Which companies are likely to infringe in the future, with which kinds of products? How intensive is infringement likely to be in terms of number of units and dollar sales?

Please understand that if you have come to the conclusion that there is no infringement now, and there will not be any infringement in the foreseeable future[45], then this patent has no current value, and the answer to the key question is, unfortunately: "Your patent may have well-crafted claims which are well-supported in the written description, and this may therefore be a 'good' patent with high quality, but these advantages are not useful because the patent has no current value." In other words, with no current or future infringement, a patent might be high-quality, but it cannot have value.

---

45 When I say "foreseeable future", I generally mean a period of 2–3 years out. Patents remain in force for 20 years from priority date, and about 17 years from the date of issuance. In theory, one could say, "Oh, the market will be very developed in 5 years, or perhaps 10 years." In reality, people in the market are very unlikely to be interested in this statement, which would be considered extremely speculative. For there to be value in a patent right now, you need to have infringement right now, or you need a clear expectation of considerable infringement in the very near future. There are some exceptions to this rule for breakthrough technologies, and there are a very few technology visionaries who are willing to bet on a long-term technology play. However, these are the rare exceptions. The vast majority of people in the market — buyers, sellers, brokers, licensees, etc. — are interested only in the near future of 2–3 years.

4. *Can infringers design around the patent claim to avoid future infringement?*

"Design around" means that a company or other entity infringes a patent claim, but can redesign or re-engineer the structure or method to stop infringing. The infringer is said to have "designed around" the claim. If this can be done only at great time and expense, then design around may be a theoretical possibility, but not a realistic option.

If design around is reasonably feasible, then the infringer may avoid incurring damages in the future, and may avoid an injunction. Under 35 USC sec. 283, an infringer is subject to an injunction to stop it from infringing, which means that it could not practice the method, or make, use, offer to sell, or sell the structure. An injunction can destroy a business, at enormous cost to the party enjoined. However, if design around is possible, then an infringer will be less concerned

In short, "design around" stops future damages from accruing and allows the infringer to avoid an injunction. The infringer is still liable for all damages up to the date of the design around, including damages that begin six years before the date the patent owner sues, up to the time of design around. Those can be major damages, but they are likely not as significant as the costs involved in shutting down a business.

Considerations of infringement, including current infringement, future infringement, and the possibility of design around, are presented in Chart 2–1.

**Chart 2-1: Evaluating Claim Scope Through Infringement**

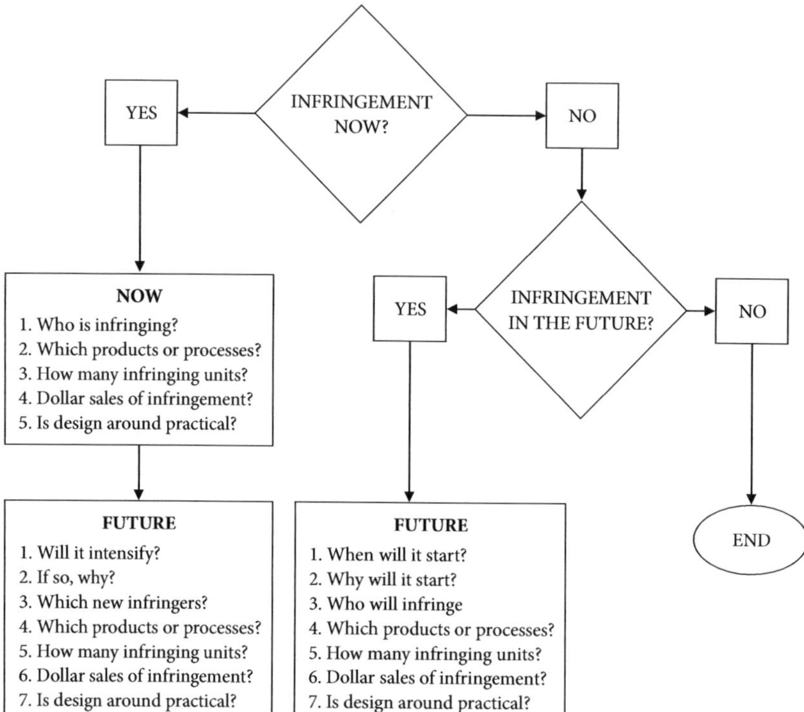


5. *The inherent tension between claim scope and claim validity.*

To complete the discussion of scope, it is useful to recognize that there is an inherent tension between claim scope and claim validity. The greater the scope of a claim, the higher the chance that the claim will include some coverage of prior art. By law, if the scope of the claim includes some prior art, the entire claim will be invalid. In this book, we will see examples where a patent owner asks the court for a narrow claim scope, and the defending infringer asks the court for a broad claim scope. Surprising, perhaps? But in these examples, if the court accepts the broader scope, the claim will be invalidated, which is what the defendant wants. In short, there is an inherent tension between scope and validity, in which broad scope risks invalidity, and strong validity is sometimes accompanied by very narrow scope.

This tension is depicted graphically in Chart 2–2.

**Chart 2–2: Scope versus Validity**

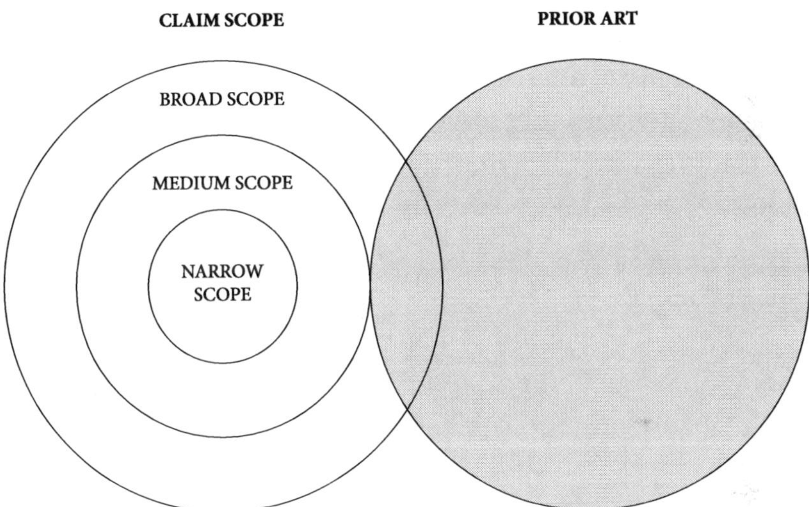


Chart 2–2 shows three possible claim scopes: Narrow, Medium, and Broad. Broad scope of course gives the widest possible coverage, but as shown in Chart 2–2, the broader the scope of the claim, the more likely that the claim will overlap prior art. If a claim overlaps prior art, even by a small amount, then properly the claim should not be allowed by a patent examiner — if such a claim were allowed in error, the claim will be subject to cancellation in future proceedings in court, at the ITC, or at the PTO. This Chart illustrates the inherent tension between the scope of a claim and its validity,

a tension which is captured in the phrase, "claim scope and claim validity are natural enemies".

### *DISCOVERABILITY OF INFRINGEMENT*

The issue of "discoverability of infringement" is analogous to the old philosophical question, "If a tree falls in a forest and no one is around to hear it, does it make a sound?" The question here is: "Assuming that the claim is valid and infringed, but infringement cannot be discovered, was there any infringement at all?" We need not be philosophers, or ask hypothetical questions, to understand that if discovery of infringement is highly unlikely, then you will never know if the claim has been infringed, and the claim is economically useless.

There are four main ways to discover infringement of patent claims.

*1. Review of literature describing the product or process*: This way is more common for products and other structure claims than for method claims. For structure claims, the main sources of product literature identifying a patent infringement are specification sheets, product descriptions, technical white papers, and other information put out by the infringer. This information is used to make direct comparison between patent claims and infringing products, thus potentially proving the infringement. By contrast, infringement of method claims often must be inferred from the results rather than identified in product literature.[46]

---

46 It is possible to review product and service literature written by either a "third party" (i.e., neither the infringer nor the patentee) or the infringer itself. Either kind of literature may be probative of infringement. Some patentees looking for infringement prefer literature by the supposed infringer, because that is considered to be, in some cases, more accurate, and also

2. *Visual Inspection*: A product or other structure may be inspected visually to discover infringement. I am not referring to the viewing of pictures available on the Internet, which is part of the review of literature discussed above. Rather, I mean that the product is obtained and inspected. The evaluator might not have the allegedly infringing product, or may lack the time or budget to obtain such a product. In such case, the evaluator would not be able to perform visual inspection. However, the patentee reviewing his or her own patent may be in a different situation than an evaluator with limited time and resources. If you have the opportunity to obtain infringing products, and to confirm the infringement by visual inspection, then this is an excellent way of establishing "discoverability" of infringement of your patent. Of course, even if you obtain an allegedly infringing product, some elements in the claim may not be accessible, and for those elements, visual inspection will not suffice.

3. *Reverse Engineering*: An allegedly infringing product may be obtained, disassembled, and reviewed in its specific components to discover and or to document the design and technology principles on which the product was engineered. In some cases, the people doing the reverse engineering may try to build the same or similar product from scratch to determine whether the principles of the original product are understood. Strictly speaking, however, the process of

---

because it is a kind of admission of activity. On the other hand, intelligent companies may "scrub" their product literature and publications specifically to reveal only what it required, and to hold back details that are not required by the customer but which may create trouble for the company. Third party literature may be more useful, in that it is typically not "scrubbed" of possible patent infringement.

tearing down the allegedly infringing product is itself "reverse engineering."

Reverse engineering is often an effective method for discovering infringement, but it can be expensive and time-consuming. Evaluators evaluating your patent for sale or license will not reverse engineer, but a corporate team reviewing competitive products for possible licensing-out of patents, or for possible litigation for infringement, may well consider this a worthwhile investment. If you are a technical expert with time, resources, and access to allegedly infringing products, you may reverse engineer to prove patent infringement.

*4. Strong Forward Citations by a Single Company*: Forward citations, as explained further in Table 2–4 below, are citations of a patent in later patents or later non-patent technical literature. It happens sometimes that the patents of one company, let's call it X, are cited very strongly by the later patents of a second company, let's call it Y. If this happens, it is a powerful indication that the two companies are active in the same technical field, and it suggests, although it does not prove, that products or services of company Y might be infringing patents of company X. This is not strictly a method to discover infringement, but it is a clue to a place where infringement might be discovered. It is a clue that is particularly valuable where discovery of infringement might otherwise be difficult.[47]

---

47 To be strictly accurate, forward citations are made by either a patent applicant or by a patent examiner, or by both, but in any case, they appear in later patents citing an earlier patent. Forward citations are discussed in much greater detail in Chapter 7, but the key thing to note now is that a patent appearing in many forward citations of a single company Y suggests, at a minimum, that company Y is likely to be interested in the subject matter of the cited patent. Strong forward citations might also indicate, although they do not prove, that some product or service of company Y might be infringing the cited patent. The inference of possible infringement becomes

*Summary of Methods to Discover Infringement:* The methods discussed here are summarized in Table 2–3 below.

**Table 2–3: Methods to Discover Patent Infringement**

| Method | Advantages | Disadvantages | Who does it? |
|---|---|---|---|
| **Review of third party literature** | Inexpensive and fast | Often technical detail is lacking to establish infringement | Evaluator; corporate team; Patentee |
| **Review of the infringer's own literature** | Inexpensive, fast, and often surprisingly effective | Sometimes insufficient | Evaluator; corporate team; Patentee |
| **Inspection of infringing product** | More detailed than literature review | More expensive than literature review; sometimes ineffective | Corporate team; Patentee |
| **Reverse engineering** | Great detail of information is generated | Generally expensive and time-consuming | Corporate team; Patentee |
| **Strong forward citations by company Y of company X's patents** | Very easy to check; provides strong indication of possible infringement; valuable particularly where discovery is difficult. | Not strictly a method of discovery; might not be tied to specific products or services of company Y; appears only over the course of years | Everyone may do this, since it is very easy to review. |

stronger if many patents of company Y contain forward citations to many earlier patents of company X, although here, too, infringement is only suggested as a possibility, and not proven.

There are also alternative approaches to discovery of infringement.[48]

Finally, you should understand an important implication of "discoverability of infringement", which is that *lack of discovery negates value*. A patent claim whose infringement is very hard to discover is a claim with low or even no value. Here are some examples:

a. *Manufacturing method claims*: If a method of manufacturing does not create a trace, then how can the method of manufacturing be discovered? By "a trace", I mean something in the product itself, or something produced by a product. For example, the internal bore of a gun barrel is manufactured in a certain way that might be discoverable by a visual inspection of the barrel. If the bore cannot be observed, the manufacturing method nevertheless might be inferable from the markings on a bullet passing through the bore. In many cases, however, the manufactured product does not indicate how the product was manufactured.

b. *Semiconductor claims*: These might be very difficult to discover in some cases. Product literature for semiconductors

---

48 Table 2–3 organizes discovery of patent infringement by methods of discovery. This is not the only way to organize, or present, discovery of infringement. Another way to allocate discovery of infringement is by relative levels of ease by which infringement may be detected. An excellent article along these lines was written by Kelce S. Wilson and Claudia Tapia Garcia (both of Research In Motion), "Patent Application Prioritization and Resource Allocation Strategy", appearing in the June, 2011 edition of *les Nouvelles*, Journal of the Licensing Executives Society International, June, 2011, at p.87. Five levels of discovery, called "detection", are listed at p.88, including (1) detection without processing an infringing device; (2) detection by consumer use; (3) detection using commonly available test equipment; (4) detection using specialized equipment; and (5) detection only by admission of the infringer. See http://www.lesi.org/docs/les-novelles-ancillary-content/Patent_Application_Prioritization_And_Resource_Allocation_Strategy.pdf.

is often not sufficiently detailed to determine infringement, and the infringement might not be easily visible, leaving the relatively expensive reverse engineering as the sole alternative for proving infringement.[49]

c. *Method claims*: Method claims are often incapable of being inspected. Therefore, evaluation of discoverability may rely upon (1) literature (if it exists) or (2) inference of how the method probably worked, based primarily on the result produced and secondarily on the inputs into the system to create the output. Since methods by their nature are actions rather than physical objects, they are often relatively difficult

---

49 In the recent case of *Carnegie Mellon University v. Marvel Technology Group, Ltd., and Marvel Semiconductor, Inc.*, U.S. District Court, Western District of Pennsylvania, No. 09–00290, a jury decided on December 26, 2012, that the defendants had infringed two semiconductor patents of Carnegie Mellon, in particular method claim #4 of US 6,201,839 and method claim #2 of US 6,438,180. The jury awarded the university $1.17 billion. See, e.g., Jad Mouawad, "Use of university's patents costs Marvel a big penalty", International Herald Tribune, December 28, 2012, p.15. How did the university discover the infringement? Among other possible methods of discovery, Marvel had more forward citations to each of Carnegie Mellon's two patents in suit than any other company. The lawsuit was filed in March, 2009. At that time, there were 57 issued U.S. patents citing Carnegie Mellon's two patents, of which 16 citations, or 28%, were by Marvel. Strong forward citations by company Y of multiple patents of company X suggest, but do not prove, strong interest by company Y in the cited patent and *possible* infringement of the cited patents by some product or service of company Y. I cannot know for a fact that Carnegie Mellon University learned of the infringement through forward citation analysis, but that is certainly a possibility. In any case, from the very focus of the parties' efforts, it was almost certain that Carnegie Mellon would have been aware of Marvel's activities, at least in a general sense. A more interesting question may be why Carnegie Mellon has chosen to sue only Marvel, and none of the other companies with multiple citations to the two patents in suit, companies such as Alcatel-Lucent, Broadcom, IBM, Qualcomm, and Seagate Technology.

to discover in comparison to products which infringe structure claims.[50]

### *(3) Proxy Fundamental Analysis — Factors*

The second kind of fundamental analysis is proxy fundamental analysis ("PFA"), where an automated method compares patents against certain pre-defined factors and produces a rating or numeric score for the patent. Typically, a higher score is meant to reflect a higher quality of patent.

There are many factors considered, by various people, to be the important factors in judging the quality of a patent in a PFA. Algorithms are created based on these factors. A patent is then placed into this evaluation factory, the patent is processed by the algorithms, and a quality scored is generated and reported. This automated analysis may be done relatively quickly for hundreds or thousands of patents, creating scores for individual patents and also an overall portfolio score.

There are two basic kinds of PFA. One kind of PFA combines multiple factors to determine a quality score related to what may be called a "meta-factor." A second kind of PFA looks only at specific factors, not at "meta-factors."

The two most commonly used meta-factors are:

(1) *The likelihood that the owner of a patent will pay to the patent office the maintenance fees to keep the patent in force*: In the U.S., maintenance fees are paid at 3.5 years, 7.5 years, and 11.5 years, after patent issuance. For fees payable to March

---

50 If all steps of a method are carried out in public, discovery of infringement may not be difficult. This is typical, for example, of what are sometimes called "business methods". It is *not* typical of what are sometimes called "manufacturing methods", which are, by their nature, often relatively difficult to discover.

18, 2013, the rates for maintenance were $1,150, $2,900, and $4,810, respectively. For fees payable on or after March 19, 2013, the rates for maintenance are $1,600, $3,600, and $7,400, respectively.[51] Most patents are not maintained through the last renewal period.[52] The theory is that if the patent owner pays the fees, the patent owner must think there is value in the patent that justifies the fees, and that is the basis of patent value. The meta-factor is *not*, "Did the patent owner pay the fees?", but rather, on the basis of some specific factors included in the meta-factor, "Is it likely that the patent owner *will* pay the fees?" The meta-factor is made up of the specific factors applied to determine the likelihood that the patent's maintenance fees will be paid.

(2) *The likelihood that the patent will be the basis of a lawsuit.* The theory is that if the patentee is willing to invest the time, effort, and money (potentially in the millions of dollars) to pursue litigation, that is a clear sign that the patentee thinks the patent has value. This subjective judgment of the patent holder is one measure of patent value.

Although PFA is not the primary focus of this book, it is important to understand its basic parameters. Some of the

---

51 For what is called a "small entity", the maintenance fees are exactly 50% of the standard rates listed above. This is true both before and after the rate increases.

52 See "Kimberly A. Moore, "Worthless Patents", Berkeley Law Journal, 2005, volume 20, pp.1521–1552, at p.1526, published electronically at http://btlj.org/data/articles/20_04_02.pdf, which suggests that historically 54% of patents are not maintained to the legal end of their life. This study was based on 96,713 U.S. patents issued in the year 1991, and is a very good study, but it needs to be updated. I am not aware of any more recent study of U.S. patent maintenance rates. The author of the study, Kimberly Moore, was formerly a professor of law, and is now a judge on the Court of Appeals for the Federal Circuit (CAFC), which is the sole appellate court in patent litigation.

factors which I consider most relevant for proxy fundamental analysis are defined in Table 2–4 below. Some of these factors are subjected to a more detailed analysis in Chapter 7.

**Table 2–4: List and Definition of Some PFA Factors**

| | Factor | Definition and Explanation |
|---|---|---|
| 1 | Number of claims in the patent. | It is believed by some that more claims are better, because more protection is obtained and because the patentee expresses its commitment by paying higher filing fees to obtain additional claims. |
| 2 | Number of issued patents and pending patent applications in the family of the patent. | A "patent family" comprises patents and applications derived from a common application. It is believed by some that more family members are better, since a higher number suggests that the owner is more interested in the subject of the patent. |
| 3 | Number of "backward citations". | A "backward citation" is a citation in the patent to earlier patents. It is believed by some that more such citations are better, since a higher number suggests that the owner is more interested in the subject and/or that the owner conducted a more thorough search of prior art. |
| 4 | Duration of prosecution of application at the PTO. | Some suggest that longer prosecutions indicate that the owner is willing to invest more to obtain the patent. |
| 5 | Technology area of the patent. | Some technology areas are believed to have greater potential for value. |

| | Factor | Definition and Explanation |
|---|---|---|
| 6 | Did the patentee obtain a certificate of correction fixing errors to the patent? | A "yes" is taken by some to indicate greater care and interest by the owner. |
| 7 | Have the maintenance fees been paid? More particularly, what is the chance that maintenance fees will be paid? This is a meta-factor. | Non-payment of fees is fatal to value, because it demonstrates no interest by the owner. However, the key is not actual payment, but rather predicted payment. It is believed by some that prediction of payment is associated with high patent quality. |
| 8 | Number of "forward self citations". | A forward self citation is a citation from a later patent owned by the same patent owner. The theory is that more are better, suggesting that the owner's additional filings suggest greater interest in the subject. |
| 9 | Was there a change in ownership of the patent? | A change of ownership is believed by some to suggest that someone was interested in acquiring the patent, which is associated with patent value. |
| 10 | Was the patent reexamined? | Some suggest that the party requesting reexamination was interested in the patent. (In addition, there is an assumption that the reexamination was "successful" in the sense that at least some of the claims were confirmed. If, conversely, all of the claims were cancelled, that would of course be a terrible reexamination result demonstrating lack of patent value.) |
| 11 | Was the patent collateralized? (That is, was the patent used as collateral to obtain a loan?) | It is thought that collateralization demonstrates value in the eyes of the lender. |

| | Factor | Definition and Explanation |
|---|---|---|
| 12 | Was the patent licensed-out? | Some believe that significant licensing revenues are a clear sign of value. |
| 13 | Was the patent litigated? | It is believed that the owner's willingness to bear heavy litigation costs suggests owner's interest. |
| 14 | Was the patent placed in a patent pool? | It costs time and money to place a patent in a pool. If the patent owner has done so, that act is considered a sign that the owner assigns value to the patent. |
| 15 | Number of forward non-self citations. | A forward non-self citation is a citation from a later patent, where the citing patent and the cited patent have different owners. It is widely assumed that more are better, suggesting high industry interest in the patent. |

## IV. Financial Analysis

Financial analysis is the second generic kind of analysis, in addition to fundamental analysis. Financial analysis is the continuation and the completion of fundamental analysis. When you ask yourself, "How do I know if my patent's any good?", what you really wish to know is, "Can this patent generate any revenues or any other tangible financial benefit for me?" A main theme of this book is that you can answer your question *only* if you have first performed a fundamental analysis of the patent, and particularly of its independent claims. However, fundamental analysis alone is not enough, since it is the financial analysis that generates the financial figures.

Although financial analysis is important, it is not the

theme or the focus of this book. Here, I will explain briefly (1) the difference between true patent value and financial patent value, (2) the components of a full patent analysis, and how they are allocated between true value and financial value, and (3) the main types of financial analysis.

### *(1) True Patent Value and Financial Patent Value*

"Patent quality" is the result when a patent has (1) well drafted claims that are (2) well supported in the written description. If in addition, there are at least (3) some current infringement (or infringement expected soon), and (4) no external events, unconnected to the patent, which weaken or destroy the patent by invalidating the claims or making them unenforceable, then the patent has true value. The first three requirements are affirmative and must occur for true value to be achieved in the first instance. The last requirement is negative in that, to maintain the value, such events must not occur.

Claims are judged according to the VSD model of review — Validity of claims, Scope of claims, and Discoverability of Infringement. These three criteria appear, in one form or another, in every kind of system for judging claim quality.

True value is not the same as financial value. The latter is a financial value that is, or at least could potentially be, attached to the claims of the patent. To determine the financial value of a patent, there must be some analysis that takes the true value of the patent as judged by VSD, combines it with a marketing analysis of claim coverage, and then applies a financial model to create an estimate of the patent's financial value. Without an understanding of the true value of the patent, the estimated financial value is nonsense, and probably would not be calculated in the first place. True value is the bedrock of financial value, and understanding true value is the key to estimating financial value.

### *(2) Components of a Full Patent Analysis*

Traditionally, there are three components of a full patent analysis:

*Fundamental Analysis*:

What are the results of the VSD analysis for this patent?

a. Validity: Are the independent claims valid?
b. Scope: Is the scope of the independent claims (including breadth of coverage and difficulty of design around) reasonable?
c. Discoverability: Is infringement discoverable?

*Market Analysis*:

What are the markets to which these claims might apply? In particular:

a. Which specific market(s) is (are) covered by the patent claims?
b. How large is each market, both now and in the future?
c. How difficult would it be for an infringer to design around the patent?

*Financial Analysis*:

Based on the fundamental and the market analyses, which financial value or range of financial values is suggested by a financial analysis? This is discussed below.

There is some overlap between fundamental analysis and financial analysis that simply cannot be avoided. To state it simply, the overlap occurs in the middle stage, called "Market Analysis," above.

Fundamental analysis includes an estimate of claim validity, which is not at all part of financial analysis. Fundamental analysis includes a review of discoverability of infringement that is parallel to a similar kind of analysis performed during financial analysis (since marketing and financial analysis can be performed only for market segments that can be identified as potentially infringing). The main overlap, however, is in review of the scope of the claims.

In an expert fundamental analysis, "EFA", a human evaluator will make an estimate of market segments that might be infringing. The evaluator might know of particular companies and products or services that may infringe. On the basis of the breadth of the claims from a legal point of view, and the evaluator's general sense of the possible markets for which patent claims may be relevant, the EFA evaluator estimates the scope of the claims.

By contrast, during a financial analysis, specific market segments will be identified, including examples of infringing technologies, products, and companies. Infringing segments will be quantified as to current infringement and growth rates of the infringing segments. Serious market intelligence is gathered and reviewed as part of the marketing analysis. Marketing review during financial analysis is more detailed than scope analysis by a human EFA evaluator, produces a deeper and more accurate picture of the market than does scope analysis, is performed generally by business developers or market managers rather than by patent professionals, and is quantified to a much more intensive degree to form the basis of the financial analysis.

With fundamental analysis of the patent and intensive marketing information, one or more methods of financial analysis are applied to determine a potential financial value of the patent. Methods of financial analysis are discussed below.

### *(3) Types of Financial Analysis*

There are three basic methods for the financial analysis of patents, which are the Income Method, the Cost Method, and the Market Method.

1. *The Income Method* says, in essence: "Figure how much cash the patent or patent portfolio is likely to generate, over what period of time (limited to the lives of the patents). Discount that cash according to some factor to derive the Net Present Value of the patent or the portfolio."

There are many variations of the Income Method, such as:

(a) *Direct cash flow*: How much cash does the company receive, or anticipate it will receive, from higher profits or from licensing revenues derived from the patents?
(b) *Relief from royalty*: Assuming the company did not own the patents, how much would the company pay to license-in a right to use the patent?
(c) *Multi-period excess earnings*: Over the moderate to long run, how much do the patents contribute above and beyond the contributions of other assets?
(d) *Incremental cash flow*: How much incremental cash is contributed by the patents?

These variations of the Income Method are discussed repeatedly, and in detail, in literature freely available on the Internet. The Income Method is, in theory, the best method of financial analysis, in that it estimates the actual benefit derived from the patents, discounted at an appropriate rate to determine the net present value of the benefit. The Income

Method is imperfect, however, because estimating future cash flows is difficult for all patents, and extremely difficult for new or untested patents.

2. *The Cost Method* relates to the cost of the individual patent, or of the patents in the portfolio. There are actually two ways of looking at this. One cost is "reproduction cost," which is the cost to make the asset being valued. If the cost of the obtaining the patent was $20,000, and the cost of maintaining the patent for its life is $10,000[53], then the "reproduction cost" may be considered to be $30,000. The reproduction cost generally produces a relatively low value for the patent. One advantage of this variation is that reproduction costs are generally well known. However, this cost is theoretically weak, since it relates to past expenses, and has no direct connection to future use or revenue streams. The Cost Method ignores the actual value of the patent in the market, and focuses only on the mechanical costs of preparing, filing, and prosecuting the patent application.

An alternative cost is "replacement cost," which means the cost for a party to continue acting, but with an alternative approach. In the world of patents, "replacement cost" refers to the total cost required for an infringer to design around (or "work around") the patent, including the costs of design around work and any additional costs for manufacturing (including, for example, re-tooling, training workers, replacing inventory, etc.).

---

53 Between October 5, 2012, and March 18, 2013, the total fees to maintain a U.S. patent through its entire legal life were $8,860. As of March 19, 2013, the total fees to maintain a U.S. patent through its entire life are $12,600. All of the numbers listed here are for an average or large entity. A "small entity", however that may be defined from time to time, pays exactly 50% of the costs of a larger entity to maintain a patent.

As an example of design around, if an invention related to a special light for a vehicle includes a claim limitation of an "incandescent bulb", a manufacturer could design around the claim by using an LED bulb. However, the manufacturer may incur significant costs for redesigning its power system to accommodate an LED bulb, scrapping infringing units in the warehouse, purchasing LED bulbs (which are generally more expensive than incandescent bulbs), adjusting sales literature, etc.

Of the two alternatives of the Cost Method, reproduction cost and replacement cost, estimating the latter may be more difficult than estimating the former, since replacement costs include more unknown variables. Possibly for that reason, "replacement cost" is not favored as the sole form of patent valuation, although it may be used with other methods of financial valuation.

3. *The Market Method* also comes in at least two forms. One form is to compare the current assets with "comparable assets," meaning patents of the same kind and quality. A second form is to attempt to analogize the patents to other kinds of assets, perhaps to goodwill or other intangible assets with known or estimated value, and form the patent valuation on that basis. As a rule, the Market Method is extremely good for real estate prices, but very poor for patent prices, since sales prices for patents are often not known and, even if they are known, patent assets are simply not comparable directly.[54]

---

54 An interesting article in this regard is by Martin A. Bader and Frauke Ruether, "Still a Long Way to Value-Based Patent Valuation: The Patent Valuation Practices of Europe's Top 500", printed in *les Nouvelles,* Journal of the Licensing Executives Society International, June, 2009, at pp.121–124, republished at http://www.wipo.int/edocs/mdocs/sme/en/wipo_insme_smes_ge_10/wipo_insme_smes_ge_10_ref_theme06_01.pdf. pp.121–124. See

*Conclusion:* Whichever method of financial analysis is selected and implemented, the financial result will be an estimate only, perhaps in the form of a range of possible values. Estimated financial value will also vary depending on who has performed the analysis, and the analyst's motivations. Although financial analysis for intangible assets such as patents is not exact, it is still necessary in a variety of business contexts, such as valuation of a company for sale or for an IPO, acquisition of a patent portfolio, or licensing-in of patents. Financial valuation typically will be based on a combination of fundamental and financial analyses. Moreover, different people looking at the same patent may well arrive at dramatically different valuations. For a creditor, for example, the main issue is coverage of debt over a relatively short period of time. Therefore, for such a creditor, certainty of payment and early cash flows are critical. For an equity investor in a company or a possible buyer of a patent, more important may be total cash flows over the entire life of the patent.[55]

---

also US 7,536,312, "Method of Appraising and Insuring Intellectual Property", issued May 19, 2009, to Robert Block, and assigned to Ocean Tomo, LLC, freely available at http://www.freepatentsonline.com/7536312.pdf. This patent discusses the three basic methods of financial valuation of patents.

55 For a patent aggregator, the motivation may be entirely different. A "patent aggregator" is an entity that combines multiple patents for a specific reason. An aggregator that acquires patents for the purpose of extracting value from potential licensees is often called a Non-Practicing Entity, "NPE" for short. An aggregator that acquires patents to keep them out of the hands of possible plaintiffs is often called a Defensive Patent Aggregator, or "DPA" for short. A DPA usually acts on behalf of multiple companies who have aggregated financial resources in order to acquire patents as a group. The motivations for aggregators may be different than the motivations for non-aggregators. For example, the financial value of a patent to an NPE may be influenced greatly by the NPE's estimate of whether it can quickly obtain financial settlements from a few early licensees. As another example, the financial value of a patent to a DPA may be affected greatly by whether the

## V. Technology Inflection Points

This book is organized such that aspects of "good patents" and patents with true value are identified throughout the book, and then summarized in Chapter 8. In accordance with that organization, Chapters 3–7 present examples of "good patents" in the form of specific cases. However, even before reviewing these examples, we can identify some aspects of good patents. Let's start by defining two terms.

*Point of Novelty*: A "point of novelty" (PON) is a part of the invention described in the patent that is new, useful, and not obvious relative to what is already known (usually called "prior art"). A person evaluating a patent should ask both:

(a) "Are *all* the points of novelty that are part of the invention well-described in the written description in the patent?", and
(b) "Assuming that the points of novelty are indeed well-described in the written description, are all the points of novelty fully covered in the patent claims?"

A "good patent" will include a clearly written description, and good coverage of each point of novelty by well-structured, minimally-limiting, and unambiguous claims. If each PON is explained, and there is a match between the explanation in the written description and the claims, that is good. If there is not a match between the written description and the claims, one of the following results may occur:

(a) If the written description is broader than the claims,

---

subject of the patent is relevant to particular companies represented by the DPA, and more specifically by whether particular companies represented by the DPA have expressed interest in acquiring the patent.

then anything in the written description that was not claimed is, by law, "dedicated to the public". That may be good for the public, but for the patentee this might be considered a catastrophic result.

(b) If the claims are broader than the written description, then the situation is not clear. It could be that the narrow description is combined with the broad claims to define clearly the meaning and scope of the claims, in which case all is well. It could be that a court rules the broad claims to be "unsupported" by the written description, in which case the claims will be invalidated, which is another very negative result.

The guidelines are very clear:

- Have well-defined claims that cover every Point of Novelty you want to protect.
- Make sure that the written description supports those claims.
- Do not include in the written description Points of Novelty which are not covered in the claims.[56]

*Technology Inflection Point*: A "technology inflection point" is a point in the existing technology that is relatively important, indeed critical, for the advancement of the technology. If you have a Point of Novelty described and claimed in a patent, that at the same time is also an inflection point for an important technology, then it is likely that your patent

---

56 Of course, the written description may be broader than the claims, if you intend to cover other parts of the written description in future patent applications. The ideal is that you intend to claim, either in the current application or in future applications, every Point of Novelty discussed in the written description.

will be valuable, perhaps extremely valuable. For example, a breakthrough in high-energy density batteries could be a technology inflection point for the adoption of electric vehicle technology.[57]

*How can you identify a technology inflection point?* The clear answer is: "find a weakness or bottleneck in the system". If you can remove that weakness, or at least widen the bottleneck, your point of novelty is likely to have value. In trying to develop valuable technology and valuable patents protecting the technology, an important first step is to find what people in the field would consider a "good problem".[58] A few examples of potential technology inflection points are presented below.

Engineers often say that 90% of the task of solving a problem is defining the problem properly. Assuming this is true, one can see that identifying and clearly defining "good

---

57 It happens that an evaluator is asked to identify patents that relate to a specific kind of technology. The question typically asked is: "Can you identify a patent in technology area X, and is technology X covered by the claims of the patent?" For example, if a client wants a patent related to advanced cellular technology, the evaluator might check to see if the patent is relevant to so-called second generation ("2G") technology, to 3G technology, to 4G technology, or to LBS, short for "location-based services." In these instances, the evaluator's client may be looking to license-in or buy patents related to a specific technology inflection point.

58 The importance of finding good problems is explained in the recent book by Jon Gertner, *The Idea Factory: Bell Labs and the Great Age of American Innovation*, (Penguin Press, New York, 2012). Bell Laboratories, the R&D arm of the Bell Telephone system from 1925 to the breakup of Bell Telephone in 1984, is arguably the greatest corporate R&D center in the history of humankind, at least in the area of ICT technologies. Bell Laboratories produced tremendous innovations in all areas of electronic technology, and led to 14 Nobel Prizes in Physics in the period 1937 — 2009. The founders of Bell Laboratories had the view that there were very many good ideas, but "[m]ainly, they [the founders] were looking for good problems" (p.33). A good problem is often found by "discovering the weak points that could be improved upon" (p.15).

problems" has great value to the practice of writing good patents (or identifying good patents that have already been issued). On the flip side, poor patents include those that solve problems that don't exist, or solve problems that are already solved by simpler, cheaper, faster, or otherwise better implementations.

*What kind of "weak points" might point to a "good problem"?* Two kinds of weak points in a technology might constitute a "good problem" which can be solved by an invention and a patent on the invention.

The first is where the weak point may be significantly improved, leading to dramatically improved results in a method or system. This includes patents that minimize or make irrelevant the weak point in the system.

The second one is "paradigm shift" away from the current method or system to something completely new and better. This is the so-called "breakthrough technology" (sometimes called "disruptive technology"). When it happens, the effects can be dramatic, but it does not happen often.

Sometimes the line between significant improvement in the current system and paradigm shift to a new system is not clear. It is difficult, sometimes, to know if a "paradigm shift" has really occurred. Either way, the key is that the new technology, and patents which cover it, significantly improve the functioning of the technology.

Following are some examples of "technology inflection points".

### *Example 1 — Motor Vehicles*

Motor vehicles are powered by an internal combustion engine, generally operating by the four phases of fuel intake, compression, combustion, and exhaust. The internal combustion engine is not more than about 30% efficient, which means that only about 30% of the potential energy in the fuel actually powers the car, while the other 70% is lost to heat, vibration, exhaust, and other non-useful effects. Because of this wasted energy and the associated emissions (both direct emissions from the engine and indirect emissions occurring during the production of gasoline), the use of the internal combustion engine is one of the chief contributors to worldwide pollution.

This is a "good problem" begging for good technical solutions. In other words, the loss of 70% of the energy, not to mention the production of massive pollution, is a "weak point" in the vehicle system. Some solutions may be directed at boosting the energy efficiency from 30% to even a few percentage points higher.[59]

Alternatively, a potentially excellent solution may be a paradigm shift away from petroleum-based internal combustion engines to something wholly different, such as hydrogen engines, nuclear engines, or battery-powered motors (in which the power source is stored chemically). "Electric cars" now being sold are battery-operated cars recharged with electricity. Based on their efficiency, which may exceed 80%, and their reduced pollution, electric motor powered vehicles may represent a paradigm shift in vehicle transportation technology.[60]

---

59 Two such solutions are described in the article by Erica Gies, "Baby steps vs. giant leaps in motors", printed in the International Herald Tribune on June 21, 2012, at p.12. The solutions described are the Scuderi split-cycle engine and the Ecomotor two-stroke engine, neither of which I will describe here except to say that they are still based on conventional burning of conventional fuel but use significantly better methods.

60 The energy calculation is more complicated than presented here, since it

*Example 2 — The Early Telephone*

In the early days of wire line communication, the telephone system suffered from two areas of weakness. These areas of weakness were vacuum tubes and switching relays. The vacuum tubes were delicate, and hard to manufacture. They consumed significant electricity, generated a great deal of wasted heat, and were unreliable. Switching relays were mechanical, with all the problems of metal fatigue, corrosion, wear-and-tear of moving parts, and physical blockage of contacts.[61] Switching relays were also relatively slow.

These weaknesses were well understood. Temporary solutions could ease the problems with better materials and improved manufacturing methods. The ultimate solution, however, was to shift from vacuum tubes and relays to solid state amplification and switching components based on the transistor. The application of solid state components to computer systems may be considered a "paradigm shift". Severe difficulties arose in creating this paradigm shift, but we can be sure that the patents on the methods and systems to solve the difficulties were very valuable. These were "good" patents.

*Example 3 — Mobile Communication*

The entire field of mobile communication is a fertile area

---

must include also the efficiency of producing the source fuel, whether that fuel is gasoline or electricity. However, under most assumptions, an electric car is significantly more energy-efficient and significantly less pollution-generating than a gasoline-powered car. The problem with electric cars is that their batteries currently have very poor energy-to-weight ratios, but intensive R&D efforts are now being made to improve these ratios.

61 This entire story is described in Gertner's book about Bell Labs, *op. cit.*, p.52.

to identify technology inflection points. Let's look at two such points.

One problem in mobile communication, as in the internal combustion engine, is wasted energy. In a mobile communication system, at any particular time communications are sent from a first point to a second point (or to multiple points in a point to multipoint system). However, because at least one of the communication points is mobile, energy must be propagated to a wide area to ensure that a communication link is achieved. Much of the transmission energy will be wasted, because mobile communication, unlike wire line communication, does not have a focused and reliable "wave guide" such as a telephone wire. How is it possible to reduce wasted energy in such a system? Would a better antenna help? How about improved processing of received signals? Would it be possible to create a kind of *mobile point-to-point communication* that could greatly improve bandwidth in existing cellular systems? One solution utilized in present-day systems is beamforming, where the antenna pattern of a transmitter is steered digitally in the direction of the receiver, thereby maximizing communication gain in that direction. Other solutions may also be used. In short, solutions that reduce wastage of energy in mobile communication systems are potential technology inflection points.

A second typical mobile problem is the reliance on batteries. For mobile devices, battery life is always an issue. How to deal with this? Incremental approaches, which may be valuable but which do not produce technology inflection points, attempt to increase the energy density of batteries. Another incremental improvement is to create more communication cells in the infrastructure, with less coverage for each cell; the result is that a mobile unit needs to use less energy to communicate with the system. All of these approaches, however incremental or fundamental, may be considered improvements of the current system. A radically different approach would be to change the method of charging the mobile device. Today, what is called "wireless charging" (although the formal name is "inductive charging" or "electromagnetic inductive charging") is limited in distance between the charging device and the mobile device. If we could increase that distance with no loss of efficiency, we would likely have a paradigm shift in battery charging technology for mobile communication systems. Patents that cover this paradigm, if the paradigm shift occurs, could be very valuable.

*Example 4 — Video on the Internet*

An enormous problem for the Internet, not today but on the near horizon, is the explosive growth of video data (particularly high-definition video data). Before that happens, people will develop new technologies for storing, compressing, transmitting, and displaying data which will help overcome this problem. Which solutions will those be? Will they be incremental? Will they be breakthroughs? These questions cannot be answered at this time. However, we can say that patents with claims that address this problem and provide solutions (temporary or permanent, partial or total, local or system-wide) are likely to be "good" patents.

*Example 5 — Data Centers*

A number of trends are converging, including video on the Internet, increasing mobile usage, and cloud computing. One result of such convergence is likely to be a proliferation of what are called "data centers" — concentrations of large numbers of servers in single locations. Such data centers consume massive quantities of electricity and are serious polluters. However, over 90% of electricity consumed is not used for power processing but rather to run backup servers and processing units. Could technologies be developed to turn off unused servers, or run servers with less electricity, or store electric energy in alternative ways (such as, for example, in mechanical flywheels or as compressed hot air)? Technologies that will improve the performance of data centers may well involve technology inflection points.

# Part II

# Examples of Good Patents and Good Patent Portfolios

# Chapter 3

# Court Cases with Good Patents

Victory in court litigation, with a multi-million dollar verdict or settlement, is a strong indication that the patent has both true value and substantial financial value. The purpose of this chapter is to give you a basic understanding of some aspects of patent litigation, and to learn lessons from victorious patents about what may constitute a "good patent".

Here is the organization of Chapter 3:

I. Introduction to Patent Litigation
II. Cases with Winning Litigation
   (1) *AT&T v. Vonage*
   (2) *Uniloc v. Microsoft*
   (3) *i4i v. Microsoft*
   (4) *TiVo v. EchoStar*

## I. Introduction to Patent Litigation

Like other forms of commercial litigation, patent litigation occurs when the opposing parties — the patent owner (who is usually the plaintiff) and the alleged infringer (who is usually the defendant) — have different views of their respective prospects in litigation.[62] If the estimates of the parties are

62 Although the patent owner is *usually* the plaintiff who brings the lawsuit, and the defendant is *usually* the alleged infringer who defends against the

far apart, the plaintiff may consider the patent to be worth a great deal against this defendant, whereas the defendant may consider the patent to be worth much less or even nothing (or possibly only "nuisance value", i.e., the minimum transaction costs to defend the litigation, sometimes paid to make the plaintiff go away). However, if the parties have similar estimates of the value of the patent in this litigation then, at least in theory, the case should be settled before trial.

The parties' estimates refer to whether the claims alleged to be infringed will be found valid or invalid, and (if they are valid) whether such claims are actually infringed by the defendant. Any rulings or procedures in the litigation that tend to narrow gaps in estimates on the questions of validity and infringement will encourage settlement.

Like all commercial litigations, patent litigation has "civil discovery", meaning each side obtains information from the other side before trial. As parties become more informed, they may or may not tend toward the same estimate of the value of specific patent claims in the litigation. This process in patent litigation of changing value estimates is much the same as the corresponding process in other commercial cases.

However, patent litigation is fundamentally different from other commercial litigation in a number of important ways:

1. Patent litigation occurs only in the federal courts, not

---

lawsuit, there is another procedure, called a "Declaratory Judgment Action", where the alleged infringer brings the lawsuit either to establish that there is no infringement, to invalidate the patent claims, or to have the patent ruled unenforceable. In other words, the possible infringer asks the court for a declaration of non-infringement, for any of a variety of reasons. In this kind of action, the alleged infringer is attempting to pre-empt litigation by the patent owner, so the alleged infringer is the plaintiff whereas the patent owner is the defendant.

in the courts of the various states. The lowest level of federal court is a district court. There are 94 district courts in the U.S., and patent litigation may begin in any one of them. A decision of the district court may be appealed to a U.S. court of appeals. There are 13 such courts of appeals in the United States, but all patent cases are appealed solely to the Court of Appeals for the Federal Circuit ("CAFC") in Washington, D.C.[63] Patent decisions of the CAFC may be appealed to the U.S. Supreme Court, which has the right to review a decision or decline to review.

2. The cost of patent litigation in the U.S. is very high. Legal and technical experts are hired. Technology analysis is complicated. Litigation costs are routinely expected to be in the millions of dollars for both sides.
3. The stakes in patent litigation are often enormous. In this chapter, we will review litigation in which the defendants were found liable for tens of millions to hundreds of millions of dollars. In Chapter 4, we will see cases where injunctions were issued against the defendant, prohibiting the sale of products in the U.S. An injunction like this can wreck a business (unless the defendant can design around the patent to stop the infringement).
4. There is procedure unique to patent cases called "the Markman hearing".[64] After the parties have performed

---

63 The United States Court of Appeals for the Federal Circuit is usually abbreviated in legal citations as "Fed. Cir.", and sometimes as "C.A.F.C." In this book, the Court will be abbreviated as "CAFC" in the text, and as the more traditional "Fed. Cir." in citations.

64 This type of hearing received its name because it was first decided by the U.S. Supreme Court, in the case of *Markman v. Westview Instruments, Inc.*

a serious amount of civil discovery,[65] but before the jury trial, there is a special hearing in which a district court judge[66] decides how various phrases and terms in the patent will be interpreted at trial. This procedure is so significant that it frequently resolves the litigation.[67] .

5. A defendant may raise defenses which are unique to patent cases. Attacks on validity of claims (i.e., the claim is "not new", or is "obvious" from prior art) have been noted above. In addition, defendants may argue that their actions or products simply do not infringe the patent. Finally, defendants may raise what are called "equitable defenses" — reasons the patent, even if valid and infringed by the defendant, should not be enforced.[68]

---

517 US 360 (1996), that patent claims are a matter of law to be interpreted by judges rather than a matter of fact to be decided by juries. The name "Markman" is not an adjective, and has no inherent meaning in this context.

65 Typically, the Markman hearing happens well after civil discovery has begun. However, this is really a question of litigation strategy and court scheduling. In some cases, one of the parties may push for an early Markman hearing. For example, a defendant may wish to have the Markman hearing scheduled before major depositions or other civil discovery — in this way, the plaintiff may have less knowledge of the defendant's products, and thus greater difficulty obtaining patent definitions more likely to cover the defendant's products.

66 Markman hearings are not mandatory, but they are often ordered by the district courts in courtroom litigation. The ITC is also permitted to order Markman hearings, and has done so on at least a half-dozen occasions. However, the use of a Markman hearing to clarify patent claims in advance of trial is much more common in the federal district courts than in the ITC.

67 Depending on the judge's decision in a Markman hearing, the plaintiff may drop the case, the defendant may decide to pay the amount requested, or the parties may reach a compromise.

68 Equitable defenses include, for example: (1) fraud against the PTO

In sum, although patent suits are similar in many ways to other commercial lawsuits, they may have a number of twists that can complicate the litigation.

## II. Cases with Winning Litigation

I will present four litigations in which a patent claim generated a great deal of revenue for a patentee, explaining why I think the victorious claim was "good".[69] The four examples are:

(1) *AT&T v. Vonage*, US 6,487,200, claim #1, a system claim. Settled for $39 million.
(2) *Uniloc v. Microsoft*, US 5,490,216, claim #19, a system claim in the Means & Function format. Judgment for Uniloc in the sum of $388 million.
(3) *i4i v. Microsoft*, US 5,787,449, claim #14, a method claim. Judgment for i4i in the sum of $277 million.
(4) *TiVo v. EchoStar*, US 6,233,389, claims ##1, 31, 32, and 61. These claims are a mix of hardware and software,

(particularly where the applicant is accused of deliberately concealing an important piece of information from the patent office), (2) patent misuse (often where the patentee tries to collect royalties after the patent has expired, or where the applicant uses the patent to violate the antitrust laws), (3) the doctrine of "laches" (where the patent owner delayed suing and the delay caused damage to the defendant), and (4) the doctrine of "equitable estoppel" (where the patent owner led the defendant to believe that no lawsuit would be filed, and the defendant relied on this belief).

69 Some claims win at trial that are not "good claims", while some claims that appear to be "good" lose at trial. It has been said that litigation is warfare, and when a person goes to war, the outcome is never certain. Even the best armies don't win every battle. Nevertheless, although the outcome of litigation, like the outcome of war, is never certain, there are some characteristics of the winning patents presented here that help us to answer the question, "How do I know if my patent's any good?"

> method and structure. They provide a good summary of some of the lessons to be learned in this chapter. Judgment for TiVo in the initial case for $74 million, with a final settlement for $500 million.

These particular patents and their claims represent a mix of method claims and structure claims (including different types of structure claims), as well as hardware and software claims.

### *Case 1: AT&T Corp. v. Vonage Holdings*

Suit brought in Federal District Court for the Western District of Wisconsin, 2007. Settled before trial, also in 2007, for $39 million.

*Background to the Decision:*

Vonage was a pioneer and a leader in Voice over Internet Protocol ("VoIP"). This technology, first implemented in the late 1990s, eventually developed into mass telephone and video telephone over the Internet. Although Vonage was a pioneer in offering services, it faced a series of lawsuits for patent infringement by plaintiffs such as Verizon (resulting in a judgment of $58M plus 5.5% royalties, against Vonage), Sprint Nextel (resulting in an $80M judgment against Vonage), and AT&T (eventually settled by Vonage's payment of $39M to AT&T). Although Vonage continues as an operating company, with annual sales of about $900 million, its overall success was hampered by these multiple patent lawsuits.

*Preview of the AT&T Patent:*

At first glance, the main patent claim, #1, appears needlessly long, complicated, and weak. However, looking deeper, its multiple claim elements describe general functions of a product called a Network Interface Unit ("NIU"). The NIU product eventually was widely adopted in the market, and US 6,487,200 was one of the earliest patents in the field. Claim #1 turned out to be surprisingly valuable. Vonage settled the case for $39 million.

The patent teaches that general claim elements are good. Even long and apparently complicated claims may prove valuable if the claim elements are general descriptions of widely adopted aspects of a product.

*Review:*

AT&T alleged infringement of claim #1 of US 6,487,200, entitled "Packet Telephone System". This patent has a priority date of April 4, 1996, which is relatively early in this field. The patent issued on November 26, 2002.

The entire claim #1 is quoted below. I use my own brackets, [ ], with enclosed element numbers, all to specify elements of the claim. These brackets and the enclosed element numbers were not part of the original claim. (The use of brackets in this way is called "parsing the claim".)

> 1. A telephone system comprising:
> [1] a wide-area packet network comprising nodes that route network packets over links that interconnect said nodes; and
> [2] a plurality of network interface units, connected to some of said nodes, each constructed to
> a) receive voice signals and encode said voice signals into network packets that are characterized as voice packets, with the encoding including compression of said voice signals,

b) receive control signals and encode said control signals into network packets that are characterized as control packets,

c) receive non-network packets and map said non-network packets onto network packets that are characterized as data packets,

d) convert receives voice packets into voice signals,

e) convert control packets into control signals, and

f) convert data packets into said non-network packets.

This is a moderately long claim, with two elements and six sub-elements. The presence of eight separate elements and sub-elements, all of which must be present for a product to infringe, is a concern.

However, despite the relatively high number of elements and sub-elements, even on the face of this one claim there are some features that should immediately elicit a positive response.

First, the entire preamble is: "A telephone system". The preamble is short, clear, and non-limiting. *Preambles do not get much better than this.* Courts sometimes use preambles to limit claim scope, other times not. That is not a concern here, as long as the infringing system could be considered a "telephone system", which is a very broad concept.

Second, there are only two structural elements, and they are both very simple:

(1) "a wide-area packet network comprising nodes that route network packets over links that interconnect said nodes". This is a very general element. Wide area packet networks were in existence years before the priority date of this packet, and have widespread application today.

(2) "a plurality of network interface units, connected to

some of said [routing] nodes". "Network interface units", or "NIU" for short, are also often called "Network interface devices" or "NID" for short, of which a "network interface card", or "NIC", is one example. In essence, an NIU allows communication between different devices in a network by converting the communications to a common protocol. The NIU, like the first structural element, is very general and widespread in usage. The reason is simple — for networks to communicate, it is vital that the products on the network use a common protocol, and the NIU insures that the various products have a common protocol.

So claim #1 has at least two very strong positives: (1) a simple preamble, and (2) two short and simple structural elements. Questions about this claim really do not concern the preamble or the elements, but rather the six sub-elements which potentially limit the scope of the second structural element.

Before we consider these six sub-elements, we need to consider the "Points of Novelty" in this invention. Where might we find the PONs in the patent?

1. In the Claims, although often, as here, it is difficult to distinguish the prior art from the PON(s).
2. In the Abstract, particularly in a sentence or phrase in the Abstract, often at the beginning or end of the Abstract, that summarizes the invention.
3. In the Description of Prior Art, particularly where the applicant defines the problem solved by the invention. (This section of the patent, "Description of Prior Art", is sometimes called "Background" or "Background of the Invention".)

4. In the Summary of the Invention, particularly where the applicant appears to summarize the invention.

In this case, the end of the Abstract includes the following sentence which attempts to summarize the invention.

> The combination of virtual circuits, with bounded delays, short packets, rapid compression and decompression, and intelligent network interface units makes it possible to build a telephone system with fewer and cheaper switches and fewer links for a given volume of traffic than heretofore possible and also permits substantial savings in provisioning and maintaining the system.

So are all these features part of the PON? You might think so, but in fact "virtual circuits", "bounded delays", "short" packets, and "rapid compression and decompression" are not discussed *anywhere* in the claims. The word "packets" appears in the claims, as does "compression" (although "decompression" does not appear in the claims). The phrase "network interface unit" appears repeatedly, and is probably the phrase appearing most frequently in the claims. In short, it appears to be the NIUs that are driving down cost and increasing system capacity.

This conclusion is confirmed by the last paragraph of the Description of the Prior Art, which reads, at column 2, lines 44–53:

> It is an object of the present invention to takes advantage of the existence of low-cost programmable devices and the advances in packet switching and transmission technology to create a telephone system which is equally adapted to voice and data communication, which requires fewer

> switches and trunk lines than existing systems, and for which programming, maintenance, provisioning, and billing are greatly simplified, and thereby to provide telephone and other telecommunications services at a substantially lower cost than heretofore possible.

This is the only "object of the invention" identified and discussed as such in the patent. It appears to relate specifically to intelligent NIU units, which we would therefore identify as the PON in this patent.[70]

Further, in the Summary of the Invention, at column 3, lines 27–34, we see the following:

> Because the telephone system is implemented using a packet network and network interface units, which can produce and respond to control packets, the telephone system can be used for data as well as voice. Further, the ability of the network interface units to produce and respond to control packets means that new services can be defined in the network interface units instead of in the network. That in turn greatly simplifies the design of devices in the network.

To summarize, in my opinion, the main PON for claim #1 is the use of network interface units to simplify system design, offer new services, and cut costs. I am not saying that

70 This "object of the invention" was presented as the very last paragraph in the section, "Description of the Prior Art". An "object of the invention" should never appear in the "Description of Prior Art", since such a placement may create confusion as to what is prior art and what is the invention. An "object of the invention" should appear only in the Summary of Invention or in the Detailed Description of the Invention. In this patent, the placement of the "object of the invention" is defective. Nevertheless, the applicant's intent seems to be reasonably clear.

packet networks are unimportant — in fact, they are essential to provide data and digitized voice. However, the essence of the invention, its "Point of Novelty", appears to be the NIUs.

That being so, what can we say about the six sub-elements of element 2 of claim 1 of US 6,487,200? Although there are many functions listed, *all of the functions listed are simple, basic, and exactly what one would need in a system based on network interface units.* If we were to simplify the sub-elements of element 2 by deleting non-essential words, we would end up with an NIU that [a] receives, compresses, and encodes, voice signals; [b] receives and encodes control signals; [c] receives and maps non-network packets; [d] converts voice packets into voice signals; [e] converts control packets into control signals; and [f] converts data packets into non-network packets. If one were defining what a general "NIU" does, these are exactly the functions one would list.

What does all this mean? Ultimately, every patent claims needs to be reviewed according to the VSD method, considering the Validity, Scope, and Discoverability of infringement. Let's do that now.

**Validity**: The general presumption must be that a patent claim is valid. This is presumed by a court, and should be presumed when you are looking at a claim. However, there are at least two reasons why you might doubt the validity of a claim.

First, you might doubt claim validity if you are aware of some prior art that might impact the claim, and that prior art is not cited in the patent. Since you may be a technical expert in the field, this can indeed happen. Patent examiners are also technical experts, but they cannot find everything, particularly not all technical papers or other non-patent prior art.

Second, you might doubt claim validity if the law has changed in a way that calls into question the validity of the patent. The presumption is that the patent claim is valid *according to the law that exists on the day the patent issues.* But the law changes. The PTO issues new guidelines. Courts change judicial doctrine. The Congress sometimes amends the patent statute, as it did in 2011.

However, barring some special knowledge or a change in the law, when you evaluate a patent claim, you should assume that it is valid, as we should do here.[71]

**Scope**: The description of the system in claim #1,

---

71 There are statistics suggesting that a significant percentage of claims might not be valid. See, for example, John R. Allison and Mark A. Lemley, "Empirical Evidence on the Validity of Litigated Patents", AIPLA Quarterly Journal, Vol. 26, p.185, (1998), stating that a study of 299 patents litigated in the period 1989–1996 shows 46% of such patents invalidated by the court. However, in my opinion, this article, and articles like it, do not overcome the presumption of patent validity. They say only that in those specific cases when patent litigation goes all the way through trial, in a significant percentage of such cases the patent claims are invalidated, but in a significant number of litigated patent cases, the claims are validated. That is about what one would expect. If a patent is relatively weak, it is likely that the plaintiff would not proceed to trial, or perhaps the matter would be settled on terms relatively favorable to the defendant. If a patent is relatively strong, the opposite would occur — the plaintiff would likely bring suit, but the ultimate result might be a pre-trial settlement on terms favorable to the plaintiff. However, where the parties to the litigation cannot agree on the validity or strength of the claims (that is, the plaintiff has a relatively favorable view of the patent while the defendant has a relatively negative view of the patent), the parties are likely to go to trial. In disputed cases like this, where the parties' have radically different view about the patent, some patents will be validated and others will be invalidated. The invalidity of some *claims in judicial decisions after patent litigation* does not prove or even suggest that the validity of any patent claim is a 50–50 proposition, but only that this *might be generally true* for some patents that have been involved in litigation all the way to judgment, which is a very small and select group of patents.

particularly the functioning of the NIU in sub-elements [a] — [f], presents a very general description of a joint data/digitized voice with local control from intelligent NIUs. Many systems will fit this description, including many public telephone systems as well as proprietary data or voice systems. This general description would be difficult for an infringer to design around. In short, claim #1 appears to have an exceptionally good scope of coverage.

**Discoverability of Infringement**: Packet networks and network interface units are easy to see in competitive systems. Perhaps not all of the functions in the sub-elements would be easy to detect, but they would be inferable, and proof could be obtained during litigation. This patent does not have any well-known problem with discoverability of infringement, such as claims focused solely on manufacturing methods. In short, discoverability looks good as well.

**Summary**: A general description of a key product in a VoIP system, with early priority date, no obvious problem to validity, good scope of coverage, and good discoverability of infringement. Claim #1 of US 6,487,200 is a good patent claim.

**Lessons Learned**: Here are some of the lessons we might learn about good patents from this patent claim:

3-1-1. ***A short and simple preamble is good.***

3-1-2. ***In a structure claim, a smaller number of structural elements is good.*** (A system claim is one example of a structure claim.)

3-1-3. ***General structural elements are good.*** The structural elements in this claim were not short in number of words, but each element was simple and general.

3-1-4. ***A large number of sub-elements will not unduly***

***narrow the main element as long as the sub-elements describe aspects or functions that you would expect to see in any product of the type described in the element.*** This is the main lesson to be learned from claim #1 of US 6,478,200.

### *Case 2: Uniloc v. Microsoft Corp.*

Full title: *Uniloc USA, Inc., and Uniloc Singapore Private Limited v. Microsoft Corporation* (decision by the CAFC in 2011)[72]

*Background to the Decision:*

The second example we will see is a kind of structure claim in the means-plus-function format. In *Uniloc v. Microsoft*, Uniloc USA and Uniloc Singapore (to be called here "Uniloc") sued Microsoft for infringement of independent claim #19 of US 5,490,216. The patent, entitled, "System for Software Registration", has a priority date of September 21, 1993, and was issued in the United States on February 6, 1996. A request for reexamination of all claims was filed on January 22, 2010, while litigation was pending. The certificate of reexamination confirming all claims was issued on October 4, 2011.

The jury found in favor of Uniloc, and determined damages of $388 million against Microsoft. That decision of the jury is, in itself, sufficient for this patent claim to pass the filtering test of a "good patent". However, the federal district court judge who presided over the trial found that the jury's decision lacked a legal basis and overturned the verdict to rule in favor of Microsoft. This decision of the trial judge was then reviewed by the CAFC, which overturned the judge's

72 The case is reported at 632 F.3d 1292 (Fed. Cir., 2011).

decision, thereby reinstating the jury decision of infringement against Microsoft. The CAFC also overturned the damage sum of $388 million, finding flaw in the theory of damages known as "the 25% rule," according to which 25% of the profits of the infringer is to be remitted to the patent holder. After the CAFC decision in January of 2011, finding Microsoft liable, the PTO issued the certificate of reexamination in October of 2011, confirming all claims. The parties then settled the case in March, 2012, at an unreported sum, but there are unofficial estimates that Microsoft may have paid more than $100 million to Uniloc.

*Preview of the Uniloc Patent:*

This was an early patent for software security, in which registration needed to be confirmed before the customer could use the product. At first glance, claim #19 looked very good, but it was vulnerable to attack because it seemed to include "local" elements at the customer site that Microsoft did not directly control. The CAFC held for Uniloc, *specifically because the preamble of claim #19 used the phrase "remote registration station"*, which, the Court said, proved that all of the elements will be at a remote site controlled by Microsoft (meaning that the claim *did not have any local elements*, despite apparent claim language to the contrary). It is relatively rare for a preamble to save a patent claim, but that is what happened here.

*Review:*

The entire claim #19 is quoted below. I add brackets, [ ], with enclosed numbers, to parse the specify elements of the claim. These brackets were not part of the claim. In addition,

I have **boldfaced** elements appearing in means-plus-function format, although there is no boldface in the actual claim.

> 19. [Preamble] A remote registration station [Transitional phrase] incorporating
> [1] **remote licensee unique ID generating means,**
> [2] said station forming part of a registration system for licensing execution of digital data in a use mode,
> [3] said digital data executable on a platform,
> [4] said system including **local licensee unique ID generating means,**
> [5] said system further including **mode switching means** operable on said platform which permits use of said digital data in said use mode on said platform only if a licensee unique ID generated by said **local licensee unique ID generating means** has matched a licensee unique ID generated by said **remote licensee unique ID generating means**; and
> [6] wherein said **remote licensee unique ID generating means** comprises software executed on a platform which includes the algorithm utilized by said **local licensee unique ID generating means** to produce said licensee unique ID.

Let's make a few preliminary observations about the claim:

First, the preamble, "A remote registration station", seems to be standard, although it later becomes very significant, as discussed below.

Second, the transitional phrase, "incorporating", is quite

irregular, but was never discussed by Federal Circuit, and seems to have been read as "comprising".[73]

Third, there are three means-plus-function elements, which are "remote...generating means", "local...generating means", and "mode switching means". For each means-plus-function element, structure must be found in the patent to support the claim element, and the infringing product must have that structure to support a finding of infringement.

What really is this patent about, particularly claim #19? The first paragraph of the Summary of the Invention in the patent summarizes the invention as follows:

> In broad terms, the system according to the invention is designed and adapted to allow digital data or software to run in a use mode on a platform if and only if an appropriate licensing procedure has been followed. In particular forms, the system includes means for detecting when parts of the platform on which the digital data has been loaded has changed in part or in entirety as compared with the platform parameters when the software or digital data to be protected was for example last booted or run or validly registered.

The CAFC summarized the patent as "directed to a software registration system to deter copying of software. The system allows the software to run within restrictions (in 'use mode') only if the system determines that the software installation is legitimate."[74]

---

73 The word "incorporating" is another non-standard transition, like "having" or "composing", which simply should not be seen in ICT patents. Stick with the standard transition "comprising".

74 *Id.* at 1296.

In simple words, the product, called a registration station, checks customer-supplied identification inputs to make sure the customer's local product (with a "local ID") is properly registered at a server (with a "remote ID"). A service will be provided *only* if proper registration has occurred, and proper registration is established by matching the local and remote IDs.

This is a very simple and very powerful concept. It is so simple and widespread today that we might forget that the inventive concept, or Point of Novelty, could be new in 1992, which is the priority date of the patent.

As with all claims involving a means-plus-function element, the court must (1) decide that the element is in fact a means-plus-function element, (2) determine the function described by that element, and (3) identify the structure described in the patent on which the function operates. The court will then interpret the claim.[75]

In this case, the trial court defined six terms from claim #19. All of these definitions were accepted by the parties, and by the CAFC. Here is a list of the six terms, the accepted definition, where the term appears in the claim, and my judgment, as an evaluator, as to whether this element is a physical structure.

---

75 On judicial analysis of means-plus-function claims, see Robert C. Kahl and Stuart B. Soffer, *Thesaurus of Claim Construction*, (Oxford University Press, New York, 2011), at pp.711–764.

**Table 3–1: Key Claim Terms in *Uniloc v. Microsoft***

| Claim Term | Definition Accepted by All Parties | Where it Appears in Claim #19 (elements) | Physical Structure? |
|---|---|---|---|
| **Licensee unique ID** | A unique identifier associated with a licensee. | [1], [2], [5], and [6] | No, it is a data structure, but not a physical structure. |
| **Remote licensee unique ID generating means. This is a means-plus-function term.** | The function is to generate a remote license. The structure is a summation algorithm or a summer and equivalents thereof. | [1], [5], and [6] | Yes, clearly a physical structure, although not defined in the claim. Appears as element #63 on Figure 8 of the patent, and as element #85 on Figure 10. |
| **Registration system** | A system that allows digital data or software to run in a use mode on a platform if and only if an appropriate licensing procedure has been followed. | [2] | Yes, but that is not helpful in analysis, since any system will meet this, provided that it performs a "registration" licensing procedure. |
| **Use mode** | A mode that allows full use of the digital data or software in accordance with the license. | [2] and [5] | No, it is a condition or state of being, but not clearly a structure. |

| Claim Term | Definition Accepted by All Parties | Where it Appears in Claim #19 (elements) | Physical Structure? |
|---|---|---|---|
| **Local licensee unique ID generating means. This is a means-plus-function term.** | The function is to generate a local license. The structure is a summation algorithm or a summer and equivalents thereof. | [4], [5], and [6] | Yes, the counterpart of the remote ID generating means. Appears in Figure 8 without a number, and as #89 in Figure 10. |
| **Mode switching means. This is a means-plus-function term.** | The function is to permit the digital data or software to run in a use mode if the locally generated licensee unique ID matches the remotely generated licensee unique ID. The structure is program code which performs a comparison of two numbers or a comparator and equivalents thereof. | [5] | Yes, a means that must be defined from the structure in the written description, and in the Figures. Appears as element #68 in Figure 8 of the patent, as element #90 in Figure 10. |

There is nothing surprising or difficult in the table above. If you are evaluating a patent claim to determine if it is "good", you will parse the elements in the claims and attempt to understand what is meant by each "key term". The claim elements above are clearly "key terms" because they address the heart of the invention (that is, the Point of Novelty).

*If you are analyzing a patent claim to determine if it is "good", it may be helpful for you to create a similar table in which you (1) identify the key terms, (2) write what you understand the term to be, and (3) note what your understanding may mean for scope of coverage. This is one way to identify the "key terms" in the claim.*

Microsoft made two main arguments on appeal to the CAFC to avoid infringement.

(1) *First Argument by Microsoft*: According to Microsoft, the algorithms Microsoft used are not the same as those algorithms described in the patent. As a result, the "licensee unique ID generating means" in elements [1], [2], [5], and [6] are not used by Microsoft, so there is no infringement.

This is a sensible argument, since there were indeed differences between the patent algorithms and the algorithms used by Microsoft algorithms. However, the argument lost. The CAFC said that claim #19 included also the "equivalent structures" (under the Doctrine of Equivalents) to the structures described in the patent, and that Microsoft's algorithms should be viewed as "summation algorithms" such as those described in the patent. In short, the CAFC looked at the definitions of "remote...ID generating means" and "local... ID generating means", both of which included "a summation algorithm...*and equivalents thereof*." The CAFC then found infringement, based on Microsoft algorithms "equivalent" to the algorithms in the patent.

Since Microsoft had agreed to the definitions of key terms above as including "summation algorithms", Microsoft was likely to lose this argument. However, even if Microsoft had disagreed with the definitions above, the decision would probably have been the same, because by law, claim elements include both the elements themselves and "their equivalents".[76]

(2) *Second Argument by Microsoft*: Microsoft said that the system described in the patent appears to require both structure at Microsoft's site (such as "remote ID generating means") and structure at the customer's site (such as "local ID generating means" and "mode switching means"). Microsoft does not own or control the customer's computer. Therefore, according to this argument, Microsoft might fulfill some of the elements of claim #19, but cannot fulfill the "local" elements such as "local ID generating means" in claim elements [4] — [6], and the "mode switching means" in element [5].[77]

This second argument lost because the Court said that claim #19 relates to only a "remote registration station", and the "remote" products in the patent are both located at Microsoft's site and operated solely by Microsoft. In other words, the claim was not "a system" including both remote stations (belonging to Microsoft) and local stations (belonging to a consumer).

---

76 As explained in Chapter 2, under the *Festo* decision, claim coverage of "equivalents" may be lost if the claims are amended during prosecution. However, neither the District Court nor the Circuit Court discussed *Festo*, so I presume that case was simply irrelevant to the decisions of the courts in *Uniloc v. Microsoft*.

77 Microsoft's argument was made under what is called "the doctrine of divided infringement", which says that if the elements of the patent claim are carried out by two separate parties, then there is no infringement. This doctrine is sometimes called the "doctrine of joint infringement", which simply means that there can be infringement by two parties only if they are in some way acting jointly. This doctrine was impacted greatly by the CAFC decision of August 31, 2012, in the case of *Akamai Technologies v. Limelight Networks*. I will not delve into the *Akamai* case except to say that it was not the law when *Uniloc v. Microsoft* was decided, and in any case, the *Akamai* does not affect any of the lessons we learn about "good claims" from claim #19 in the *Uniloc* case.

Rather, claim #19 was about a single part of the system, the "remote station", which belonged solely to Microsoft. The fact that the system itself included different structures, some at Microsoft's site, some perhaps at the customer's site, was not relevant, since these other structures are merely descriptive of the system in which the remote station is located. In essence, the decision is that claim #19 is about a product called a "remote registration station", even though the word "system" appears in elements [2], [4], and [5], of claim #19.

The phrase "remote registration station" in claim #19 appears *only in the preamble*. In this case, the preamble saved the claim. Microsoft's argument might have won, if the claim were about a system, but the claim was restricted to a single part of the system, as we learn in the preamble of claim #19. It is not unheard of, but still a bit unusual, for the preamble to have this kind of impact, but that is what happened here.

Let's go one step deeper, however. There are 20 claims in U.S. patent 5,490,216. Of these, claims 1–16 and 19 are structure claims. Of the structure claims, claims 1–16 are all "registration *system*" claims, which might have been defeated by Microsoft's second argument. Claim #19 is the only structure claim that is a device claim, here a "remote [hence Microsoft] registration station". So Microsoft's second argument lost.

**Validity**: There is no obvious problem that calls validity of claim #19 into doubt. The means-plus-function format used in elements [1], [4], and [5], might be interpreted narrowly, and is disfavored by some patent practitioners. The format is not invalid, however. In addition, the priority date of this patent, 1992, is very early. An early priority date is not a guarantee of no prior art, but it is still a good date. Nothing in the prosecution history suggests any problem of patent or claim validity.

**Scope**: The general concept of claim #19 is very broad. Infringers would likely have difficult designing around the claim. Design around is not impossible, however.

This claim apparently requires that a local ID and a remote ID be generated every time software is registered. What if it were possible, instead, for an ID to be pre-generated and pre-stored at either the local location (the user's computer) or at the remote location (the company's server)? In such case, there might not be "generating means" in the system, and hence no infringement. Another possible structure would be to locate the switching mode at the company's site rather than on the user's computer, which might also avoid infringement. So there might be a possibility of design around, which could reduce the effectiveness of any injunction against future infringement, but which would not reduce legal damages for past infringement.

Regardless of any possibility of design around, claim #19 seems to cover one of the most natural forms of software, so the scope of the claim must be considered to be significantly above average.

**Discoverability of Infringement**: As noted before, three general ways of discovering infringement are: (1) visual inspection, (2) reviewing product literature, and (3) reverse engineering. It might be possible to open a consumer product to see the "locally generating means". However, even if not visually discoverable, infringement in a case like this is almost certainly discoverable, at least by reasonable inference, from product literature and from the way a system such as software registration works.

**Summary**: This was a relatively early patent in the area of software security and, specifically, a system to register new software added to a hardware platform. Independent structure claim #19 is relatively broad, but complicated by the fact that some of the claim elements are in the means-plus-function format. The claim language was a bit unusual at points, particularly the use of "incorporating" as a transitional phrase, but such language did not impact the outcome of the litigation.

**Lessons Learned**: Here are some of the lessons we might learn about good patents, from patent claim #19 in U.S. 5,490,216, litigated in *Uniloc v. Microsoft*.

3-2-1. ***Sometimes the preamble can save the entire patent***. In this case, Uniloc defeated Microsoft's second argument sole because the preamble to claim #19 said a "remote registration station", rather than a "registration system".

3-2-2. ***A non-traditional or non-standard word might not matter, as long as everyone knows what you mean***. In this case, the word "incorporating" is non-standard as a transition from preamble to claim body, but this non-standard term did not harm Uniloc.

3-2-3. ***Clarity of the "key claim terms" is critical***. That clarity can be the difference between victory or defeat in court, and hence it is a major part of determining whether a claim is "good". This is true for all claims, but particularly for the means-plus-function elements. For this claim #19, some key terms were defined very broadly, such as "software" and "platform", which undoubtedly helped the plaintiff. Other terms, such as "generating means", were mentioned and discussed but never defined, leading to attacks by the alleged infringer. *Clear and broad definitions of key terms add greatly to the value of a claim. This is the main lesson to be learned from U.S. 5,490,216.*

3-2-4. ***Formal defects in a patent are potentially bad, but may not matter if everyone knows what you mean.*** Here are some formal defects in the patent that simply did not make any difference in this case.

1. A key term, "local licensee unique ID generator", appeared in Fig. 8 and was discussed in the patent, but had no patent element number in the Figure.
2. The terms "software", "platform", and "use mode" were explicitly defined in a section entitled "Definitions", located at Column 2, lines 13–48. However, for reasons not clear to me, the Definitions section is located at the end of the section entitled "Description of the Prior Art". The Definitions should be at the beginning of the "Detailed Description of the Invention", or perhaps somewhere in the "Summary of the Invention". Definitions of key claim terms should not appear in the section "Description of the Prior Art" because, by convention and by good patent practice, you should avoid confusion between what is prior art and what is part of your invention. Placing part of the invention, including "Definitions", with the "Prior Art", is incorrect.
3. The section entitled "Brief Description of the Drawings" discussed six embodiments, numbered first through sixth. In the section, "Detailed Description of the Preferred Embodiment", there are descriptions of the First, Second, Third, Fifth, Sixth, and Seventh,

> Embodiments. The Detailed Description forgot to describe a "Fourth Embodiment", and the various "preferred embodiments" are therefore misnumbered in the Detailed Description.

Formal errors like this present a sloppy appearance but in the end did not prove damaging because people knew what was intended. *In this case, a single patent claim generated a jury verdict of $388 million and a final settlement said to be over $100 million. For all its formal flaws, claim #19 proved to be good.*

### *Case 3: i4i Limited Partnership v. Microsoft Corp.*

Federal District Court for the Eastern District of Texas, 2007) and (CAFC, 2010)[78]

*Background to the Decision:*

The third example we will look at presents a method claim. In *i4i Limited Partnership v. Microsoft Corporation*, i4i — a company based in Toronto, Canada, specializing in XML text editing — sued Microsoft for infringement of the independent method claims of US 5,787,449. This patent, entitled, "Method and System for Manipulating the Architecture and the Content of a Document Separately from Each Other", has a priority date of June 2, 1994, and was issued on July 28, 1998. The allegation was that Microsoft Word's XML editing infringed the patent.

There was extensive litigation here. i4i filed suit in the

[78] The District Court opinion is at 670 F.Supp.2nd 568, and the CAFC opinion is at 598 F.3d 831.

District Court of the Eastern District of Texas on March 8, 2007.[79]

A jury verdict for the plaintiff was decided on May 20, 2009. On August 11, 2009, the District Court granted all of i4i's motions for enhanced damages, issued an injunction against Microsoft, and denied Microsoft's motions to reverse the jury verdict or order a new trial. Microsoft was ordered to pay $240 million. On March 10, 2010, the Federal Circuit Court affirmed the opinion of the District Court. On June 9, 2011,

---

79 Both this case and the next case in this chapter, *TiVo v. EchoStar Communications Corporation*, were brought by plaintiffs in the Federal District Court for the Eastern District of Texas. This particular Court is one of those most favored by patent plaintiffs. For patent litigation, district courts are sometimes rated by their speed (called "time-to-trial"), their success rate for plaintiffs, and their size of damage awards. For the time period 1995–2011, the Eastern District of Texas was sixth in speed at 2.17 years to trial, second in plaintiff success rate at 55.7%, and fifth in median damage awards at $8.8 million per award. It had the second most patent decisions in the time period with 80 decisions, trailing only the District Court of Delaware which had 105 decisions. Overall, the Eastern District of Texas is rated as the third best in the nation for patent plaintiffs, trailing only the Eastern District of Virginia (which, however, has been much less popular as a venue with only 17 reported patent decisions) and the District of Delaware (which has overall results very similar to those in the Eastern District of Texas, but a slightly lower success rate for plaintiffs and a substantially higher median damage award). All statistics come from a report prepared by the accounting and consulting firm of PricewaterhouseCoopers, PwC, *2012 Patent Litigation Study: Litigation continues to rise amid growing awareness of patent value*, (2012), at http://www.pwc.com/en_US/us/forensic-services/publications/assets/2012-patent-litigation-study.pdf, chart 7d on p.21 and chart 8 on p.23. For whatever the specific reasons, plaintiffs believe that they can quickly achieve positive trial verdicts in the Eastern District of Texas, and they therefore tend to bring patent lawsuits in that federal district. The legendary bank robber Willie Sutton, when asked why he robbed banks, is said to have answered, "Because that's where the money is." Same thing here — whether it is true or not in recent years, patent plaintiffs believe they can receive quick and favorable verdicts in the Eastern District of Texas. They evidently believe "that's where the money is".

the United States Supreme Court affirmed the judgment of the Federal Circuit Court.[80]

In general, both the District Court and Circuit Court opinions are relevant for us. The Supreme Court opinion had to do with the legal burden of proof to show patent invalidity under 35 USC sec. 282, and therefore is not relevant for us here.[81] A reexamination request was filed for US 5,787,449 on November 21, 2008, which was after the lawsuit had been filed but before the jury verdict. The certificate of reexamination, issued on July 27, 2010, after the Circuit Court opinion but before the Supreme Court opinion, confirmed all of the method claims (14–20) and did not address the system claims (1–13).

*Preview of the i4i Patent:*

This was an early patent for using software to process different elements of a document. Microsoft had a very strong argument against the patent, because the claims used

---

80 The Supreme Court decision has been published as *Microsoft Corp. v. i4i Ltd. Partnership*, 564 US — (Docket No. 10–290). The sole question to the Supreme Court concerned interpretation of the section of the patent statute known as 35 United States Code sec. 282. Section 282 requires the courts to presume that a patent, and every claim in the patent, is valid. However, this presumption may be rebutted by a patent defendant. The question before the Supreme Court was, "What is the standard of proof to show that a patent is invalid?" The Supreme Court held, in a unanimous 8–0 opinion, that a patent defendant must show invalidity by "clear and convincing evidence", a relatively high burden of proof, much higher than the burden known as "preponderance of the evidence", which is the standard for most civil litigation. The Supreme Court decision is interesting, but not relevant for us here, except to note that it supports the general rule that a patent evaluator should assume claim validity, the V in VSD, unless there is strong evidence to doubt claim validity.

81 Of course, invalidity of a claim is an important defense, and would kill the claim. However, the Supreme Court's decision is not related to our discussion of this specific patent.

the word "metacode" and Microsoft said, correctly, that its Word product did not use what the industry generally calls "metacodes". This argument would have won, except that the written description of the patent explicitly defined the word "metacode" in a non-traditional way that *did indeed* cover Microsoft's products. The courts found for i4i, and Microsoft was liable for $240 million.

The main lesson to be learned here is that non-traditional usage of a key claim term is permitted *only* if the key claim term is explicitly defined in the patent to include this non-traditional usage. Definitions of key claim terms are critically important contributions to patent quality, especially when the definition is something other than the industry norm.

*Review:*

This is a patent for defining the architecture or structure of a document, and also the content of a document. "Architecture" or "structure" means encoding in a form that allows a computer to understand the text. Much of the structure is captured in a form that is called "metacodes". The patent itself presents structures and methods to process and store both content and structure in a "metacode map".

The basic allegation of i4i was that Microsoft infringed the patent starting in 2003 when Microsoft introduced into its Word software the possibility of XML editing.

The entire claim #14 is quoted below. I have parsed the claim with brackets [ ] and numbers, but these are not part of the original claim. In addition, many key terms in claim #14 were explicitly defined in the Summary of the Invention section of the written specification, and I have **boldfaced** key claim terms that were so defined there.

14. A method for producing a first map of **metacodes** and their addresses of use in association with mapped content and stored in distinct map storage means, the method comprising:
[1] providing the mapped content to mapped content storage means;
[2] providing a menu of metacodes; and
[3] compiling a map of the metacodes in the distinct storage means, by **locating**, **detecting** and **addressing** the **metacodes**; and
[4] providing the **document** as the content of the document and the **metacode map** of the document.

We could discuss any or all of these terms, but let's focus on the terms in dispute between i4i and Microsoft. Here they are:

**Table 3–2: Key Claim Terms in *i4i v. Microsoft*[82]**

| Claim Term | Definition in the Patent | Definition by the District Court | Where it Appears |
|---|---|---|---|
| **Map of metacodes, also called a metacode map** | "A multiplicity of metacodes and their addresses associated with mapped content." Col. 4, lines 17–19. | "A data structure that contains a plurality of metacodes and their addresses of use corresponding to mapped content." | Claim #14 [Preamble], [3], and [4] |

82 Unlike the prior Table 3–1, Table 3–2 has no column called "Physical Structure", because we are analyzing here a method claim, not a structure claim. Of course, every method does operate on a specific structure, but

| Claim Term | Definition in the Patent | Definition by the District Court | Where it Appears |
|---|---|---|---|
| **Metacode** | "Includes, but is not limited to a descriptive code, which controls the interpretation of the data, i.e., it differentiates the content." Col. 4, lines 14–17. | "An individual instruction which controls the interpretation of the content of the data." | Claim #14 [Preamble], [2], [3] and [4] |
| **Distinct map storage means, and mapped content storage means, and mapped content storage** | There are all discussed in the patent, but NOT DEFINED. | (See definition of "Distinct", in the box below.) | Claim #14 [Preamble], [1], and [3]. |
| **The specific word "distinct" in the phrase "distinct mapped storage means"** | Discussed extensively in the patent, but NOT DEFINED. | "Distinct map storage means" defined as "a portion of memory for storing a metacode map." "Mapped content distinct storage means" defined as "a portion of memory for storing mapped content." | Claim #14 [Preamble] [Element 3] |

identifying the structural elements in this method claim is not necessary or helpful.

Microsoft raised several arguments. Let's look at two of them, and their resolution.

(1) *First Argument by Microsoft*: Microsoft argued that "metacodes" include what are called "delimiters", which are characters or symbols that indicate, in effect: "Up to now you have been receiving content, but here comes description of the content". Graphically, Content bits => Delimiter => Description bits. Microsoft Word does not include delimiters. Therefore, according to Microsoft, Word does not use "metacodes" and hence there is no infringement.

This is a reasonable argument for Microsoft, because it focuses on a key term in the patent claim, rather than on a court definition derived from a key term. The argument might have won for Microsoft except, again, the patentee, i4i, had defined "metacode" in a manner that was very beneficial to the patent, the District Court adopted this definition, and Microsoft could not overcome the definition. The accepted definition of "metacode" was "code which controls the interpretation of data". Under this definition "metacode" does not require a "delimiter".

The District Court said:

(1) During the Markman hearing, Microsoft raised a similar argument and lost.
(2) There was sufficient evidence to allow the jury to rule for i4i, using the District Court's definition of "metacode".

If the patent had relied on the word "metacode", *without any definition in the patent*, there is a very good chance Microsoft would have won the case, because the accepted technical definition of "metacode" requires a "delimiter", something that Microsoft's Word does not use. However, *when you are writing your patent, you are not limited to standard industry definitions of the key terms, as long as you clearly define the terms in the way that you want and that serves your interests.*

i4i did not rely on the industry definition of "metacode" (which would have limited the claims and caused i4i to lose the case) but instead expanded the definition to be "individual instruction which controls the interpretation of the content of the data". This definition does not require a "delimiter" or anything like it, so the definition expanded the scope of the claim. Without this definition, "metacode" would have meant, by implication, "as defined in the industry", and the standard industry definition of "metacode" would have meant that Word did not infringe the patent.

*(2) Second Argument by Microsoft*: The word "distinct" appears in the key claim term as "distinct map storage means", which is the preamble to claim #14. The word "distinct" also appears in element [3] as part of "the distinct storage means", which presumably meant, "the distinct map storage means" (although the word "map" did not appear in element [3]). Microsoft made a two-pronged argument based on the word "distinct":

1. The "metacode map" and the "content" must be stored in entirely separate files. That is what is meant by "distinct". However, in Microsoft Word, there are not "distinct files", so Microsoft does not infringe.

The CAFC considered this argument, found nothing in the patent or in prosecution history that required storage in separate files, and so rejected this argument.

2. The patent requires that editing of the "content" be

"distinct" from editing of the "metacode map". In Microsoft Word, however, editing is not "distinct" and therefore Microsoft does not infringe.

This was Microsoft's best argument in the case, in my opinion.[83] There are multiple statements in the written description showing that content and structure (whereby "structure" means "metacode map") are "separate" in some way. The argument might have won for Microsoft. However, the CAFC rejected the argument for three reasons:

First, the general patent rule is that a limitation is not added to the claims unless the patentee intended to add this limitation. That intent was not clear, according to the Court.

Second, "separate" does not mean "independent". Microsoft erroneously equated the two words, but that is wrong, and there is nothing in the patent to require "independence" of editing content and the metacode map.

Third, although the words "distinct" and "separate" are not defined anywhere in the patent, the patent states in the paragraph at Column 7, lines 6–16, that the invention "provides the ability to work solely on the metacodes". Similarly, in the paragraph at Column 7, lines 17–25, the patent states that the invention "further provides the ability to work solely on the content". According to the CAFC, the word "ability" means "option", but does *not* mean requirement. Since this is an optional feature only, it cannot be a limitation on the claims.

---

83 It is Microsoft's best argument because, as noted in the text, there are many statements in the patent showing that content and structure are "separate". The CAFC also found this to be a strong argument, stating that editing was a "closer question" than the argument as to separate files. 598 F.3d at p.843. In the end, however, the CAFC ruled for i4i and against Microsoft.

The CAFC rejected Microsoft's interpretation of the word "distinct", and i4i won the litigation.

A good result for i4i? Yes it was, *but this decision might easily have gone the other way*. Had the Court accepted Microsoft's argument about the word "distinct", Microsoft would have won, and i4i would have left with nothing, rather than a judgment for $240 million.

The reason Microsoft's argument to avoid infringement was so powerful is that *nowhere in the patent is there a definition of "distinct", or "separate", or "distinct and separate". Nowhere is it stated that these terms do not mean "independent". Nowhere is it stated that these operations are optional rather than mandatory. Nowhere is it stated that simultaneous manipulation of metacodes and content is also possible.* The absence of definition for these key terms gave Microsoft an opening to make its best argument in the case.

The wise drafter of a patent always tries to predict what will be important to a court in another 5 or 10 years. In the case of this patent US 5,787,449, the patent drafter defined many of the key claim terms, but did not define the word "distinct". The lack of definition for this one word gave Microsoft an opening to its strongest argument, which might have won the day.

A VSD analysis of claim #14 of US 5,787,449 might look like this:

**Validity**: The history suggests no problem of patent invalidity or limitation. There was a very active prosecution history, including five Office Actions, and several prior art references that were eventually overcome by claim amendment and argumentation.

However, validity issues came up not in the history of

US 5,787,449, but in its post-grant reexamination. The reexamination proceeding, initiated by the defendant Microsoft, is relevant. Initially, the PTO found all of the claims to be both non-new and obvious relative to two pieces of prior art. Ultimately, the PTO rejected these two pieces of prior art, and confirmed the claims, *specifically because the preamble has the key term "addresses of use", which did not appear in the two references.* Hence, the references were not relevant, and here, too, i4i won. In this case, also, a key term appearing in the preamble saved the claim.

When limitations are placed in a preamble, a court may find them to be part of the claim or may find them to be general descriptions which are not part of the claim. Here is an important lesson: "*Don't put limitations in the preamble, but only in the body of the claim.*" If you ignore this lesson, you never can be sure if a court (as in the *Uniloc* case) or the PTO (as in the *i4i* reexamination) will determine that these limitations are not part of the claim, and disaster may ensue. *To be certain that a limitation will be applied by both the PTO and the courts, placed the limitation in the body of the claim, not in the preamble.*

**Scope**: There are two important things to say about scope in this case:

First, the form of the patent, and particularly of claim #14, is very good, suggesting a broad scope. There are only four elements in claim #14, all short and all general.

Nevertheless, there are a couple of concerns here. For one thing, why is the preamble so long and complicated? There is always a question whether the preamble will be limiting. In other words: will the preamble be read together with the body of the claim? If the answer is unclear, then there is doubt about what the claim actually says. In this case, a long and complicated preamble, which introduces multiple terms used in the body of the claim, may well be judged as part of the claim. To avoid confusion, the best practice is to make the preamble as short and simple as possible. Put limitations in the body of the claim, not in the preamble.

The lack of clarity in claims undermines patent quality.

Second, although the claim *as interpreted by the courts* is good, I doubt any evaluator would have been able to accurately predict the true value of this patent. The problem is the presence of the word "metacode" in the claim. An evaluator, looking at the patent before litigation, would likely say, "Well, Microsoft Word does not use delimiters, which are a central feature of metacodes, which means that Microsoft does not use metacodes, so Microsoft does not infringe this claim." Or perhaps the evaluator might say, "The patentee's definition of 'metacode' is such that Word might in fact infringe the patent, so I will give the patent a positive evaluation, but I will discount the value due to the doubt about whether Word actually infringes".

How could i4i have avoided this confusion? In other words, how could the patentee have created even more value by removing doubt from the mind of any possible buyer or licensee about the scope of the patent claims? One way would have been for the patentee to use a term other than the industry term "metacode." What if the patent, instead of using the word "metacodes", had employed a non-standard phrase like "data controllers" or "control interpreters", or some other term invented by the patentee? Since no one would know what that term means, the term would not be interpreted as "metacode".

Rather, the evaluator would search out the written description to try to discover what the patent means by "data controller".

Now let's go one step further. Suppose the patentee had defined "data controller", in the "Summary of Invention" or in the "Detailed Description of the Invention", to be the following:

> A "data controller" controls the interpretation of the content of data. It may set off content from instructions, or may differentiate one kind of content from another kind. *A "data controller" may or may not be a type of metacode, but it is not required to have all of the specific elements of a metacode such as delimiters.*

I wrote the italicized sentence to show how a definition such as this might have anticipated and destroyed any argument, by Microsoft or by any other software provider, that its products do not use "metacodes" and therefore cannot infringe claim #14. A definition such as this would have removed any doubt, and would have thereby strengthened the patent significantly.

This definition might have been included in the patent, but it was not. *There is great danger in using a technical term having a standard industry definition, when the patent means something different from the standard definition.* This kind of non-standard usage confuses the PTO, courts, juries, and patent evaluators. If people reading your patent cannot understand easily the scope of protection, the patent cannot be as good as it should have been.

*Remember always that a patent is both a description and a communication tool. Similarly, patent value is based both on the content in the patent and by what you communicate to potential buyers, licensees, courts, and other interpreters of the patent. If you fail to communicate what you mean, you cannot maximize the value of your patent.*

**Discoverability of Infringement**: There is no apparent obstacle to the discovery of infringement. Although the method might not be evident to the "naked eye," it is surely discoverable by review of technical literature and by inference from the results generated by the method. The specific patent questions, such as definitions of "metacode" or the word "distinct", are not clear, as explained, but the lack of clarity of key claim terms is not what we mean when we ask, "Is the infringement reasonably discoverable?" The answer here is: yes, infringement is reasonably discoverable.

**Summary**: This is a patent with good definitions and good claims. Microsoft had a very difficult time in this case, in large part because many of the key terms had been defined in the patent. The District Court, and later the CAFC, adopted essentially the definitions of i4i, and these definitions were not to Microsoft's benefit. When you write your own claims, make sure you know what the key terms are, and define the key terms, in either the claims or in the written specification, in a way that benefits you. The "key terms" are those that define the "Points of Novelty" in your patent. Identify and clarify the PONs, and then the key terms supporting the PONs.

The patent must be written clearly, so that people understand it. If people are confused by your patent, they generally will discount it. Keep this in mind when you write definitions of key terms, and select words or phrases that will remove undesirable ambiguity from key terms (such as the word "metacode" vs. "data controller") so that you retain control over the meaning and scope rather than leaving them ambiguous.

**Lessons Learned**: Here are some of the lessons we might learn about good patents from patent claim #14 in U.S. 5,787,449, litigated in *i4i v. Microsoft*.

3-3-1. ***Method claims are like structure claims in that both are more valuable if the preamble is short and simple, and if the elements are few and general.***

3-3-2. ***Method claims are not like structure claims in that structure claims will include many structural elements whereas method claims will have no structural elements and may not be limited to any structural implementation.*** If this difference seems obvious to you, consider the next two lessons.

3-3-3. ***Identify and define the key claim terms in your method claims.*** The key terms are those which define the critical features of each PON. This is true of structure claims also, but it is even more true of method claims. Why more so?

a. In structure claims, the key terms are almost always structural terms. In method claims, the key terms may be structural, but they are also commonly gerunds ("-ing" verbs).[84] Key terms in method claims may also be adjectives. In the i4i case, the adjective "distinct"

84 "Structural" and "method" elements must not be combined in one claim. That would make the claim "indefinite", and hence invalid under 35 USC sec. 112(2). However, a method claim may include a step or function running on a particular piece of hardware. This hardware, even though it is not itself an "element" in the claim, is a key claim term that supports the method claim. *Elements are not at all the same as key claim terms. A structure claim must have only structure elements, and a method claim must have only method elements, but a structure claim may be supported by key method terms and a method claim may be supported by key structure terms.*

became a key term in the claim, but the lack of a definition for this word in the patent suggests strongly that the patentee did not realize it would be a key term.

b. By their nature, structural terms are usually more concrete and more understandable to buyers, licensees, and other evaluators, than non-structural terms. Non-structural terms, which often appear in abundance in method claims, tend to be vaguer and generally require some kind of explanation or definition. These distinctions are not always true, but generally they are.

3-3-4. ***Pick very carefully the words you use to represent your key terms.*** Ask yourself: "Did I pick the best words to represent my key terms? What do those words tell the reader of the patent? Are they clear? Do they maximize the scope and potential value of my claims?"

## *Case 4: TiVo, Inc. v. EchoStar Communications Corp.*

*Fed.Cir. 2008*[85]

*Background to the Decision:*

The fourth example we will review in this chapter is different from the prior examples. In *TiVo, Inc. v. EchoStar Communications Corporation*, TiVo sued EchoStar for infringement of the four independent claims of US 6,233,389. The patent, entitled "Multimedia Time Warping System", has a priority date of July 30, 1998, and was issued on May 15, 2001. The patent covers what is called "time-shifting television", which means recording audio and visual TV signals in digital format for later replay. Time-shifting is possible for

85 516 F.3d 1290 (Fed. Cir., 2008), *cert. denied*, 129 S.Ct. 306 (2008).

both programs previously recorded in their entirety and for programs being recorded at the time certain sections were replayed. In short, this is an early patent for digital video recorders ("DVRs").

There was extensive litigation in this case over seven years, including multiple court decisions and a reexamination proceeding at the PTO. The main events of litigation are:

**Table 3-3: Some of the Events in *TiVo v. EchoStar***

| Date | Event in the Litigation | Venue |
|---|---|---|
| **April, 2006** | A jury finds that EchoStar has infringed claims 1, 31, 32, and 61, of the patent, and awards TiVo $74 million in damages. | |
| **August, 2006** | August, 2006: The District Court issues an injunction against EchoStar. 446 F.Supp.2d 664 (E.D.Tex. 2006) | District Court I, later affirmed in part, reversed in part, and remanded, in Federal Circuit I |
| **November, 2007** | November, 2007: The PTO reexamines the patent, and confirms all claims. | Reexamination I |
| **January, 2008** | The Federal Circuit Court affirms the District Court as to claims 31 and 61, but finds that EchoStar has not infringed claims 1 and 32. The Federal Circuit affirms the award of damages. 516 F.3d 1290 (Fed. Cir. 2008), *cert. denied*, 129 S.Ct. 306 (2008) | Federal Circuit I |

| Date | Event in the Litigation | Venue |
|---|---|---|
| **November, 2008** | PTO agrees to reexamine the patent again, but this time the reexamination will be limited to only the two claims, 31 and 61, that were found infringed by the Federal Circuit Court. | Reexamination II |
| **June, 2009** | EchoStar has redesigned the product, and argues that the new product is not infringing. TiVo says the new product is infringing. The District Court finds the new product infringing, and holds EchoStar in contempt for violating the earlier injunction. 640 F.Supp.2d 853 (E.D.Tex. 2009) | District Court II, later affirmed in Federal Circuit II, then affirmed in part, vacated in part, and remanded in Federal Circuit III (en banc) |
| **September, 2009** | The District Court awards TiVo another $200 million for further infringement. 655 F.Supp.2d 661 (E.D.Tex. 2009) | District Court III |
| **March, 2010** | In a 2–1 decision in favor of TiVo, the Federal Circuit Court upholds the injunction against EchoStar. 597 F.3d 1247 (Fed.Cir. 2010) | Federal Circuit II |
| **February, 2011** | The U.S. PTO issues a reexamination certificate, confirming claims 31 and 61. | Reexamination II |
| **April, 2011** | In a hearing with all the judges of the court (called “en banc”), the Federal Circuit Court rules 7–5 to uphold the injunction against EchoStar. 646 F.3d 869 (Fed. Cir. 2011) (en banc) | Federal Circuit III |

| Date | Event in the Litigation | Venue |
|---|---|---|
| **April, 2011** | Having lost in Reexamination II and Federal Circuit III, EchoStar settles the case, taking a license to patent US 6,233,389 and paying to TiVo $500 million. | |

*Preview of the TiVo Patent:*

This is one of the earliest patents for recording television programs for later replay. The patent has sixty-one claims, of which fifty-nine claims are hardware, and two are software. Every internal indication is that the software patents were added as an after-thought to what TiVo thought was a hardware patent. The CAFC, however, found the fifty-nine hardware claims were not infringed, but the two software claims were infringed. After multiple rounds of litigation, EchoStar paid TiVo $500 million.

The main lesson to learn is that claim diversity in a patent can save the day.

*Review:*

Our review of this patent and its litigation will be different than our review in the prior examples. The *TiVo* case is similar to other examples we've reviewed, but there is one key difference in the structure of the independent claims in the patent.

US 6,233,389 has four independent claims. TiVo sued EchoStar for infringement of these four claims alone. The four claims were classified by the courts in the litigation as "hardware claims", numbers 1 and 32, or "software claims", numbers 31 and 61. It is important for you to understand here the structure of these claims (although the content of the claims is less important for present purposes).

Let's compare the two hardware claims first. Just skim Table 3–4 below:

**Table 3–4: Hardware Claims in *TiVo v. EchoStar***

| Hardware Claims | Claim #1 (method claim) | Claim #32 (apparatus claim) |
|---|---|---|
| **Preamble** | 1. A process for the simultaneous storage and play back of multimedia data, comprising the steps of: | 32. An apparatus for the simultaneous storage and play back of multimedia data, comprising: |
| **Element** [1] | accepting television (TV) broadcast signals, wherein said TV signals are based on a multitude of standards, including, but not limited to, National Television Standards Committee (NTSC) broadcast, PAL broadcast, satellite transmission, DSS, DBS, or ATSC; | a module for accepting television (TV) broadcast signals, wherein said TV signals are based on a multitude of standards, including, but not limited to, National Television Standards Committee (NTSC) broadcast, PAL broadcast, satellite transmission, DSS, DBS, or ATSC; |
| **Element** [2] | tuning said TV signals to a specific program; | a module for tuning said TV signals to a specific program; |

| Hardware Claims | Claim #1 (method claim) | Claim #32 (apparatus claim) |
|---|---|---|
| **Element [3]** | providing at least one Input Section, wherein said Input Section converts said specific program to an Moving Pictures Experts Group (MPEG) formatted stream for internal transfer and manipulation; | at least one Input Section, wherein said Input Section converts said specific program to an Moving Pictures Experts Group (MPEG) formatted stream for internal transfer and manipulation; |
| **Element [4]** | providing a Media Switch, wherein said Media Switch parses said MPEG stream, said MPEG stream is separated into its video and audio components; | a Media Switch, wherein said Media Switch parses said MPEG stream, said MPEG stream is separated into its video and audio components; |
| **Element [5]** | storing said video and audio components on a storage device; | a module for storing said video and audio components on a storage device; |
| **Element [6]** | providing at least one Output Section, wherein said Output Section extracts said video and audio components from said storage device; | at least one Output Section, wherein said Output Section extracts said video and audio components from said storage device; |
| **Element [7]** | wherein said Output Section assembles said video and audio components into an MPEG stream; | wherein said Output Section assembles said video and audio components into an MPEG stream; |
| **Element [8]** | wherein said Output Section sends said MPEG stream to a decoder; | wherein said Output Section sends said MPEG stream to a decoder; |

| Hardware Claims | Claim #1 (method claim) | Claim #32 (apparatus claim) |
|---|---|---|
| **Element [9]** | wherein said decoder converts said MPEG stream into TV output signals; | wherein said decoder converts said MPEG stream into TV output signals; |
| **Element [10]** | wherein said decoder delivers said TV output signals to a TV receiver; and | wherein said decoder delivers said TV output signals to a TV receiver; and |
| **Element [11]** | accepting control commands from a user, wherein said control commands are sent through the system and affect the flow of said MPEG stream. | accepting control commands from a user, wherein said control commands are sent through the system and affect the flow of said MPEG stream. |

The obvious point is that these two hardware claims are practically the same, *although claim #1 is a method claim and claim #32 is a structure claim*. The comparison in Table 3–4 teaches that the basic idea of a claim often may be stated in both a method form and a structural form, as occurred here.

Why did the courts call claims 1 and 32 "hardware claims", particularly since claim #1 is a method claim? The answer is that both claims are talking about how a certain piece of hardware is composed, and what the various parts of the hardware do. If this is not clear, let's clarify by comparing software claims 31 and 61. Again, just skim Table 3–5.

## Table 3–5: Software Claims in *TiVo v. EchoStar*

| Software Claims | Claim #31 (method claim) | Claim #61 (apparatus claim) |
|---|---|---|
| **Preamble** | 31. A process for the simultaneous storage and play back of multimedia data, comprising the steps of: | 61. An apparatus for the simultaneous storage and play back of multimedia data, comprising: |
| **Element [1]** | providing a physical data source, wherein said physical data source accepts broadcast data from an input device, parses video and audio data from said broadcast data, and temporarily stores said video and audio data; | a physical data source, wherein said physical data source accepts broadcast data from an input device, parses video and audio data from said broadcast data, and temporarily stores said video and audio data; |
| **Element [2]** | providing a source object, wherein said source object extracts video and audio data from said physical data source; | a source object, wherein said source object extracts video and audio data from said physical data source; |
| **Element [3]** | providing a transform object, wherein said transform object stores and retrieves data streams onto a storage device; | a transform object, wherein said transform object stores and retrieves data streams onto a storage device; |
| **Element [4]** | wherein said source object obtains a buffer from said transform object, said source object converts video data into data streams and fills said buffer with said streams; | wherein said source object obtains a buffer from said transform object, said source object converts video data into data streams and fills said buffer with said streams; |

| Software Claims | Claim #31 (method claim) | Claim #61 (apparatus claim) |
|---|---|---|
| **Element [5]** | wherein said source object is automatically flow controlled by said transform object; | wherein said source object is automatically flow controlled by said transform object; |
| **Element [6]** | providing a sink object, wherein said sink object obtains data stream buffers from said transform object and outputs said streams to a video and audio decoder; | a sink object, wherein said sink object obtains data stream buffers from said transform object and outputs said streams to a video and audio decoder; |
| **Element [7]** | wherein said decoder converts said streams into display signals and sends said signals to a display; | wherein said decoder converts said streams into display signals and sends said signals to a display; |
| **Element [8]** | wherein said sink object is automatically flow controlled by said transform object; | wherein said sink object is automatically flow controlled by said transform object; |
| **Element [9]** | providing a control object, wherein said control object receives commands from a user, said commands control the flow of the broadcast data through the system; and | a control object, wherein said control object receives commands from a user, said commands control the flow of the broadcast data through the system; and |
| **Element [10]** | wherein said control object sends flow command events to said source, transform, and sink objects. | wherein said control object sends flow command events to said source, transform, and sink objects. |

Here again, the two claims are strikingly similar, even though claim #31 is a method claim and claim #61 is an apparatus claim. Moreover, these claims, whether drafted as methods or structures, were accurately classified by the courts as "software claims" in the sense that they are discussing procedures controlled by software. In fact, many of the terms, particularly those related to the word "object", are classic software terms.

What does all this mean? There were two kinds of products alleged to be infringing, the DVRs in the "50X" product line, and the DVRs in the "Broadcom" product line. The jury found that both product lines infringed all four of the patents, although the jury found that the Broadcom line infringed the software claims only by the Doctrine of Equivalents.

Here is a tabular summary of the jury's decision:

**Table 3–6: Jury Decision in *TiVo v. EchoStar***

| Claims | 50X DVR Product Line | Broadcom DVR Product Line |
|---|---|---|
| **Hardware claims (1 and 32)** | Literal Infringement | Literal Infringement |
| **Software claims (31 and 61)** | Literal Infringement | DOE Infringement |

The jury awarded $74 million in damages to TiVo. In District Court I, the judge presiding at trial added an injunction against EchoStar's sale of infringing products, 446 F.Supp.2d at 671.

When the dispute came to the CAFC, that court ruled that the Broadcom DVRs did not fulfill element [4] of the hardware claims, since the products did not "separate" data into different buffers. The CAFC also ruled that the 50X DVRs did not fulfill element [7] of the hardware claims, since these products did not perform what is called "interleaved assembly" of data streams. So here is how the CAFC ruled:

**Table 3–7: CAFC Decision I in *TiVo v. EchoStar***

| | **50X DVR Product Line** | **Broadcom DVR Product Line** |
|---|---|---|
| **Hardware claims (1 and 32)** | NO Infringement | NO Infringement. |
| **Software claims (31 and 61)** | Literal Infringement | DOE Infringement |

Thus, the CAFC found the hardware claims #1 and #32 not infringed at all, but upheld the infringement of the software claims #31 and #61, 516 F.3d at 1312.

There was additional litigation between the parties, much of it listed in Table 3–3 above. Of particular importance for us is Federal Circuit III, decided April 20, 2011.[86]

EchoStar attempted to avoid the injunction by designing around the infringement — redesigning its software and putting the *new software* packages into the *existing hardware*. This might have worked to avoid an injunction, because again, the existing hardware had been found not to infringe, and new software might avoid infringing software claims #31 and #61.

In a 7–5 decision in Federal Circuit III, the CAFC rejected EchoStar's position. The majority held that the injunction covered *any DVR functionality* in infringing units, whether such units were modified by new software or not, 646 F.3d at 690. In opposition, the minority opinion of the five dissenting

86 *TiVo Inc. v. EchoStar Corp.*, 646 F.3d 869 (Fed. Cir. 2011) (en banc).

judges argued that EchoStar should have been able to avoid the injunction by redesigning the software, *ibid.*[87] Decision is by majority rule, however, so TiVo won this round of the litigation. The parties settled the case shortly after Federal Circuit III, with a $500 million payment from EchoStar to TiVo, all based on software claims 31 and 61 in the patent US 6,233,389.

Software claims won the day for TiVo. Although no claims were invalidated at any point in the litigation, the defendant was found by the CAFC not to infringe the hardware claims.

Does this mean that the software claims were simply "better" than the hardware claims? Consider this: by a 7–5 vote, the CAFC ruled that the injunction could not be avoided by redesign of software. But if two votes had gone the other way, that is, *if 7 judges had ruled for the defendant EchoStar instead of for the plaintiff TiVo on the question of design around,* then the CAFC would have ruled, in essence:

> The infringements were software infringements, and the defendant changed the software so that it was not infringing. Therefore, the products became non-infringing, which means that the injunction no longer applies (although damages must still be paid for past infringement).

Why is this relevant? Consider the effort involved to modify infringing hardware or infringing software. Modification of

---

87 The particular phrasing of the argument between the majority and the minority was whether EchoStar should be found in contempt of the lower court's injunction as a result of EchoStar's attempt to install modified and non-infringing software in its products. The majority barred this attempt to avoid infringement, finding that EchoStar was required to "disable" the DVR functionality of its products. The minority wanted to allow the installation of non-infringing software.

time-shifting hardware would probably have been very difficult, perhaps even impossible. Modification of hardware might have required design and manufacturing changes which would have been relatively difficult and relatively costly in comparison to simply inserting modified software. Engineering design would of course be required for either hardware or software modifications, but, as a general rule, redesigning and remanufacturing hardware is often more difficult then re-engineering and inserting new software code.

Here is the point: In many cases, infringement of hardware claims is harder to show but, once shown, may resist a defendant's efforts to avoid an injunction by design around. By contrast, infringement of software claims might be easier in some cases, but a defendant might be able to design around the infringement with software redesigns that do not involve costly manufacturing. Each type of claim tends to have its own advantages and disadvantages, as illustrated in this case.

*In this litigation, only the software claims succeeded. On the other hand, the software claims were relatively open to design around by defendant EchoStar to avoid an injunction.* In this case, by the slimmest possible majority of 7–5, the CAFC did not accept EchoStar's software design around as non-infringing. It was this ruling about design around and the expected cost of the injunction, rather than the monetary judgment, that put enormous pressure on EchoStar to settle the case. However, this decision might have gone the other way. If two judges had joined the minority, then the decision would have been 7–5 to accept the design around, meaning no injunction against EchoStar.

*Please be clear — it was this last decision rejecting EchoStar's argument about design around that created a $500 million* *settlement. If the ruling on design around had gone the other way (i.e., accepting EchoStar's argument), there would have been no injunction. There might still have been a settlement for past damages, but almost certainly the settlement sum would have been much less than $500 million.*

One key to the strength of this patent is the mix of claims by hardware and software, as well as by method and structure.

We did not analyze an individual claim here, but rather a group of claims. A traditional VSD analysis of claims 1, 31, 32, and 61, might look like this:

**Validity**: In the reported court cases, there were no challenges to the validity of the claims. The PTO conducted two reexaminations of the claims, and confirmed all claims reviewed. Validity was not an issue, and in fact the certificates of reexamination strengthened the validity of the claims.

**Scope**: The patent covered some of the basic DVR functionality. The potential market is enormous. In short, these are good claims, covering a critical functionality, in a large market. The two key questions related to infringement of the original products and whether the design around effort avoided infringement. In the end, EchoStar was not permitted to design around, for reasons unique to the case. *Scope of patent coverage is determined both by the original liability of infringers and by the patent's ability to defeat attempts at design around.*

**Discoverability of Infringement**: To people in the industry, this should not be a problem. Some functionality is easily visible, and some may be inferred from known functionality. One way or another, infringement would not be likely to stay secret for long.

**Summary**: This is a patent that addresses an important functionality in a major market. The independent claims cover multiple implementations, including hardware device, hardware method, software device, and software method. This mix of claims created great potential value, which resulted ultimately in $500 million to patent owner TiVo.

This is an excellent patent to teach how a court, or any evaluator, looks at patent claims. In particular, unlike the prior examples, a key part of the value has to do with the entire suite of independent claims, and not just one independent claim.

In this case, the software claims triumphed for the plaintiff, while the hardware claims did not. In that sense, the software claims were superior to the hardware claims, since the software claims appear to have had broader scope. In another way, the hardware claims are superior, because generally they are harder to design around than software claims. EchoStar tried to design around the infringed software claims, and five dissenting judges supported this effort, but the majority of seven judges did not, so EchoStar ended up settling the litigation for $500 million.

**Lessons Learned**: Here are some of the lessons we might learn about good patents, from patents claims 1, 31, 32, and 61, in U.S. 6,233,389, litigated in *TiVo v. EchoStar*.

Some of the basic lessons have already been discussed. For example, the independent claims here tended to be relatively long, with about ten elements. Lengthy claims, and multiple elements, are not favored. Indeed, in this case, the hardware claims were found not infringed because only one element was found not to be implemented by the defendant's products. On the other hand, we have also learned that even long claims, with many elements, may be valuable, *if the elements are general.* Here, the elements were general, and they did capture the infringing DVRs.

The interesting and unique lessons of this case, however, are those related to the group of independent claims, 1, 31, 32, and 61.

3–4–1. ***A single patent is like a patent portfolio in that the true value is based on all relevant claims rather than on a single claim.*** Obviously, a multi-patent portfolio has more patents, and will almost certainly have more claims, than a single patent. Nevertheless, the general principle is that the aggregation of multiple types of claims can itself create patent value. This principle, which might be called "claim aggregation to create value" applies to both individual patents and portfolios of patents.

3–4–2. ***"Relevant claims" that create value are independent claims protecting a central Point of Novelty.*** Here there were four independent claims, all focused on DVR functionality. Hence, all of the independent claims were deemed relevant because they focused on the main PON.

In this case, there were four claim sets, hardware 1–30, software 31, hardware 32–60, and software 61. The long claim sets, 1–30 and 32–60, were found irrelevant, since the CAFC decided that EchoStar had not infringed either "hardware method claim #1" (hence not any of claims 2–30 depending on #1) or "hardware apparatus claim #32" (hence on any of claims 33–60 depending on #32). Independent claims #31, "software process", and #61, "software apparatus", stand alone, with no dependent claim. The impression is that the patent drafter and inventors devoted great time and thought to the 59 hardware claims, and just threw in the two software claims at the end, almost as an afterthought. In the final analysis, however, the 59 hardware claims lost while the 2 software claims won.

*For breadth of claim coverage, the key is not "claims" in general, but rather "independent claims" and, particularly, "independent claims focused on the Point of Novelty".*

3-4-3. ***Claim mix can be key to both a patent and a portfolio of patents.***

There are at least three ways to think about the mix of claims:

a. *Method claims* (which often tend to be vaguer and broader, but more subject to attack for lack of validity and more subject to design around by an infringer) *versus structure claims* (which often tend to be clearer with clear infringement, and which are harder to design around, but which are very likely to be narrower in scope than method claims).
b. *Hardware claims versus software claims*, which was the issue here in *TiVo v. EchoStar*. The software claims were found to have a greater scope of coverage: they won while the hardware claims lost. But the software claims were also subject to possible non-infringing software to avoid an injunction. In Federal Circuit III, 5 judges said that EchoStar should be permitted to avoid the injunction in this way, but 7 judges held for TiVo.

   In this particular case, the hardware claims lost while the software claims won. However, what would have happened if EchoStar had used, *in its original products*, "non-infringing software"? In that case, the software claims could not have won, and TiVo's only chance would have been to focus on the hardware claims. The relative strength of the hardware and software claims depends to a large degree on the specific facts of the case. Again, *it is the mix of claims that is particularly strong rather the individual claims.*

c. *Client-side versus server-side claims.* This claim mix may appear as consumer-oriented claims versus supplier-side claims, or manufacturer claims versus distributor claims, or others. Try to consider all sides, whether you are writing or evaluating a patent.

3-4-4. ***The line between method and structure claims is often blurry.*** With a few words, "method claims" may be transformed into "apparatus claims" and vice versa. That is what we have seen in US. 6,223,389: the lines between 1 (method) and 32 (apparatus), or between 31 (method) and 61 (apparatus), are blurry indeed.

There may be cases where that is not true, that is, where a sharp line separates method and structure claims. However, there is often blurriness, accidental or intentional, between the two claim types. Patent protection is maximized by covering multiple aspects of the same Point of Novelty. Therefore, as a general rule, a patent writer should draft both structure and method claim, because this mix of structure and method claims is likely to enhance patent value.[88]

---

88 Not every patent must have both structure and method claims. Some inventions are extremely structure-oriented, others extremely method-oriented. Further, the writer may concentrate on only one type to save costs of filing and prosecuting the application. However, apart from valid exceptions such as these, one should try to include both structure and method claims in a patent.

## Chapter 4

# ITC Cases with Good Patents

People often look to the courts to enforce a patent. However, a patent may also be enforced at an administrative body known as the United States International Trade Commission ("ITC"). This chapter is about patents that won hearings at the ITC. The purpose of this chapter is to give you a basic understanding of some aspects of litigation at the ITC, and to learn lessons from victorious patents about what may constitute a "good patent". Here is the organization of Chapter 4:

I. A Comparison of ITC Proceedings to Court Litigation
II. ITC Cases with Winning Litigation
  (1) *Broadcom v. Qualcomm*
  (2) *Trend Micro v. Fortinet*
III. Five Additional Lessons Learned from Five ITC Cases
  (1) Buying Patents — If You Need Patents Fast, Buy Them (Broadcom)
  (2) Improved Markush Type Claims (Magnequench International and Sumitomo Special Metals)
  (3) A Patent Thicket May Have Great Strength (Fuji Photo Film)
  (4) Even the Best Patent Can Be Destroyed By a Mistake During Prosecution (Ideations Designs)

(5) The Uncertainty Principle of Patent Value (Funai Electric Corporation)

## I. Comparison of ITC Proceedings to Court Litigation

In Chapter 3, we looked at a few examples where patent claims won big in court. Courts, however, are not the only forum for patent litigation in the U.S. In this chapter, we will consider another forum, known as the United States International Trade Commission (or "ITC"). The ITC is an administrative body, not a court. It is a popular forum for patent plaintiffs, and becoming more so. To understand what the ITC does, and why it is so popular, let us compare ITC proceedings to court litigation.

The ITC has two significant disadvantages relative to the courts:

(1) Unlike courts, *the ITC can only order a special type of injunction (called "an exclusion order") to stop or prevent importation of infringing products.* The ITC cannot order damages or monetary compensation to a plaintiff. By contrast, federal courts can offer all kinds of remedies, including both injunctions and damages.

(2) Unlike courts, *the ITC may hear and decide only cases in which an infringing product or component was imported into the United States.* The ITC may not hear a case where the product was made, sold, and used solely in the U.S. The federal courts have no such restriction and may hear any patent case.

But the ITC has some substantial advantages over federal courts:

(1) *Litigation at the ITC is very fast,* typically going from complaint to final order within about 16–18 months. The

federal courts set their own schedules. In theory, the courts could be as fast as the ITC, but in reality, they are almost always behind, often far behind.[89]

Speed means two things. First, if the plaintiff has a strong case, then it will likely win an injunction, probably much sooner than would have been possible in court litigation. Second, the accelerated litigation schedule of the ITC puts tremendous pressure on both parties, but particularly on the defendants, to get ready for trial. This is not primarily a question of money, even though patent litigation costs can easily run to millions of dollars. Rather, it is a question of executive time and attention for litigation. Executives typically prefer to use their time running their business rather than preparing for litigation.

In sum, speed of litigation is potentially an enormous advantage of the ITC for patent owners.

(2) *The ITC can order two kinds of injunctions that cannot be ordered by the courts.*

One kind of injunction issued by the ITC is called an "Exclusion Order", which may be either a Limited Exclusion Order ("LEO") or a General Exclusion Order ("GEO"). The difference are not critical for present purposes (although some differences are discussed in this Chapter 4 below, in the case of *Broadcom v. Qualcomm*). The key thing to keep

---

89 In the period 2005–2011, the median "time-to-trial" for a patent litigation in the United States federal district courts was about 30 months, PwC study, *op. cit.* p.21, which is much longer than the typical experience at the ITC. However, there is a very significant variation among the courts, with two courts actually having a median time-to-trial less than the time of the ITC — Eastern District of Virginia at about 12 months and Western District of Wisconsin at about 13 months, *ibid.*, chart 7d at p.22. Apart from these two courts, the ITC historically has been faster than the district courts, and in fact much faster than the great majority of the district courts.

in mind is that either type of injunction will stop current or future importation into the United States of products found by the ITC to infringe claims of U.S. patents.[90]

The second kind of injunction issued by the ITC is a "Cease & Desist Order", which means, in effect: "If there are infringing products that have already been imported and are now located in the U.S., the defendant will stop selling or offering to sell such products".

Taken together, the Exclusion Order and the Cease & Desist Order effectively end the importation to and sale in the United States of infringing products.

Don't federal courts have the power to issue injunctions and Cease & Desist Orders, just like the ITC? Yes, courts have such power, but no, not "just like the ITC", because the courts are subject to specific legal constraints for granting injunctions. Before 2006, if a court found for the plaintiff in a patent case, an injunction would follow almost automatically. In 2006, however, the U.S. Supreme Court in *eBay v. MercExchange*[91] ruled that injunctions no longer would be granted automatically in patent cases. In the future, it was decided, the lower federal courts would be required to apply, in patent cases, the four standard criteria for granting injunctions.[92]

---

90 An Exclusion Order is issued only if (a) the defendant is engaged in an "unfair act or method" such as a patent infringement, (b) the product is imported, or sold after being imported, and (c) there is a "domestic industry" for the product that may be harmed by the infringing import.

91 547 U.S. 388 (2006).

92 The four standard criteria are (1) the patent owner suffered an irreparable injury; (2) remedies available at law are inadequate to compensate for that injury; (3) an injunction is warranted based on the balance of hardships between the plaintiff and defendant, a remedy in equity is warranted; and (4) the public interest would not be harmed by a permanent injunction.

Does this restriction matter? Very much so! Before *eBay*, winning patent plaintiffs *in federal court cases* received injunctions in about 95% of cases. After *eBay*, plaintiffs received injunctions in only about 75% of cases.[93]

By contrast, at the ITC, 100% of winning plaintiffs before *eBay* received injunctions, and 100% of winning plaintiffs after eBay received injunctions.[94] This is not surprising, for two reasons:

1. The ITC lacks authority to order damages. If the ITC were to find a violation of law but refuse to order an injunction, the ITC would be saying, in effect, that there is a legal violation within the ITC's jurisdiction but the ITC will grant no remedy for this violation. In my opinion, the ITC will simply not do this. Courts, on the other hand, can and do order large damages (which the ITC may not do), but often deny injunctions.

2. The federal courts are part of the judicial branch of government and, as such, are subject to legal precedents of the Supreme Court, including *eBay*. The ITC is an administrative body, part of the executive branch of government. The ITC is bound by statute, but is not bound by judicial doctrine such as that created in *eBay*. Thus, the ITC is not required to apply the same criteria required of courts in considering plaintiffs' requests for injunctions.[95]

---

93 Colleen V. Chien and Mark A. Lemley, "Patent Holdups, the ITC, and the Public Interest", Cornell Law Review, Vol. 98:1, 2012, pp.9–10.

94 *Id.*, Fig. 3 on p.16.

95 The ITC is not subject to the *eBay* case, but rather to provisions of the Tariff Act of 1930, which appears in 19 United States Code chapter 4. See, for example, Gene Quinn, "Happy 5th Anniversary: The Impact of eBay v. MercExchange", IPWatchdog, a leading intellectual property law blog, published May 15, 2011 (http://www.ipwatchdog.com/2011/05/15/

To be sure, there are certain criteria by which the ITC must judge a request for injunction. These include the "economic prong" (the subject of the case is part of a U.S. domestic industry) and the "technical prong" (the plaintiff is practicing the patent in some way). The ITC also considers, in theory, the possible effects on competition, and on consumers, prior to issuance of an Exclusion Order. These criteria, however, have not been impediments to the granting of injunctions in ITC patent cases.

Given the advantages and disadvantages of both court litigation and ITC litigation, one might expect that in major cases a patent owner would sue in both places. That, in fact, happens not infrequently. In this Chapter 4, we will look at examples of patents where the ITC found infringement and ordered an injunction against the defendant. In some but not all of these cases, the ITC decision was appealed to the CAFC. We will consider issues from both ITC decisions and CAFC decisions, but our focus will be on the ITC litigation.[96]

---

happy-5th-anniversary-ebay-v-mercexchange/id=16894/.) There are many other writings to the same effect. The point is that the criteria for granting injunctions in patent cases are substantially different at the ITC than at the federal courts.

96 As noted, in major cases, a patent owner may sue both in federal court and at the ITC. However, if an injunction is important to the patent owner, and if the patent owner cannot afford litigation in both forums, or if the patent owner wants to obtain the relatively rapid relief that may be obtained at the ITC, the patent owner may sue at the ITC *rather than* in federal court. Indeed, in the conclusion to their article, Chien and Lemley note, *op. cit.*, p.43, that "*eBay* has had the unintended consequence of driving patentees to the ITC in hopes of obtaining an injunction no longer available in the federal district courts." As Professors Chien and Lemley note, it probably was not the Supreme Court's intention to drive patent owners away from courts and to the ITC, but that surely was a predictable result of the *eBay* decision and, according to the professors, that outcome did come to pass.

## II. ITC Cases with Winning Litigation

We will now consider two ITC cases in which the ITC found for the plaintiff patent owner, and ordered an injunction against the infringing defendant.[97]

### *Case 1: Broadcom Corp. v. Qualcomm, Inc.*

ITC Case No. 337-TA-543: Broadcom Corporation as the plaintiff, alleging infringement of a patent for circuits in a mobile handset, against Qualcomm, Inc.

*Background to the Decision:*

Broadcom Corporation of Irvine, California, and Qualcomm, Inc. of San Diego, were involved in patent litigation against each other, in a variety of forums, from 2005 to 2010. Patent litigation began in both federal court and the ITC in 2005.[98]

The ITC litigation is entitled, "In the Matter of Certain Baseband Processor Chips and Chipsets, Transmitter and Receiver (Radio) Chips, Power Control Chips, and Products Containing Same, Including Cellular Telephone Handsets".

---

97 In ITC litigation, the patent owner who sues, which would be called the "plaintiff" in court litigation, is called rather the "complainant". Similarly, in ITC litigation, the sued party, who would be called the "defendant" in court litigation, is called the "respondent". Although "complainant" and "respondent" are the correct terms technically, to avoid confusion I will stick with the traditional courtroom names — I will call the party who sues the "plaintiff" and the party who is sued the "defendant."

98 Antitrust arguments were later added to the court litigation, and Broadcom was part of a group asking the governing body of the European Union, the European Community, to investigate Qualcomm's allegedly monopolistic behavior in Europe, but we will confine our review here to the patent litigation.

It was a case brought by Broadcom alleging Qualcomm's infringement of various claims in US 6,714,983, entitled, "Modular, Portable Data Processing Terminal for Use in a Communication Network", filed in 1995, and issued in 2004.[99]

*Preview of the Broadcom Patent:*

We will focus on claim #1 for "one or more circuits adapted for use in a mobile computing device." This circuit may be classified as a "device" or "component" claim.

In the ITC case, Broadcom received an injunction against Qualcomm, and the entire litigation between the two parties was eventually settled with Qualcomm paying $891 million to Broadcom. This case, and the settlement payment of almost one billion dollars, turned on a single word in claim #1. We will identify that single word, determine why it was so important, and understand why Broadcom won the case.

*Review:*

To understand what happened in the case, scan the actions and dates summarized below:

99 As a result of what happened in the case, the following parties eventually became involved as what are called "intervenors" in the proceeding: Kyocera Wireless, LG Electronics Mobilecomm, Motorola, Samsung, Sprint Nextel, and Verizon Wireless. Those parties, and their involvement, will not be reviewed here, but it is noteworthy that this was a case of interest to many players in the mobile handset business.

**Table 4–1: Events in the *Broadcom v. Qualcomm* Litigation**

| Event | ITC Litigation | Federal Court Litigation |
|---|---|---|
| **Broadcom sues** | June, 2005 | May, 2005 |
| **First decision** | The Administrative Law Judge ("ALJ") — the ITC officer who hears the patent complaint — finds for Broadcom: October, 2006 | Jury finds for Broadcom: May, 2007 |
| **First review of decision** | ITC affirms the ALJ: June, 2007 | Federal District Court grants injunction against Qualcomm: December, 2007 |
| **Appellate review by CAFC** | October 14, 2008 | September 24, 2008 |
| **RESOLUTION OF CASE (April 2009)** | Settlement. Qualcomm agrees to pay Broadcom $891 million over four years. April, 2009 | |
| **Reexamination** | PTO issues reexamination certificate. October, 2010 | |

The ITC litigation began in June, 2005, with Broadcom's complaint that Qualcomm was infringing various claims in five patents. During the course of the litigation, Broadcom withdrew its complaint as to two of the patents, two of the remaining patents were found by the ALJ to be non-infringed, and the ALJ found that Qualcomm had infringed five claims in the fifth patent, US 6,714,983. These five claims were numbered 1, 4, 8, 9, and 11. Of these five claims, only #1 is an independent claim, and all of the other claims are dependent on claim #1. Here is claim #1 of US, 6,714,983. (I have parsed the elements by adding brackets "[ ]".)

> 1. [Preamble] One or more circuits adapted for use in a mobile computing device comprising:
> [1] a terminal adapted to receive battery power for at least one of the circuits;
> [2] communication circuitry comprising
> [2a] a reduced power mode and
> [2b] being adapted to use a first wireless communication and a second wireless communication different from the first wireless communication to transmit data to access points,
> [2c] the communication circuitry reducing power by controlling the frequency of scanning for the access points; and
> [2d] processing circuitry arranged to process data received from the communication circuitry.

In his written opinion in 2006, the ALJ discussed and interpreted six patent terms from this patent, taken from elements [1], [2a], [2b], and [2c], above. However, in its written opinion of October 14, 2008, the CAFC said the following:

> Because the ITC correctly construed ***the critical disputed claim term*** in Broadcom's patent, and because the ITC correctly rejected Qualcomm's invalidity arguments..., this court affirms the ITC's holding that the '983 patent is not invalid. [Emphasis ***in boldface italics*** added.][100]

---

100 Kyocera Wireless Corporation LG USA v. ITC, No. 2007–1493 (Fed. Cir., Oct. 14, 2008), slip opinion at pp.3–4. This case, including both the ITC and court decisions, had industry-wide importance. As a reflection of that fact, Kyocera was joined as plaintiff by Qualcomm, and by many Qualcomm

The CAFC believed that one particular term in claim #1 was "critical" to the decision in the case. In fact, a single word decided the entire case.

Take a look at claim #1 again, quoted above. In your opinion, which do you think is "the critical disputed claim term"? In particular, which single word within that term decides this billion dollar case?

I will give you a hint. The following were the terms interpreted by the Administrative Law Judge in this litigation. The single word that determined the entire case appears in one of these claim terms.

**Table 4-2: Key Claim Terms for Claim #1 of US 6,714,983**

| Element Number | Claim terms interpreted by the Administrative Law Judge |
|---|---|
| [1] | "terminal" |
| [1] | "a terminal adapted to receive battery power for at least one of the circuits" |
| [2a] | "communication circuitry comprising a reduced power mode" |
| [2b] | "communication circuitry...being adapted to use a first wireless communication and a second wireless communication different from the first wireless communication to transmit data to access points" |

customers or other interested parties who could be negatively impacted by the ITC decision. These other companies included Motorola, Inc., Samsung Electronics, LG Electronics Mobilecomm USA, Sanyo Fisher, T-Mobile USA, AT&T Mobility, Sprint Nextel, Palm, Pantech Wireless, Pantech Co., Pantech & Curitel Communications, UT Starcom, High Tech Computer, Shenzhen Huawei Communication Technologies, Research In Motion, Foxconn International Holdings, and Casio Hitachi Mobile Communications.

| Element Number | Claim terms interpreted by the Administrative Law Judge |
|---|---|
| [2c] | "reducing power by controlling the frequency of scanning for the access points" |
| [2c] | "the communication circuitry reducing power by controlling the frequency of scanning for the access points" |

Have you identified the billion dollar word?

Here is a second clue. Above are the six terms reviewed and interpreted by the ALJ. The key claim term was element [2b] above. Now can you guess which single word in element [2b] decided the entire case?

The word is "different".

When you are reading independent claims, and you come to a word like "different", that word should jump off the page, tap you on the nose, and say, "Hey! Look at me! I'm important!" This kind of word, a comparative adjective, is almost guaranteed to create problems, *unless* the word is explicitly defined, or clearly explained, in the patent's written description.

Almost all of the other terms are technical terms, well known in the industry, or relatively easily definable in a patent. The word "different" is a commonly used word, and non-technical. Specifically for those reasons, it is likely to create problems. Here are some questions, for example, that arise when element [2b] says that there is a second wireless transmission "different" from a first wireless transmission:

- How is it “different”?
- Why is it “different”?
- To what degree is it “different”?
- What is the effect of the patent element being “different”?

One might hope, for the plaintiff’s sake, that the patent applicant has defined this word. Unfortunately, non-technical words — which can prove the most ambiguous and confusing of all — are almost never defined in patent specifications. That is the case here, too. There is no definition of the word “different” in US 6,714,983.

The entire case turned on this one word, so let’s make sure we understand the arguments about this one word. The plaintiff Broadcom argued:

> [T]he plain language of claim 1 requires that the claimed communication circuitry be capable of using two different wireless communications for transmitting data to access points....[T]he two different wireless communications must be air interface protocols. Broadcom cites to the specification and prosecution history in support.[101]

Therefore, according to the plaintiff Broadcom, “different” refers to two types of “wireless communication” which must be what are called “air interface protocols” or “air interfaces”, such as “narrowband radio frequency”, or “frequency-hopping spread spectrum”, or “direct-sequence spread spectrum”, or “infrared”.

---

101 Quoted from Investigation No. 337-TA-543, Publication 4258, Volume 2 of 2, at page 119. I have deleted specific references to the patent and to the prosecution history.

The defendant Qualcomm responds:

> [T]he term "wireless communication" should be construed broadly and... the applicants could have chosen a narrower claim term, such as "air interface" if a narrower claim was intended. According to Qualcomm, the term "different" as applied to wireless communications is extremely broad and is not limited to just one form of difference, such as an air interface. Qualcomm cites to the specification in support of the breadth of the term. Qualcomm asserts that the patent never uses the term "air interface" and that prosecution history makes clear that the different wireless communications were not limited to different air interfaces. Qualcomm asserts that, adopting Broadcom's claim construction would amount to rewriting the claim as follows: "communication circuitry... being adapted to use a first wireless communication **[using a first air interface]** and a second wireless communication **[using an interface]** different from **[that used in]** the first wireless communication to transmit data to access points."[102] [The **boldfaced and bracketed insertions** are in the original text, and were not added.]

*Paradoxically, the patent owner is arguing for a narrow interpretation of the claim, while the defendant is arguing for the broadest possible interpretation!* How did this happen? Wouldn't we expect to see the patent owner seeking a broad claim, and the defendant seeking a narrow one? Yes, that is what we would expect, but the exact opposite happened here. Why?

102 *Ibid.* at pp. 119–120.

The answer can be found by examining the prior art. Communication circuitry that could communicate with two different access points was well known in the art before this patent. In fact, defendant Qualcomm cited three U.S. patents, any one of which might have invalidated claim #1 *if* the word "different" includes "two communications using *the same* communication method". A broad interpretation of the word "different", which the defendant Qualcomm wanted, may have caused the claim to be invalidated by prior art.

The ALJ, however, interpreted "different" narrowly, in concurrence with Broadcom's position, and the ITC agreed with him. On appeal, the CAFC also agreed with Broadcom, but we need to understand *exactly why* the CAFC agreed. The CAFC gave two reasons in its written opinion for its agreement with a narrow definition of the word "different".

First, the phrase "access point" is found in Figures 11, 47, and 48 of the patent. Qualcomm relied on Figure 11, where multiple access points are shown, and the only discussion is that Figure 11 shows a Local Area Network (which, presumably, would have a single air protocol). The court, however, relied on Figure 47 rather than Figure 11, and a discussion in column 39 which says: "The [first] access point...provides for communication via one type of radio communication while [the second] access point provides for another. For examples, [the first] access point...may provide a long-distance digital cellular link while [the second] access point...provides for a local spread spectrum link." In other words, according to the CAFC, this quote from the patent suggests that there are at least two *different types* of radio communication, which was also Broadcom's argument.

Second, according to the CAFC, Figure 11 is *merely one example* of a particular method of communication. The Court said:

> This Figure does not change claim 1's requirement for a device "adapted to" use two different communications. The specification provides the necessary context for the difference between the claimed first and second wireless communications. The difference envisioned by the claim is a difference in their method of communication. In other words, the ITC properly construed the meaning of the term "different".[103]

The Court's first argument in support of Broadcom is, on balance, not convincing, in my opinion. Qualcomm says, in effect: Yes, we agree that the patent includes different protocols, but only in some embodiments such as Figures 47 and 48. In other embodiments, such as Figure 11, the same protocol is used, so that the word "different" should be interpreted naturally to mean "two different access points whether or not of the same protocol". Qualcomm has a strong argument here. The patent owner could have defined "different" in the claim, or could have referred to "air protocol", but neither thing appears in the patent. The ALJ, the ITC, and the CAFC all interpreted the word narrowly to save the claim. However, that narrow interpretation is not how Broadcom presented the word "different" in the patent.

The Court's second argument, however, is a winner for Broadcom. Element [2b] in claim #1 is "communication circuitry...being adapted to use...different [communications]

---

103 *Kyocera Wireless v. ITC* slip opinion at p.11.

to transmit data to access points". The focus here is not on method but rather on structure which is "adapted to" use methods. However, structure "adapted to" use two or more methods might sometimes use two methods and other times might use only one, while the structure is at all times "adapted to" use as many methods as required.

The phrase "adapted to" is what I call a *structural tag* in the patent. This is language attached to what would otherwise be a process or method claim element, but which by its inclusion converts the element into a structural element. The structural tag does *not* limit the element to the specific method, but simply says the structure can perform that method. A structural tag can enhance greatly the value of a claim, hence also the value of the patent. That is exactly what happened here, in the *Broadcom v. Qualcomm* ITC case.

So claim #1 in US 6,714,983, would seem to be a "good patent claim", yes? But hold on a second!

The CAFC rejected the ITC's Exclusion Order, and told the ITC to reconsider this remedy.[104] In its Order, the ITC forbade the importation or sale of Qualcomm chips, and also of wireless devices with the chips, *even if the wireless devices were made, imported, and sold not by Qualcomm, but rather by some Qualcomm customer that was not part of the ITC litigation.*

Can the ITC do that? Can it issue an order that applies to people who were not even in the case? Yes, but only if the

104 I said "rejected", which is the way most of us would think about it. The legal jargon is not "rejected" or "reversed", but rather "vacated and remanded". It was "vacated" because it was simply voided, not changed into something else. It was "remanded", because the court was saying, "Yes, we understand an Exclusion Order may be required, but not the one you wrote, so please try again."

Order is a "General Exclusion Order" ("GEO"), and not if the Order it is a "Limited Exclusion Order" ("LEO"). For the ITC to issue a GEO, however, it must first find that a LEO will be circumvented by the infringers, or that there is both a pattern of patent infringement and an inability to identify the source of infringing products. The ITC did not even discuss either condition. Instead, the ITC issued an LEO, but with *general* exclusion, and that is simply beyond the ITC's legal authority to do. So the remedy that Broadcom remedy was procedurally incorrect. Therefore, when the CAFC rejected the decision of the ITC, the CAFC was *not* saying that the substantive decision of infringement was wrong, but was saying instead: "For the ITC to issue this kind of exclusion order, with the record before us, is simply beyond the legal authority of the ITC. The ITC must try again — either to change the order to an LEO (hence, Qualcomm's customers would not be affected by the ITC order) or to make factual findings sufficient to support a GEO".

What does this all mean? Technically, *Qualcomm won this round of litigation at the CAFC*. How did that happen? Both the ITC and the CAFC found no direct infringement by Qualcomm, because, among other things, Qualcomm did not import or sell products with the reduced power mode, element [2a]. The ITC, however, found Qualcomm guilty of the indirect infringement called "induced infringement", in that Qualcomm enabled and encouraged others to infringe.

There is induced infringement only where there is:

(1) at least one direct infringer,
(2) the inducer does something to help cause the direct infringement, and
(3) the inducer had an intention to cause the infringement.

In this case, the ITC found that all three requirements had been met.[105]

The CAFC did not discuss at all requirement (1), "direct infringer", and seemed to accept "as a given" that other handset manufacturers were infringing the patent *specifically because of their use of the Qualcomm chip.*

The CAFC noted a mountain of evidence for requirement (2) Qualcomm acts to help cause infringement, including:

- providing software that creates an infringement when combined with the handset hardware,
- training the infringers, and
- providing the infringers with documentation and customer support.

These are acts that might have enabled infringement, which is necessary by requirement (2) for induced infringement.

The CAFC, however, reversed the lower court on requirement (3) Qualcomm's intent to cause infringement. The ITC found that Qualcomm intended to perform the acts it performed, but the CAFC said that the legal standard for intent is whether Qualcomm had a specific intent to encourage the infringement. Thus, Qualcomm's liability was cancelled by the CAFC, and the case was sent back to the ITC to see if Qualcomm had the required intent to encourage infringement. Qualcomm therefore won this round of the litigation.

---

105 The CAFC, in the *Akamai* case decided August 31, 2012, changed the law in this area. However, *Akamai* was not the legal standard at the time *Broadcom v. Qualcomm* was decided. Moreover, *Akamai* applies only to method claims, whereas we have a product claim here. In any case, the *Akamai* decision has no bearing in this case on the lessons we are trying to learn here about what makes a good patent.

*Since defendant Qualcomm clearly won the last round of litigation, how can this be a "good patent" for Broadcom? Even more puzzling, why would Qualcomm, after winning this round of litigation, turn around and agree to pay $891 million?*

Qualcomm's state of mind, which is relevant to a charge of "induced infringement" in the ITC case, was left open by the court in the ITC litigation. However, in the parallel litigation starting in federal court, which is noted in the last column of Table 4–1 above, a significant decision was made that left little doubt about what would happen in the next round of litigation.

The CAFC's opinion in the ITC case was rendered on October 24, 2008. Three weeks earlier, on September 24, 2008, a different group of CAFC judges (with one judge overlapping in both cases) decided the appeal in the *Broadcom v. Qualcomm* federal court case. There were different patents in the court case, but like US 6,714,983, these other patents also covered dual-mode transceivers. What makes the CAFC decision in the federal court case interesting is that in the federal court case (as opposed to the ITC case) the CAFC found Qualcomm guilty of induced infringement, because Qualcomm:

(1) knew of Broadcom's patents (that is, US 5,657,317, US 6,389,010, and US 6,847,686 in the federal court case),

(2) did not change its own products to avoid the Broadcom patents or even explore ways to do so,

(3) did not instruct its customers how to avoid infringing Broadcom patents, and

(4) did not seek legal opinions on the question of infringement.[106]

Let's summarize what happened here:

1. In the ITC case, the ITC found that Qualcomm's customers directly infringed Broadcom's patent. The CAFC, reviewing the ITC opinion, did not rule on this point, but apparently assumed that was true. *The assumption by the CAFC in the ITC litigation is that Qualcomm's customers would be directly liable for infringement. Qualcomm could not perceive this assumption as positive. Indeed, the CAFC ruling, which appears to include this assumption, would almost certainly be perceived by Qualcomm as extremely negative.* The CAFC decision in the ITC case was rendered on October 14, 2008.

2. At almost the same time, on September 24, 2008, a different panel of the CAFC decided, in the federal court litigation, that Qualcomm had indirectly infringed some patents and, in particular, had induced infringement of those patents. Prior to CAFC *Akamai*, inducement to infringement was determined only if there is another party or parties directly infringing, which in this case would mean Qualcomm's customers using Qualcomm's infringing products.

These two cases, decided together, determined the matter. This is a bit complicated, so let us illustrate with the following Table 4–3.

---

106 *Broadcom Corporation v. Qualcomm, Inc.* 543 F.3d 683 (Fed. Cir. September 24, 2008), at p.700.

**Table 4-3: Two CAFC Decisions in the *Broadcom v. Qualcomm* Litigation**

| | **Lower Court or ITC** | **CAFC Decision** | **Implications** |
|---|---|---|---|
| **Federal court case** | District Court Held: (1) Qualcomm infringed directly. (2) Qualcomm induced infringement. (3) Affirms jury determined damages of $19.64 million. (4) Adds injunction against Qualcomm. | September 24, 2008: (1) Invalidates the claims from one of three patents infringed (2) Affirms all other decisions of the District Court. | By its affirmation of the finding of induced infringement, the CAFC necessarily agreed that users of the infringing products must themselves be direct infringers. |
| **ITC Case** | ITC Held: (1) Qualcomm did not infringe directly. (2) Qualcomm induced infringement. Injunction ordered against all products including the infringing components. | October 14, 2008: (1) Affirms the ITC's decision of no direct infringement by Qualcomm. (2) On induced infringement, the ITC used the wrong standard of "intent" by Qualcomm. Vacated and remanded for another decision by the ITC. | A. On (2), the CAFC assumed, but did not decide, that Qualcomm's customers had directly infringed. B. CAFC said the ITC must review and decide again. If Qualcomm had the required intent, an injunction may issue against Qualcomm, and possibly against all products including infringing components. |

Each of the CAFC decisions above was decided unanimously by a panel of three judges, with only one judge serving on both panels. This is significant particularly for the charge of indirect infringement, because Qualcomm can be liable for inducing to infringe only if someone else, here Qualcomm's customers, has directly infringed. In essence, five of the total of twelve CAFC judges either held implicitly (in the federal court case) or assumed (in the ITC case) that Qualcomm's customers infringed various patents of Broadcom.

3. Qualcomm won the last round of the ITC litigation only on the very narrow ground that the ITC had applied an incorrect legal standard in its determination of Qualcomm's "intent to induce infringement". The ITC would need to change its procedure, and decide again. That is not a strong support on which Qualcomm could lean.

4. There were no other rounds of litigation, because all the litigation then settled. However, if there had been another round of litigation in the ITC case, what probably would have happened? There are several possibilities:

a. The plaintiff, Broadcom, might have sought only a narrow exclusion order (called a "Limited Exclusion Order" or "LEO") preventing Qualcomm from importing and selling its own chips. This would have required Broadcom to prove that Qualcomm had the intent required for induced infringement. In the circumstances, a Limited Exclusion Order is the narrowest remedy Broadcom could seek, but even this remedy would be very negative for Qualcomm.

b. Instead of a limited ITC order, perhaps Broadcom would seek to obtain a more comprehensive exclusion order (called a "General Exclusion Order" or "GEO"), by meeting the requirements to obtain the GEO. A GEO would bar importation of sale of products including Qualcomm components, and *would be disastrous both for Qualcomm's customers and for Qualcomm's public reputation*. This option would also require Broadcom to prove Qualcomm's intent, and to meet other criteria, but it was a very severe threat to Qualcomm.

c. Alternatively, instead of trying to change the exclusion order in the ITC case, Broadcom might have chosen instead to initiate an entirely new ITC complaint, this time naming all of Qualcomm's customers as direct infringers, not just as "intervenors" (which is what they were in the original ITC case). In the ITC case, the ITC had ruled, and the CAFC assumed to be correct, that Qualcomm's customers were all direct infringers of Broadcom patent US 6,714,983. In the federal court case, the CAFC affirmed the District Court finding of induced infringement of US 5,657,317 and US 6,389,010. Broadcom had the option to file actions for direct infringement, either at the ITC or in federal court, or both, against Qualcomm's customers. This also is an extremely serious threat. Liability for its customers would be a terrible result for Qualcomm.

5. The Court's rejection of the ITC's injunction means, perhaps ironically, that Qualcomm won the last round of litigation in the ITC case. However, few companies could survive such a "victory". In the end, Qualcomm had little choice but to settle the case by making a large settlement payment, spread out over four years.

The results in the ITC litigation all hinged on the ITC and court interpretation of the word "different" in claim #1 of US 6,714,983. Were it not for the ruling on this single ambiguous word, Qualcomm might have won the ITC case. In the end, Qualcomm settled by agreeing to pay $891 million.

**Validity**: Validity is determined at a particular point in time. The estimate of validity can change, depending on what has happened in litigation involving the patent. In this case, let's call claim validity prior to the litigation (that is, before 2005) the "prospective validity estimate", and let's call claim validity from the time of the litigation the "retrospective validity estimate". These two estimates vary dramatically.

Looking prospectively, that is, before the litigation, the claims in US 6,714,983 might be valid, but there is significant doubt because of the argument that Qualcomm made in the case. Prior to the ITC litigation, one might think that the word "different" means "multiple communications with the same protocol" and, on that basis, the claims might be invalidated as being anticipated by multiple earlier patents. (This was Qualcomm's argument.) Therefore, prospective claim validity — that is, the estimate of validity prior to litigation — appears moderate to weak, because of the word "different".

This weakness could have been avoided if the patent had defined "different" to mean different air protocols. However, the absence of definitions of key claim terms is a relatively common defect in patents, even in otherwise "good patents". The absence of definitions for *non*-technical claim terms is particularly common, because these are every day words that everyone seems to understand (except that these words suddenly become unclear and confusing in the body of a patent claim!).

The absence of a definition is clearly a defect. Nevertheless, the patent claims were strengthened by the use of structural tags in the elements of claim #1, such as "adapted to".

It is too bad for the patentee that only four of six parts of claim #1 had structural tags, but at least the most critical element [2b], had one. It is also too bad that claim #1 has three different structural tags, namely, "adapted for" in the preamble[107], "adapted to" in element [1] and element [2b], and "arranged to" in element 3. Having three different structural tags, when they all seem to say exactly the same thing, simply creates confusion. Perhaps equally bad, none of the three forms appearing in claim #1 is the most traditional tag — probably the most traditional language for a structural tag is "configured to", and its use would have been entirely appropriate throughout all of the claims of US 6,741,983. Using structural tags to expand the scope of claim #1 was a very good idea, but the implementation was imperfect.[108]

The lack of a definition for "different" is bad, but the use of the structural tag "adapted to" in element [2b] provides at least a partial remedy. On balance, therefore, "Validity" appears to be of medium quality, *looked at prospectively*, that is, before litigation.

Retrospectively, however, the view of validity is much different. Both the ITC and the CAFC found the claims of 6,714,983 to be valid. In addition, the PTO reexamined all of the claims in the litigation (1, 4, 8, 9, and 11) and confirmed their validity on October 5, 2010.

This was not an ordinary reexamination. This reexamination included a massive quantity of potentially damaging prior art, including 60 U.S. patents, and several hundred technical standards and technical publications. Not only did the PTO confirm all the reviewed claims, but in addition the patentee

---

107 The preamble of claim #1 is, "One or more circuits adapted for use in a mobile computing device". The structural tag is "adapted for".

108 Element [3] of claim #1 is, "processing circuitry arranged to process data received from the communication circuitry". The structural tag is "arranged to".

added new claims 26–41, all based directly or indirectly on structure claim #1. From a retrospective view, that is to say after litigation, the validity of claims in 6,714,983 has been proven to be extremely high. In other words, the litigation and the PTO reexamination have greatly strengthened the estimate of claim validity.

**Scope**: There is a spectacular scope of coverage, without doubt. Although the wireless handset market is massive today, it was also important and growing when the patent was filed in 1995, and even more so when litigation began, in 2005. The particular problem addressed by the patent, which is the energy drain on a wireless handset battery, is one of the most significant problems in the business, both in 1995 and today. The solution offered in the patent to this problem, which is to reduce the on-duty cycle, is a basic solution that is used widely in the market.

**Discoverability of Infringement**: Prospectively, that is, prior to litigation, I would estimate discoverability as moderately high. Infringement is not apparent to the naked eye but should be discoverable by a review of product literature, and by inference from the operation of products that include the chips which are the subject of the claims. Retrospectively, the discoverability rating is even higher, since discoverability clearly did not present any problem to Broadcom or to the ITC.

**Summary**: This is a very good patent covering an important feature in a large market. There was some doubt about the validity of the patent due to the risk that a broad interpretation of the word "different" (sought by the defendant) might have caused the claims to be invalidated by prior art. Litigation, however, resolved this doubt.

Those who may still doubt the Pyrrhic nature of the Qualcomm "victory", or dispute its subsequent decision to settle the case, might consider the following analogy:

Suppose that you personally are sued for money, and the judge rules as follows:

> *You* are not liable. However, because of what you did, your spouse, your children, your parents, your colleagues at work, your best friend, and the man you buy a newspaper from every morning, are all liable, and they are all going to pay a lot of money when this comes to court again.

As you walk out of the courthouse thinking about your "victory", the plaintiff walks up and says to you, "I have another idea. Instead of my suing all these people, pay me an amount equal to about 3 or 4 months of your annual profit. Then I won't sue you or anyone else". Now here is your choice: Will you become *extremely* unpopular by allowing all the people you care about — let's call these people your "customers" — to be hauled into court and inevitably be forced to pay large sums of money to the plaintiff? Or will you agree to pay a sum of money, spread out over four years that, while certainly significant and onerous, will not bankrupt you or forever alienate your customers?

You now understand why, instead of continuing with this increasingly difficult litigation, a victorious Qualcomm chose to settle and pay Broadcom $891 million over four years. Qualcomm is a great company, possibly the most successful developer and monetizer of technology in history, but even Qualcomm can't win 'em all.

**Lessons Learned**: Here are some of the lessons we might learn from patent claim #1 in US 6,714,983, litigated in the ITC litigation of *Broadcom v. Qualcomm.*

4–1–1. ***Patent cases almost always turn on a very limited number of key claim terms, often a single term.*** Here, the term "different" in element [2b] of claim #1 was critical.

4–1–2. ***Explicit definitions in the patent of critical terms can make or break the case.*** It is impossible to define every term used. When you write a patent, however, try to imagine which terms might raise questions and define those terms to your advantage. When you are reviewing an allowed claim, identify the critical terms in the independent claims, and connect them, if you can, with definitions or explanations of those terms in the patent.[109]

---

109 The PTO recently issued a request for public comments on ways to facilitate patent examination "and bring more certainty to the scope of issued patents". Federal Register / Vol. 78, No. 10 / Tuesday, January 15, 2013 / Notices, p.2960, United States PTO Docket No. PTO-P-2011–0046, "Request for Comments on Preparation of Patent Applications", available at http://www.gpo.gov/fdsys/pkg/FR-2013–01–15/pdf/2013–00690.pdf. The goal, greater clarity of claims, is admirable, but its attainment is very far from certain. For example, the PTO has suggested the need for a "glossary of potentially ambiguous, distinctive, and specialized terms used in the specification and/or claims". *Id.* at p.2961. The problem with this suggestion, as noted by one commentator, is that drafters of patent applications simply cannot "*know ahead of time which claim terms will be at issue in examination or litigation years down the road.*" Courtenay C. Brinckerhoff, partner at Foley & Lardner, LLP, "USPTO considers best practices to improve patent application quality", published on February 18, 2013, in *Lexology,* a newsfeed service published in cooperation with ACC, the Association of Corporate Counsel, and at http://www.foley.com/uspto-considers-best-practices-to-improve-patent-application-quality-02–14–2013/. Although I support the PTO's goal of claim clarity, as a drafter of patent applications I am in substantial agreement with Ms. Brinckerhoff's belief that clarity of all claim terms, or even of the key claim terms that will arise in litigation, is unattainable. Still, we must do the best we can, and one purpose of this book is to help drafters of patents

4–1–3. ***Although many patents do define terms, these definitions are most often for technical terms only. Ironically, however, the non-technical terms are often the ones that cause the big problems.*** Non-technical terms are rarely defined, perhaps because applicants believe that "everyone knows what the non-technical terms mean". However, the opposite is true. Often the technical terms do not create issues (or those issues are not "critical") because technical terms are either understood in the industry or clearly defined in the patent, whereas undefined non-technical terms create difficulties. In this case, the word "different" turned out to be both unclear and critical to the outcome of the case. Comparative words, in particular, can cause problems.

4–1–4. ***Structural tags in patent claims can win the case.*** Structural "tags" help establish claim terms as "structural" rather than as "methods". At the same time, they may expand the scope of a structure claim by indicating the ability of the structure to perform a function, but not requiring that the function be performed in the infringing product.

Probably the most common structural tag is "configured to", but "designed to" and "constructed to" can also work. In this case, the tags used were "adapted for", "adapted to", and "arranged to". Structural tags can save a claim, and therefore an entire case, just as the tag "adapted to" saved this case for Broadcom.

4–1–5. ***Claim scope and claim validity are natural enemies.*** The greater the scope of a claim, the more likely that claim will be disallowed by the PTO during examination, cancelled by the PTO during reexamination, unenforced by the

---

identify and define what are likely to be the key claim terms in the applications they draft.

ITC, or invalidated by a federal court during patent litigation. In this case, the defendant argued for a broader interpretation of the term "different" and if that interpretation had been accepted, the claim scope would have expanded greatly but the claim would have been found invalid. In this case, the narrower interpretation of the plaintiff was accepted by both the ITC and the CAFC, resulting in a narrower claim scope but a valid claim.

4-1-6. ***Three factors determine claim value***: (1) ***the market size*** of the main subject, (2) the importance of ***the technical issue*** or problem discussed by the patent, and (3) the simplicity and clarity of ***the solution presented*** in the claims. In this case, the market for wireless handsets is vast, the technical problem addressed (reduction of power consumption to save battery life) is a crucial problem, and the solution (lengthening the duty cycle for the handset's scan of access points) is both simple and clear.

4-1-7. ***Value is created by both direct and indirect infringement***. When you ask yourself, "How do I know if my patent's any good?", make sure to ask "Who might be a direct infringer?" and also "Who might be an indirect infringer?" In this case, the defendant Qualcomm was found to be only an indirect infringer, but additional pressure was added on the defendant by the implicit assumption of the CAFC that the defendant's customers were direct infringers.

4-1-8. ***There may be many battles in a patent war***. Don't feel the war is lost after losing a single battle. Recognize that another round of legal combat may change what happened in a previous round. Here, an incorrect legal standard was applied by the ITC, and so the exclusion order against Qualcomm was voided by the CAFC, but that only meant that there would be another round of battle in which the correct legal standard would be applied. Although the plaintiff lost this round on a technicality, the plaintiff was likely to win the next round. In the next round of litigation, the plaintiff might have changed the form of remedy in the main case or might have filed a new ITC complaint with new defendants, initiating (or threatening to initiate) steps against Qualcomm's customers who would likely be found liable as direct infringers of Broadcom's patent. As it turned out, this step proved unnecessary and never happened.

### *Case 2: Trend Micro, Inc. v. Fortinet, Inc.*

ITC Case 337-TA-510: Trend Micro, Inc., as the plaintiff, alleging infringement of a method claim for blocking computer viruses, against Fortinet, Inc.

*Background to the Decision:*

Trend Micro, Incorporated, of Cupertino, California, is an electronic security company founded in Los Angeles in 1988. The headquarters were moved first to Taipei, Taiwan, and later to Tokyo. The company has a strong presence in Cupertino, California, and annual sales in 2012 of about $1.18 billion.[110]

Fortinet is a company based in Sunnyvale, California with 2012 sales of about $534 million.

110 Trend Micro's reported sales for 2012 were 93.839 billion Japanese yen. Based on an average Yen/Dollar rate of 79.79 in 2012, this would translate to about $1.18 billion.

*Preview of the Trend Micro Patent:*

Trend Micro sued Fortinet in a case entitled, "In the Matter of Certain Systems for Detecting and Removing Viruses or Worms, Components Thereof, and Products Containing Same". Trend Micro alleged infringement of US 5,623,600, "Virus Detection and Removal Apparatus for Computer Networks". We will look at independent claim #4, claim #8 (which is dependent on claim #4), and independent claim #13. Each of these claims is a "method for detecting viruses in mail message". In various forms of litigation in the case, all of the structure claims were invalidated (which we will not review), and independent method claim #4 was cancelled by the patent office on reexamination, but the patent retained value because dependent claim #8 was found valid, and became the new independent claim after claim #4 was cancelled.

Litigation continued between the two parties for about eight years, ending in a cash payment from Fortinet to Trend Micro of $9 million in 2011. Although the size of this settlement is far less than the settlement in the *Broadcom* case, we are interested here in the principles of patent value and this case provides a very good example.

*Review:*

US 5,623,600, filed September 26, 1995, and issued on April 22, 1997, is one of Trend Micro's earliest U.S. patents. Trend Micro asserted this patent against a number of companies, including Fortinet, Inc., in this ITC action. The litigation of the two parties over this patent included these highlights:

(1) In 2004, Trend Micro sued Fortinet in Federal District Court for the Northern District of California, alleging infringement of the patent.

(2) Also in 2004, Trend Micro sued Fortinet at the ITC, in case 337-TA-510, seeking to stop importation and sale of products alleged to infringe the patent. The administrative law judge, "ALJ", found claims 1 and 3 to be invalid, but found that claims 4, 7, 8, and 11–15 to be valid and infringed. The ITC opted not to review this decision of the ALJ, thus upholding the decision without additional review.

Both the ITC case and the 2004 federal court litigation were settled by a payment from Fortinet to Trend Micro.

(3) In 2008, Fortinet (the defendant in the prior actions) sued Trend Micro, again in Federal District Court for the Northern District of California, seeking a declaratory judgment that the patent claims were invalid due to prior art.[111] However, Trend Micro voluntarily issued to Fortinet a "covenant not to sue", which is a promise, here to Fortinet, that Trend Micro would not sue to enforce the patent. Since there was no longer any real dispute between the parties, the Federal District Court dismissed this lawsuit.

(4) In 2009, Trend Micro filed suit in California state court to enforce the royalty payments required by the settlement agreement between the parties.

(5) In 2010, Fortinet asked the PTO to reexamine US 5,623,600 on the basis of prior art not considered by the patent examiner in the original prosecution. Fortinet sought to invalidate all the claims in the patent. The reexamination application number at the PTO is 90/011,022.

---

111 This kind of lawsuit, brought by a patent licensee seeking to invalidate the patent on which the license is based, is permitted under the U.S. Supreme Court decision of *Lear, Inc. v. Adkins* 395 U.S. 653 (1969). Such a lawsuit is commonly called a "*Lear* challenge", or is said to be based on the "*Lear* Doctrine".

(6) On March 25, 2011, Fortinet made a second request for reexamination, on the basis of new prior art not presented in the first request for reexamination. Fortinet sought to invalidate claims 1, 4, 7, 9, and 11 in the patent.

(7) The parties settled all court litigation by a payment from Fortinet to Trend Micro of $9 million, made in the last quarter of 2011. This payment did *not* affect the reexamination proceedings at the PTO, which continued, and which we will review here.

(8) On December 17, 2012, the PTO issued a reexamination certificate for US 5,623,600. The final decision cancelled claims 1–7, 9, 11–12, and 14–22 due to prior art; found claim #8 and claim #13 patentable as amended; confirmed the patentability of claim #10; and determined new claims 23–27 to be patentable.

Although all of this litigation may seem complicated, it is not particularly complex in comparison to other patent wars in recent years involving information & communication technologies. A patent war often results when two companies have widely divergent views of the value of a particular patent. In this case, the parties disagreed about the value of US 5,623,600, and the result was protracted litigation.

The critical thing for us in this litigation is the ultimate fate of the claims of US 5,623,600. Let's focus on three claims.

**Table 4–4: Decisions about Claims 4, 8, and 13, of US 5,623,600**

| | 337-TA-510: Administrative Law Judge and the ITC | Patent Examiner: Initial Decision in Reexamination 90/011,022 | BOPAI in Reexamination 90/011,022 (appear within the patent office) | Reexamination Certificate issued December 12, 2012 |
|---|---|---|---|---|
| **Claim 4** | Claim is valid and infringed | Claim is cancelled by prior art | Agrees that claim is cancelled by prior art. | Claim is cancelled, and therefore dead. |
| **Claim 8** | Claim is valid and infringed | Claim is cancelled by prior art | Reverses and finds claim is valid and confirmed. *Claim is alive.* | Claim is patentable as amended. |
| **Claim 13** | Claim is valid and infringed | Claim is valid and confirmed | No appeal of examiner, meaning claim is still valid and confirmed. Claim is alive. | Claim is patentable as amended. |

In these three very different rulings, claim #4 was found valid but then invalid (win, lose, lose, lose), claim #8 was reviewed and found valid, then invalid, then valid in the last rounds (win, lose, win, win), and claim #13 was found valid, then valid and confirmed (win, win, win, win). The third round, which is the decision of the BOPAI ["Board of Patent Appeals and Interferences", the PTO's appellate board], essentially determines the outcome, but the final disposition is made only in the fourth round here, by issuance of the reexamination certificate.

Here is claim #4, which I parse in brackets:

> 4. [Preamble] A computer implemented method for detecting viruses in data transfers between a first computer and a second computer, the method comprising the steps of:
> [1] receiving at a server a data transfer request including a destination address;
> [2] electronically receiving data at the server;
> [3] determining whether the data contains a virus at the server;
> [4] performing a preset action on the data using the server if the data contains a virus;
> [5] sending the data to the destination address if the data does not contain a virus;
> [6] determining whether the data is of a type that is likely to contain a virus; and
> [7] [7a] transmitting the data from the server to the destination without performing the steps of determining whether the data contains a virus and
> [7b] performing a preset action if the data is not of a type that is likely to contain a virus.

The ALJ in the ITC action interpreted nine claim terms. Of these nine, only one term appeared in claims 4, 8, and 13. Of the nine, a second term appeared in claims 4 and 13, but not in claim #8. These two terms were the key claim terms that decided the entire case. Can you guess which they are? I will give you some hints.

First, I will quote the other claims, as amended upon

reexamination.[112] Claim #8 is dependent on claim #4, and is a further requirement for element [3] above:

> 8. The method of claim 4, wherein the step of determining whether the data is of a type that is likely to contain a virus is performed by comparing an extension type of a file name for the data to a group of known extension types.

In the patent, "extension type" is defined at column 7, lines 35–41, to include examples such as ".txt", ".bmd", ".pcx", ".tif", ".exe", ".zip", and ".com".

Here is claim #13, as amended upon reexamination.[113] It is somewhat long, but here, too, the same two critical terms appear.

> 13. [Preamble] A computer implemented method for detecting viruses in a mail message transferred between a first computer and a second computer, the method comprising the steps of:
> [1] receiving a mail message request including a destination address; electronically receiving the mail message at a server; scanning the mail message for encoded portions; determining whether the mail message contains a virus;
> [2] performing a preset action on the mail message if the mail message contains a virus;
> [3] sending the mail message to the destination address if the mail message does not contain a virus; and
> [4] wherein

112 The amendment to claim #8 was to change the word "or" in the last line to "of". This was simply a clerical or typographical error that was corrected.

113 The amendment to claim #13 was to change the word "contains" in element [3] to "contain". This was another clerical or typographical error that was corrected.

[4a] the step of sending the mail message to the destination address is performed if the mail message does not contain any encoded portions; the server includes a SMTP proxy server and a SMTP daemon; and

[4b] the step of sending the mail message comprises transferring the mail message from the SMTP proxy server to the SMTP daemon and transferring the mail message from the SMTP daemon to a node having an address matching the destination address.

Are you able to guess the two key claim terms that decided the case? Here are two more hints, which should help you greatly:

1. Each of the two key claim terms is a single word.

2. In Fortinet's second request for reexamination, Fortinet quoted the CEO of Trend Micro, Ms. Eva Chen, regarding what she thought this patent was all about, in essence what she thought was the "Point of Novelty" of the patent. Ms. Chen said this:

> **In the patent [5,623,600], we are not claiming that we invented the antivirus scanner. We are not claiming that we invented the proxy server. But the *<u>concept</u>* of using these two together so that you can stop the virus during... [transmission] is new.**[114]

The key patent claim term that appears in all three claims is

---

114 Fortinet's REQUEST FOR EX PARTE REEXAMINATION UNDER 35 USC SECTIONS 302–307, March 25, 2011, http://www.fortinet.com/legal-docs/March2011_600_Patent_Reexam_Request.pdf, at p.6. This quote was derived from Robert McMillan, "Trend Micro: Barracuda Suit Not About Open Source", *PC World*, June 13, 2008, at http://www.pcworld.com/article/147085/article.html. These emphases in boldface, italics and underlining did not appear in the *PC World* article, but do appear in Fortinet's REQUEST.

the word "virus". The second patent claim term, which appears in claims 4 and 13, is "server". These two terms together, "virus" and "server", essentially determined the outcome of the case.

The typical problem that comes up with a word like "virus" is that it is undefined in the patent and so creates confusion about what should be included or excluded. In a case where prior art will knock out one definition of key claim term, but will not knock out another definition, the lack of clarity could lead to disaster, because there is no way to be certain how the claim will be interpreted by the ITC or by a court.

There was no disaster in this case, however, *for the simple reason that the patentee properly defined this key term in the written description.* A complication arose but made no difference, because this key term had been properly defined. Here is the definition of the term "virus", from column 1, lines 45–57 of the written description of US 5,623,600:

> A computer virus is a section of code that is buried or hidden in another program. Once the program is executed, the code is activated and attaches itself to other programs in the system. Infected programs in turn copy the code to other programs. The effect of such viruses can be simple pranks that cause a message to be displayed on the screen or more serious effects such as the destruction of programs and data. Another problem in the prior art is worms. Worms are destructive programs that replicate themselves throughout disk and memory using up all available computer resources eventually causing the computer system to crash. Obviously, because of the destructive nature of worms and viruses, there is a need for eliminating them from computers and networks.

As you see, "virus" was clearly defined, and it was defined to be something allied to, but different from, computer "worms".

In the decision of the ALJ, two issues came up about the definition of the word "virus". Astoundingly, the ALJ ruled in both cases in favor of Fortinet's position, and against Trend Micro, even though Trend Micro defined this term in the patent. Why are these rulings astounding? Look at the issues:

First, how to interpret the word "virus"? The defendant Fortinet says that "virus" means "malicious code". The patentee, Trend Micro, essentially copied the definition from the patent, and said that "virus" is:

> A section of malicious code that is buried or hidden in another program. When executed, the malicious code may attach itself to other programs, open a backdoor for a hacker..., destroy data, perform a prank, or other actions harmful to the server or recipient client computer.

Isn't this exactly the definition that appeared in the patent? I think so, but the ALJ said that defendant Fortinet was right, not patentee Trend Micro.[115]

Second, the Commission staff advising the ALJ concluded that the term "virus" also "covers a form of malicious code referred to as a worm."[116] The patent itself has two distinct

---

115 The parties' positions, and the ALJ's decision, appear in Final Initial and Recommended Decisions of Administrative Law Judge Paul J. Luckern, at pp.33–37. This document is part of the larger document entitled, "In the Matter of Certain Systems for Detecting and Removing Viruses or Worms, Components Thereof, and Products Containing Same", Investigation No. 337-TA-510, Publication 3936, July, 2007. http://www.usitc.gov/publications/337/pub3936.pdf.

116 *Id.* at p.34.

definitions, one for "virus" and one for "worm", quoted above. Nevertheless, the ALJ ruled that "virus" includes "worm".[117]

What effect did these definitions have on the case? Zero! How can that be? *I suggest that the definition for "virus" in the patent robbed the term of any possible harmful consequence for the patentee.* Is a "virus" equal to "malicious code", or only "malicious code that is buried or hidden in another program"? The question was not relevant to the decision. Does "virus" include "worms", or not? This was also irrelevant. *The patentee lost on the nuances of the definition, but this loss did not affect the outcome.* Once the main definition was clear, no serious attack could be mounted against Trend Micro on the basis of the term "virus".

There were other attacks on "virus", but they were not based on this particular definition of the term. Rather, the patent examiner in the PTO reexamination found claim #4 to be "obvious", and hence invalid under 35 USC sec. 103(a). The examiner cited one piece of prior art for elements [1] — [4], a second piece of prior art for elements [5] — [7b], and said, "it would have been obvious" to combine these two pieces of prior art, meaning it would have been obvious to determine the likelihood of a virus even without scanning, then taking some action. Thus, according to the PTO, claim #4 was obvious relative to prior art. Although Trend Micro may appeal this decision to the CAFC, claim #4 appears to be invalid, at least for now.

This is where claim #8 comes into play. Claim #8 is "dependent" on #4, meaning that #8 includes *all of the elements* of claim #4, but also adds the new element in claim #8. That is

---

117 *Id.* at p.37.

the way dependent claims work. With claim #4 presumably dead, the dependent claim #8 comes "alive" and becomes independent. Here's what new independent claim #8 says, including all of the elements of cancelled claim #4, plus the additional element of claim #8 at the end:

> 8. [Preamble] A computer implemented method for detecting viruses in data transfers between a first computer and a second computer, the method comprising the steps of:
> [1] receiving at a server a data transfer request including a destination address;
> [2] electronically receiving data at the server;
> [3] determining whether the data contains a virus at the server;
> [4] performing a preset action on the data using the server if the data contains a virus;
> [5] sending the data to the destination address if the data does not contain a virus;
> [6] determining whether the data is of a type that is likely to contain a virus; and
> [7] [7a] transmitting the data from the server to the destination without performing the steps of determining whether the data contains a virus and
> [7b] performing a preset action if the data is not of a type that is likely to contain a virus,
> [8] where the step [6] of determining whether the data is of a type that is likely to contain a virus is performed by comparing an extension type of a file name for the data to a group of known extension types.

All of the Preamble and elements [1] — [7b] are from

cancelled claim #4, and only element [8] is from the dependent claim #8. Without doubt, the PON of new claim #8 is in element [8], since the examiner and BOPAI have already determined that elements [1] — [7b] taken together are invalid as being obvious over prior art.[118]

How did claim #8 do in reexamination? The examiner also found claim #8 to be "obvious", hence invalid by 35 USC sec. 103(a). The examiner already identified [1] — [7b] in two pieces of prior art. Now the examiner adds a third piece of prior art which says, as quoted by the ALJ: "The way a file is scanned depends on the type of file...to be scanned and the validator employed". Is this the same as step [8] above? The ALJ said, "Yes, it is the same, so claim #8 is invalid".[119]

However, the decision of the examiner about claim #8 was appealed to the appellate board ("BOPAI") at the PTO, which disagreed, saying:

> the Examiner does not demonstrate that... [the third piece of prior art] discloses comparing an extension type of a file name to a group of known extension types. At best,... [the third piece of prior art] appears to disclose only scanning e-mail attachments for viruses and that the type of scanning may vary based on the type of data scanned.[120]

---

118 It would be more accurate, strictly speaking, to say that element [8] *in combination with the other elements* constitutes the PON. However, even with this more accurate expression, it is clear that it is the addition of element [8], derived from claim 8, that gives the new claim its patentability.

119 The decision of the examiner is reported in the Examiner's Answer, Ex Parte Reexamination of U.S. Patent No. 5,623,600, Control No. 90/011,022, mailed December 7, 2011, at p.31.

120 Decision on Appeal, U.S. PTO Board of Patent Appeals & Interferences, Ex Parte Trend Micro, Inc., Reexamination of US 5,623,600, Appeal 2012-0052505, Control Number 90/011,022, mailed July 17, 2012, at p.11.

The patent says that some extension types, such as ".exe", ".zip", and ".com", are inherently dangerous, may be infected, and will therefore be scanned before sending. Other types, such as ".txt" and ".gif", are not likely to contain viruses and so, under claim #8, will not be scanned before being transmitted. The third piece of prior art, cited by the examiner, does not say that the filtering will be by extension type. Thus, according to the decision of BOPAI, claim #8 remains valid. This decision was adopted by the reexamination examiner, who confirmed claim #8 in the reexamination certificate issued December 17, 2012.

As for claim #13 in the ITC case, the ALJ stated that this claim is essentially the same as claim #1 (which the ALJ invalidated) and claim #4 (later invalidated in the reexamination), except that claim #13 has an SMTP proxy server, and an SMTP daemon (a kind of background computer program). The ALJ found this claim to be valid, and infringed by the defendant. Upon reexamination, claim #13 was confirmed, because none of the cited prior art included element [4b] from claim #13. That is, none of the prior against claim #13 included "the step of sending the mail message comprises transferring the mail message from the SMTP proxy server to the SMTP daemon and transferring the mail message from the SMTP daemon to a node having an address matching the destination address." Hence, element [4b] in claim #13 was the Point of Novelty in claim #13.

So, in essence, whereas independent claim #4 and dependent claim #8 had trouble, and claim #4 was eventually invalidated by the PTO, independent claim #13 was never rejected by any examiner, any ALJ, or the ITC. If so, why not focus the discussion of *Trend Micro v. Fortinet* on claim #13? Isn't claim #13 the true hero of this story?

No, it is not. There is a fundamental problem with claim #13 that disqualifies it from being a "good" claim. The fundamental problem with claim #13 is that it includes the limitations that there be an SMTP proxy server, that there be an SMTP daemon, and that the method of claim #13 requires message transfer from the SMTP proxy server to the SMTP daemon, and from the SMTP daemon to a destination address. The main problem with claim #13 is that it is strictly limited to SMTP implementations.

To focus any claim on a single specific protocol is potentially very problematic. Focusing on a specific named protocol may increase your chance of having the claim allowed and confirmed, but it will also, at the same time, raise questions whose answers can reduce drastically the scope of claim coverage. What kinds of questions could reduce the scope of a claim that has been limited to a single protocol? These kinds of questions:

(1) Which versions of the protocol are included in the claim? Here, for example, SMTP was first defined in 1982, but revisions and refinements were made through at least 2008. Are all of these revisions and refinements included in the "SMTP proxy server" and the "SMTP daemon" in claim #13?

(2) Not just which "versions", but indeed, which protocols are intended? SMTP is one protocol. However, in 1995, which is also the year that US 5,623,600 was filed, Extended SMTP, also called ESMTP, was defined. Is ESMTP included as part of SMTP protocol in the patent claims, or is ESMTP separate and excluded? Is ESMTP a "revision or refinement" and, if so, is it included in claim #13?

(3) Which features are not included in the protocol? SMTP is a "push only" protocol. It sends messages from a server toward the consumer. The protocol is silent about pulling messages from a server. Hence, since SMTP does not manage two-way initiation of messages, and it is not suitable for management of email systems or even for management of email boxes. Any company that engages solely in pulling messages down cannot be an infringer, since it is not performing an SMTP method.

(4) What happens if the alleged infringer omits a feature that is required in the protocol? There are many versions of the protocol. The latest version, which I believe is RFC 5321, is about 117 pages long, including dozens of definitions, commands, syntactic principles, procedures and specifications. If a party leaves out one command or procedure, is it still implementing an "SMTP procedure"? Could it still be liable for infringing claim #13? Would the answer be different, or the same, if the party deliberately left out one command or one procedure, specifically to avoid infringement of claim #13?

(5) What happens if the technology changes, so that a new protocol is created? Unless the ITC or a court chooses to extend claim #13 to the successor technology of SMTP, there will no longer be any infringement. Will the ITC or the court extend "SMTP" to SMTP's successor protocol?

We could go on, but *the point is this: to use one specific protocol in the claims is potentially extremely limiting. By contrast, to use a protocol in the written description merely as one example is acceptable.* However, if you are going to do that, why not instead add a broad and generic definition, plus several examples, all in the written description?

In this case, the patent uses, but does define or explain,

the terms "SMTP", "SMTP proxy", "SMTP proxy server", and "SMTP daemon", although all of these terms are used in element [4] of claim #13. Using a specific protocol in a claim, without definition or explanation, adds to the chances that the claim will be found valid, but may limit severely the scope of the claim. In this case, it is impossible to know how a court or the ITC would interpret claim #13. For that reason, claim #13 is not a "good patent claim", regardless of what may happen in a particular hearing or litigation.

**Validity**: Looked at prospectively, claims 4 and 8 are problematic. Although there are many claim elements in claim #4, the elements are all very general, which suggests that prior art might be found to invalidate the claim. That is in fact what happened in this case, and it might have been predicted as a serious possibility. Claim #8 is also problematic. Although narrower than claim #4, it adds filtering by file type, and that additional limitation is also fairly generic. Prospectively, the validity of both claims, #4 and #8, is problematic

Retrospectively, the story is very clear. Claim #4 has been cancelled in reexamination, and is unlikely to be resurrected in any form. Claim #8 has been confirmed in reexamination. It is always possible that Fortinet or another possible infringer might find additional prior art that could invalidate claim #8, but for now, the validity of claim #8 looks solid.

For the reasons noted above explaining the narrow scope of claim #13, the probability of claim #13 being considered valid is very high, and therefore it is likely to have value as long as SMTP remains a major email protocol.

**Scope**: Claims 4 and 8 have good scope. The 1995 priority date of the patent is early. The elements in both claims are general, which is good for claim scope. The clarity of the concept of sorting data by type, and applying analysis according to the sort, is well done. On the other hand, #13, as explained above, has a narrow claim scope.

**Discoverability of Infringement**: Infringements should be reasonably discoverable by Trend Micro.

**Summary**: Trend Micro used an early priority patent for over ten years to generate income from a variety of electronic security companies, and to help solidify its position in the market. In that sense, US 5,623,600 turned out to be a very good patent for Trend Micro. Some of its claims have issues of scope or validity and, to that extent, this was not a "great patent." However, US 5,623,600 has proven to be an interesting patent, in a field with strong growth, and covering communication systems and methods with widespread implementation.

**Lessons Learned**: Here are some of the lessons we might learn from patent claims 4, 8, and 13 in US 5,623,600, litigated in the ITC litigation of *Trend Micro v. Fortinet*.

4-2-1. ***Claim diversity is key for a "good" patent***. In this case, all of the structure claims, including the system claims and the apparatus claims, were invalidated either at the ITC (claims #1–3) case or on reexamination at the PTO (claims #18–22). Of the twenty-nine method claims, twenty-one were invalidated in the reexamination, but eight method claims survived. In particular, claims 8 and 13, which were found in the ITC case to have been infringed by Fortinet, survived reexamination, and in that sense, they have been strengthened rather than weakened by the reexamination. *The diversity of claims in US 5,623,600 allowed the patent to survive the loss of all structure claims and two-thirds of the method claims.*

4–2–2. ***The Point of Novelty in an independent claim is often (but not always) found in the last element of the claim.*** There is a natural tendency to list the prior art elements first, and novelty afterwards. That often happens when a new element is added to avoid the rejection of a patent examiner or ALJ. In this case, the PON of claim #4 is the last element [7], and the PON of claim #13 is the last element [7b].

4–2–3. ***Dependent claims back up independent claims, and become independent themselves when the original independent claim is invalidated.*** If you knew for certain that your independent claim would never be invalidated, then you would never write claims dependent on that independent claim. This is a rule of logic. Every dependent claim is narrower than the independent claim on which it relies. If you know that the independent claim would never be invalidated, then the dependent claims would be worthless. In real life, however, independent claims are invalidated, as happened here in the reexamination of claim #4. When that happens:

a. A dependent claim, such as claim #8, becomes the independent claim, including all of the prior elements (here the elements of claim #4) and the elements of the dependent claim (here the single element of claim #8); and
b. The PON of the new independent claim cannot be an element in the old and cancelled independent claim (here #4), but must be at least one element in the former dependent claim (here #8), either by itself or in combination with the elements of the cancelled independent claim.

4-2-4. ***Good independent claims produce good breadth of coverage. Good dependent claims produce good depth of coverage.*** You should have both good breadth of claims (i.e., strong independent claims) and good depth of claims (i.e., strong dependent claims) to have a "good patent". Good breadth will allow you to include many defendants and many products in the scope of infringement. Good depth means that if some of the independent claims are knocked out, the dependent claims may still survive.

4-2-5. ***Definitions of key claim terms can deflect attacks on the claims.*** Here, the claim term "virus" was well-defined in the specification and never became a serious focus of attack in either the ITC action or the reexamination. In fact, the ALJ rejected the particular version presented by the patent owner, and instead agreed with the defendant's interpretation. The adoption of a particular definition might be critical, but here it was not, because the fact that there was a definition at all fended off a host of possible attacks on claims 4 and 8. By contrast, there were no definitions of "SMTP", "SMTP server", or any other claim term involving "SMTP", absences that weaken the scope of claim #13.

4-2-6. ***Even if patents are not great, good patents may be good enough.*** US 5,263,600 has been good for Trend Micro, generating licenses and royalty revenues. This patent has almost certainly deterred some potential competition. The ITC case weakened the structure claims by invalidating the system claims, and the reexamination weakened the patent generally by invalidating all apparatus claims and most method claims. However, some method claims remain valid, and may be very valuable.

## III. Additional Lessons from the ITC Cases

### *(1) Buying Patents — If You Need Them Fast, Get Them*

Consider ITC Case No. 337-TA-543, involving Broadcom and Qualcomm, and the parallel federal court litigation discussed above. In both the court litigation and the ITC action, Broadcom sued on a mix of patents, some of which had been filed by Broadcom (meaning that Broadcom was the original assignee), and others of which Broadcom acquired after issuance. Here are the results in tabular form:

**Table 4–5: *Broadcom versus Qualcomm* — Sources of Patents**

| Litigation | Initial Patents | Results |
|---|---|---|
| **ITC 337-TA-543** | Broadcom sued on five patents. Of these, Broadcom was the original assignee of three patents (6,359,872, 6,583,675, and 6,714,983), and Broadcom had acquired from two patents from other companies (5,682,379 and 6,374,311). | *Broadcom wins on US 6,714,983, a patent originally assigned to Broadcom.* The other four patents dropped out of the case. |
| **Litigation in Federal District Court, appealed to the CAFC** | Broadcom sued on three patents. Of these, Broadcom was the original assignee of one patent (6,847,686), and Broadcom had acquired two patents from other companies (5,657,317 and 6,389,010). | *Broadcom wins on 5,657,317 and 6,389,010, which were the two patents it acquired from other companies.* The CAFC invalidates one claim and finds no infringement in 6,847,686, which was the patent originally assigned to Broadcom. |

There was no overlap of patents in the two cases — the five patents in the ITC action were different than the three patents in federal court litigation.

It makes no difference whether you filed the patents or bought the patents from a third party. If you need patents to obtain royalties, or to stop someone from obtaining royalties from you, and you don't have the patents, consider going to the market and getting them.

Many of the cases presented in this book might have gone better for the defendants if they had had, or subsequently acquired, patents to assert against plaintiffs.

### *(2) Improved Markush Claims*

The Markush style, as explained in Chapter 1, is a claim in which one element includes two or more members of the group, and an implementation of the claim may use any one of the members of that group. This style is found often in BCP patents, but less frequently in ICT patents. It is sometimes considered a weak format, because if any implementation is found in the prior art, including any one of the members of the group, the entire claim element, and hence the entire claim, will fall.

Nevertheless, there are ways to use Markush style claims for maximum effect. One way is to create a number of independent claims, where each claim has its own combination of the various members of the group. Prior art might knock out one or two of the independent claims, but it would be unlikely to knock out all of the independent claims (unless, of course, the invention is not new at all).

Consider, for example, ITC Case No. 337-TA-413, entitled, "In the Matter of Certain Rare-Earth Magnetic Materials and

Articles Containing the Same", *Magnequench International, Inc., of Indiana, USA (formerly a division of General Motors), and Sumitomo Special Metals Co., Ltd., of Japan, versus Houghes International, Inc., of Great Neck, New York*, and nine other defendants from the United States, Republic of China — Taiwan, and the People's Republic of China — PRC. The relevant patent is US 4,496,395, entitled "High Coercivity Rare Earth-Iron Magnets". The relevant claims are numbers 13–18, which are various kinds of permanent magnets and permanent magnet alloys. These claims appear below. I have marked each Markush element in a claim with brackets "[ ]". Do not read the claims in detail, but skim them to identify various members of the Markush group.

13. A permanent magnet alloy having an inherent intrinsic magnetic coercivity of at least 5000 Oersteds at room temperature comprising iron and one or more rare earth elements taken from the group consisting of [1] neodymium and [2] praseodymium.
14. A permanent magnet having an inherent intrinsic magnetic coercivity of at least 5000 Oersteds at room temperature which comprises one or more light rare earth elements taken from the group consisting of [1] neodymium and [2] praseodymium and [3] at least 50 atomic percent iron.
15. A permanent magnet having an inherent intrinsic magnetic coercivity of at least 5000 Oersteds at room temperature and a magnetic ordering temperature above about 295° K. which comprises one or more rare earth elements taken from the group consisting of [1] neodymium and [2] praseodymium, and [3] at least about 50 atomic percent iron.

16. A permanent magnet alloy having an inherent intrinsic magnetic coercivity of at least 5000 Oersteds at room temperature and a magnetic ordering temperature above about 295° K. comprising one or more rare earth element constituents taken from the group consisting of [1] neodymium, [2] praseodymium or mischmetals thereof and [3] iron or [4] iron mixed with a small amount of cobalt where the iron comprises at least 50 atomic percent of the alloy.
17. A permanent magnet containing a magnetic phase based on one or more rare earth elements and iron, which phase has an intrinsic magnetic coercivity of at least 5,000 Oersteds at room temperature and a magnetic ordering temperature above about 295° K., the rare earth constituent consisting predominantly of [1] neodymium and/or [2] praseodymium.
18. A permanent magnet based on [1] neodymium and [2] iron, which phase has an intrinsic magnetic coercivity of at least 5,000 Oersteds at room temperature and a magnetic ordering temperature above about 295° K.

Each of claims 13–16 appears in a classic "Markush" format. Although claim #17 is not in the standard Markush format, because it makes no reference to a "group", it nevertheless appears to be a Markush claim based on the "and/or" conjunction at the end of the claim. Claim #18 includes both neodymium and iron, but the conjunction between them is "and", so claim #18 is *not* a Markush claim, because both of these chemical elements must appear in the magnet.

If one of the Markush claim members is found in prior art, the claim will fall. For example, claim #17 will fall if prior art is found to contain all of the claim elements with only neodymium, or only praseodymium, or with both neodymium and praseodymium.

It would be possible to eliminate the Markush format claims completely, by simply writing each claim separately with only one metal, but such a rewrite would have multiplied greatly the number of claims, and hence would have increased significantly the cost to receive an allowance of the patent. The presentation in US 4,496,395 is a reasonable compromise, in which the various metals in the claims, that is, neodymium, praseodymium, iron, and iron alloy with cobalt, are distributed among multiple Markush format claims, such that if some of the Markush claims are invalidated by prior art, the other claims may still survive.

The key lesson to be learned is that although Markush format claims are less common in ICT technology areas, there is a way to formulate such claims for maximal protection against later invalidation.

### *(3) A Patent Thicket May Have Great Strength*

In ITC Case No. 337-TA-406, entitled, "In the Matter of Certain Lens-Fitted Film Packages", *Fuji Photo Film Co., Ltd., of Japan v. Achiever Industries of Hong Kong*, and twenty-six other defendants from various countries in Asia, Europe, and North America, there were a total of fifteen patents alleged to have been infringed, including eleven standard utility patents, one reexamination utility patent, and three design patents. All 15 of the patents focus on photographic "film units" (i.e., handheld disposable cameras), photographic film packaging, methods for assembling photographic film packages, and the ornamental design of handheld cameras.

A patent "thicket" is a group of patents working together

to protect various aspects of the same general invention. That is what we have in this case. Here is a quick glimpse of the thicket, focusing only on the claims found by the ITC to have been infringed:

**Table 4–6: Fuji Photo Film Patent Thicket in ITC Case 337-TA-406**

| Aspect Patented | Patents Focused on this Aspect of the Subject | Number of Patents in the Thicket Focused on this Aspect | Number of Independent Claims in the Thicket Infringed by Defendants |
|---|---|---|---|
| **Film units = hand-held cameras** | US 5,361,111<br>US 5,381,200<br>US 5,408,288<br>US 5,436,685 | 4 | 9 |
| **Film packaging** | US 4,833,495<br>US 4,855,774<br>US 4,884,087<br>US 4,954,857<br>US 5,063,400<br>US 5,235,364<br>RE. 34,168 | 7 | 19 |
| **Methods for assembling film packaging** | US 4,972,649 | 1 | 2 |
| **Ornamental design of hand-held cameras** | Des. 345,750<br>Des. 356,101<br>Des. 372,722 | 3<br>(all design patents) | 3 |
| **TOTALS** | | **15** | **33** |

Thirty-three independent claims were found to have been infringed, including claims related to the entire system (the camera), one aspect of the system (the packaging), the method of making the packaging, and the design of the system. There were many more claims in the patents, including a total of fifty independent claims and one-hundred sixty-four dependent claims, each claim covering one of the four aspects patented (i.e., system, packaging, method, and design).

Some of the independent claims were strong, while others were not. The key point is, however, that the patents work together in a thicket to protect multiple aspects of the same general concept. A patent thicket, as a rule, provides stronger protection than a single patent. That is often true even if the individual patents in a thicket are not strong in themselves.[121]

### *(4) Even the Best Patent Can Be Destroyed By a Mistake During Prosecution*

ITC Case No. 337-TA-365, entitled, "In the Matter of Certain Audible Alarm Devices for Divers", *David A. Hancock*

---

121 There was very extensive court litigation associated with this ITC case. One of the leading decisions was *Jazz Photo Corporation et al. v. ITC and Fuji Photo Film, Co., Ltd.*, 264 F.3d 1094 (Fed.Cir.2001), *cert. denied* 122 S.Ct. 2644 (2002), in which the CAFC affirmed the ITC's finding of liability as to some products, but reversed the ITC and found no liability solely as to cameras "repaired" in the United States. There are at least seven other court decisions related to the ITC litigation, but none of them are relevant here, except to note the following: Several of the defendants in this case, particularly but not only Jazz Photo Corporation, fought vigorously against Fuji Photo Film and also against the ITC. Fuji Photo Film did not win in all of these actions, but the great majority of the ITC defendants were found liable, Jazz Photo Corporation was driven to bankruptcy in large part by this litigation, and in general, Fuji Photo Film derived great strength and benefit from its thicket of patents focused entirely on hand-held cameras.

*and Ideations Designs of Seattle, Washington v. Duton Industry of Taiwan and IKH International of Torrance, California*. The relevant patent is US 5,106,236, entitled, "Audible Alarm Device for Divers and Others". Claim #1 was found to be infringed, but all six claims in the patent are involved in the lesson.

In this case, the patent applicants filed both the U.S. application that eventually became US 5,106,236 and a European patent application on the same subject. While both applications were pending before the PTO and the EPO, respectively, the EPO issued an office action citing prior art in the EPO case. *Although cited in the European case, this prior art was also clearly relevant to the pending U.S. application*. Nevertheless, the patent applicant never brought the EPO prior art to the attention of the U.S. examiner. How this happened is not clear, but the defendant in the ITC case, Duton Industry, sought to make the U.S. patent unenforceable on the ground of "inequitable conduct" before the U.S. PTO.

In a patent case before the PTO, the applicant has *no duty to search for prior art that might be relevant to the application*. However, if the applicant happens to know of prior art that might be relevant, then the applicant and the applicant's attorney are required to present that prior art to the U.S. examiner. A deliberate attempt to hide prior art from a U.S. examiner is considered "fraud" against the PTO, and, if discovered, will cause the entire patent, including all claims in the patent, to be unenforceable against all parties. In *Hancock v. Duton Industry*, the defendant alleged Hancock's conduct to be inequitable due to Hancock's failure to disclose the EPO prior art to the PTO. The ITC considered two issues:

First, was the EPO prior art relevant to the U.S. application, such that it should have been disclosed to the U.S. examiner? The ITC concluded affirmatively: the EPO prior art should have been disclosed to the U.S. examiner.

Second, did the U.S. applicants intend to deceive the PTO? This was not clear. The European patent agents did receive the EPO Office Action, but it is not clear if they ever sent a copy to the U.S. patent attorneys, and the applicants, who were based in the U.S., testified that they were not aware of the prior art cited by the EPO.[122] The defendant then argued that the knowledge of the applicants' English agents must be "imputed to" the applicants.[123] However, the legal standard to establish fraud on the PTO requires the defendant to show, by "clear, unequivocal, and convincing evidence", that the patent applicant "intentionally misled" the PTO. In this case, the plaintiff, or its agents, may well have been negligent, but not demonstrably fraudulent. Therefore, fraudulent conduct was not found, the patent was not invalidated, and the plaintiff won this case.

The plaintiff might have lost if different people had reviewed the same facts, or if the facts had been a bit different. For example, if the English agents had sent the EPO Office

---

122 Why didn't the European patent agents scan the EPO Office Action, and send it by email? US 5,106,236 was filed in 1990, and issued in 1992, long before anyone had ever heard of electronic mail or "document scanning". I assume, but cannot say for certain, that the common English practice would have been to mail a copy to the American lawyers. The record of the case, however, does not explain what happened here.

123 "Imputed to" is a legal doctrine that says, roughly, whatever the agent knows is also assumed to be known to the principal, *whether or not the agent actually tells the principal.* If that had been the standard for finding fraud, plaintiff Hancock might have lost this ITC case. The standard, however, as noted by the ITC, is "intentional" deception, and that was not proven by the defendant in this case.

Action to the U.S. patent attorneys, the ITC might have found inequitable conduct. The potential consequences (i.e., unenforceability of the entire patent) of such actions, or of failure to act, are serious. This kind of problem should never arise.

The lesson here is that even a good patent can be wrecked by a mistake in prosecution of the patent application. *The combination of good claims, a good written description, and broad scope of claim coverage, create valuable patents, but external events, such as failure to reveal information to the PTO, can destroy value.*

### (5) The Uncertainty Principle of Patent Value

ITC Case No. 337-TA-617, "In the Matter of Certain Digital Televisions and Certain Products Containing Same and Methods of Using Same", *Funai Electric Corporation of Osaka, Japan v. Vizio, Inc. of Cupertino, California*, and thirteen other defendants from the U.S., Taiwan, Hong Kong, and the People's Republic of China. The patent is US 6,115,074, entitled, "System for Forming and Processing Program Map Information Suitable for Terrestrial, Cable or Satellite Broadcast". In its decision on April 10, 2009, the ITC found the claims valid and determined that the defendants had infringed independent claim #1, "apparatus for decoding [an MPEG] datastream", claim #5 dependent on claim #1, and claim #23, "method for decoding MPEG compatible packetized program information". The key lesson to be learned is the uncertainty of patent litigation.

The defendants tried to work around US 6,115,704, but the ITC found that these work-around products also infringed. However, this decision of the ITC was appealed to the CAFC which found, in its decision on May 26, 2010, that although the pre-litigation products ("legacy products") may have infringed, the work-around products did not fulfill any of the following elements:

**Table 4–7: Non-Infringing Work-around Products in ITC Case 337-TA-617[124]**

| Claim | Claim element not in the work-around products |
|---|---|
| 1 | [Preamble] "for decoding" |
| 1 | Element [1] "for identifying" |
| 1 | Element [2] "for identifying" |
| 23 | [Preamble] "for decoding" |
| 23 | Element [2] "suitable for use" |

Since claim #1 was not infringed, the narrower claim #5, dependent on #1, was also not infringed. The result is that although the "legacy products" infringed, the "work-around products" did not. The ITC, which is bound by the decision of the CAFC on appeal, then modified its Limited Exclusion Order to forbid only the sale of legacy products, but to permit the future importation and sale of all "work-around products". In essence, the future aspects of the ITC injunction were cancelled.[125]

While this litigation was going on, two of the defendants

124 The decision of the CAFC is reported at *Vizio, Inc. v. International Trade Commission*, 604 F.3d 1330 (Fed. Cir. 2010). The CAFC's holding as to the various claim elements that were not in the work-around products is on p.1343.

125 The ITC is not bound by judicially created doctrines, such as the rule for deciding injunctions as set forth in *eBay v. MercExchange*. However,

asked the PTO to reexamine US 6,115,074. The two requests were made in August and December, 2007. A reexamination certificate was issued on May 10, 2011, in which *all 25 of the claims in the original patent were cancelled* due to the additional prior art reviewed by the examiner. However, during reexamination, Funai presented substitute claims which were allowed as new claims 25–44. New claim #25, "apparatus for decoding" is roughly comparable to cancelled claim #1, and new claim #35, "method for decoding a datastream of MPEG...information", is roughly comparable to cancelled claim #23. However, each substitute claim after reexamination is longer, with more limitations, than the claim it replaced. It is impossible to know whether the defendant products that infringed the old claims would also have been found to infringe the new claims after the reexamination.

In the other words, the ITC confirmed the validity and scope of the claims in the ITC case. The CAFC then slashed the claim scope by finding the claims not applicable to design around products. The PTO then slashed the claim scope again by canceling the old claims but allowing new, narrower claims. Although US 6,115,074 as written had claims which seemed to cover fundamental aspects of MPEG data transmission, which is a very large market, the court and the patent office both reduced claim scope substantially.

What does all of this mean? Even if you have a patent with claims that look excellent, you can never be sure what will happen to it. Claims may be invalidated, or reduced in scope, by the ITC, or by the CAFC on appeal, or by the PTO in a reexamination. In this case, for example, both the CAFC and

---

decisions of the ITC may be appealed to the CAFC, and the ITC must comply with the decision of the CAFC *in the particular case.*

the PTO reduced significantly the scope of the claims. If there is parallel litigation at a federal district court, which happens very often, claim scope may be reduced by the district court judge in a Markman hearing, or the claims may be later limited or invalidated by the CAFC.

In physics, the Heisenberg Uncertainty Principle says that we can never know both the position and direction of a particle at the same time. I propose an Uncertainty Principle of Patent Value, as follows:

> *No matter how good your claims look, or how many times you have won in litigation, something can always happen that will impact the entire patent and might even leave you with nothing.*

This is not merely the patent version of the old Murphy's Law of, "Anything that can go wrong, will go wrong". I'm not saying that anything *will* go wrong, but only that many things *can* go wrong, and at different levels. Patents are enormously complicated, even more than most legal subjects, for two reasons:

1. Patents include an interweaving of law and technology not found in any other legal field;
2. Patents include so many different players, in so many different arenas, all of whom can impact greatly both the validity and scope of the patent claims. There are, for example, the PTO on original examination, the PTO on reexamination, the PTO appellate board, the ITC, the federal district courts, the CAFC, the Supreme Court, and the Congress (which passed major amendments to the patent statute in 2011).

The validity of claims, and claim scope, are always subject to change. From this Uncertainty Principle of Patent Value, we may draw three inferences:

First, if you are planning to go to litigation to enforce a patent or to cancel a patent, do not forget that litigation is war, and one can never be certain what will happen in war.

Second, if you engage in any kind of patent commerce, including buying or selling patents, licensing-in patent rights in exchange for making payments, licensing-out patent rights in exchange for receiving payments, joint ventures based on patents, or any other activity, bear in mind that patent rights may always be changed, either for the good (through positive rulings) or the bad (through invalidations or reduced claim scope). Prices paid must include appropriate consideration of the risks involved with patents. Contracts based on patents should also include provisions appropriate to deal with the uncertainties of patent value.

Third, prepare as best you can, by learning lessons of good patents and determining, in advance of legal action or business transaction, the answer to the question: "How good are your patents?"

# Chapter 5

# Sales of Good Patents

Patents were once considered somewhat esoteric. News stories about patents were assigned to business sections, or relegated to legal journals. In recent years, however, patent sales and patent litigation have often become front page news. The purpose of this chapter is to help us understand why this change has happened, and to learn lessons about "good patents" from patents that were sold for substantial sums. We will look at a standalone sale of one patent and at a patent sold as part of a large portfolio.

Here is the organization of Chapter 5:

I. Why Do Patents Attract So Much Attention?

II. What Creates Sale Value in Patents?

   (1) Sale of an Individual Patent — US 5,133,079: This was the first patent sold in a public patent auction for more than $1M. What made it so valuable?

   (2) Sale of a Patent as Part of a Portfolio — US 5,774,670: This is one of the patents acquired by Microsoft in the AOL patent portfolio purchase for $1.056 billion, and is considered to be one of the patents that created real value in the AOL portfolio. How and why did this patent contribute to the portfolio price?

## I. Why Do Patents Attract so much Attention?

Patents have become hot news in recent years, and that trend appears likely to continue. Why? We can point to three key factors:

### *(1) Large-scale Patent Purchases*

First, there have been enormous purchases of patent portfolios in recent years. The largest is Google's purchase of 17,000 wireless technology patents from Motorola Mobility for $12.5 billion, announced in August, 2011 and completed in May, 2012.[126] Other notable transactions include:

- The purchase in July, 2011 — by a consortium of Apple, EMC, Ericsson, Microsoft, RIM and Sony — of 6,000 patents from Nortel for $4.5 billion. The patents cover 3G and 4G wireless technology, optical networks, Voice over IP, and semiconductors.
- Microsoft's purchase in April, 2012 of 800 patents and applications from AOL for $1.056 billion.[127] The purchased patents were primarily in the area of Internet communication (on-line communication, browser and search technology, multimedia, and ecommerce) as well as wireless, and security.
- A consortium's purchase in December, 2012, of 1,100

126 In fact, Google bought the company Motorola Mobility, not just its patents, but commentators suggest the main motivation was to strengthen Google's patent position to better defend its Android operating system for mobile devices. Further, the transaction included, in addition to the 17,000 issued patents, an additional 6,800 pending applications.

127 The deal included also a license from AOL to Microsoft for another 300 patents.

digital imaging patents from Kodak for $525 million. The consortium, represented by Intellectual Ventures and RPX, included Adobe, Amazon, Apple, Facebook, Fuji Photo Film, Google, HTC, Huawei, Microsoft, RIM, Samsung, and Shutterfly.

- Intel's purchase in June, 2012, of 1,700 wireless patents (3G, 4G, and Wireless LAN) from InterDigital for $375 million.

These are very large numbers in aggregate. Moreover, the prices-per-patent are significant, ranging from $220,000/patent for the InterDigital portfolio up to $1.32M/patent for the AOL portfolio. Numbers like these, not surprisingly, draw attention to commerce in patents.

### *(2) High-profile Patent Battles Among Major Companies*

Second, there have been several patent battles, more correctly patent "wars" between major companies, ranging over multiple cases in multiple countries in North America, Europe, Asia, and Australia. These wars fill the business press, and also capture popular attention. The current war between Apple and Samsung is, as of this writing, only the latest example. What will be the next war? Google is believed to have purchased Motorola Mobility in part to protect the Android operating system. Some commentators believe Microsoft purchased the AOL portfolio to target mobile commerce, and to go after the Android operating system. Is that the next war? No one really knows, but all these conflicts attract attention to patent commerce.

### *(3) The Nature of Modern Economies*

Third, the nature of life today boosts the value of patents. Modern economies are built primarily on intellectual capital — ideas, know-how, inventions, methods of operation, etc. Recall Chart 1–1, showing the radical shift in corporate value from tangible assets to intangible assets (which is to say, to intellectual capital) between 1975 and 2010. Legal instruments such as patents, copyrights, and trademarks embody a significant part of this intellectual capital.

When people buy patents, they are acquiring the intellectual capital which the patents represent and protect. As intellectual property has become more important in recent decades, patents have become more interesting and valuable. It is doubtful that we will return to an economy in which tangible assets create most corporate value. The importance of creativity, innovation, and know-how will continue to grow, and with them the importance and value of patents.

## II. What Creates Sale Value in Patents?

### *Sale of an Individual Patent — US 5,133,079*

*Background:*

Ocean Tomo describes itself as an "intellectual property merchant bank". Founded in 2003, Ocean Tomo held the first ever public auction of patents in April, 2006. At that auction, only one patent sold for more than $1M. That patent, US 5,133,079, is entitled, "Method and Apparatus for Distribution of Movies". The patent has a priority date of July 30, 1990, and was issued on July 21, 1992. The patent was purchased for $1.54M (including a 10% sales commission of $140,000) by a company involved in the United States cable television business.[128]

*Preview:*

This patent focuses on an important technology that covers a market application (that is, downloading movies) of great importance to a major industry, and has an early priority date. Offsetting these advantages, the patent has a few major problems in its method claims, and some other problems, much less serious, in its structure claims. The claim defects might have been avoided with different claim language, or they might have been corrected by applying one or more of the three well-known techniques in the written description, that is, (1) definition of claim terms, (2) examples of claim terms, and (3) claim elements in the patent drawings. The method claims alone might not justify the purchase price paid. However, the purchase price is justifiable by the structure claims in combination with the hot technology area of the patent, the patent's early priority date, and the broad market coverage of the claims. This is a case in which we might say the quality of the patent high, but the financial value was even higher due to the subject area and priority date of the patent.[129]

---

128 This patent appears as an Appendix at the end of this book.

129 I said previously that only a high-quality or "good" patent can have high value, and this is one of the main differences between "patent quality" and "patent value". This relationship between quality and value is demonstrated graphically in Preface Chart 1. Is US 5,133,079 an exception to this rule? The answer depends on whether you view "quality" objectively or subjectively. From an objective point of view, not related to the viewpoint of any evaluator, US 5,133,079 is a reasonably good patent, with reasonably good claims but some problems. From a subjective point of view, however, the specific buyer of the patent saw high quality, and hence high value, due to the buyer's specific concern that the patent might be used to harm companies in the

*Review:*

This patent was purchased for $1.54 million. Why would a company in the cable television business value this patent so highly? When a patent is purchased, the buyer is demonstrating interest either in

(1) asserting the patent to receive licensing revenues, or trial damages, or otherwise generating value, or

(2) preventing another party from asserting this patent against itself or other companies.

Either way — whether purchased for offensive (assertive) or defensive (non-assertive) purposes — the buyer will base a patent's valuation on the amount of money it believes the patent can generate over a period of time.

Various financial models have been used to determine the value of patents. These models determine one or more scenarios of revenue generation at some point in the future, then discount expected future sums by various risks and by what is perceived to be an appropriate capitalization rate. The result is the expected present value of the patent.

Although a detailed review of financial modeling of patent values is not within the scope or this book, various models suggest that companies can expect possible future payments in the range of 20 — 50 times what they are willing to pay for a patent today. The estimate for a specific patent (or for a specific portfolio of patents) will vary according to the perceived value of the patent(s), the perceived risks of claim invalidation, the financial discount rate, and other factors. Overall,

---

cable business. Concepts such as "Objective Patent Value" and "Subjective Patent Value" will be discussed below in Chapter 7. For now, we can say that US 5,133,079 had both quality and value, as established by the willingness of a buyer to pay about $1.5 million for the patent in 2006.

however, we can say that a patent purchased today is likely to be deeply discounted from its possible payout at some point in the future. If the range cited above is accurate, it would suggest that a company paying $1.54M for a patent today expects that the patent might generate revenue within the range of $30M — $75M over the remaining life of the patent.[130]

To the best of my knowledge, patent US 5,133,079 was never licensed or litigated. Based on the assumption of no action taken on the patent, and the fact that it was purchased by a company actively involved in the U.S. cable television business, the natural conclusion is that the patent was purchased to prevent its assertion against companies such as cable television companies.

What in this patent might have concerned the cable television industry?

The title is "Method and Apparatus for Distribution of Movies", and its Abstract begins with the following definitional phrase: "A new and useful method and apparatus for distribution of movies for viewing on a customer's television

---

130 These financial models include a host of risks associated with patents, including possible loss at trial, invalidity, non-infringement, bad Markman hearings, adverse reexaminations, changes in the technology to reduce damages, design arounds to prevent future infringement, etc. These risks are cumulative. The model also includes projections of revenue generation, including estimates of market size, market growth, degree of infringement, and design arounds. In addition, an annual discount factor, possibly 20% or higher, is used to bring future value to present value. Finally, different parties evaluating a patent will estimate different values based on the specific interests of the evaluators — some evaluators will place greater value on early cash flow, other evaluators may be more or less sensitive to risk, etc.

The model above is applicable to individual patents and also to small patent portfolios. However, the assumptions of risk and market projections may change dramatically when evaluating the purchases of large portfolios rather than the sale of individual patents or small groups of patents.

set". This is a patent about the electronic distribution of movies to people's homes, a core function of this industry. The priority date of July, 1990 is relatively early for patents related to sending movies in compressed digital format to customer homes.

Let's consider the independent claims in the patent. There are two independent claims, method claim #1 and apparatus claim #8. The other method claims, 2–7, all depend on claim #1, and they will therefore incorporate all of the defects in claim #1 discussed here. The sole independent structure claim is claim #8. The other structure claims, 9–16, all depend on claim #8, and they will therefore incorporate all of the defects in claim #8 discussed here.

Let's look first at independent method claim #1:

> 1. A method for distribution of movies for viewing on a customer's television set, the method comprising the steps of:
>
> (a) compressing and digitizing audio visual data corresponding to an entire movie and storing the compressed, digitized data at a remote source;
>
> (b) sending digitized compressed signals containing audio visual data corresponding to the entire movie selected by the customer from a source to a receiver of the customer;
>
> (c) passing the signals to a converter to convert the signals to corresponding electronic signals;
>
> (d) passing the electronic signals to processors where they are decompressed and converted to signals compatible with conventional television sets; and
>
> (e) passing these converted signals to a conventional television set for viewing by the customer.

There are several problems with claim #1:

The first problem is in element (a), and relates to word order. We see first "compressing" and then "digitizing" of data. That is, if the order of words reflects the true intent, the patent describes a process in which analog data is compressed, after which the compressed analog data is converted to digital data. Although there is such a thing as "analog compression", the method described here — first compression, then digitization — is not what people typically mean when they say that they will transmit digitized compressed signals. Indeed element (b) states that "digitized compressed signals" are transmitted, a phrase which reverses the order of "digitizing" and "compressing" from element (a). I suggest that element (b) is the correct order, and is probably what the patentee intended, but the confusion of element (a) remains.

Supporting the view that element (b) describes the true order of steps in the method, the only figure in the patent showing either digitization or compression, Figure 1A, illustrates clearly, beyond any doubt, that the data is first digitized and only then compressed. The order of words in element (a) is wrong. Element (a) should say, "digitizing and compressing audio visual data". This appears to be a sloppy presentation, but let's generously interpret element (a) to mean, "data is both compressed and digitized, but not necessarily in that order". That fixes the problem with element (a), although it is uncertain if a court or the ITC would be willing to apply the same fix to element (a).

The second problem in claim #1, also in element (a), is the appearance of an adjective which is limiting and apparently unnecessary. Why does element (a) say, an "entire" movie? The inclusion of this word might mean that sending only clips of the movie, rather than the entire movie, would not be infringing. Thus, advertising trailers would not be infringing. Why was it necessary to add the word "entire"? Would it not have sufficed to say, for example, "data corresponding to a movie" (deleting the word "entire" from element [a]), or perhaps to say, "data extracted from a movie"?

In contrast to independent method claim #1, independent apparatus claim #8 refers apparently to "a pre-determined movie" or "the movie". The word "entire" does not appear in any of the structure claims. Therefore it is not clear why the word "entire" was added to method claim #1 but not to apparatus claim #8.[131]

The third problem in claim #1, introduced by element (b), is the splitting of infringement between two parties, known as "divided infringement". Element (a), and that part of element (b) related to "sending signals", are conducted by a system operator on the "server side", meaning the network operation center or centralized digital movie library. By contrast, the part of element (b) related to "a receiver of the customer", and all of elements (c), (d), and (e), occur at the customer's house, that is to say, on the "client side".

Divided infringement can undermine the enforceability of the claim, and hence reduce its value.[132]

---

131 It is possible that the word "entire" was added during prosecution, but the prosecution history is not available on-line to check this possibility. However, if the word "entire" were added to method claim #1 during prosecution, then why was that word not added to apparatus claim #8? The different presentation of structure and method claims leads one to suspect that the word "entire" was included in the original claim #1 and not added in prosecution.

132 Under the law existing up to the CAFC's decision in *Akamai* on August 31, 2012, method claims with divided infringement were often unenforceable. After *Akamai*, divided infringement might not be an insurmountable barrier

The fourth problem with claim #1 is that element (c), which requires "passing the [digitized compressed] signals [containing audio visual data] to a converter to convert the signals to corresponding electronic signals", seems to exclude all systems in which signals are not converted. To complicate matters, in element (d), the electronic signals from element (c) are further "decompressed and converted to signals compatible with conventional television sets".

The problem here relates to the idea of signal conversion. "Conversion" or "signal conversion" is a key claim term in US 5,133,079. What is meant by that term? In particular, which systems are included within that term?

There seem to be three possibilities.

First, systems that include a fiber optic backbone, in which audio and visual movie signals are first converted from electronic to fiber optic, then transported on the backbone, then converted from fiber optic to electronic, and finally converted back from electronic signals to audio-visual signals suitable for showing on a television set.[133]

Second, all-electronic signals, meaning that the communication backbone was coaxial cable, so an electronic signal is

---

to enforcement of method claims with joint infringers. Divided infringement and its implications are discussed in Chapter 2. Whatever may be the ultimate resolution of the doctrine of divided infringement, the patent was purchased long before the *Akamai* decision, and that case played no role in the buyer's determination of the value of this patent.

133 The last conversion in this example is essentially from digital data in electronic form to analog data suitable for showing on a television set. From the time this patent was filed in 1990, through its purchase in 2006, and to June 12, 2009, when all major television systems in the United States were converted to digital, the main standard for televisions in the United States was analog. It is not clear that this last conversion would be required on today's digital systems.

sent to the backbone, and then to a customer's receiver where it is converted to a signal suitable for showing on a television set.

Third, a hybrid system including both fiber optic and coaxial backbones.[134]

Conversion" or "signal conversion" is a key claim term in US 5,133,079. To understand the scope of the claims, the critical question is, "What is meant by the key claim term 'signal conversion'?" Lack of clarity in the meaning of "signal conversion" is a serious problem in method claims 1–8, and it is the main problem in structure claims 9–16.

Please recall that there are three ways to clarify a key claim term in the draft of a patent.

(1) *Definition of the key claim term*: There is no definition, in the claims or in the written description, for "conversion", "converter", or any similar form of the key term.

(2) *Examples of the key claim term*: There are indeed many examples of "conversion" or "converter" in the written description, but all of them appear to be either electronic to optical or optical to electronic. For example, in the Summary of the Invention, at column 2, lines 13–16, it is written, "[Electronic distribution of movies] may be achieved for example through existing coaxial cable or fibre optic networks. If coax cable is used electrical to optical conversion…is not required."

---

134 A hybrid system is certainly a possibility, and in two forms. First, separate backbones might run from the site of the system operator to different groups of customers. Second, the entire system may include a fiber optic backbone, but at some points in the system, there may be a conversion from fiber optic to coaxial cable, and the coaxial cable would then be connected to the customer's home. If the claims in US 5, 133,079 do not cover electronic systems, then they would seem not to cover any part of a system that includes a coaxial cable backbone.

This example tells us that one example of "conversion" is electrical to optical. To the same effect are examples in the Detailed Description of the Invention, column 4, lines 39–42, and column 4, lines 42–46. The difficulty here is that all of the examples describe specifically electrical to optical "conversion".

Can "conversion" mean anything other than between electrical and optical? The examples above make clear that the written description includes cases where there is not electrical to optical conversion, so something else must be intended, but the patent gives no examples of this "something else".[135]

(3) *The key claim term is an element in a figure*: Figure 2 is a "video distribution bus", and shows only "optical converter" invention element 36. However, Figure 3 is also a "video distribution bus", and Figure 3 shows both "optical to electronic converter" 36, and a dotted line for "Coax (Alternative)" which bypasses the optical converter 36. It therefore seems to be the intent of Figure 3 to show two possible systems, one with a fiber optic backbone, and the other with a coaxial backbone

---

135 Please note that this example uses the phrase "electrical conversion", whereas claim #1 uses the phrase "electronic conversion". Is there a difference between these two words appearing in the patent, "electrical" and "electronic"? Both words are used repeatedly throughout the patent, but with no definitions. I assume that the patentee intended the same meaning, but this is without question a sloppy presentation, and it suggests the danger inherent in using two different terms for one concept. In patents, we want a one-to-one correspondence between terms and concepts. If there are two terms for one concept, as appears to be the case here, confusion results. If there is one term for two different concepts, confusion results. In this patent, as we will see, the one claim term "conversion" seems to mean "electrical to optical", "digital to analog", and possibly also "analog to audio-visual". This is an example of what I call "term stretching". However, term stretching is inappropriate, because a single term cannot cover multiple concepts without causing confusion.

(with no fiber optics). The continuing problem, however, is that none of this clarifies what is meant by "conversion", apart from the now well-known electrical to optical form.

Let us sharpen our understanding of the problem. As noted above, there are multiple examples of optical conversion, so if a system has a fiber optic backbone, there is no difficulty. Both the examples noted above, and Figure 3 explained above, demonstrate clearly that the patentee intended to include not only fiber optic systems but also entirely coaxial systems with no fiber optics. However, if there is no fiber optic backbone, then element 1 (c) has no function at all — there is no conversion to an "electronic signal" as required in element (c), because the original signal on coaxial cable is already "electronic", hence there is no "conversion". Element 1 (d) still makes sense, because the "electronic signals" (here, the signals *from the coaxial backbone, not from the optical converter*) are converted to television signals — the probable intent was electronic digital signals to electronic analog signals. So the real problem is, "If the system intended is entirely electronic as with a coaxial backbone, then element (c) is redundant because the necessary signal conversion is done in element (d). Therefore, a coaxial system could not be intended in claim #1. Is there anything in the patent that suggests otherwise?"

We have explained already that there is nothing in the written specification, no definition, example, or figure, that can explain away the redundancy of element 1 (c) and hence the exclusion of coaxial systems from the scope of claim #1. Is there any way to save claim #1 to include all-electronic systems? There is a doctrine by which courts interpret patent claims, called the "doctrine of claim differentiation". Under this doctrine, each claim in the patent is interpreted to cover an aspect of the invention different than the aspects covered in the other claims. In other words, claims may not be interpreted in a way to make any claim redundant. This doctrine may be used, in some cases, to create a broader interpretation for an independent claim.

This doctrine is *not to be used* by a drafter of patent applications. A drafter can never be certain that a court will actually apply this doctrine, and if the court does apply the doctrine, can never be certain what the court will decide is the "differentiation" between two claims. The other methods of clarifying claims i.e., definition of terms, examples of usage, and appearance as elements in a patent drawing, are simple, effective, and free of doubt. The doctrine of claim differentiation is used by courts and other evaluators of patents[136], but should never be used by a patent drafter to explain a key claim term.[137]

---

136 An evaluator — such as a court, the ITC, a legal advisor, a professional evaluator or consultant, or a person involved in patent commerce — must take the patent as it comes. The evaluator cannot influence the patent as it exists, and must instead rely on all tools of evaluation for existing patents. A good evaluator prefers key claim terms to be defined in the patent, or shown as examples, or depicted in a figure. If none of the those methods appear in the patent, then for lack of any better option the evaluator must rely on the doctrine of claim differentiation. That is the lot of the evaluator, who takes the patent as it comes, but the patent writer shapes the document, is not limited to claim differentiation, and should not rely on this doctrine to change the interpretation of claims.

137 An analogy: Suppose you go to a casino in Las Vegas, or Monaco, or Macau. You have been throwing dice, but not successfully. You've lost all of your money, and most of your clothes. You are now down to your underwear, and you have one last throw of the dice to win it all back, or lose everything. That is a bit like what happens when you rely on the doctrine of claim differentiation to interpret key claim terms. The doctrine of claim differentiation only comes into play in the desperate circumstances when a key claim term has not been properly defined or explained in the patent.

Could the doctrine of claim differentiation be applied in US 5,133,079 to expand the scope of claim #1 to include all-electronic systems (that is, no fiber optics)?

Claim #6 is "A method according to claim #1 wherein the digitized compressed signals are sent from the source in optical signal format." Claim #7 is "A method according to claim #1 wherein the digitized compressed signals are sent from the source via coaxial cable." Taken together with the doctrine of claim differentiation, these two claims must mean that system can include either a fiber optic backbone or a coaxial cable backbone or possibly both (although this latter possibility is not entirely clear). Does this solve the problem? Unfortunately, it does not do so, since claims #6 and #7 are different implementations of element 1 (b), not of element 1 (c). Even with these two claims and the doctrine of claim differentiation, element (c) seems to serve no purpose in an all-electronic system such as coaxial cable. The only way to make sense of claim #6 or claim #7 is to read element (c) out of claim #1. Certainly a court might do that, on the assumption that this is the true intent of the patent, but a court also might not do so. Reliance on the doctrine of claim differentiation here still leaves doubt about the scope of claim #1 and about the scope of all of the method claims.

Supporting the claims is one of main functions of the remaining parts of the patent, including the written description and the figures. As noted, there are a number of ways to support the claims in the written description and figures,

---

Certainly you might find yourself in these desperate circumstances, but why in the world would you deliberately choose to put yourself in such a situation? If you are writing a patent, explain key terms by definitions, examples, or figures, and do not rely on the doctrine of claim differentiation.

which would avoid the problem presented in element 1(c) and ensure that all-electronic communication systems are included. Here are three ways that the written description might have been drafted to avoid this confusion about the term "conversion":

1. *Definition of the key claim term*: Define "signal conversion" to include fiber optic to electronic, electronic to fiber optic, *or electronic from a master library to electronic in a television set*. This is not the standard definition of "conversion", but the patentee may write definitions, and therefore could have defined "signal conversion" in a favorable way that supports inclusion and expands scope. Alternatively, the patentee might have used different terms altogether, and then defined them — for example, "source to receiver transform", or "digital-to-analog adaptation". Different terms might have been used, but unfortunately, the one term "conversion" is applied to several different concepts.

2. *Examples of the key claim term*: The patentee could have added examples of "signal conversion" to include fiber optics to electronic, electronic to fiber optic, *or from other forms of electronic, such as a master signal to a digital receiver, or from a digital receiver to a digital-to-analog converter*. Again, even without an explicit definition, examples will expand the scope of a claim.

3. *The key claim term as an element in a figure*: The patentee could have included an element in a figure with electronic to electronic conversion. Unfortunately for the patentee, the figures include fiber optic to electronic conversion and show that coaxial transmission does not require such conversion. There is no suggestion that electronic to electronic may also be a type of "signal conversion". (There is indeed a

digital-to-analog converter in Figure 5, but this explains element 1(d), not element 1(c).) There was a missed opportunity here, which might have been corrected by simply adding another element in the figures.

In sum, the written description apparently does not support including in claim #1 any system that is all-electronic, because the inclusion of element (c) in claim #1 appears to require conversion from electronic to optical and back to electronic, but does not include an all-electronic system.

There are four deficiencies with method claim #1, as discussed above. The deficiencies place in doubt both the meaning and the scope of claim #1.

Turning now to consider independent structure claim #8, and the dependent structure claims 9–16, we find a very different story than in method claims 1–7.

Here is independent structure claim #8:

> 8. An apparatus for enabling a customer to electronically receive and play on a television set a pre-determined movie, the apparatus comprising:
>
> (a) receiver means to receive from a remote source data in digitized compressed signal format containing audio visual data corresponding to the movie;
>
> (b) a converter to be electronically associated with the receiver means to convert the signal data to corresponding electronic signal data;
>
> (c) a video processor to be electronically associated with the converter to receive the electronic video signals, decompress them and convert them to electronic video signals compatible with the television set to provide a video image of the movie on the television set; and
>
> (d) an audio processor to be electronically associated

with the converter to receive the audio electronic signals from the converter, decompress them and convert them to electronic audio signals compatible with the television set, the video processor and audio processor to be electronically associated with the television set to provide an audible sound tract of the movie through the television set.

There are at least two issues related to claim #8. First, there is a potential problem with the form of elements (a) and (b). Why are these elements written in the means-plus-function format? Neither of the other elements, (c) and (d), are written in means-plus-function format. Element (a) might easily have been written as, "a receiver to receive from a remote source", and (b) might have been rewritten as "the receiver" rather than "the receiver means". With these rewrites, the means-plus-function format would not have applied.

The means-plus-function format is permitted by law, but 35 USC sec. 112(6) requires that, in such a format, the "claim shall be construed to cover the corresponding structure, material, or acts described in the specification...." Unfortunately, the term "receiver means" does not appear at all in the written description. This term is not defined in any way. The word "receiver" appears once in the Abstract, and four times in the Summary of the Invention, but the word "receiver" is also not defined in the patent.

For lack of an alternative, we must ask again, "Can an ambiguous term, here 'receiver means', be clarified by the doctrine of claim differentiation?" Claim #15 says, "the receiver means is adapted to receive [optical] data from...an optical converter", and claim #16 says, "the receiver means is adapted to receive data...from a coaxial cable." These two claims do not define or explain "receiver means". They are, rather, a type of structural tag that explains how the "receiver means" may be configured. Perhaps a court would use claims 15 and 16 to conclude that "receiver means" in claim #8 includes, at a minimum, an optical receiver and a receiver of all-electronic data from a coaxial cable. Perhaps the court would reject this interpretation, since the claim #15 does not say, "the receiver means are an optical receiver", nor does claim #16 say, "the coaxial cable is all-electronic, and the receiver means is a receiver of electronic data". The problem with the doctrine of claim differentiation is that even if we know it will be applied, which seems to the case here, *we cannot say for certain how it will be applied.*

The question remains: does the specification adequately support the claim term "receiver means", even though the patent has no definition of "receiver", no definition of "receiver means", no element in the figures called "receiver" or "receiver means", and no clear resolution from the doctrine of claim differentiation? You may understand by the way I have asked this question that I am uncertain whether the court would find the claim term "receiver means" adequately supported or not. In the end, I believe the answer is yes, a court would likely accept the word "receiver" as sufficient structural support for "receiver means" and would not invalidate claim #8 as being indefinite.[138] All of this uncertainty was created by the failure of the patentee to take action that would have clarified the term "receiver means" and removed all doubt.

---

138 That is only my guess. No one can be sure what a court would rule, but this was probably the industry understanding of "receiver" circa 1990–1992.

Here are some solutions that the patentee might have found to resolve ambiguity about the claim term "receiver means":

*Solution 1*: Use "receiver" rather than "receiver means" in the claim.

*Solution 2*: Add a clarifying definition in the Summary or in the Detailed Description, such as "the term 'receiver means' shall include a receiver or other combination of hardware and software components sufficient to receive either optical or electronic information signals".

*Solution 3*: Add examples of "receiver means" in the written description.

*Solution 4:* Add a new element, numbered and with the name "Receiver", to Figures 2 and 3. Discuss this new element in the written description.

The second issue I see with structure claim #8 is element (b), which references a "converter" that is "electronically associated with the receiver means" and which acts "to convert... signal data to corresponding electronic signal data". We have already noted, in the discussion of element (c) of claim #1, that there is a problem with "electrical" or "optical" conversion. Does element (b) in claim #8 suffer from the same problems as element (c) in claim #1? Let's compare these two claim elements:

**Table 5–1: Comparison of "converter" in Claims 1 and 8 of US 5,133,079**

| **Method Claim #1, element (c)** | **Apparatus Claim #8, element (b)** |
|---|---|
| (c) passing the signals to a converter to convert the signals to corresponding electronic signals. | (b) a converter to be electronically associated with the receiver means to convert the signal data to corresponding electronic signal data. |

Is there a difference between these two elements? Although the language is similar, I would argue that yes, there is an important difference, and the elements are not the same.

Claim #1 is a method claim, requiring actions. Element #1(c) works fine for an electronic to optical to electronic system, but it is impossible in an all-electronic system because no such conversion is performed. Therefore, all-electronic systems, such as a cable system having only electronic signals, are apparently not covered by claim #1.

By contrast, in element 8(b), there may be an optical converter in the system, the converter may be connected in some way to the receiver means, and the purpose of the converter may be to convert optical signals. If the system is fiber optic, then there is no problem, since the converter will be present and active. *However, even if the system is all-electronic, this is also sensible, because the optical converter need only be present, not necessarily active.* If the system is converting electronic and optical signals, then the converter in element 8(b) is active, and the system is covered by the claim. If the system is all-electronic, the converter still exists but it is inactive — the rest of the elements of claim #8 may still be present in the all-electronic system, and hence the all-electronic system will infringe claim #8, provided, of course, that the infringer has an optical server somewhere in the system.

In this sense, structure claim #8 may cover both optical systems and coaxial or other all-electronic systems, whereas method claim #1 appears to cover only optical systems. Therefore, in this case, the structure claim has greater scope of coverage than the corresponding method claim, which represents an exception to the general rule that method claims are usually broader than corresponding structure claims.[139]

I do not see any issues with element 8(c), related to a video processor, or with element 8(d), related to an audio processor.

**Validity**: All of the method claims might be unenforceable due to the doctrine of divided infringement (especially prior to the *Akamai* case in August, 2012). Beyond that, even if the method claims were enforceable, they would apparently not apply to all-electronic systems (such as coaxial systems lacking a fiber optic backbone) for the reasons indicated.

With the structure claims, one major concern is a possible lack of structural support for element (a) of claim #8, which

139 You might ask whether it would be sensible for a customer's system to include an optical converter, even though the backbone is not optical at all. Such a system can definitely be imagined. Let us say that customer systems are being sold with optical converters because some systems have switched to fiberoptics, while other customer systems are still coaxial. Products may be designed with both modes of operation so as to work with either system. The simultaneous existence of two kinds of technical systems is very common when technology is transitioning from one kind of system to another. There is quite often a transition period when both kinds of systems co-exist, or when individual products must operate on both kinds of system. So certainly there may be systems that infringe claim #8 because they have an optical converter, even though the converter will operate only in optical applications and not in all-electronic applications.

is the "receiver means" in claim #8. This problem could have been avoided by not phrasing element (a) in the means-plus-function format. The problem might have been resolved by adding to the written description a definition of "receiver means", by adding to the written description examples of what is meant by "receiver means", or by adding a "receiver" as a visual element in the figures. If claim #8 were litigated, it would probably survive, but one can never be certain what a court will do. Better to have avoided the uncertainty and risk in the first place by adding a better definition.

**Scope**: Virtually every cable operating company offering downloadable movies via a fiber optic network might be caught by the claims in this patent, particularly by the structure claims. In that sense, the claims, if valid, would have a broad scope that would surely be of great concern to the cable industry when the patent was purchased in 2006.

**Discoverability of Infringement**: There is no problem here. Cable operators would advertise downloadable movies as a service to consumers, so discovery would not prove difficult. The same holds true for manufacturers of infringing products: although these products might not be advertised directly to consumers, they would be readily available to the patentee, and discovery of infringement by the products would not be difficult.

**Summary**: This was a patent with great value, due to the generality of its topic, the wide scope of its claims, and its early priority date. True, the claims had some problems, particularly the method claims, although even these claims would seem to cover systems with fiber optic backbones.

The structure claims present a different story. The

generality of the elements of apparatus claim #8 makes this claim, and indeed all the structure claims, powerful. These claims cover the most basic structure of a system for receiving and playing digitized, compressed movies. It is true that claim #8 and therefore all of the structure claims, suffer from the lack of a clear definition of the phrase "receiver means" in element [8a] — however, the lack of such a definition may not have been fatal to the structure claims had they gone to litigation.

In short, this patent, with its broad scope and early priority date, would seem to justify the $1.54 million purchase price paid at public auction, despite some serious problems with the method claims and some lesser problems with the structure claims.

**Lessons Learned**: Here are some lessons we might learn about good patents, from patent claims 1, 6–7, 8, and 15–16 in U.S. 5,133,079, issued to Ballantyne and Mulhall, and sold for $1.54M in the first public patent auction.

5–1–1. ***A patent's area of technology, markets covered, and priority date, are critical to patent value, and might overcome its technical flaws.*** This patent was flawed: the absence of specific structure and discussion of a 100% coaxial implementation places the method claims in doubt, and the unclear definition of "receiver means" raises questions as to viability of the structure claims. Nevertheless, the burgeoning market for electronic downloading of movies, combined with this patent's 1990 priority date, created substantial value and justified the purchase price paid.[140]

140 If there are technical flaws in the claims of the patent, these flaws may be resolved or at least limited in a continuation application based on the

5-1-2. ***Patent value should not change whether the patent is acquired for offensive or defensive purposes.*** This patent was probably purchased for defensive purposes, to keep it out of the hands of people who might have asserted the patent against major companies. However, the reason for the patent's acquisition should make no difference to the patent's value. Valuation is based on an estimate of how much money the patent might be able to generate in licensing, litigation, or threats to exclude competition.

5-1-3. ***If you use "means-plus-function" language in a claim, make sure you define the structure that supports the term "means".*** There was no apparent reason to use the language "receiver means" in element (a) of claim #8. The single word "receiver" would have been sufficient, and would have been adequately supported in the patent. This language rendered the entire claim, and the structure claims which depend on it, vulnerable to attack for possible lack of support in the written description. However, there are legitimate reasons to use such a format for a key claim term, and once the term "means" is selected, the drafter must explain in the written description (not just in the claim itself) what the term means.

5-1-4. ***Changing law can help or hurt patent value.*** The doctrine of "divided infringement" was not an issue when the patent was filed in 1990, nor when it is was issued in 1992. It later became a pressing issue, which threatened to invalidate all the method claims in this patent. Then along came CAFC *Akamai*, decided in August, 2012, which said that such claims

original patent. However, a continuation application is possible only if it is filed before the earlier application issues as a patent. This is one reason that patent owners frequently file continuations before the earlier application issues as a patent.

might be used to prove induced infringement even if direct infringement could not be proven.[141]

5–1–5. ***Structure claims are sometimes broader than method claims.*** In US 5,133,079, the method claims seem to cover only electronic to optical to electronic systems, while the structure claims cover both those systems and all-electronic systems (including all-electronic coaxial systems of cable television companies).

5–1–6. ***Value may be created by the prospect of either direct or indirect infringement.*** Sometimes, all of the value in a patent is created by the possibility of indirect rather than direct infringement. For this patent, direct infringement is likely to occur in the customer's home, making the customer a direct infringer. However, the supplier of a product that induces infringement, and/or the system operator sending data onto an infringing product might be ruled indirect infringers. The possibility of indirect infringement by manufacturers and system operators created significant value in this patent. That was true prior to *Akamai*, and it became more true after *Akamai* rehabilitated method claims that formerly would have been unenforceable due to the doctrine of divided infringement.

5–1–7. ***The doctrine of claim differentiation is a useful doctrine for patent evaluators, but should not be used by patent drafters.*** When the interpretation or scope of a claim

141 The possibility that changing law may impact patent claims is just one more reason that having a good claim mix is very important to the value of a patent, as well as to a patent portfolio. Although some claims may be impacted negatively by the change in law, other claims will survive and maintain their original strength. Changes in law may also increase the strength of claims — as a result of the CAFC *Akamai* case, formerly unenforceable method claims became enforceable on a theory of indirect infringement.

is unclear, and there are no other clues, the evaluator must and should use the doctrine of claim differentiation to understand the claim. This judicial doctrine is useful, however, only where the key claim term lacks other explanation (i.e., no definition, no examples, and no invention element in a drawing, as happened here with the key claim term "receiver means"). Since you can never be certain if and how a court will apply the doctrine, it is much better to explain key terms by definition, examples, and drawings rather than to rely on claim differentiation.

### *Sale of a Patent as Part of a Portfolio — US 5,774,670*

*Background:*

Netscape, a Silicon Valley company founded in 1994, was the pioneer and leading company in Internet browsers throughout the 1990s. The company was acquired by AOL in 1999 for about $10 billion. However, its share of the browser market fell from over 90% in 1995 to almost nothing in the ten years from 1995 to 2005, eclipsed mainly by Microsoft's browser, Internet Explorer.

Netscape generated about 75 U.S. patents, including a handful of design and reexamination patents, but mainly standard utility patents. US 5,774,670, entitled "Persistent Client State in a Hypertext Transfer Protocol Based Client-Server System", is one of Netscape's earliest patents. The patent's filing date, and its priority date, is October 6, 1995. It was issued on June 30, 1998. The patent was transferred to AOL when AOL purchased Netscape. In April, 2012, AOL sold a portfolio of 800 patents to Microsoft for $1.056 billion. Commentators have suggested that patent 5,774,670 might have been one of the patents contributing significantly to the billion dollar value of the portfolio sold.

*Preview:*

US 5,774,670 is a good patent, perhaps the most beautiful of all those presented in this book. It has good claims, albeit with some problems we will discuss. It has good support for the claims in the written description. Given the subject matter, Internet cookies, and the early priority date, this patent could be worth tens of millions of dollars, or even more. Thus, this patent might indeed help justify the billion dollar price Microsoft paid.

The patent was asserted by AOL against various defendants in litigation. During one litigation round, it was learned that Netscape, the original patentee, engaged in business discussions with a company called MCI, and in fact sold to MCI a product containing the invention discussed and claimed in the patent. The sale occurred in September, 1994. One year and 28 days after the sale, the application for patent 5,774,670 was filed with the PTO. By the U.S. patent statute, if a product is sold that contains an invention, an application for that invention may be filed within one year of the sale, *but not one day more.* The record is not entirely clear as to what happened, but it seems that Netscape thought, incorrectly, that the date which triggered the one-year period was the public announcement of the product, not the private sale to MCI. Had Netscape been correct, then the filing date of October 6, 1995 would have been fine. But Netscape erred.

The result is that this high-quality patent, which should have been very valuable, became economically worthless. It is still useful for us, however, as a lesson in what a good patent is and how even the best patent can be devalued by external events.

*Review:*

This patent appears to have a broad scope of coverage, for several reasons.

First, the word "hypertext" and the phrase "hypertext transfer protocol" in the title establish this as an Internet patent. When we further understand that the subject matter of the patent is Internet cookies, potentially broad coverage is clear.

Second, the phrase "client-server system" in the title, and the extensive use of the terms "client" and "server" throughout the patent, tell us that this patent might have general applicability, applying to both the client side (i.e., the customer side) and the server side (i.e., the system operator).[142]

Third, the 1995 priority date is relatively early in the field of Internet patents, and particularly early for Internet cookies.

The combination of early priority date, hot technology area, and coverage of both client-side and server-side usages, suggest that this patent may cover *all* communication systems involved with or using Internet browsers.

This patent was owned by the original assignee, Netscape, when the patent was issued in 1998. In 1999, AOL bought

---

142 I have already discussed the structure of a telecom system as including both the client side and the server side. I have indicated that claims in a patent should be directed to both sides. Solely by its title, this patent was likely to claim both the client-side and the server-side usages, which indeed turned out to be the case. In patents for telecommunication systems, having some claims on the client side and others on the server side is a good mix. In contrast, individual claims that include both "client elements" and "server elements" *within a single claim* are bad, because such claims risk non-enforceability due to the doctrine of divided infringement.

Netscape, and this patent transferred to AOL as part of the purchase. In early 2012, AOL was actively seeking buyers for this portfolio. Microsoft was an interested buyer, and patents in the Internet space, such as US 5,774,670, were generally within Microsoft's realm of interest. In April, 2012, this patent was one of 800 patents sold by AOL to Microsoft for $1.056 billion.

More specifically, it seems that Microsoft in particular was interested in the AOL patents. MDB Capital Group, an investment house that promotes itself as "Wall Street's only IP investment bank", has gathered statistics on the companies that cite AOL patents in their own patents, that is, companies with forward citations to the AOL patents. Far and away the company with the most citations is Microsoft, with 1,331 citations to the AOL patents compared to IBM with 570 forward citations to the AOL patents, followed by AT&T, Yahoo, and Google.[143] On the basis of forward citations, Microsoft would appear to be a natural fit for the AOL portfolio. Patent 5,774,670 appears to have been of special interest — as of the date of the Microsoft/AOL transaction, it had been cited in 43 Microsoft patents, which was far higher than the average number of Microsoft citations to other AOL patents.

Microsoft paid $1.056 billion for AOL's portfolio. This corresponds to an average of about $1.32 million per patent. Common sense, confirmed by experts, suggest that a portfolio like this, involving multiple subjects and multiple patents issued over a period of time, is not valued by simply taking

143 These numbers are taken from Jay Greene and Stephen Shankland, "Why Microsoft spent $1 billion on AOL's patents", CNET News, April 9, 2012, http://news.cnet.com/8301-10805_3-57411434-75/why-microsoft-spent-$1-billion-on-aols-patents/. I have not independently verified these numbers.

the number of patents and multiplying by an assumed value per patent. Rather, values are assigned to specific patents, and these assigned values drive the overall value of the portfolio.[144]

Commentators have suggested that US 5,774,670 may have been one of the key patents that drove the portfolio value. Why might that patent be so valuable? The patent deals with Internet "cookies", which are small pieces of data, stored on either the consumer's computer or the operator's computer, typically containing a history of the contacts between this client and this server and/or other information of value in the client-server interaction. "Cookies" are used very extensively in on-line commerce, allowing operators to suggest possible products and services of interest to a consumer, to effectively target advertising based on the specific interests of that consumer, and to create databases of marketing information useful to sellers of products and services. The general topic of the patent, Internet "cookies", is broad and valuable.

The patent has five independent claims, including #1 (a method), #9 (a computer-readable medium on a client), #10 (a computer readable medium on a server), #11 (a network of computer systems), and #14 (a computer system). Thus, claim diversity within this one patent is very good. Although Netscape asserted infringement of only claims 1, 9, 10, and 14

144 A sensible way to value such a large portfolio is to determine the value of a few key patents in specific markets, and then aggregate the value, perhaps increased by the number and various subject matters of the other patents. Using an average value of "price/patent" might make sense in comparing different transactions after the fact, but it makes no sense in actually valuing the portfolio prior to the sale. Portfolio valuation in this detail is more properly within the realm of financial analysis than fundamental patent analysis, but the latter will form a basis for the former, just as true patent value is a basis for financial patent value.

(not including claim #11), let us consider all five to understand the diversity of claims in the patent.

Here are the independent claims, which I parse with bracketed numbers and words added:

> 1. [Preamble] A method of transferring state information between an http server and an http client, said method comprising the steps of:
> [1] requesting a file on said http server from said http client;
> [2] transmitting said file from said http server to said http client;
> [3] transmitting a state object from said http server to said http client; and
> [4] storing said state object on said http client.
>
> 9. [Preamble] A computer readable medium on an http client containing executable program instructions for performing a method comprising:
> [1] requesting a file on a http server;
> [2] receiving said file from said http server;
> [3] receiving a state object which specifies state information from said http server;
> [4] storing said state object on said http client.
>
> 10. [Preamble] A computer readable medium on an http server containing executable program instructions for performing a method comprising:
> [1] receiving a request for a file on said http server from an http client;
> [2] transmitting said file from said http server to said http client;

[3] transmitting a state object which specifies state information from said http server to said http client.

11. [Preamble] A network of computer systems comprising:
[1] a client system having a client processor and a client computer readable medium coupled to said client processor, said client computer readable medium containing program instructions for receiving a state object which specifies state information and for storing said state object on said client computer readable medium;
[2] a server system having a server processor and a server computer readable medium coupled to said server processor, said server system coupled to said client system through a network medium, said server computer readable medium containing program instructions for transmitting a file from said server system to said client system and for transmitting said state object to said client system.

14. [Preamble] A computer system, said computer system comprising:
[1] a processor;
[2] a memory coupled to said processor;
[3] a computer readable medium coupled to said processor, said computer readable medium containing executable program instructions for:
[3a] requesting a file on a server;
[3b] receiving said file from said server;
[3c] receiving a state object which specifies state information from said server; and
[3d] storing said state object in one of said memory and said computer readable medium.

There is an immediate problem that casts doubt on the

enforceability of two of these five claims. Can you see what the problem is? Would it help if I hint that this problem is very serious for claims 1 and 11, but does not apply to claims 9, 10, or 14?

The problem is, once again, the "doctrine of divided infringement". Consider claim #1. Elements [1] (requesting a file) and [4] (storing information) are performed on the client side, while elements [2] (sending the file) and [3] (sending information) are performed on the server side. This is a classic problem of divided infringement. Unless we can say that the server controls the client, or the client controls the server, under the law prior to CAFC *Akamai*, this problem might destroy all value from claim #1. After CAFC *Akamai*, the patent owner still cannot prove direct infringement, but might be able to prove indirect induced infringement.

The problem is more serious in claim #11. Element [1] is a client system, and element [2] is a server system. There are only two elements in the claim, but they create divided infringement! CAFC *Akamai* on its face states that it applies only to method claims, not to structure claims, so unless and until that decision is extended to system claims, claim #11, and claims #12 and #13 which depend on claim #11, would probably be invalidated if the patent were to come to trial today. Claim #11 was not asserted by AOL at trial, possibly due to the problem of divided infringement (although there is no record of the reason for the exclusion of this claim from litigation).

Look at the other three independent claims, 9, 10, and 14. Do you see anything striking about them? They are all the same, but in different forms! In claim #9, there is a computer readable medium, which we will assume for the moment to be a type of memory that enables requesting information, getting it, and storing it. In claim #10, there is a computer-readable memory that receives a request for information, then sends the information. These two claims are mirror images, one on the client side, and the other on the server side. Since we do not have both client and server elements in either claim #9 (all client elements) or claim #10 (all server elements), there is no issue of divided infringement in claim #9 or claim #10.

Claim #14 is a computer system that must be tied to the client side, although "client" is not mentioned. The claim includes a processor, which is in all "computer systems" by definition of the word "computer", a memory, also in all computer systems, and then a computer readable medium that enables requesting information, getting it, and storing it, all of which occurs on the client side.

In addition to being very similar, and with no problem of divided infringement, claims 9, 10, and 14 are noteworthy for having few elements, simple elements, and very sparse limitations. The claim elements are "requesting a file", "receiving a file", "storing" the information, and "transmitting the information". What could be more general than these kinds of elements? This kind of language is typical of a patent that establishes a new technical concept, which is what US 5,774,670 did.

This patent was the subject of litigation in the case of *Netscape Communication v. Valueclick*, No. 1.09cv225, Eastern District of Virginia. Four memoranda opinions were written in this case in the period October, 2009, to April, 2010, after which the parties settled the case on undisclosed terms in May, 2010.[145] I will summarize here the first two of the

145 All four of the opinions are entitled, *Netscape Communications Corp. v. ValueClick, Inc.*, all issued by the Federal District Court for the Eastern

four opinions as they relate to specific issues relevant to us here.[146] All of the opinions were by Federal District Court Judge Thomas S. Ellis III.

First opinion of October 22, 2009: This was the Markman opinion, setting forth the interpretation of specific elements in the claims. By decision of Judge Ellis, "computer readable medium" will be construed as "storage device"; "state information" will be construed as "information, such as a cookie, that specifies and identifies a characteristic, or a condition of a client and/or a server"; and "state object" will be construed as "data having a predetermined structure that specifies state information", or in other words, the data structure of the cookie.

The key ruling is that "cookie" is definitively read into the claims by the judge. Further, the parties themselves agreed on the interpretation of "computer-readable medium", so there was no dispute on that term. As to "state object" and "state information", the judge adopted the plaintiff Netscape's

---

District of Virginia, abbreviated as E.D.Va. The opinions are reported as follows: First opinion of October 22, 2009 — 684 F.Supp.2d 678 (2009); Second opinion of January 29, 2010 — 684 F.Supp.2d 699 (2010); Third opinion of April 2, 2010 — 704 F.Supp.2d 554 (2010); Fourth opinion of April 15, 2010 — 707 F.Supp.2d 640 (2010).

146 The first opinion, of October 22, 2009, is Judge Ellis' interpretation of the claims after the Markman hearing. This opinion is discussed in relevant part, below. The second opinion, of January 29, 2010, is his invalidation of claim #1 due to early disclosure of the invention. The second opinion is at the heart of this part of the book, and is discussed below. The third opinion, of April 2, 2010, is his rejection of Netscape's motion to reconsider the invalidation of claim #1. The third opinion reinforces the second opinion, and is an interesting opinion in itself, but since it is not necessary for our purposes, it is not discussed here. The fourth opinion is his ruling on various arguments by Netscape to exclude from prior art certain technical papers. This opinion is not relevant for our purposes, and is not discussed here.

opinion, not defendant ValueClick's opinion, thereby strengthening the claims.[147]

Second opinion of January 29, 2010: This is a very important opinion for us, because it demonstrates how external events, unrelated to either the patent or the prosecution history, can destroy a "good patent".

The judge found that the original owner of the patent, Netscape, tried to sell a product containing claim #1 more than one year before the patent was filed. This creates what is called an "on-sale bar" to claim #1. Thus, according to the judge, claim #1 is invalidated.[148]

Claim #1 is an independent method claim, and each of claims #2–8 directly depend on it. The defendant argued that claims #2–8 also should be invalidated by the on-sale bar. Judge Ellis considered this argument, but ruled that the record before him did not clearly demonstrate whether these claims had also been part of the products offered for sale by Netscape more than one year before the patent. Thus, he refused to invalidate claims #2–8.[149]

Even after claim #1 fell, independent claims 9, 10, and 14 remained. Each of these claims has a relatively unusual structure, which is a computer-readable medium that includes

---

147 To understand how judges decide Markman issues and thereby interpret elements in patent claims, read Judge Ellis' first opinion of October 22, 2009, at 684 F.Supp.2nd 678. The Judge's summary of the principles of claim construction is concise and clear.

148 In essence, the judge was saying, "This claim was already stale on the day it was first presented to the PTO. It never should have been allowed". If so, why did the PTO allow claim #1? The PTO is generally not aware of events "external" to the patent. Almost certainly, the PTO was unaware of business negotiations or commercial sales involving Netscape and other companies.

149 Judge Ellis' decisions to invalidate claim #1, but not claims 2–8, appear at 684 F.Supp.2d 719.

program instructions for carrying out a method. So are these structure claims or method claims? By law, a claim that contains both a structure and a method is invalid as violating 35 USC sec. 112(2) because it is indefinite. The reason for this law is clear: if the claim is not clearly structure or method, one could not know whether the infringement occurs when the structure is completed or only when the method occurs. Such confusion renders the claim invalid.

The defendant argued that claims 9, 10, and 14 were neither clearly structure nor method and thus "indefinite", which would render them invalid. However, Judge Ellis rejected this argument:

> [C]laims 9, 10, and 14...do not require a user to execute a claimed method; rather, the claimed computer systems are simply described as *capable* of performing the method, not as actually performing the method. Thus,... [a person with a technical background reading the patent] would have adequate notice that the...patent is infringed only when an apparatus capable of performing the desired functions is made, not when the apparatus executes the claimed method. [684 F.Supp.2d at 722–723. The italicized emphasis appears in the original opinion by Judge Ellis.]

In Chapter 4, we said essentially the same thing in the ITC case *Broadcom v. Qualcomm*, involving US 6,714,980. The claims in that patent used language such as "adapted for", "adapted to", and "arranged to". In the Netscape patent considered here, we have another example in which the structure is "capable of" performing a method, but still remains structure. Whatever the formulation, if the phrase makes clear that the structure is "enabled" in some way to do something, this is clearly a structural element, not a method. Therefore, there will *not* be a forbidden mix of a method element in a structure claim. Therefore, the claim will remain valid.

**Validity**: Claim #1 is dead by Judge Ellis' ruling.

*There is significant doubt about the validity of any of claims 2–26. Although Judge Ellis invalidated only claim #1, this decision casts doubt on the validity of the remaining independent claims, 9, 10, and 14 due to the on-sale bar.* The simple reason is that the four elements in claim #1 comprise all of the elements of claims 9 and 10, plus all of the elements related to the Point of Novelty in claim #14. (Claim #14 also includes a processor and a memory, but these seem to be generic elements present in every computer system, not part of the PON.)

As of the last reported litigation, only claim #1 was invalidated, and the other claims survived. Judges do not like to invalidate claims prior to trial, and will certainly not do so if there is a disputed fact. Judge Ellis' refusal to invalidate any of the other claims prior to trial may well have been correct procedurally. However, from a substantive view, the continuing validity of the other claims was rendered unclear due to the external events of August-September, 1994, all of which occurred more than one year before the patent application was filed on October 6, 1995.

**Scope**: The claims as allowed had a marvelously broad scope. Even after claim #1 was invalidated in litigation, the surviving independent claims 9, 10, and 14 have excellent scope, and would justify a very high valuation of this patent. However, the dubious validity of these claims more than offsets their broad scope.

**Discoverability of Infringement**: I see no particular

difficulty in discoverability. Although infringement is not viewable by the naked eye, it would be inferable from the way the system works, and discoverable from technical and product literature accompanying the browser, or by various means of "cookie detection" by inspection or by software analysis.

**Summary**: Was this patent one of the handful of patents that contributed substantially to the billion dollars plus that Microsoft paid for the AOL patent portfolio? It could have been. The subject, the priority date, and the scope of claims would have supported this argument. But external events destroyed its value, and in the end this patent probably contributed little or nothing to the value of the AOL patent portfolio.

US 5,774,670 is a "high-quality patent". However, its economic value was wrecked by outside actions. Netscape's two disclosures of the invention to an outside party, and an offer to sell products including the invention, were all made more than one year prior to the filing of the application. These actions cast serious doubt on the validity of the claims, under the "on-sale bar", 35 USC sec. 102(b). These actions, together with a failure to file early, were catastrophic mistakes that destroyed the value of the patent more than 15 years after the events, more than 14 years after the patent application was filed, and more than 11 years after the patent issued. External, value-destroying events can have a long life.

**Lessons Learned**: Here are lessons we might learn about good patents, from claims 1, 9, 10, 11, and 14 in U.S. 5,774,670, issued to Netscape Communications, sold to AOL, resold to Microsoft.

5–2–1. ***Even the greatest patent can be destroyed by***

***external action unrelated to the patent.*** This patent was beautiful, both artistically and economically. Unfortunately, the economic value was destroyed by actions totally unrelated to the patent.

5-2-2. ***Heavy forward citation by one company suggests possible interest in buying a patent portfolio.*** The AOL portfolio, including US 5,774,670, was heavily cited by Microsoft, which turned out to be the buyer. Heavy forward citation by a company suggests, although does not prove, strong interest in the patent by the citing company. Chapter 7 discusses forward citations in greater detail.

5-2-3. ***Even after an independent claim falls, dependent claims might survive.*** Claim #1 was invalidated, but claims 2-8 remained alive. The loss of claim #1 diminished the patent's value, and cast doubt on the status of the remaining method claims, but the dependent claims were not invalidated.

5-2-4. ***Structural tags can protect structure claims from being invalidated.*** By law, a claim may not include both structural and method elements. Any such claim would be invalid under 35 USC sec. 112(2) as "indefinite." However, the structure may "contain instructions for the method", or be "configured to operate the method", or "be adapted for" the method, or "be capable of" implementing the method, or otherwise enabling the method, without destroying the claim. These are not methods, but rather structures of a component or device that is "ready" to perform the method.

## Chapter 6

# "Essential" Patents in Pools

This chapter is about patents that have been placed by their owners into a "patent pool" for aggregated licensing by a patent pool administrator. The purpose of this chapter is to give you an understanding of what a patent pool is, and why patents entering a pool may be candidates to be classified as "good patents". We will also learn some lessons about good patents from four patents that were placed into two different patent pools.

Here is the organization of Chapter 6:

I. What are Patent Pools?

II. A Classic Example of a Patent in a Pool (MPEG-2)
*US 5,606,539 (U.S. Philips Corporation)*: A patent for encoding and decoding electronic signals. This patent, essential to implementation of the MPEG-2 standard, was accepted into the MPEG-2 patent pool administered by MPEG-LA.

III. Patent Pool Case Studies: Power Control Technology in a Cellular System

Introduction: There is a brief introduction describing some of the basics of power control in a cellular system.

Three Cases: The introduction is followed by three patents that deal with power control essential to the implementation of the W-CDMA FDD standard for third generation wireless systems. These patents were accepted into the W-CDMA patent pool administered by Sipro Labs Telecom. By examining three patents that are focused on the same technology and that address the same technical problem within the technology, we will see how the potential value of good patents can be realized by aggregating the patents in a group. In this sense, a patent in a pool is "good" specifically because it is a member of the pool. The three cases are:

(1) *US 6,430,398 (Sharp Corporation)*: A patent for power control in a mobile system
(2) *US 6,549,785 (Sharp Corporation)*: A patent for power control in a mobile system
(3) *US 6,885,875 (Siemens Aktiengesellschaft)*: A patent for regulating power in a mobile system

## I. What are Patent Pools?

A "patent pool" is a group of two or more companies, often called a "consortium", which have patents related to a single technology and place these patents into a single group to be licensed as a package.[150]

[150] The characteristics of a patent pool, and in particular the comparison between a patent pool, a "patent platform", and traditional bilateral negotiations for licensing, are discussed extensively in my prior book, *Technology Patent Licensing*, at Chapter 2, entitled, "A Comparison of Licensing Methods", pp.66–87. See also the book by Sunita K. Sreedharan, *An Introduction to Intellectual Asset Management*, (Kluwer Law International, London, 2010), Chapter 7, "Marketing of Intellectual Assets", which examines various means by which intellectual property may be monetized, and particularly pp.180–186, which discuss patent pools.

A patent may be accepted into a pool only if the patent has been determined by an independent technical and legal expert to be "essential" to implementation of the technical standard covered by the pool.[151]

All of the patents in the pool must be essential to the same technology.[152]

---

151 This kind of essentiality, applicable to a technical standard, is known as "technical essentiality". Such a patent is said to be "technically essential". Another kind of essentiality, known as "commercial essentiality", is where a specific feature is essential to the commercial success of a product or method, but the patent is not essential to implementation of a standard. For example, there are technical standards related to the operation of a smartphone — patents essential to those standards are "technically essential". However, some of the functions on a smartphone that help create consumer demand, such as multi-touch technology, may not be captured in technical standards — patents essential to such functions could be "commercially essential", even if they are not "technically essential". See, for example, John Paczkowski, "Google Says Some Apple Inventions Are So Great They Ought to Be Shared", in the online publication AllThingsD.com, wholly owned by Dow Jones & Company, member of the Wall Street Journal Digital Network, July 20, 2012. The patents discussed in Chapter 6 are "technically essential" to particular standards. Determining whether a patent is "commercially essential" is complicated, the legal implications of this determination are not always clear, and commercial essentiality is not discussed further in this book.

152 Inclusion in the pool of a *non*-essential patent would likely be a violation of antitrust law, called in Europe "competition law". A misstep in this area of law could subject the administrator of the pool, and the companies which contributed their patents, to action by government bodies and possible liability in private lawsuits. The determination of patent essentiality to a standard is discussed extensively in my prior book, *Technology Patent Licensing*, in Chapter 3, entitled, "The Determination of Essentiality", pp.88–141. Antitrust law, and its impact on patent pools, is discussed in *Technology Patent Licensing* in Chapter 5, entitled, "Antitrust Liability: The Lurking Fear", pp.178–239. Chapter 5 discusses various requirements of the Antitrust Division of the United States Department of Justice, the Competition Directorate of the European Commission, and the Japanese Fair Trade Commission.

Why is acceptance into a pool a sign that the patent has value? Such acceptance indicates that an independent expert, knowledgeable in both patent law and the technology area of the patent, has determined that one or more claims of the patent are "essential" to implementation of the standard. The patent cannot enter into the pool until the expert has rendered this opinion. This opinion means that any party implementing the standard, by making a product according to the standard, or by importing the product into the U.S., or by selling the product in the U.S, or by using the product in the U.S, is likely to be infringing the patent.[153]

The independent expert is not a court of law. Only a court, or a regulatory body such as the ITC, can make a final determination of infringement. The expert's opinion, however, is an indication that infringement is likely. If the standard in question is a widely adopted technical standard, such as MPEG-2 or W-CDMA, infringement means that many companies, and possibly millions of product units, may be liable for damages. The expert's opinion, therefore, is a strong confirmation of the patent's quality and economic value, at least as to the specific claims found by the expert to be "essential" to implementation of the technical standard.

153 The determination of essentiality is not limited to U.S. patents. Patent pools can and routinely do determine essentiality to the same technical standard of Asian and European patents. It should be remembered, however, that the analysis of a patent, including both the validity and scope of its claims, is determined by the national law of the patent. Thus, for example, a U.S. patent will be reviewed *under U.S. law* for its essentiality to a technical standard, a German patent *under German law* for essentiality to the same standard, a South Korean patent *under South Korean law* for essentiality to the same standard, etc. U.S. law is particularly relevant here only because this book reviews U.S. patents rather than the patents of any other country.

Four patent pool administrators actively administer multiple patent pools:

1. MPEG-LA, short for MPEG-Licensing Administrator, was founded in 1996 and is based in Denver, Colorado. It administers patent pools for technologies such as MPEG-2, MPEG-4 Visual, IEEE 1394, VC-1, ATSC, and AVC/H.264. The patent pool for MPEG-2 is probably the most successful patent pool, financially, of all time. It has 27 licensors, 1,415 licensees, and has generated substantially more than $1 billion in revenue.

2. Sipro Lab Telecom, founded in 1994, is based in Montreal, Canada, and administers pools for electronic audio technologies such as G.729, G.723.1, G.279.1, and G.711.1. The patent pool for W-CDMA was launched by the company 3G Licensing, and Sipro became the administrator for this pool in early 2011.[154]

3. Sisvel International, founded in 1982 and based in Turin, Italy, administers patent pools for technologies such as MP3, MPEG Audio, DVB-T, DVB-T2, UHF-RFID, and cdma2000.

4. Via Licensing, a wholly owned subsidiary of Dolby Laboratories, Inc., founded in 2002, is based in San Francisco, California, and administers patent pools for technologies such as Advanced Audio Coding, 802.11a-j, MPEG-2 AAC, MPEG-4 SLS, and OCAP tru2way interactive digital cable.

---

154 A particularly useful feature of the W-CDMA pool is that the pool identifies which claims in the included patents were found to be essential. Other administrators, such as MPEG-LA and Sisvel, publish the numbers of patents found to be essential, but not the specific claims.

In addition to these four, there are bodies which manage a single pool for a particular technology. Examples include the RFID consortium, the DVD 6C licensing agency, the 3C DVD patent pool administered by Philips Electronics, and the AVC patent pool management organization.[155]

Why do patent owners choose to place their intellectual property in a pool? One reason is that the owners may maximize patent value with a licensing and litigation campaign involving all the patents in the group. In particular, the strength of the patent aggregation is that it will cover many different aspects of the technology. Moreover the threat of litigation against potential licensees is magnified by the aggregation of patents, because:

(1) The costs of litigation are shared, giving the owners as plaintiff a cost advantage.

(2) The defendant is faced with many patents, all of which have been found by technical experts to be essential to a standard. The likelihood of finding infringement of at least some of the patents is therefore high.

(3) Because so many patents are directed at the defendant, there is almost no incentive for the defendant to try to invalidate one or two of the patents.

(4) The relatively modest joint licensing rate typically offered by the administrator often makes it worthwhile for a licensee to take the license rather than fight the lawsuit.

155 This list is taken from *An Introduction to Intellectual Asset Management*, *op. cit.*, pp.185–186.

## II. A Classic Example of a Patent in a Pool (MPEG-2)

*Background:*

US 5,606,539, “Method and Apparatus for Encoding and Decoding and Audio and/or Video Signal, and a Record Carrier for Use with Such Apparatus”, priority date of June 5, 1990, issued to U.S. Philips Corporation on February 25, 1997. This patent presents methods and structures for preventing both “overflow” and “underflow” of a data memory buffer. When the data inflow is not matched to the limits of the memory buffer, whether due to overflow or underflow, data can “stall”, causing a video scene or an audio stream to freeze or break up.

*Preview:*

This patent relates to one aspect of data decoding, which is a key function of an MPEG system. The invention is a small yet significant improvement, contributing to the standard. The scope of the claims is not clear due to statements in the description which seem to link the patent to a failed technical standard. The owner, Philips, chose to unlock the potential value in this patent by placing it in a patent pool. Why Philips did so is not known, although the unclear scope of the claims may be one reason why Philips opted to include the patent in a pool rather than to monetize the patent directly.

*Review:*

The prosecution history for this patent is not available online and, to the best of my knowledge, the patent was never reexamined or litigated.[156] Therefore, this analysis relies solely on the patent itself.

The patent does not refer to "MPEG" or to the specific standard "MPEG-2", but it was found by MPEG-LA to be essential to that standard, and thereby incorporated into the MPEG-2 patent pool.[157]

MPEG-LA lists the patents found to be essential, although it does not list the specific claims that were judged and found essential. Therefore, to really understand the patent, and why it might be "essential", we need to look at the four independent claims: #1, #18, #23, and #29.

156 To be precise, it appears that the owner of the patent, U.S. Philips Corporation, has not initiated any lawsuits based on this patent. However, when a licensing administrator sues a potential licensee, many of the patents in the pool become part of the lawsuit. This patent, for example, was part of lawsuits initiated by MPEG-LA against Lenovo, and Vizio, respectively. In theory, it would be possible to include in a lawsuit all of the patents in the pool, since they are all essential to implementation of the standard, and therefore likely to have been infringed. In practice, however, a few patents are selected, typically the ones most relevant to the alleged infringement, and only these selected patents are used as the basis of the lawsuit.

157 Actually, MPEG-LA, like most pool administrators, hires patent law firms to do the evaluations of essentiality. MPEG-LA itself does not judge the essentiality of a patent, but rather accepts the finding of the technical and legal experts in the patent law firm.

**Table 6–1: Independent Claims in U.S. 5,606,539**

| Claim #1 | Claim #18 | Claim #23 | Claim #29 |
|---|---|---|---|
| [Preamble] A method for encoding an audio and/or video signal into an encoded signal which can be decoded by a decoding device including a decoder buffer for receiving the encoded signal and a decoder for decoding the encoded signal, the method comprising: | [Preamble] An encoding apparatus for use with a system for encoding and decoding an audio and/or video for signal, which system includes the encoding apparatus for encoding the audio and/or video signal into an encoded signal, and a decoding apparatus having a decoder buffer for receiving the encoded signal and a decoder for decoding the encoded signal, the encoding apparatus comprising: | [Preamble] A decoding apparatus for use with a system for encoding and decoding an audio and/or video signal, which system includes an encoding apparatus for encoding the audio and/or video signal into code blocks making up an encoded signal, determining a delay time parameter for a code block of the code blocks and inserting the delay time parameter into the encoded signal, and the decoding device for decoding the encoded signal, the decoding device comprising: | [Preamble] A method for decoding an audio and/or video signal encoded in successive code blocks making up an encoded signal, which encoded signal further includes a delay time parameter, the method comprising: |

| Claim #1 | Claim #18 | Claim #23 | Claim #29 |
|---|---|---|---|
| [1] encoding successive portions of the audio and/or video signal into corresponding successive code blocks making up the encoded signal; | [1] means for encoding successive portions of the audio and/or video signal into corresponding successive code blocks making up the encoded signal; | [1] a) means for obtaining the delay time parameter from the encoded signal; | [1] a) obtaining the delay time parameter from the encoded signal; |
| [2] determining a delay time parameter for a code block of the code blocks, which delay time parameter represents a length of time during which the code block is to be stored within the decoder buffer before decoding by the decoder in order to ensure that the decoder buffer will not experience overflow or underflow of the code blocks; and | [2] means for determining a delay time parameter for a code block of the code blocks, which delay time parameter represents a length of time during which the code block is to be stored within the decoder buffer before decoding by the decoder in order to ensure that the decoder buffer will not experience overflow or underflow of the code blocks; and | [2] b) a decoder buffer for receiving the code blocks from the encoded signal; and | [2] b) supplying the code blocks of the encoded signal to a decoder buffer; and |

| Claim #1 | Claim #18 | Claim #23 | Claim #29 |
|---|---|---|---|
| [3] inserting the delay time parameter into the encoded signal. | [3] means for inserting the delay time parameter into the encoded signal. | [3] c) a decoder for decoding the code blocks after receipt by the decoder buffer, which decoder decodes the code block when the code block has been stored in the decoder buffer for a length of time represented by the delay time parameter which ensures that the decoder buffer will not experience overflow or underflow of the code blocks. | [3] c) decoding the code blocks after receipt by the decoder buffer in a manner whereby at least one of the code blocks is decoded when that code block has been stored in the decoder buffer for a length of time represented by the delay time parameter which ensures that the decoder buffer will not experience overflow or underflow of the code blocks. |

Several aspects of the patent claims are attractive:

1. Encoding and decoding are set forth in parallel claims. Encoding method claim #1 corresponds to decoding method claim #29, and encoding apparatus claim #18 corresponds to decoding apparatus claim #23. This is a nice, clean structure.

2. None of the claims include both encoding and decoding in the same claim. That is to say, each claim is either encoding (therefore server-side) or decoding (therefore client-side),

but not both. Hence, there is no possible problem of divided infringement.

3. Each independent claim has exactly three elements, and each element is relatively clear.

The Point of Novelty presented by this patent seems to be the creation, insertion, and use of a time stamp into each block of data. This time stamp is called a "delay time parameter" and sets the length of time for which the block of data shall be in the decoder buffer (that is, in a memory in the decoder), after which the block of data will be decoded. If timed correctly, decoding will allow presentation, without stall, of both the video and the audio. The elimination of stall in video appears to be the improvement provided by the claims.

The four independent claims seem to support this PON very well. So these claims are presented well and provide a general solution to a general problem. Would this therefore be a "good patent"?

There is a question about the two structure claims, #18 (the encoder) and #23 (the decoder). There are three claim elements in claim #18 for the encoder, and they are all written in the means-plus-function format. Claim #23, the decoder, also has three elements, although only the first element is written in the means-plus-function format. Is there sufficient "means" in the written description to support the means-plus-function elements of these claims?

There are fourteen figures in this patent, but the only structural figure is FIG. 2, so all of the structural support for claims 18 and 23 must reside in FIG. 2. The more precise question then becomes: "Is there enough structure in FIG. 2 to support the 'means' in the structure claims?" FIG. 2 is critical to our understanding of this patent, so let us look at that figure now.

**Chart 6–1: FIG. 2 of US 5,606,539**

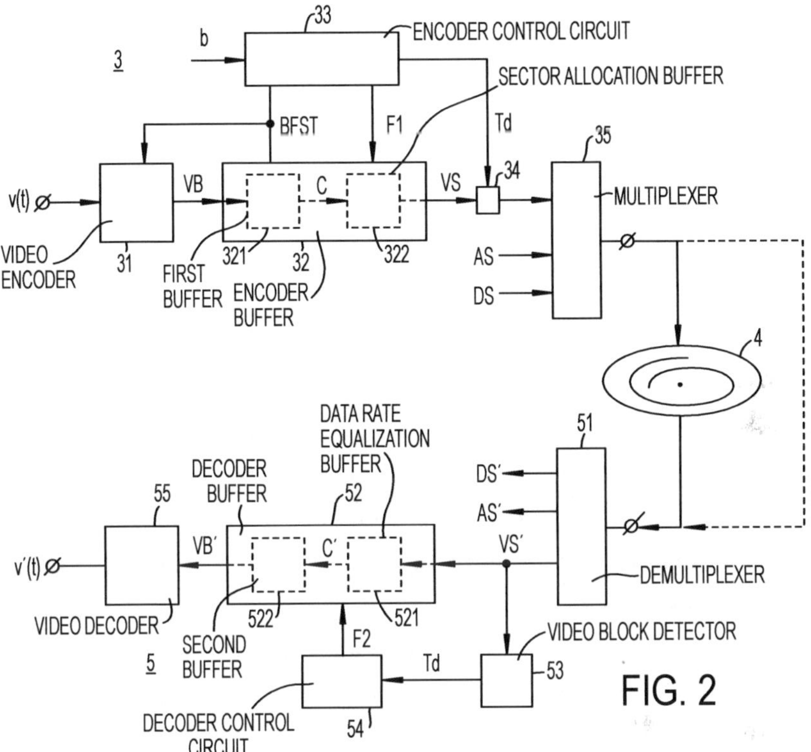


FIG. 2 has a top half and a bottom half. The top half is a detailed block diagram of an encoder, while the bottom half is a detailed block diagram of a decoder. Slightly more than 50% of the section, "Detailed Description", relates specifically to this FIG. 2, and every invention element appearing in FIG. 2 is discussed in the Detailed Description. Therefore, I would say that there is enough structure in FIG. 2 to support claims 18 and 23 . The fact that some of the claim elements appear in the "means-plus-function" format does not seem to be a problem, because supporting structure is illustrated in the figures and explained in the written specification.

Nevertheless, one problem remains. The title of the patent, and the claims in the patent, seem to be general and "medium-neutral," that is, applicable to all forms of electronic communication. However, the Abstract refers to a CD: "One or more audio and/or full motion video signals...(and possibly computer data), are recorded on an interactive compact disc". FIG. 2, the only structural figure, has an encoder on the top and a decoder on the bottom. These two structures, the encoder and decoder, are connected *only* by element number 4 in FIG. 2, which appears at the right of FIG. 2 above, and which is described repeatedly in the patent as "a compact disc". It therefore seems that the invention is *not* medium-neutral, but limited rather to implementations where a CD is used to transfer data from an encoder to a decoder.

Because of the specific structure shown in FIG. 2, and the way in which element 4 of FIG. 2 is described, the patent might be limited to implementations with compact discs. The market for compact discs was very large at the time this patent was filed in 1994, and also when the patent was issued in 1997 but sales have been declining for years in favor of online downloading and flash drives.[158] The patent will expire in 2014, but in any case, as a standalone patent limited to the CD market, this patent's market may have peaked and started to decline more than ten years ago.

However, since the CD market was very large during the life of this patent, wouldn't this still be a "good patent"?

---

158 More than 200 billion CDs were sold between first sales in 1982 and 2007 — BBC News, "Compact disc hits 25th birthday", August 17, 2007, at http://news.bbc.co.uk/2/hi/technology/6950845.stm. Sales however, have declined by more than 50% in the period 2000–2010 — Joseph Plambeck, "As CD Sales Wane, Music Retailers Diversify", New York Times, May 30, 2010: http://www.nytimes.com/2010/05/31/business/media/31bestbuy.html.

Unfortunately, the answer is not so obvious. The Abstract refers not merely to a "compact disc", but rather to "an interactive compact disc". The word "interactive" appears only one other time in the patent, in the Background section, which says, at column 1, lines 27–29, "The interactive compact disc (CDI) on which data for text and graphic images and digital audio is stored has been developed in the last few years". This seems not to be any type of "interactive compact disc", but rather specifically a compact disc in CDI format. Perhaps you are asking yourself, "CD or CDI, does it really matter?"

Philips created a company-specific technical standard called the Philips CD-i (Compact Disk Interactive standard), announced first in 1986, with first products shipped in 1991, and used primarily for interactive electronic gaming based on the interactive compact disc. This technical standard, like many technical standards, and particularly technical standards that are championed by a single company, failed. The standard was not adopted by the technical community or by consumers. US 5,606,539 was issued in 1997, but Philips stopped the development of video games based on CD-i in 1998. This patent, US 5,606,539, was based on a failed technology. Does the market failure of the format also mean that the patent is a failure, hence not a "good patent"?

This is a critical question, but its answer remains unclear because the scope of the claims is unclear. There are two reasons that explain why the claim scope is unclear, the first relating to the patent itself, and the second relating to Philips' submission of the patent to the MPEG-2 pool.

The first reason for claim scope unclarity is that the written specification and the patent figures appear in such a way that it is very difficult to know the scope of the claims. There are three possibilities:

1. The first possible scope is based on the words "interactive compact disc". This phrase appears once in the Abstract of the written description, and once in the in the Background, but nowhere else in the patent. In addition, the acronym "CDI", which seems to stand for "Compact Disc Interactive", appears four times in Background section, but nowhere else. There is no reference anywhere in the patent to the Philips CD-i technical standard, which failed shortly after issuance of the patent. Bottom Line: Did Philips mean to restrict this patent to interactive compact discs? Would that be the ruling of a federal court, or of the ITC? If so, this patent would be of little value even on the day it was issued, and would have lost all value after the failure of the CD-i standard.

2. The second possible scope is based on the phrase "compact disc", but without the word "interactive". The phrase "compact disc", without the word "interactive", appears once in the Background section, and four times in the Detailed Description section. The phrase appears in the discussion of the only structural figure in the patent, FIG. 2, where illustrated element number 4, connecting the encoder to the decoder, is referred to only as "compact disc", never as "interactive compact disc". Would it be a good thing for the patent scope to include all "compact discs", and not just "interactive compact discs"? Hundreds of billions of CDs have been sold worldwide since inception of the CD technology. If patent US 5,606,539 covered all CDs, that coverage would be a very good thing, even though the market for CDs peaked in the year 2000, and is in serious decline today. However, I am not sure

if a court would accept that the claims include all compact discs rather than just interactive compact discs.

3. The third possible scope is that the patent is not limited to compact discs at all, but rather includes all electronic communication where an encoder and a decoder act to avoid problems of data overflow and underflow in the decoder buffer. This would be a tremendously broad scope, almost to the point where one would expect challenges to validity based on prior art. Is this a reasonable possibility for claim scope? The claims do not at any point mention "CD", "compact", or "disc", which suggests that the claims are *not limited* to CDs. Here is the very first paragraph of the written description, at the start of the section Background of the Invention, column 1, lines 16–26:

> The invention relates to a method of encoding audio and/or video signals for transmissions via a transmission medium. More particularly, the transmission medium is preferably an optically readable disc. **Nevertheless, the transmission medium may also be** a magnetic tape or disc, or **a direct connection between a transmitter and a receiver**. The invention also relates to a transmission medium on which audio and/or video signals are recorded, to an encoding apparatus for encoding and transmitting the audio and/or video signals, and to a decoding apparatus for receiving those signals after unloading and transmission. [Emphasis **in boldface** added.]

If the connection may be "direct", rather than by using an "optically readable disc" such as a CD, magnetic tape or disc, *then the patent might also cover online downloading, the predominant way of receiving information via the Internet today.*

*If that is the correct interpretation of the claim scope, then this patent could be worth tens of millions of dollars, or more.*

On the other hand, one must ask:

1. If "direct connection" is also intended, why are "CD" and "interactive compact disc" mentioned repeatedly throughout the written description? Also, why does the sole structural diagram, FIG. 2, show a CD, element 4 at the right of FIG. 2, as the only medium of transferring information between an encoder and a decoder?

2. Does "direct connection" require a physical connection between a transmitter and a receiver, with no intermediary? Connections through the Internet require intermediate hardware, so if "direct" means "without intermediate hardware", then on-line downloading is not covered by the claims of this patent. However, if "direct" means flowing directly from a transmitter to a receiver over a transmission network, then "direct connection" might include downloading via the Internet.

3. If the sole support for this broad reading of the patent is in the Background section of the patent, why does the same Background section repeatedly mention "interactive compact disc" or "CDI"?

4. Why does the phrase about "direct connection between a transmitter and a receiver" appear in the Background section? This is an error. The phrase about "direct connection" does not belong in the Background section. *No part of an invention should be discussed in the Background section, ever.* Every definition related to the invention should be in the Summary, or even better, in the Detailed Description. Every explanation that is meant to broaden the scope of the invention, or to list additional embodiments of the invention,

should be in the Summary and/or the Detailed Description. Philips was correct to put what might be a broadening of the invention into the written description, but it was definitely incorrect to put the broadening into the Background section. This defective placement, together with the general lack of clarity about what the patent means, creates a situation where there are three possible scopes of claim, from narrow and of negligible value (CD-i) to broad (CD) and finally to vast value (Internet). It is impossible to say which way a court would rule.

A second reason explaining why the scope of the claims is unclear is that Philips chose to submit this patent to an essentiality review, and to licensing through the MPEG-LA MPEG-2 patent pool. Why did Philips do that? If the patent had been judged by Philips to be truly medium-neutral, then the patent might cover all forms of electronic communication between an encoder and a decoder, and this single patent would be worth many millions of dollars. In that case, Philips might have licensed the patent itself, and made much more money in the form of licensing royalties paid directly to Philips. By placing its patent in the pool, Philips gave up the possibility of individual patent value, but gained a share of a revenue stream worth over $1 billion. One possibility is that Philips itself had some doubt about the scope of the claims.

We do not know for certain why Philips chose as it did. While the patent claims are very good, the written description supporting the claims is confused and creates uncertainty as to the true scope of the claims. I have said before that a "good patent" is one with good claims and good support in the written description. In this case, we have good claims, but we lack good support in the written description, which contains ambiguous and confusing language. These weaknesses may have contributed to Philips decision to "play it safe" by joining the patent pool.

**Validity**: The estimate of validity depends here on the estimate of scope. If the claim scope is restricted to interactive compact discs, the chances of validity are extremely high. If the claim scope includes all compact discs, chances of validity are reasonably good. If the claim scope is extremely expansive, with all forms of "direct connection" between an encoder and a decoder, including Internet connections, then even with the priority date of June 5, 1991, there is a serious chance that prior art could be discovered to either anticipate the patent or to make its claims obvious. As has been noted previously, broad scope of claim and claim validity are natural enemies. The natural tension between scope and validity is illustrated here: a broad scope of the independent claims would likely have problems with validity, whereas a relatively narrow scope of such claims would create high chances of validity (but lower claim value).

**Scope**: This is the main question. Of the three possible interpretations noted above, I cannot say how a court or the ITC would rule. One interpretation (downloads) creates extremely broad claim scope, a second interpretation (transfer by CDs) creates moderate claim scope, and a third interpretation (transfer by the CD-i disk format) creates almost zero claim scope.

**Discoverability of Infringement**: According to any interpretation of scope, I do not see a serious problem with discoverability of infringement. Compact discs, whether interactive or not, will be visible. Direct connection would be easily discoverable by following the description of the service, or by making technical inferences as to how the service works.

**Summary**: Philips created an invention and a patent in an interesting area, with multiple additional patents covering the same topic. US 5,606,539, with the similar patents, were all placed into the pool of patents essential to implementation of the MPEG-2 standard. This was probably a safe way to go. Instead of going to high-cost, high-risk litigation, Philips ensured it would obtain value from these patents through the pool. This is one reason patent owners pool their intellectual properties — to generate revenue without the cost, risk, and potential resulting ill-will that may be incurred by initiating litigation against alleged infringers.

**Lessons Learned**: Here are some lessons we might learn about good patents, from claims 1, 18, 23, and 29 in US 5,606,539, issued to Philips and placed in the MPEG-2 patent pool.

*6-1-1.* ***Draft the written description so as not to limit claim scope.*** Here, the claims alone might have had broad coverage, but unclear terms in the written description created serious uncertainty as to what the claims intended to cover.

*6-1-2.* ***Definitions of technical terms related to the invention belong in the Detailed Description, and/or the Summary, but never in the Background.*** If such definitions are placed in the Background section, this placement will create confusion as to whether the definition is part of the prior art or part of the invention. This also applies to any phrase that intends to either expand the scope of claims or provide a new embodiment of the invention — *put these phrases in the Summary or Detailed Description, not in the Background.*

6–1–3. ***Means-plus-function claims are generally not favored, but they are acceptable when the "means" are explained clearly***. In this case, there was only one structural figure, which makes the focus clear, particularly when supported by illustrations of the "encoder" and "decoder" in FIG. 2. In addition, more than 50% of the Detailed Description was devoted to structural FIG. 2, so there was adequate discussion of the structural "means" sufficient to support claims 18 and 23 in means-plus-function format.

6–1–4. ***Tying an invention to one technical standard is dangerous***. If you must cite a standard, make sure to state that the standard is only one of multiple alternatives. In this case, mention of "interactive compact disc" or "CDI" was, in my opinion, counter-productive, unless there was no other way to have the patent accepted by the examiner. Use only the limitations that are required to obtain the patent.

6–1–5. ***Patent pools offer a potential path to unlock value from a patent***. Philips has had about 100 patents in the MPEG-2 patent pool. Most have now expired, but some remain active. Each patent created value by increasing Philips' share of the greatest revenue stream ever created by a patent pool. Of course, no other patent pool has been as successful as MPEG-2, so results in a different pool may not match Philips on a patent-by-patent basis. Nevertheless, if you have a patent that has claims essential to the implementation of an important technical standard in the ICT space, and if there is a pool covering this technology, consider placing your patents in the pool.

## III. Patent Pool Case Studies

### *A. Power Control Technology in a Cellular System*

In all electronics, power is important. More power often means improved performance, but it means also increased cost of electricity and usually a higher failure rate for electronic components. In radio communications, power is even more important than in electronics generally, because the usefulness of remote units ("handsets" in cellular systems) is limited to the life of the units' batteries.

Battery life for cellular handsets has increased, but only gradually. One reason is that transmission and reception components have been among the least adaptable to replacement by low-power digital components. In addition, although battery life has improved, the power demands on products tend to increase at a much greater rate than the rate of improvement in battery life. In sum, despite some improvement in battery life, power consumption and battery life are likely to continue being important issues for the foreseeable future.

There are three basic kinds of wireless air protocol, sometimes called "radio link protocol" or "channel access method". Power considerations are different for these three protocols.

One kind of air protocol divides radio bandwidth into multiple frequencies. This is called a "frequency division" protocol. An example is OFDM, a 4G cellular protocol. Virtually all radio systems use frequency division — in other words, communication channels are allocated to different frequencies in all radio systems.

A second kind of air protocol divides a single "channel", or frequency, according to time slices. This is called a "time division" protocol. Probably the outstanding example is GSM, which in its time was the most widely adopted 2G protocol in the world.[159]

The third basic kind of air protocol enables multiple channels to share the same frequency at the same time. Each pair of transmitters and receivers operates according to a specific code that allows the pair to focus on their own communications and to ignore all other communications on the same channel at the same time but using a different code. The classic analogy people use to explain this is to assume several pairs of people in one room, where the people are all talking at the same time but the two members of each pair are speaking a language that is different than the languages spoken by other pairs in the room. Since all the people talk at the same time, there is no time division, and since they all talk within the narrow band of human voice frequencies, there is no frequency division. However, each pair of people is speaking a different language, which allows that pair to focus on their conversation and ignore all the other conversations in the room. The specific language spoken by a pair of people is that pair's "code", and the air protocol allocating communication this way is called the "code division" protocol. There are several examples of the code division protocols, including CDMA, a 2G cellular protocol popular in the U.S. and South Korea, and the 3G protocols W-CDMA and cdma2000.[160]

Division by frequency, time, and code, are the three basic

---

159 GSM, a second generation protocol, is still important, but it is gradually being replaced by 3G, primarily W-CDMA, and by 4G, primarily LTE.

160 In reality, this analogy is imperfect, because human ears are not completely language-selective, so the speech of others, even in different languages, will have some negative impact. By contrast, in code-division electronic communication systems, the codes are designed to have very little "overlap", sometimes called "interference" or "cross-talk". Still, the general

kinds of air protocols, and thus the three ways to establish radio links between transmitters and receivers. There are very many specific protocols, generally defined in technical standards, but all rely on one or a combination of these three basic protocols.[161]

This introduction to air protocols is necessary for you to understand, because code division multiple access (CDMA) technology is fundamentally different from both frequency division multiple access (FDMA) technology, and time division multiple access (TDMA) technology. In FDMA, each communication is at a different frequency. In FDMA, there are very narrow bandwidths between active frequencies that guard against interference, but as a general matter, communication in one frequency tends not to disturb or be disturbed by communications in other frequencies. "Disturbance" in this sense is usually called "interference".[162] Similarly, in TDMA systems, different communication channels use different time

---

idea is clear — code division systems operate differently than frequency division and time division systems.

161 Some believe there is a fourth basic air protocol, called "packet mode multiple access", but others disagree because this might be considered a hybrid of time division and code division. Some believe there is a fifth basic air protocol, called "spatial division multiple access", but others say this is simply a technique for increasing system capacity by sectorizing space and reusing frequencies. For our purposes, fourth and fifth protocols are simply not important. It is sufficient that you understand the three basic air protocols based on frequency division, time division, and code division.

162 I have simplified. Strong power allocated to one frequency may cause "adjacent-channel interference" to nearby channels. There is also "harmonic interference", "inter-modulation interference", and other kinds of problems caused by one communication link to another communication link. Nevertheless, the general point is that under normal circumstances, communications on different frequencies will not typically interfere with one another.

slots, with brief unused periods between usable time slots, so that in normal circumstances, communications in different channels will not interfere with one another.

In contrast to TDMA and FDMA systems, CDMA systems are highly sensitive to differences in power levels of different communications. The reason is that multiple communications are happening at the same time, in the same frequency, within the same physical space. In the analogy to human speakers, imagine that all the speakers in the room are speaking at one volume level, and then one of the pairs starts shouting its conversation. Communication will degrade rapidly and drastically for the non-shouting pairs, even if each pair of people is speaking a different human language.

Therefore, it is critical in CDMA systems to control transmission power so that the energy of one communication does not interfere with or overwhelm communications operating in the same channel but using different codes. As a practical matter, CDMA systems try to equalize power levels of communications in the same channels. Therefore, although power control is a major issue in all radio systems, it is particularly important in CDMA systems. Consequently, technical standards defining CDMA systems, such as the W-CDMA standard, give significant attention to power control. As a further result, technologies are developed and covered by patents that focus specifically on transmission power control for CDMA systems. Sipro Lab Telecom's W-CDMA patent pool includes several patents essential to those parts of the standard that deal with transmission power control.[163]

The discussion in the rest of this chapter focuses on three

163 The W-CDMA standard is sometimes called by the names 3GPP, 3GPP FDD, UMTS, or UTRAN. For our purposes, these describe the same

patents, two from Sharp Corporation and one from Siemens, which offer different solutions to the problem of power control in CDMA systems. These three solutions are not mutually exclusive and can be implemented together. Each invention represents a small improvement, which is nevertheless valuable, as we will now consider.

## *B. Three Cases*

### *US 6,430,398: Power control in a mobile system*

*Background:*

US 6,430,398, essential to the implementation of the W-CDMA 3GPP FDD standard for third generation wireless systems, is entitled, "Method for Improving Performance of a Mobile Radiocommunication System Using Power Control". The patent has a priority date of 1999, was issued in 2002, and was assigned initially to the French company Alcatel (now called Alcatel-Lucent). Alcatel was never a licensor under the W-CDMA patent pool — US 6,430,398, together with next patent, US 6,549,785, were submitted to the patent pool by the Japanese company Sharp.[164]

---

technical standard. W-CDMA will be used except where quotations use other terms.

164 These two patents were assigned originally to Alcatel, which later granted Sharp a temporary but exclusive license to both patents. Sharp then submitted the patents to the W-CDMA patent pool. For our purposes, the exact nature or duration of the transfer to Sharp is not important, except to keep in mind that (1) Sharp is referenced in this book as the owner of these two patents, and (2) despite Sharp's temporary ownership or control, the patents were originally owned by a European company. European companies often use the Jepson format of claim, called in Europe the "two-part form", which is the format used in claim #1 of US 6,430,398 and claim #1 of US 6,549,785.

*Preview:*

There are many patents related to CDMA power control. Each such patent improves a different aspect of power control. Although the individual improvements may be small, the combination of the improvements in all the patents may have a major positive impact on system performance.

*Review:*

The independent patent attorneys who reviewed and judged the patents submitted to the W-CDMA patent pool, determined claims 1, 3, 4, 5, 11, 12, 13, 23, and 25 to be essential to various parts of the 3GPP FDD standard. I will focus here on independent method claim #1.

Here is claim #1:

> 1. A method for improving performances of a mobile radiocommunication system using a power control loop which controls power according to a transmission quality target value, and an adjustment process for adjusting said transmission quality target value, *a method wherein said adjustment process is controlled based on an assessment of the convergence of said power control loop around said transmission quality target value.* [Emphasis in italics added.]

This claim is noteworthy for several reasons.

First, the claim is written in the Jepson format, which was explained in Chapter 1. In this format, there is a clear distinction between what is considered by the patentee to be prior art, and what is considered to be the invention. In the quotation above, everything in normal typeface is considered by the patentee to be prior art, and everything *in italics* is the

Point of Novelty ("PON"). In this case, the admitted prior art, meaning the part of claim #1 above in normal typeface, is clearly prior art, not solely because the applicant has admitted it as prior art, but because it truly is not new. Since the applicant's "admission of prior art" in the Jepson format does not really concede anything, I would not discount this claim due to its format.

Second, the claim is noteworthy because it relates specifically to CDMA, and most particularly to the form of CDMA known as W-CDMA. The beginning of the invention states, in the section "Background of the Invention", at column 1, lines 13–17:

> The present invention is more particularly applicable to mobile radiocommunication systems of CDMA... type. In particular, the present invention is applicable to UMTS....

There are three problems with the quotation above.

1. It says, "the present invention". Why add this limitation? Much better would be to say, "according to some embodiments of the invention..."

2. In general, the patentee should describe the invention only in the Summary or in the Detailed Description, not in the Background section as was done here.

3. Why add any limitation by technical standard? In theory, power control can apply to all air protocols. A sentence should be added to the description, after the quotation above, along the lines of: "Although particularly suited to CDMA, and especially to UMTS, alternative embodiments are applicable also to GSM, cdma2000, OFDMA, and all other wireless air protocols". This sentence should be placed in the Summary

of the Invention, or perhaps in the Detailed Description, but definitely not in the Background section.

Third, the claim is noteworthy because its Point of Novelty, which is the part of the claim above *in italics*, is a clear and simple idea. Further, the PON addresses a general problem. The method in claim #1 is to set a target value for a power level of a transmission, where the level is based on the quality of the signal received by a receiver. The system then monitors the signal quality of the received signal, and increases or decreases the transmission power to approach the desired quality of the received signal. If the desired quality cannot be achieved, that is a sign that the target value of the transmission power may need to be adjusted (up if the received quality is poorer than desired, or down if the received quality is higher than desired).

However, what is to be done when the power control loop does not even approach the targeted signal quality, almost certainly due to some temporary interference or disruption? Claim #1 states that if this is the case, then there is some kind of temporary problem, and the target value will not be increased until the situation is resolved. This is a simple and elegant idea that improves power control for the entire system. It is also essential to implementation of the 3GPP FDD standard, according to the independent experts who judged claim #1 to be an "essential claim" and thereby allowed this patent into the W-CDMA patent pool.

**Validity**: I have no reason to doubt the validity of this patent. To the best of my knowledge, it was not subject to reexamination or litigation. Further, the simple innovation expressed in the italicized portion of claim #1 above, while not groundbreaking, is valuable nevertheless. A simple and small improvement is likely to be valid. The Jepson format here is helpful, because there are no great admissions of prior art, and the claim is very easy to understand.[165]

**Scope**: The scope of the patent is not particularly broad, but what gives this patent value is that it has been judged essential to the W-CDMA standard *by being part of the W-CDMA pool.* To generate value with a single patent having limited scope is not easy. If the patent is asserted in licensing negotiations or in litigation, the alleged infringer might not give it much weight because, after all, there are very many patents that deal with power control, while this particular patent is relatively narrow in scope, and there are likely other patents of greater concern to the infringer. For a patent like this, there are basically two realistic ways to generate value:

(1) Assert the patent as one of a group of patents covering the same standard and owned by the same party. The aggregation of multiple patents may create a "patent thicket" that will capture the infringer's attention. We saw an example of a patent thicket in Chapter 4 with Fuji Photo Film.

(2) Put the patent into a patent pool, as Sharp did here.

**Discoverability of Infringement**: Infringement will not be viewable by the naked eye, but should nevertheless be discoverable by documentation or by inference from the way the system works in the field. I would not expect a serious problem here.

**Summary**: This is an interesting patent, with a small but

165 As one commentator has said, "Jepson claims are... relatively easy for jurors and courts to understand during litigation". Robert D. Fish, *Strategic Patenting, op. cit. at* p.108.

valuable innovation, which can produce significant value when asserted with a group of patents either as part of a package from the patentee or as a package asserted by the administrator of a patent pool.

**Lessons Learned**: I will discuss lessons learned together with the second Sharp patent, below.

### *US 6,549,785: Power control in a mobile system*

*Background:*

US 6,549,785, essential to the implementation of W-CDMA 3GPP FDD standard for third generation wireless systems, is entitled, "Method for Improving the Performance of a Mobile Radiocommunication System Using a Power Control Algorithm". The patent has a priority date of 1999, was issued in 2003, and was assigned initially to Alcatel (now Alcatel-Lucent), later submitted to the W-CDMA patent pool by Sharp.

*Preview:*

This is the second of the two Sharp patents related to power control in a mobile system. The approach in this patent is different from the approach of the first patent. Indeed, the two approaches complement each other technically, and add value to one another when licensed together.

*Review:*

The patent attorneys who reviewed and judged the patents submitted to the W-CDMA patent pool determined that claims 1, 6–8, 11, 13, 33, and 38 are essential to various parts of the 3GPP FDD standard. Let us focus on independent method claim #1.

This patent has strong similarities to US 6,430,398 previously discussed, but there are significant differences as well. Although both were assigned initially to Alcatel, they have different inventors and are not part of a single patent family.

Let's compare the first claims of each patent side-by-side [**boldface** added]:

**Table 6-2: Comparison of Claim #1 in U.S. 6,430,398 and Claim #1 in U.S. 6.549,785**

| US 6,430,398 | US 6,549,785 |
|---|---|
| 1. [Preamble with admitted prior art] A method for improving performances of a mobile radiocommunication system using a **power control loop** which controls power according to a transmission quality target value, and an **adjustment process** for adjusting said transmission quality target value, a method [Jepson improvement] wherein said **adjustment process is controlled based on an assessment of the convergence of said power control loop around said transmission quality target value.** | 1. [Preamble with admitted prior art] A method for improving performances of a mobile radiocommunication system using a **power control algorithm** for controlling a transmit power according to a transmission quality target value, and an **adjustment algorithm** for adjusting said transmission quality target value **according to transmission requirements**, said method including, [Jepson improvement] upon the occurrence of **a change in said transmission requirements,** applying a corresponding change to said transmission quality target value, so as to **adjust it in an anticipated way**, said adjustment in an anticipated way **corresponding to adjustment based on a fixed criteria in addition to said adjustment algorithm.** |

The similarities between these two claims are obvious.

Both are method claims in Jepson format. Both seek to deal with power control in CDMA systems, specifically W-CDMA systems. Each patent has the same third paragraph in its Background of the Invention, which states that the "present invention is in particular applicable to mobile radiotelecommuncation systems of CDMA…type. In particular, the present invention is applicable to UMTS…" (US 6,430,398 at column 1, lines 13–17, and US 6,549,785, at column 1, lines 15–19.)

However, despite these similarities, there are clear differences between the two claims quoted above, as indicated in the boldfaced words. In particular:

1. US 6,430,398 deals with the specific problem where power convergence on a target value is not possible due to a temporary situation. One example given is that the transmitter is already operating at maximum power, which cannot be increased. A second example given is that the system is already overloaded, so signal quality cannot be increased, and an increase in transmission power would just add more interference. The solution proposed is *not* to increase the target value when power convergence has not occurred. This solution recognizes that there is a temporary interference that needs to be resolved before the power convergence method is applied.

2. By contrast, US 6,549,785 does not cause a change in the power loop nor suspend application of the adjustment process in the target value. Rather, *it does the opposite by temporarily speeding up adjustment of the target value*. This patent notes temporary circumstances which may occur and which would require this action.

I understand that these last two paragraphs may be technically difficult, so let me summarize succinctly. The first patent,

US 6,430,398, suspends temporarily the process of adjusting the "transmission quality target value" because there is some temporary interference problem which prevents application of the process. The second patent, US 6,549,785, does not suspend the adjustment process, but rather supplements the process with an additional change to make the adjustment process faster, to meet higher data needs. In short, the first patent *suspends the process*, whereas the second patent *accelerates the process*. Although these are approximately opposite methods, they both achieve small improvements in power control.[166]

It may seem surprising or contradictory that two diametrically opposed approaches can both contribute to the goal of improved communication, but this is indeed one way that creativity can occur in technology development and in patent generation. If a problem can be solved by performing X, one may ask, "What would happen if we did the exact opposite of X?" Here, performing X solves one problem of power control (that is, the existence of temporary interruptions), while performing "anti-X" solves a different problem of power control (that is, the need to hasten the adjustment process due to rapidly changing but temporary data requirements). Putting these two patents together creates unique value, providing complementary solutions to related but slightly different power control problems.

Both patents include structure claims as well as method claims. However, in both cases the structure claims are based for the most part on the method claims. It is advantageous,

---

166 In US 6,549,785 it is probably considered possible to either speed up or slow down the adjustment process, but the examples noted in the patent all apply to speeding up a continuing process rather than slowing it down.

and increases value, for a patent to achieve "claim diversity" with both method and structure claims.

**Validity**: I see no obvious problem with validity of claims.

**Scope**: As with the earlier patent, claim scope is relatively narrow, dealing with only one specific problem of power control. However, this patent, like the earlier one, correctly includes both method and structure claims, increasing its overall scope.

**Discoverability of Infringement**: For the same reasons noted in the earlier Sharp patent, there appears to be no particular problem with discoverability of infringement.

**Summary**: This is another interesting patent with a small but valuable innovation which produces significant value, especially when asserted with a group of patents either as part of a package from the patent owner or by the administrator of a patent pool. The fact that this patent creates value by doing approximately the opposite of what was done in US 6,430,398 makes it a particularly intriguing case.

**Lessons Learned**: Here are some lessons we can learn about "good patents" from the two Sharp examples, claim #1 of US 6,430,398, and claim #1 of US 6,549,785.

6–2–1. ***In some cases, a Jepson claim works well.*** A Jepson claim is a claim in which the preamble recites prior art, and the body of the claim describes "an improvement" to the prior art. Although this style of claim is common among European companies such as Alcatel and Siemens, it tends to be disfavored by American companies out of concern that the admissions in the claim preamble will unduly restrict the scope of the patent. The concern is not unreasonable, and is indeed well-founded in some cases. In other cases, such as in the Sharp patents, Jepson claims work well. We have two such examples here of good patent claims in the Jepson format.

6–2–2. ***References in a patent to a technical standard can be good or bad.*** In the Philips case discussed above, reference to the company-specific standard, CDI, was very restrictive, since the reference could limit the patent to a narrow standard that died in the market place. Both Sharp patents here make reference to CDMA technologies, and indicate that the inventions are suited particularly to such technologies. But unlike Philips' failed CDI format, CDMA technologies are currently the most widely adopted cellular standards in the world, including most major cellular systems (with the exception of GSM systems, which are TDMA based). In this case, the reference helped define the focus of the invention, without greatly diminishing the patent's value.

6–2–3. ***To write good patent claims, think creatively***. In this pair of Sharp patents, one patent solves a power problem by doing X, while the other patent solves a similar problem by doing "anti-X". Both approaches, although apparently contradictory, nevertheless contribute to improved system performance, especially when used together. "Out of the box" contrarian thinking can add value.[167]

6–2–4. ***Don't add unnecessary limitations.*** Patents should not say, "in this invention" or "in the present invention". This kind of language occurs not infrequently, and may be used by

---

167 It is of course true that patents follow inventions, not vice versa. However, the particular technique evidenced in the Sharp patents, that is, using both X and anti-X as two solutions to a single problem, is a technique for creative thinking that applies both to the development of innovative technology and to the drafting of patents to protect technology.

a court to limit the scope of a patent. Say instead: "in some embodiments of the current invention" or, even better, "in some alternative embodiments". These alternative phrasings achieve the same goals without limiting claim coverage.

## *US 6,885,875: Regulating power in a mobile system*

### *Background:*

US 6,885,875, essential to the implementation of the W-CDMA 3GPP FDD standard for third generation wireless systems, is entitled, "Method and Radiocommunication System for Regulating Power Between a Base Station and a Subscriber Station Using a Power Control Algorithm". The patent has a priority date of 1998, was issued in 2005, and was assigned initially to the German company Siemens Aktiengesellschaft. Only claim #25 was evaluated and found essential.

### *Preview:*

There should be only one Point of Novelty (PON) in an independent claim. That seemed to be true in claim #25. However, a surprising thing happened during prosecution of the application. Although the applicant thought the PON was in element number [2] of the claim, the examiner at the PTO presented prior art which showed that element [2] was not new, and the examiner allowed the claim because of a PON in element number [4]. When this shift happened, one of the terms in element [4] became critical to understanding the scope of the entire claim. Unfortunately, this term, which formerly seemed not important but suddenly become a key claim term, is not clearly defined or otherwise explained anywhere in the patent. In fact, depending on how this term is interpreted, the scope of claim #25 may be (1) almost worthless, or (2) moderately reasonable, or (3) extremely broad. As with the Philips case cited above, uncertainty of claim coverage may have contributed to the patent owner's decision to put the patent in a pool.

*Review:*

The only claim found essential to the technical standard by the independent experts is claim #25, which reads as follows, with parsing in brackets [ ] by me:

> [Preamble] A method of controlling power in a radio communication system having a radio interface, comprising:
> [1] receiving a transmission from a second radio station at a first radio station;
> [2] determining a transmission power correction instruction that corresponds to a transmission power of the second radio station, the transmission power correction instruction corresponding to a variable power adjustment increment, the variable power adjustment increment being adjustable in a subscriber-dependent manner and a time-dependent manner; and
> [3] transmitting the transmission power correction instruction to the second radio station during a transmission of the first radio station;
> [4] wherein the variable power adjustment increment is temporarily increased after an end of an interrupt of transmission between the first radio station and the second radio station. [Brackets [ ] added to identify claim elements.]

What is the problem that claim #25 comes to solve? As

described above, the problem is that changes in transmission power levels, which are important factors in a CDMA system, occur in pre-defined, or what the patent calls "static," steps. Pre-defined changes are sometimes not the best ones, however. This invention, as described in the Summary section, column 2, is to allow variable increments of power which are "subscriber-dependent" and "time-dependent" rather than "static" or "pre-defined". That is the Point of Novelty, as described by the patentee, who says explicitly that variable increments are in "contrast to the prior art". This PON appears in element [2] of claim #25.

After explaining the PON, the patent goes on to present "an advantageous further development of the invention", which is that the "transmission condition" of the radio environment is measured repetitively and, based on this changing condition, power is incrementally changed. By this invention, power change may be "variable", not "static", so the invention allows better power control when the transmission condition changes.

During prosecution, some surprising things happened with claim #25. First, the examiner rejected claim #25, finding one U.S. patent including claim elements 1–3, and a second U.S. patent, 6,337,988, owned by Alcatel, including element 4 of claim #25. The examiner determined that it would have been obvious to combine the teachings of these two patents, and hence claim #25 was deemed "obvious" and thus not allowable.

At this point, claim #25 in US 6,885,875, might have died, because the two U.S. patents cited by the examiner seem to include all of the elements of claim #25. However, although the United States patent application for US 6,885,875 was filed at the PTO on April 2, 2001, its priority date is based on an original application at the German patent office, in the German language, filed on October 9, 1998. By contrast, the Alcatel patent used to knock out element [4] of claim #25 had a priority date of April 12, 1999. That is to say, the priority date of the Alcatel patent is two years before the Siemens patent was filed in the U.S. (hence, claim #25 and many other claims of the Siemens patent would be invalidated), *but six months after the German language application at the German patent office*. Siemens then translated the German application into English, and showed that element [4] of claim #25 had been filed in October, 1998, *six months before the Alcatel patent*. As a result, the United States patent examiner "withdrew" the Alcatel patent as prior art, meaning that the Alcatel patent no longer applied to the Siemens application. Therefore, claim #25 was allowed, specifically because no prior art remained against element [4].

The patent applicant did a good job rescuing claim #25 from oblivion, but look what happened in the process. Although Siemens thought that the PON was in element [2], which is variable power adjustments, the claim was allowed only because the PON became element [4], which reads, "the variable power adjustment is temporarily increased after the end of an interrupt of transmission between the first radio station and the second radio station".

So the value of claim #25 became dependent on the answer to the question, "What is an 'interrupt of transmission'?" Unfortunately, this claim term is *never defined in the patent*. In fact, the word "interrupt" appears *only one time*, in element [4] of claim #25. That does not help define what has now become the patent's only key claim term.

Variants of "interrupt" appear in the patent. For example, the word "interrupted" appears one time, in column 2, line 42, where it is said, "the control loop is interrupted for a certain time...." Also, the word "interruption" appears several times in a discussion of what is called "slotted mode transmission", which means, in essence, that when a mobile conversation is handed off from one base station to a different base station, there is a break or "interruption" in the transmission. This is also known as a "hard handover," in contrast to a "soft handover" in which there is no interruption.

"Interrupt" itself is not defined anywhere in the patent.

There are three different possibilities for what the term "interrupt" means, with massive consequences for the scope of claim #25. Here are the possibilities:

(1) First possibility: "Interrupt" element [4] applies only to the "interruption" condition listed for slotted mode, which might limit the claim to systems that have "hard handover" of communication from one base station to a second base station. Unfortunately, hard handover is a much poorer quality of communication than soft handover, because with hard handover there is a physical break of communication. W-CDMA systems use soft handover, and that is one advantage of W-CDMA systems. If claim #25 is limited to only "hard handover", then the claim might not include W-CDMA systems, and therefore the scope of the claim would be very narrow.

(2) Second possibility: "Temporary increase" in power level adjustment appears only in element [4], not in the rest of claim #25. So perhaps element [4] can apply to every transmission parameter where the change in power level is "temporary". The patent discusses three such cases. These are

slotted mode hard handover, column 4, line 33, "fast fading" caused by a rapidly moving mobile station, column 5, line 24, and "soft handover", column 5, line 65. In each case, the power adjustment is "temporarily increased", so a court might rule in a Markman hearing that "interrupt" includes all three cases, and not solely "slotted mode hard handover". This would be much better than the first possibility, and would give reasonable scope of coverage to claim #25.

(3) Third possibility: Seven "transmission condition parameters" are listed in column 2 of the patent, including all three of the parameters noted above, plus four other parameters (such as the number of antennas in operation, the balance between downlink and uplink communication, and others). A court might conclude that any of these seven parameters could be "interrupts", so they might all be included within the scope of claim #25. Such an interpretation of the key claim term "interrupt" would give claim #25 a very broad scope of coverage.

To the best of my knowledge, this patent was never reexamined or litigated. I don't know how a court would rule on scope of coverage. I suppose that the patent lawyers who reviewed claim #25 for the W-CDMA patent pool either decided, or at least assumed, that the scope of this claim is either the second or the third possibility, because if claim #25 had been judged to be the first possibility only, this patent would not have been admitted into the patent pool. In the end, only a court can decide, but the confusion might have been avoided if the key term "interrupt" had been clarified in the patent (a) by definition, (b) by examples, or (c) by illustration in a figure.

**Validity**: There was a serious validity challenge at the PTO, but it was overcome by translating and presenting the German patent office application which provided an early priority date for 6,885,875. Beyond that, I see no problem with validity to the allowed claim #25.

**Scope**: This is the whole difficulty. There are three possibilities, which we could summarize as (1) so narrow as to be of limited value, (2) reasonably useful, and (3) very broad. The key claim term that would determine the scope of claim is the word "interrupt" in element [4] of claim #24, but the patent does not explain this term, and I do not know how a court would interpret that word.

**Discoverability of Infringement**: Infringement should be reasonably discoverable by publicly available product literature or by inference from operation of the system.

**Summary**: This is a good Siemens patent that was almost killed by an earlier Alcatel patent, but saved when Siemens presented to the PTO the English translation of the original German application on which the U.S. patent depends. However, when the patent was saved, the PON shifted from what Siemens thought it was, variable power adjustment, to "temporary increase of power adjustment" in specific cases. This change had two effects. First, it narrowed the scope of the patent generally. Second, it suddenly attached great importance to the claim term "interrupt". The term "interrupt", and its variant forms "interrupted" and "interrupted", are used but not defined in the patent. The effect of no clear definition of a key term is to blur the scope of the claims, and hence reduce the patent's value.

**Lessons Learned**: Here are some lessons we might learn

about good patents from claim #25 of Siemens' U.S. patent 6,885,875:

6–3–1. ***What you think is the Point of Novelty of your patent may not be what the PTO or a court thinks.*** You do not decide what makes your patent novel. That is decided by other people, first by the patent office, and perhaps later by a court. Certainly you may guess about what is new and argue your case, but you cannot be sure. Here, the PON allowed by the patent examiner was different than what Siemens described. Had Siemens understood what would become the PON, it would likely have removed the source of confusion by explaining the term "interrupt" though a definition, examples, or invention element in one of the figures.

6–3–2. ***A claim should have only one Point of Novelty.*** If Siemens thought that the PON for claim #25 was in element [2], why did it write element [4] into the claim? Rather, it should have written the first three elements into claim #25, then added element [4] in a dependent claim. This is not a legalistic triviality. The claim as written, with elements 1–4, is much narrower than a claim with only elements 1–3. If you think that a certain element is the PON, put any other innovation into an entirely separate claim. That gives you the best possible scope for your claims, and facilitates a "good" patent. Identify the one and only one PON in each independent claim.

6–3–3. ***A single undefined claim term can undermine an entire patent.*** The lack of a definition for "interrupt" significantly damages the measurability of this patent's scope.[168]

168 It might be argued that the definition of "interrupt" is critical whether the PON is in element [4] or in element [2], since in either case the term can limit the scope of claim #25. This is a reasonable argument, but I would

6–3–4. ***Use consistent terminology.*** Claim #25 uses the word "interrupt" and no other variation. The written description does not use that word, but instead uses "interrupted" and "interruption". Claim #25 would be stronger if only one word, whether "interrupt" or "interruption", had been used in claim #25 and the written description. Shifting terminology between a claim and the written description will weaken the claim.

6–3–5. ***In a Jepson claim, place in the preamble only prior art.*** Claim #25 in US 6,888,875 illustrates the potential problem with a Jepson claim, specifically because claim #25 was *not* a Jepson claim. If it were, the preamble would have included elements [1], [3], and [4], since the applicant considered element [2] to be the Point of Novelty, a Jepson claim includes only one PON: the "improvement to the existing art" and all other elements of the claim go into the preamble as "admitted prior art". If that had happened, [4] could not have become a PON during prosecution, since the applicant would have previously admitted [4] to be prior art. Therefore, if the claim had been in Jepson format, with elements [1], [3], and [4] in the preamble and [2] as the PON, when the examiner rejected element [2], claim #25 would have fallen. The great

respond to it as follows: (1) The argument simply reinforces the prior lesson that element [4] should have been introduced in a dependent claim, and should not have been part of claim #1. (2) Had Siemens understood that the innovation was in [4], it probably would not have permitted this lack of clarity to arise. (3) Even if the argument is correct in theory, in practice the review of "interrupt" is likely to be more severe when it is understood that this term represents the novelty in the claim rather than a mere description of a prior art function.

risk of the Jepson format is that all elements in the preamble are *presumed* to be prior art.[169]

The two great advantages of the Jepson claim are: (1) it ensures that only one PON is in an independent claim, which is correct claim drafting, and (2) it focuses all attention on the one element considered by the applicant to be the PON. This is probably the reason that Jepson claims are easy for juries and judges to understand. The great disadvantage of the Jepson format is that everything must go into the preamble except the one PON, and everything in the preamble is, by definition of this claim format, prior art by the applicant's own admission. For that reason, Americans tend not to use the Jepson claim. *However, there is nothing inherently wrong with the Jepson format, as long as you are certain that the elements in the preamble are truly prior art and not part of the invention.*

**Lessons Learned from the group of Sharp's US 6,430,398, Sharp's US 6,549,785, and Siemens' US 6,885,875:**

6-General-1. ***A general problem (such as power control) may be broken down to smaller problems***. Each such smaller problem may be the subject of its own Point of Novelty, and each such PON may be covered in a separate patent (or in different independent claims within one patent).

6-General-2. ***Small innovations are important, particularly if they are deemed essential to a technical standard***. If you can cover, in one patent or in a group of related patents,

---

169 These are the consequences of placing material in the preamble of a Jepson claim. This applies, however, only for U.S. patents. As explained in Chapter 1, the corresponding patent in Europe is called a "two-part form". In a two-part European patent claim, the material in the preamble is not considered to be an irrevocable admission of prior art by the patent applicant, unlike the irrevocable admission in a U.S. Jepson claim.

multiple approaches to the same problem, this diversity strengthens your claims and the value of your intellectual property.

6-General-3. ***Generally, the value of small innovations may be maximized by licensing or litigating the innovations as a package.*** A patent pool does this by offering a group license to many patents (or by suing for infringement of multiple patents, if the suspected infringer refuses to take a license).

All innovations in these three patents focus on the same problem: power control in CDMA cellular systems. Although these innovations represent real contributions, they are small and gradual improvements rather than breakthroughs, which are difficult for a patentee to license or litigate in isolation. These incremental innovations properly belong as part of a package, such as that offered by a patent pool.

6-General-4. ***A private package is possible with a strong portfolio.*** If a single company has a strong portfolio of patents focused on a specific technology — including a significant number of patents with incremental innovation and at least a few patents with high value — then the company may license the collection of incremental innovations as a private package. These incremental innovations, such as the inventions presented in the last three patents considered, would add value to such a portfolio and would receive additional value from being part of a portfolio.

## Chapter 7

# Seminal Patents

After a patent is issued, it may receive citations in later patents. These citations are called "forward citations". If the forward citation is from a patent that is owned by the same entity that also owned the cited patent, the forward citation is called a "forward *self*-citation". If the cited and citing patents have different owners, then the citation is called a "forward *non-self* citation".

Most patents generate a few forward citations over their lifetimes. Some generate dozens. A few patents, however, generate very large numbers of forward citations. A large number of forward citations is a characteristic of what I call "seminal patents", the subject of this chapter. The four characteristics of a "seminal patent" are: (1) early priority date for the technology; (2) many forward citations; (3) important technology; and (4) significant market. These characteristics will be discussed in the text. Strong forward citations alone are not sufficient to define a "seminal patent." However, they are sufficient in themselves to cause an evaluator to examine the patent in detail to determine if it is indeed a "seminal patent".

The purpose of this chapter is to explain why forward non-self citations have been selected as a gateway factor in this book, to explain why such citations may or may not indicate patent quality and value, to compare such citations to other factors not selected as gateways factors, and to seek to understand how "seminal patents" contribute to the idea of patent value.

We will consider four patents, each with hundreds of forward non-self citations. Although Chapter 7 completes our review of good patents, this chapter is somewhat different from earlier parts of this book. Each of Chapters 3 (patents winning in court), 4 (patents winning at the ITC), 5 (patents sold), and 6 (patents accepted into a patent pool), includes discussions ending with "Lessons Learned" by each patent. By contrast, Chapter 7 includes, in addition to "Lessons Learned" for individual patents, discussions of the patent portfolios of various companies and "Lessons Learned" for patent portfolios (that is, lessons for patent portfolios in addition to lessons learned for individual patents). In other words, whereas Chapters 3–6 addressed the question, "How do I know if my patent's any good?", this Chapter 7 discusses both that question and also the question, "How do I know if my patent *portfolio's* any good?"

Here is the organization of Chapter 7:

I. The Significance of Forward Non-Self Citations
   (1) Why might forward non-self citations be useful indicators of patent value?
   (2) Why might forward non-self citations *not* be useful indicators of patent value?
   (3) What role do forward non-self citations play in seminal patents?
   (4) Why are forward non-self citations different from other factors in proxy fundamental analysis?

II. Three Cases of Companies with Seminal Patents

(1) Check Point Software Technologies (2 patents): US 5,606,668 and US 5,835,726
(2) Scientific Atlanta/Silanis Technology (1 patent): US 5,606,609
(3) Qualcomm (1 patent): US 5,414,796

For each case, I will introduce the company, the technology, and the patent. I will explain why this is a "seminal patent". I will then analyze one or more claims from each patent, and conclude with "lessons learned" for both individual patents and for portfolios of patents.[170]

## I. Significance of Forward Non-Self Citations

Our examination of seminal patents may be introduced by discussing questions which consider the suitability of this factor relative to others typically used in proxy fundamental analysis.

*(1) Why might forward non-self citations be useful indicators of patent value?*

If a patentee or patent examiner makes a non-self citation

---

170 Is it worthwhile to view a "portfolio" as somehow different than individual patents in the portfolio? The "patent portfolio theory" is a concept championed by Gideon Parchomovsky and R. Polk Wagner of the U. of Pennsylvania Law School, who wrote an article entitled, "Patent Portfolios", *University of Pennsylvania Law Review*, Vol. 154, No. 1, pp.1–77 (2005), in which they said, "the true value of patents lies not in their individual worth, but in their aggregation into a collection of related patents — a patent portfolio", at p.1, and also at pp.5–6, 51, 53, and 77. Why? For two reasons, according to the professors, which are "scale" at pp.32–37 (meaning, roughly, intensive, in-depth patenting of multiple aspects of the same topic) and "diversity" at pp.37–42 (meaning, roughly, broad patenting of the particular topic and of topics allied to the main topic, designed to cover changes in technology, market, and most especially in the patent law). See also the discussion of US 5,623,600, Lesson 4-2-4, in Chapter 4.

to an earlier patent[171], that is a sure sign that the citing party finds the earlier patent "interesting and relevant" to the technology discussed in the citing patent. For example, let's assume a particular patent issued to Cisco Systems makes a citation back to hypothetical US A,BCD,EFG, issued to IBM. For hypothetical US A,BCD,EFG, this is a forward citation from Cisco Systems. The citation means that Cisco Systems finds patent US A,BCD,EFG "interesting and relevant" to the invention described in the later Cisco patent.

The phrase, "interesting and relevant", means just that and no more. It means that the cited patent captured the attention of the citer (was "interesting") and the citer felt that the cited patent was important enough ("relevant") to appear on the face of the citing patent. However, in our hypothetical example, the citation does *not* mean necessarily that Cisco thinks the claims in US A,BCD,EFG are valid (the V in VSD), or broad in scope (the S in VSD), or easy to discover in infringing products and methods (the D in VSD). In short, the forward citation by Cisco does *not* mean necessarily that Cisco thinks US A,BCD,EFG has value in the market or is a "good patent".[172]

---

171 There are actually three kinds of forward citations. There are forward self-citations, which are not relevant for the current discussion. There are forward non-self citations by technology companies and entrepreneurs with new technology, and those are discussed here. There are also forward non-self citations by patent examiners who are examining the later patents. For the purposes of this discussion, "non-self citations" include both those made by companies and entrepreneurs on the one hand, and patent examiners on the other hand. There might or might not be differences between these two kinds of non-self forward citations, but both of them are validations by a third party that the cited patent is interesting and relevant, so both are included here.

172 Under what is called "Rule 56", appearing at Title 37 of the Code of

Still, we are considering a large block of forward non-self citations, not just a single citation from Cisco. If many patents cite back to US A,BCD,EFG, that means that US A,BCD,EFG has many forward citations, far more than the average number of forward citations. The presumption is that if many people are citing back to a patent, then the cited patent is possibly:

1. Early in its priority date for this technology area (because if there were earlier patents in the same field, the earlier patents would be cited rather than US A,BCD,EFG); and also

2. Of general applicability (since so many people are citing to that patent).

*(2) Why might forward non-self citations **not** be useful indicators of patent value?*

A high number of forward non-self citations suggests early priority and broad applicability of the cited patent. Such priority and applicability may be indicators of strong objective quality in the cited patent, but they are *not determinative*, for two main reasons:

First, they relate to the entire disclosure of the cited patent, that is to say, they relate to everything in the cited patent, rather than to the claims specifically. Patent citations, whether

---

Federal Regulations, section 1.56, a patent applicant has a duty to disclose to the patent office "all information material to patentability" of the applicant's invention. This is sometimes called the "materiality" duty of disclosure, but it is *not* what we mean when we say that a forward citation suggests that an earlier patent is "interesting and relevant". The earlier patent might indeed affect the patentability of the later invention, in which case the earlier patent would indeed be "material". However, the earlier patent may also be cited because it is interesting background material, or because it is specific prior art on which the new invention is based, or for other reasons that make the forward citation appropriate but which do not make the cited patent "material" to patentability of the new invention. In other words, the group of "interesting and relevant" patents includes, and is broader than, the group of "material" patents.

forward or backward, are to an entire patent, not to any one section of the cited patent. That makes sense, because the citation, whether forward or backward, is looking at the entire earlier patent as interesting and relevant prior art. All parts of the earlier patent are prior art for later patents, not just the claims, and it cannot be known for certain if the forward citation was made for the claims or for some part of the written description.

Second, even if it could be proven, or reasonably inferred, that a forward citation relates specifically to the claims of the earlier patent, that would relate only to the subject of the claims, not to the quality of the claims and certainly not to their financial value. A citation to the claims of the earlier patents means that the earlier patents are of interest and relevance in the building of the new technology in the later patent. It is not a statement that the claims in the earlier patent are valid (V), or broad in scope (S) , or easy to discover in infringing products and methods (D).

*(3) What role do forward non-self citations play in seminal patents?*

A seminal patent is one that represents a kind of "breakthrough" in the technology area of the patent. We could also consider this patent "fundamental" in the sense that later technology, and later patents, build on a seminal patent.

For a patent to be seminal, it must fulfill several requirements. First, it must be an early patent in its technical field — if not, then earlier patents are likely to be the seminal patents in that field. Second, the patent must address a major technical problem, and provide a solution to that problem. Patents with incremental solutions were presented in Chapter 6, but seminal patents, presented in this chapter, are the opposite of incremental — they tend to define a field of technical work. They are "game-changers." Third, the coverage of the patent, as represented by the scope of its claims, must be broad enough to cover many players in a large market. If the claims are limited or defective in some way, the patent cannot be seminal. If the market is small, the patent cannot be seminal.

A large number of forward citations is not, strictly speaking, a requirement for a patent to be seminal, but I have nevertheless added it as a requirement for purposes of this book. The reason is that patents that have strong interest and relevance to an industry, which are those that have hundreds of forward non-self citations, are much more likely to be seminal than patents that have only a handful of such citations. This is not to deny that patents with few forward citations may be seminal, and it certainly does not mean that every patent with hundreds of forward citations is seminal. Nevertheless, hundreds of forward non-self citations are a strong indication that the patent might have value, and that the patent might justify the time and expense of an expert fundamental analysis. I have therefore added strong forward citations as a fourth requirement of a "seminal patent", for the purposes of review in this book. These citations act as a gateway, similar to the gateways in Chapters 3 and 4 (litigation victory in federal court and the ITC, respectively), Chapter 5 (sale), and Chapter 6 (membership in a patent pool).

*(4) Why are forward non-self citations different from other factors in proxy fundamental analysis?*

Given these basic arguments for and against forward non-self citations, why are such citations different from the other PFA factors listed in Chapter 2? There are three reasons: (a) logic, (b) control, and (c) argumentation. Let's consider these reasons:

*a. Logic as a reason to differentiate forward non-self citations from other PFA factors.*

It makes sense that if a patent is reviewed and cited heavily by other technology companies, by entrepreneurs in their own patents, or by patent examiners reviewing later applications, there is probably something interesting, relevant, *and also valuable* in the patent. That is not necessarily true, but it is likely. Some of the specific forward citations might not suggest claim quality or patent value, but remember that we are discussing patents with hundreds of forward non-self citations, compared to an average patent which receives no more than a handful of forward citations throughout its entire life, if any.[173] Of the hundreds of forward non-self citations, some

173 Every patent discussed in this chapter has at least 200 forward non-self citations. This number is much greater than the number of citations received by a typical patent. A report was published recently by the prestigious Brookings Institution, entitled Patenting Prosperity: Invention and Economic Performance in the United States and its Metropolitan Areas, February, 2013, available at http://www.brookings.edu/~/media/Research/Files/Reports/2013/02/patenting%20prosperity%20rothwell/patenting%20prosperity%20rothwell.pdf. Table 2 at page 9 of this report shows that the average number of forward citations for a patent within eight years of the patent's issuance was 9.8 forward citations for patents filed within the period 1991–1995. Table 2 also presents statistics by technology areas — among the ten top technology areas for numbers of patents, the highest average number of forward citations was 18.9 for computer software. Every patent discussed in this Chapter 7 has more than 200 forward non-self citations. It is true that the numbers of citations for the four patents discussed in Chapter 7 are not restricted to eight years from the time of patent issuance. However, for each of these four patents, most of the forward citations, meaning well above 100, were made within the first eight years after issuance. The four patents discussed in Chapter 7 have many more forward citations than the average number received by all U.S. patents, and many more than the numbers received by patents in technology areas such as communications,

are likely to refer only to the technology in the patent, or perhaps to various definitions or other formal aspects of the cited patent. However, it is likely that at least some of these citations mean, "This is a patent which contributed significantly to the invention described in the citing patent."

This implication of value in the cited patent is an implication only, not a certainty, but it is strongly suggested by the fact that there are hundreds of such citations.[174]

*b. Control as a reason to differentiate forward non-self citations from other PFA factors.*

Various PFA factors were defined in Chapter 2. Let's call up these factors again, but organized in a new way.

---

software, semiconductors, computers, and other areas reported in Table 2 of the Brookings report.

174 I find only three articles that downplay the value of forward citation analysis. These articles are (1) James E. Bessen, "The Value of U.S. Patents by Owner and Patent Characteristics", *Boston University School of Law Working Paper no. 06–46*, (2006), (2) Alfonso Gambardella, Paola Giuri, and Myriam Mariani, with the assistance of Serena Giovannoni, Alessandra Luzzi, Laura Magazzini, Luisa Martolini, and Marzia Romanelli "The Value of European Patents: Evidence from a Survey of European Inventors: Final Report of the PatVal EU Project", (2005), and (3) Alfonso Gambardella, Dietmar Harhoff, and Bart Verspagen, "The Value of European Patents", *European Management Review*, Vol. 5, pp.69–84, (2008). Article (3) is an EU report that accompanies the survey presented in article (2). All of these three articles say essentially the same thing — forward citation analysis *does help explain patent value*, but explains a relatively small amount of patent value, because, as Professor Bessen says, "Patent citation statistics may be more meaningful as measures of the value of the underlying technology [rather than of the patent]", Bessen, *op. cit.* at p.23, and because, in the EU articles, there is "noise" in the forward citation statistics, which means that the true significance of a forward citation is not always clear, in the opinion of the authors of the EU articles.

**Table 7–1: PFA Factors Classified by Control of Factors[175]**

| **Pre-Issuance PFA Factors:** ***Solely within the patentee's control*** | **Post-Issuance PFA Factors:** ***Solely within the patentee's control*** | **Post-Issuance PFA Factors:** ***Joint Control — patentee and third parties*** | **Post-Issuance PFA Factors:** ***Solely within the control of third parties*** |
|---|---|---|---|
| 1. Number of claims in the patent.<br>2. Number of items in the patent family.<br>3. Length of prosecution at the PTO.<br>4. Number of backward citations.<br>5. Technology area of the patent. | 6. Certificate of correction.<br>7. Payment of maintenance fees.<br>8. Number of forward self-citations. | 9. Ownership transfer from patentee to third party (typically by sale to a third party).<br>10. Patent is reexamined at the PTO.<br>11. Patent is "collateralized".<br>12. Patent is licensed-out.<br>13. Patent is litigated.<br>14. Patent has been placed in a pool. | 15. Number of forward non-self citations. |

Of the many factors cited in the literature of scholars and commentators, *forward non-self citations are the only factor that is wholly beyond the control of the patent owner*. In other words, this factor is the only one that is solely within the control of independent third parties. All the other factors in Table

175 The concept of dividing the factors between pre-issuance and post-issuance is taken from Colleen V. Chien, "Predicting Patent Litigation", Texas Law Review, vol. 90, pp.283–328 (2011). I am indebted to Professor Chien for this insight. I have added to her division the concept of "control", for which I am solely responsible.

7–1 include the involvement of the patent owner to some degree, and to that extent, such factors may be measures of Subjective Patent Value (that is, from the patentee's perspective). However, we are seeking measures of Objective Patent Value, and for that purpose, the appropriate determiner of value would seem to be independent third parties, not the patent owner.

*c. Argumentation as a reason to differentiate forward non-self citations from other PFA factors*

Most of the factors in Table 7–1 can be argued either way. That is, one could argue that the presence of the factor suggests patent strength, but one could also argue that the presence of the factor suggests weakness. That applies for factors 1 (number of claims), 2 (size of patent family), 3 (length of prosecution), 4 (backward citations), 5 (technology area), 6 (certificate of correction), 8 (forward self-citations), 10 (reexamination), and 13 (litigation). Not only can arguments can be made either way, but in fact various commentators have taken opposing positions on these factors.

This is a complicated topic, the material is voluminous, and PFA is not the focus of this book. For those reasons, I will not now enter into all the arguments about the meaning of the various PFA factors. However, I will present here a brief explanation of two factors often emphasized in PFA, which are factor 13, the tendency of a patent to be litigated, and factor 7, the likelihood a patent will be maintained over its legal life.

First, factor 13. Anyone who wants to understand PFA should read two articles, both authored by Professor John R. Allison, Professor Mark A. Lemley, and the CEO of Lex Machina, Inc., Mr. Joshua Walker. The first article is, "Extreme

Value or Trolls on Top? The Characteristics of the Most-Litigated Patents", in *University of Pennsylvania Law Review*, Vol. 158, No.1, pp.101–137, (December, 2009). The authors, basing themselves on extensive prior research, suggest that the most valuable patents are those which are most litigated. They present various characteristics of the most-litigated patents. The second article is "Patent Quality and Settlement Among Repeat Patent Litigants", *Georgetown Law Review*, Vol. 99, pp.677–712, (2011). In this second article, the authors report their findings that, in opposition to the first article and contrary to their expectations, the most litigated patents are the patents most likely to lose at trial. In the Conclusion of the second article, the authors write:

> [W]hat we found was dramatic and unexpected. The patents and patentees that occupy the most time and attention in court... — the very patents that economists consider the most valuable — are astonishingly weak. Nonpracticing entities and software patentees almost never win their cases. *Ibid.* at 712.

Just before the Conclusion of this article, there is a paragraph entitled, "Do We Understand Patent Value?" If you wish to understand PFA analysis, read this paragraph very carefully.

> Whatever the explanation for the poor performance of the most-litigated patents, such performance calls into question the evidence economists have long relied upon to demonstrate patent value. The connection between patent claims, forward citations, backward citations, and application family size...and the value of patents...is well-established in the economic literature...The fact [is]

> that... the very patents that by every economic measure are the most valuable ones turn out to be much weaker than other litigated patents... [T]he voluminous literature that measures the value of patents based on these characteristics, and the value of innovation based on the number of patents that have those characteristics, stands on rather shakier ground than previously thought. *Id.* at 711.

Hence, the second article suggests that to assume a correlation between "frequency of litigation" and "patent value" is simply unwarranted. That is not at all the same as, and does not include, *successful* litigation. In my mind, successful litigation is clearly a gateway to a human review and a possible finding of Objective Patent Value, but the evidence in the *Georgetown Law Review* article seems to suggest that "litigation" in general (as opposed to *successful* litigation) is neither a gateway for deeper review nor a legitimate factor for a proxy fundamental analysis.

The quotation from the Georgetown article above does not break out "forward citations" by self-citation or non-self citation. As might be inferred, I would disagree strongly with any suggestion that forward *non-self* citations are either totally irrelevant or suggestive of weak patent value. The opposite is the case, in my opinion.

Second, factor 7. Payment of maintenance fees is perhaps one good measure of Subjective Patent Value, that is, value in the eyes of the patentee. However, it does not establish Objective Patent Value, for two reasons. First, there are many motivations for a patentee paying or not paying fees, and it is impossible to identify Objective Patent Value as the sole reason, or even as the main reason, for payment of maintenance fees. Second, consider that that about 46% of issued patents are maintained through the final fee, but 54% are allowed to lapse without payment of all the fees.[176] More than 8.5 million U.S. patents have been issued. Is it realistic to conclude that we can identify the features of a good patent on the basis of several million patents that have been maintained, or several million that have not been maintained? I am doubtful that that is a realistic approach. A high degree of granularity is required to reach reliable conclusions, and we must be skeptical whether that degree is achieved where each paradigm, that is, the paradigm for renewal and the paradigm for non-renewal, totals millions of possible items.[177]

As to the remaining PFA factors in Table 7–1, I agree that they may be predictors of value. They are not sufficient in themselves to prove value, but they suggest that a fuller analysis may be worth performing. These include factor 9 — transfer of ownership (considered as "sale" in Chapter 5 of this book), factor 11 — collateralization, factor 12 licensed-out to a licensee, and factor 14 membership in a patent pool (considered in Chapter 6 of this book). To these factors I would add also ***successful*** litigation (considered in Chapters 3 and

176 As previously noted, historically perhaps as many as 54% of patents are not maintained to the legal end of their life. The exact percentage is not important for our purposes. The important point is that many patents are maintained to the end of their legal lives, but many are not.

177 I am aware that some of the models based on prediction of tendency to pay fees are based on multiple factors, rather than on a single giant factor called "payment of renewal fees" or "tendency to pay renewal fees". Additional factors can improve a model, but in the end, we are still faced with the fact that an enormous number of patents are renewed, and an equally enormous number are not renewed. There is serious doubt that the specific features of Objective Patent Value can be determined by these models, although these models might be helpful in determining the Subjective Patent Value that the patentee places on its own patent.

4 of this book), which is not at all the same thing as factor 13 "litigation". These are all valid factors, or rather what I have called "gateways" to EFA analysis. Their validity is based on some kind of validation not by the patentee, but rather by an outside party (such as a patent buyer, a lending bank, a licensee, patent pool evaluators, or a court). They are valid also because they all involve money, meaning that the outside party in some way assigns value to the patent which is either monetary or which may be converted into money.

Factors 9 and 11–14 are *superior* to forward non-self citations in that they do involve money, whereas forward non-self citations do not involve money. However, these factors are also *inferior* to forward non-self citations in that (1) only forward non-self citations are completely outside the control of the patentee, (2) forward non-self citations involve multiple companies citing the patent, whereas each of factors 9 and 11–14 involve only a single party acting (buying, lending on, licensing-in, delivering a verdict, or certifying as essential to a technical standard), and (3) there is a high degree of argumentation, and therefore ambiguity, about the objective value of these other factors, whereas the broad consensus of commentary does judge forward non-self citations as positive indicators of objective value, especially with regard to breakthrough or seminal patents.

Obviously, forward non-self citations are just one relevant factor in judging a patent, but this factor is uniquely able to help identify patents which represent game-changing paradigm shifts in a particular technology area. For this reason, strong forward non-self citations are a gateway for the patents presented in this chapter.

## II. Three Companies with Seminal Patents

Four patents are discussed below, two from Check Point Software, one from Scientific Atlanta and Silanis Technology, and one from Qualcomm. Each has hundreds of forward non-self citations, which means that each one has many more such citations than the vast majority of U.S. patents. I have selected these four, rather than others with strong forward citations, because each covers a technology that was very important to an industry at the time the patent was issued. These patents, covering an important technology, with hundreds of forward non-self citations, I call "seminal".

I will review individual seminal patents and conclude with "Lessons Learned" for individual patents. I will also review, in varying details, the patent portfolios of Check Point Software, Scientific Atlanta, Silanis Technology, and Qualcomm, concluding this review with "Lessons Learned for Patent Portfolios".

### *Check Point Software, US 5,606,668 and US 5,835,726*

#### *a. Introduction to Check Point Software Technologies, Ltd.:*

Check Point Software Technologies, Ltd. (called here "Check Point" for short) is a public company (NASDAQ: CHKP) founded in 1993, currently employing about 2,300 people at its international headquarters in Tel Aviv, its U.S. headquarters in Silicon Valley, and various offices around the world. The company provides software and security appliances (that is, a combined hardware and software security system) to confirm the identity of remote users accessing a network, to control access if required, and to block the entry of viruses, worms and other undesirable agents. Its products and services also guard against hacking, identity theft, and spyware. With annual sales of about $1.25 billion, and a profit margin of close to 44%, this company was one of the pioneers, and is currently one of the leading companies in the world, in firewall protection and virtual private networks.

The industry in which Check Point operates is highly competitive, and characterized by intensive technological development. Not surprisingly, the company invests significantly in R&D. Here is a brief snapshot of Check Point's R&D intensity from 2006 to 2012.

**Table 7–2: Financial Summary for Check Point Software[178]**

| | 2006 | 2007 | 2008 | 2009 | 2010 | 2011 | 2012 | CAGR |
|---|---|---|---|---|---|---|---|---|
| **Revenues ($M)** | 575 | 731 | 808 | 924 | 1,098 | 1,247 | 1,343 | 15.2% |
| **R&D ($M)** | 53 | 77 | 87 | 84 | 96 | 103 | 103 | 11.8% |
| **R&D/ Revenues** | 9.2% | 10.5% | 10.7% | 9.0% | 8.7% | 8.2% | 7.7% | |

Since its founding, Check Point has generated the following patents and applications:[179]

---

178 Information in this Table 7–2 comes from Check Point, and is available at http://www.checkpoint.com/corporate/investor-relations/earnings-history/index.html.

179 Data about U.S. patents and patent applications is from the U.S. PTO web site, www.uspto.gov. Information about European, German, Japanese, and International patents and patent applications is from the web site www.freepatentsonline.com. I have used dates of publication for applications and dates of issuance for patents, rather than dates of filing. I have removed duplications where I found them — if a particular application resulted in a patent, the patent will appear in Table 7–3 but not the application. All data was collected on May 22, 2013.

## Table 7–3: Check Point Software's Patent Activity[180]

| | US pats | US apps | EU pats | EU apps | DE pats | JP pats | Int'l apps | Totals |
|---|---|---|---|---|---|---|---|---|
| 1994 | 0 | 0 | 0 | 0 | 0 | 0 | 0 | **0** |
| 1995 | 0 | 0 | 0 | 0 | 0 | 0 | 0 | **0** |
| 1996 | 0 | 0 | 0 | 0 | 0 | 1 | 0 | **1** |
| 1997 | 1 | 0 | 0 | 0 | 0 | 0 | 1 | **2** |
| 1998 | 1 | 0 | 0 | 0 | 0 | 0 | 0 | **1** |
| 1999 | 0 | 0 | 0 | 0 | 0 | 0 | 0 | **0** |
| 2000 | 0 | 0 | 1 | 0 | 1 | 0 | 0 | **2** |
| 2001 | 0 | 0 | 0 | 0 | 0 | 0 | 1 | **1** |
| 2002 | 1 | 0 | 0 | 0 | 0 | 0 | 0 | **1** |
| 2003 | 0 | 1 | 0 | 0 | 0 | 0 | 0 | **1** |
| 2004 | 0 | 0 | 0 | 0 | 0 | 0 | 0 | **0** |
| 2005 | 2 | 2 | 1 | 0 | 0 | 0 | 3 | **8** |
| 2006 | 0 | 2 | 1 | 1 | 2 | 0 | 0 | **6** |
| 2007 | 2 | 3 | 0 | 0 | 0 | 0 | 0 | **5** |
| 2008 | 2 | 1 | 0 | 0 | 0 | 0 | 0 | **3** |
| 2009 | 4 | 1 | 0 | 1 | 0 | 0 | 1 | **7** |
| 2010 | 5 | 7 | 1 | 1 | 1 | 0 | 0 | **15** |
| 2011 | 5 | 1 | 0 | 0 | 0 | 0 | 0 | **6** |

180 In addition to the data in the Table 7–3, there are fifteen more U.S. applications which were filed by Check Point, but which are not listed because they have been allowed as patents, and their inclusion would have caused a double-counting of patent items.

| | US pats | US apps | EU pats | EU apps | DE pats | JP pats | Int'l apps | Totals |
|---|---|---|---|---|---|---|---|---|
| 2012 | 10 | 5 | 0 | 0 | 0 | 0 | 0 | **15** |
| 2013 | 3 | 2 | 0 | 0 | 0 | 0 | 0 | **5** |
| **Totals** | **36*** | **25**** | **4** | **3** | **4** | **1** | **6** | **79** |

(In addition, there is one Canadian patent in 2001, one Korean patent in 2002, one Singaporean patent in 2002, and one Chinese patent in 2003. Adding these four items creates a total portfolio of 83 patents or applications that did not issue as patents.)

* Check Point has been involved in 42 issued U.S. patents. Of these, the company filed and prosecuted 16. The other 26 were gained as assets in companies Check Point acquired in 2004, 2009, and 2010.[181] Of the 26 patents acquired, Check Point apparently prosecuted 20 of them, while 6 patents were filed and prosecuted entirely by others. For the sole purpose of determining portfolio strength, all patents, however acquired or prosecuted, should be included in Table 7–3. For the sole purpose of evaluating investments in patents, patents that were prepared and prosecuted by others should not be included in the Table, irrespective of the relatively minor costs of maintaining an issued patent. Table 7–3 reflects in particular investment in patents, and so does not include the six patents filed and prosecuted entirely by other parties. I have no knowledge as to whether the patent portfolios of these three corporate acquisitions had any bearing on the acquisitions, nor do I know what, if any, part of the purchase prices were allocated to the acquired patents.

**All 25 of the U.S. applications were filed by Check Point, and have not yet resulted in patents. In addition to these, a further 14 were acquired as part of the corporate acquisitions, have not yet resulted in patents, and are mostly quite old (12 of the 14 were filed in 2006 or earlier). The applications listed here include only those filed by Check Point, and not those which were acquired.

Let us summarize all this information in Table 7–4.

---

181 Check Point acquired patents or applications when it bought Zone Labs for $205 million in 2004, the Nokia Security Appliances Division for an unpublished sum in 2009, and the company Liquid Machines for an unpublished sum in 2010.

**Table 7–4: Snapshot of Check Point Software's Patent Portfolio**

| | US pats | US apps | EU pats | EU apps | DE pats | Other pats | Int'l apps | Totals |
|---|---|---|---|---|---|---|---|---|
| **Filed and prosecuted by Check Point** | 16 | 25 | 4 | 3 | 4 | 5 | 6 | **63** |
| **Only prosecuted by Check Point** | 20 | 0 | 0 | 0 | 0 | 0 | 0 | **20** |
| **Filed and prosecuted by others** | 6 | 14 | 0 | 0 | 0 | 0 | 0 | **20** |
| **TOTALS** | **42** | **39** | **4** | **3** | **4** | **5** | **6** | **103** |

In short, it appears, according to my best estimate, that Check Point has filed and prosecuted about 63 patent items, prosecuted another 20, and acquired (but apparently not prosecuted) about 20 more. Also by my estimate, Check Point owns about 55 patents (U.S., European, German, and other), and 48 applications.[182]

182 The numbers in Tables 7–3 and 7–4 for issued U.S. patents assigned to Check Point are almost certainly correct (within a very small margin of error), because all U.S. patents are published after issuance. However, although the number for assigned U.S. patents is probably correct, the overall number, 103 items, is probably low, for several reasons.

1. Most jurisdictions, including those in the table, publish patent applications after eighteen months, but the applications remain secret during those eighteen months, and cannot be reflected in Table 7–3 or Table 7–4.
2. In the U.S., an applicant may request to have its applications unpublished until a patent issues, which may increase the number of filings unknown to the public.
3. There may be pending applications, or even patents, in countries other

What would be the investment to obtain this kind of portfolio? Although I am not privy to Check Point's corporate records, let's make some reasonable assumptions. Let's assume that:

1. To file and obtain a patent in the U.S. costs an average of $20,000, to which we will add another $10,000 for renewal fees and other costs after issuance. Total investment in 36 issued U.S. patents, according to these assumptions, would amount to about $1.08 million. However, Check Point prosecuted but did not file 20 of these 32 patents, so its total cost for these 20 patents is probably about $200,000 less than our estimate.

---

than the U.S., Germany, Japan, Canada, Korea, Singapore, and China. Such items would not be captured in Table 7–3 or Table 7–4.

4. A company is *not* required to file assignments with the PTO, although good patent practice suggests that should be done. As a practical matter, patents that have been financed by a company are generally assigned to that company at the PTO, but this is not legally required. If, contrary to the standard practice, patents and applications of Check Point inventors have not been formally assigned to Check Point, then such patents and applications cannot be captured in a patent search of "Check Point patents and applications", and such items would not appear in Table 7–3 or Table 7–4.

Despite these reasons for possible underestimates, I suggest that the Table 7–3 is probably a relatively accurate depiction of Check Point's patent activity and Table 7–4 is a relatively accurate snapshot of Check Point's patent portfolio, at least in the U.S. Why? The number of issued U.S. patents formally assigned to Check Point is certainly accurate within a very small margin of error. As for pending applications, it is impossible to know the exact number, particularly for the most recent applications, but the numbers through about 2010 are likely accurate. For European and Asian patents and applications, I have presented what I could find with a search of the web sites indicated. There may well be more items in these locations, although given that almost 80% of the patent items in Tables 7–3 and 7–4 are in the U.S., that Check Point has a significant presence in Silicon Valley, and that the U.S. is likely the #1 market in the world for Check Point's technology, it is likely that Tables 7–3 and 7–4 capture the great bulk, albeit not all, of Check Point's patent activity and current portfolio.

Total cost estimated for these 35 U.S. patents is therefore $1,080,000 minus $200,000 = $880,000.[183]

2. Initial cost of a U.S. application is about $10,000–$12,000, with an additional $8,000–$10,000 to prosecute the application to its conclusion. Although obviously not all U.S. patents have been fully prosecuted, let's assume they are (or at least the clear majority are)[184], so the total cost for the 25 U.S. applications filed and prosecuted by Check Point might be estimated at about $500,000.[185]

---

183 I cannot make any allocation of cost to the six patents filed and prosecuted by others, since I do not know if Check Point made any investment in these patents.

184 For present purposes, this is a reasonable assumption. Although it is not simple to determine the allowance rate of U.S. applications, and the allowance rate changes over time, multiple sources suggest a long-term allowance rate of about 50% over the past ten years, and a possibly higher rate in the 1990's. See, for example, PTO's estimate of AVERAGE MONTHLY ALLOWANCE RATE — PPH RATE VS USPTO OVERALL RATE, showing a monthly allowance rate between 40% and 58% in the period October 2009 — September 2011 at www.uspto.gov/about/stratplan/ar/2011/vl_mda02_03_fig6.html.

See also Sean Tu, "Luck/Unluck of the Draw: An Empirical Study of Examiner Allowance Rates", 2012 Stanford Technology Law Review 10, at ¶36, quoting an allowance rate of 54% in 2006, but an average of 66% for the entire period 1993–1999. For present purposes, the exact number is not needed. By definition, applications prosecuted to patent have incurred the full cost of preparing and prosecuting the application, so full costs have been incurred for at least 50% of applications as a whole. As for applications that were abandoned rather than prosecuted to completion, even these incurred the full cost of preparing the application, and they incurred, on average, at least part of the cost of prosecution by responding to Office Actions. Estimates of cost incurred to build a patent portfolio cannot be exact, but they can be sufficiently accurate to give at least a reasonable approximation of costs incurred, which is all that is required for present purposes.

185 There are another 14 applications in the portfolio that were not prepared or filed by Check Point. The company might have invested something in these 14 applications, but I have no knowledge of such investment, and in any case it could not change the basic picture.

3. There are costs for the European patent, but there are no maintenance costs, so let us assume $20,000 per European patent, for a total of $80,000.[186]

4. The cost of preparing and prosecuting a European patent application, whether or not the application is ultimately successful, are likely to approach the cost of obtaining a European patent. At $20,000 per European application, total cost would be $60,000.

5. German, Japanese, Korean, and Chinese patents might cost the same as a U.S. patent, but let's add another $5,000 for translation fees, giving a total cost of $35,000/patent, for a total cost of $245,000 for seven patents. (This may be too high, but let's make the assumption nevertheless.)

6. Costs of an international application, called a "PCT" application, are about the same as simply preparing a U.S. application, except the filing fees are higher. Let's assume an average cost of $15,000 per international application, for a total cost of $90,000.

7. Singapore and Canada patents are likely to cost about the same as the U.S. patents, so let's assume an additional $60,000 for these two items.

---

186 A European patent may be "validated" in individual European countries, and enforced only in countries in which validation has occurred. There will be standard national maintenance fees due for each country in which a European patent has been validated. These maintenance fees are not included here as part of the European patent, but they would need to be added for countries in which national stage validation has occurred. All of this may be changed by the European Unity Patent which is scheduled to come into existence at the beginning of 2014. It may be expected that overall European patent costs will decline, perhaps dramatically. I express no opinion on the European Unity Patent, or on future costs of patent protection in Europe, but I do say that none of these future costs affect past investments in patents, and so these changes are not relevant when we consider Check Point's historical investment in patents.

Total investment is therefore about $1.92 million, to generate and maintain all 83 of the items listed in Table 7–4 as having been filed and/or prosecuted by Check Point. Let's round this up to $2.0 million.[187] Is $2.0M a reasonable level of investment for a company such as Check Point?[188]

Let's compare this investment, and the portfolio generated, to the following:

1. The average cost of a single patent litigation in the United States is more than $2M, so Check Point's total investment in patents probably does not equal the cost of one U.S. litigation.[189]

2. The costs of litigation are comparatively minor in comparison to the business costs of losing a case and being required to pay millions in damages and/or being barred from selling one's products in the U.S. That has not happened to Check Point, but many of the cases in Chapters 3 and 4 demonstrate that it is possible.[190]

---

187 This estimate does not include engineering or management time, only out-of-pocket expenses.

188 Whether Check Point's investment is $1.92 million, or $2 million, or even $4 million, is of little importance. It is the general order of magnitude that is important, and that is reflected by the number of patents and applications in the portfolio.

189 Various studies suggest that patent litigation costs depend to some degree on the amount at stake in the litigation. However, for all but nominal amounts, expected costs exceed $2M. For example, a study conducted by the American Intellectual Property Law Association ("AIPLA"), which is likely the leading organization in the U.S. for patent attorneys, estimates total litigation costs at $650,000 for up to $1M at risk, $2.5M for up to $25M at risk, and $5M for suits involving more than $25M. Jim Kerstetter, "How much is that patent going to cost you?", CNET News, (April 5, 2012), http://news.cnet.com/8301-32973_3-57409792-296/how-much-is-that-patent-lawsuit-going-to-cost-you/.

190 Check Point has been involved in at least two patent litigations in the U.S., including a lawsuit filed by Intellectual Ventures against Check Point

3. In the last seven years alone, the company has had revenues of about $6.7B, and has invested about $600M in R&D. Assuming $2M invested in patents, as reflected by the portfolio appearing in Table 7–4, the rate of investment in patents is about 0.33% of the investment in R&D. Some companies in technology fields apply a rough rule of thumb that says investment in patents should equal at least 1% of the investment in R&D, although this ratio is likely to be higher in fields with rapidly changing technology or for technological startups. At least by this rule, Check Point appears under-invested. Other factors affect the rate of patent investment, but $2M for a company of this size, in an area as technologically dynamic as firewalls, seems light.[191]

---

in December, 2010, and a lawsuit filed by Check Point asking for declaration of non-infringement of SRI patents, filed in June, 2012.

[191] I do not have in hand a study that compares the R&D investments and patent investments of technology companies. Such a study should be done and would provide important insights, but I am unaware of the existence of any such study. Therefore, I am not able to offer hard evidence to support my statement that a benchmark for patent investment is 1% of R&D investment. Nevertheless, I believe this be true, for two reasons.

First, macro-evidence, that is, on an economy-wide level, supports this as a rough rule of thumb. For example, in the Brookings study, *op. cit.* at p.8, it is stated that average R&D investment per issued patent has been about $3.5M since 1975; assuming a fully-loaded cost to acquire and maintain a patent of $27,000 — $30,000, this would imply an investment in patents at about 0.77% — 0.86% of R&D investment. Similarly, we could compare total U.S. R&D investments for the three years 2009–2011, to the total U.S. patents issued in those years based on an application from an American entity; assuming again a fully-loaded cost of $27,000 — $30,000 per patent, the total range of patent investment/R&D investment for these three years is about 0.58% — 0.78%. U.S. R&D numbers from Battelle Memorial Institute, *2012 R&D Global Funding Forecast*, p.8, http://battelle.org/docs/default-document-library/2012_global_forecast.pdf, and Martin Grueber of Battelle Memorial Institute, *Re-Emerging U.S. R&D*, December, 2009, http://www.rdmag.com/articles/2009/12/re-emerging-us-r-d. U.S. utility patents solely of

4. The size of the portfolio in the United States, which is a total of 81 items (including acquired patents and applications), might not be reasonable for a company of this size, in a technology market as sophisticated and intensive as firewalls, in the biggest commercial market in the world. In particular, Check Point's U.S. patent portfolio appears to be significantly smaller than the portfolios of its major competitors.[192] This

---

U.S. origin from U.S. Patent & Trademark Office, *U.S. Patent Statistics Chart Calendar Years 1963–2012*, in the category "Utility Patent Grants, U.S. Origin", http://www.uspto.gov/web/offices/ac/ido/oeip/taf/us_stat.htm.

Second, it accords with my personal experience and with what I would consider common sense. I worked with Motorola in the 1980's, and this was the benchmark for patent investments. I have heard anecdotal evidence to the same effect. As an independent patent lawyer servicing corporate clients, I am fully aware of the relative place of patents in the hierarchy — patents may be considered important, but they are a small percentage of R&D investment.

Even this benchmark, 1% of R&D investment, is only an average. The actual patent investment can and will vary from company to company, for a variety of reasons. One would expect, for example, that startup companies, or companies in fields of intense technological development, or companies that have deliberately chosen a strategy of patent investment, may have ratios higher than 1%. Still, 1% of R&D investment is a reasonable starting point for analysis of a technology company's interest in patents.

192 In its 2012 annual report to the U.S. Securities & Exchange Commission, Check Point lists thirteen companies as its prime competitors. *Check Point 2012 Annual Report (Form 20-F), p.6.* U.S. patent and application data is available for all these companies, and revenue data is available for all of these companies except WatchGuard. In comparison to these companies, Check Point's patent portfolio is much smaller, both in absolute numbers and *also as a ratio of patents/revenue*, than Cisco Systems, Fortinet, Hewlett-Packard, IBM, Juniper Networks, McAfee (subsidiary of Intel), Microsoft, and Symantec. Of the remaining five competitors, Check Point's portfolio is the same size but worse per revenue than the portfolio of SonicWall (subsidiary of Dell), larger in number of items but worse per revenue than the portfolios of both Sourcefire and Websense, and larger than Watchguard's portfolio (but the absence of revenue figures for Watchguard makes this comparison not very useful). Of the thirteen main competitors, Check Point is greater in number of patent items and better in patents per revenue than

book focuses on the quality of patents, rather than on the size of portfolios, but when portfolios are judged, both quality and quantity matter.

5. We review below Check Point's two earliest patents. These two patents are very good, and surely have provided Check Point an umbrella of protection for its development over the past decade.[193] Very high quality of patents can offset a deficiency in quantity, at least to some degree. These two

---

only one company, Palo Alto Networks (which itself seems to have picked up its patenting activity significantly in the very recent past). To summarize, Check Point's portfolio is inferior in number of items to eight of its thirteen main competitors, and to at least eleven of its thirteen main competitors as a percentage of revenue devoted to patent activity. Check Point compares favorably only with Palo Alto Networks, which seems to be catching up with rapidly increasing patent investments. Overall, in comparison to its main competitors, Check Point cannot reasonably rely on the *quantity* of its portfolio, so it must rely on the *quality* of its portfolio, which is discussed in the main text below.

193 One commentator on the litigation involving Intellectual Ventures ("IV") noted that Check Point's patent 5,606,668 pre-dates all of IV's patents in the litigation and, by implication, might be used to invalidate some or all of IV's patent claims. See "Intellectual Property Analysis of Intellectual Ventures' U.S. Patent No. 5,987,610", December 16, 2010, by Patently Obvious™, at http://m-cam.com/sites/www.m-cam.com/files/20101216_IntellectualVentures_v_McAfee.pdf.

The invalidation of the patent claims of competitors or other suing parties is one of the ways a patent provides an umbrella of protection. However, it should be understood that this kind of protection is particularly useful, in that the ability to invalidate later applications *never goes away*, even after the patent has expired. Therefore, the expiration date is irrelevant for purposes of using the patent as prior art against other patents. By contrast, a patent's expiration date is relevant for the owner's ability to threaten infringement lawsuits — upon expiration, the patent can no longer generate an injunction against the infringer, and six years after expiration, the patent can no longer generate legal damages for the patent owner.

excellent patents, however, will expire in February, 2014. What will happen then?[194]

*b. Introduction to Check Point US 5,606,668 and US 5,835,726:*

These two patents will be discussed together, because of their similarly, as described below.

US 5,606,668 is entitled "System for Securing Inbound and Outbound Data Packet Flow in a Computer Network". The patent was filed on December 15, 1993, and issued on February 25, 1997. The independent claims that will be reviewed here are method claim #1 and method claim #8. The basic subject of this patent is to create a security rule, use the rule to filter inbound and outbound data packets, and then accept or reject the transmission. As of May 22, 2013, this patent had 436 forward non-self citations.[195]

US 5,835,726 is entitled, "System for Securing the Flow of and Selectively Modifying Packets in a Computer Network". The patent was filed on June 17, 1996, and was issued on November 10, 1998. It has three independent claims: method claim #1, method claim #18, and system claim #24. This patent is what is called a "continuation-in-part" of patent 5,606,668, which means that this patent includes much of the material in the earlier patent, but adds additional material of its own, and bases at least some of the claims on the new material. As of May 22, 2013, this patent had 402 forward non-self citations.

---

194 It is clear from the Table 7–3 that Check Point has boosted its investment in U.S. patents over the past few years. This is a step in the right direction. Nevertheless, its patent position will weaken when two of its seminal patents, US 5,606,668 and US 5,835,726, expire in 2014.

195 U.S. forward citations are determined by reviewing the U.S. PTO web site at www.uspto.gov, or by the private site www.patentbuddy.com, or both.

In a "continuation-in-part" ("CIP") patent, claims that are based on the old material should have the priority date of the earlier patent, while claims based on the new material should have the priority date of the new application. Here, for example, the claims in US 5,835,726 based on the earlier patent will have a priority date of December 15, 1993, while the claims based on new material will have a priority date June 17, 1996. However, despite the different priority dates, these two patents will expire at the same time. Written on the face of US 5,835,726, is the notice, "The term of this patent shall not extend beyond the expiration date of Pat. No. 5,606,668". This notice is known as a "Terminal Disclaimer", and it means exactly what it says: the later patent, US 5,835,726, and all of its claims, will expire ("terminate") together with US 5,606,668, on February 25, 2014.

Why is there this "Terminal Disclaimer" on the patent? The examiner reviewing the application decided that the claims in the later application are not patentably distinct from the claimed invention of the related patent.[196] This type of rejection, and the use of a Terminal Disclaimer to overcome the rejection, is not unusual. However, this type of rejection appears only where the claims in the two patents are not patentably distinct from one another, which was the case here.

*c. Why are these two patents "seminal patents"?:*

I have suggested four criteria for such patents — (1) they

196 This kind of rejection occurs where there are two patents on the same invention or related inventions, and the patents have common inventors or owners. The rejection is called a "double patenting" rejection, and is intended to prevent the illegal extension of a patent life beyond the time period set forth in the patent law. This is a standard kind of rejection that is typically resolved by a Terminal Disclaimer.

have relatively early priority dates, (2) they have hundreds of forward non-self citations, (3) they address a major technical problem, and (4) the scope of their claims cover a significant market.

The first and second criteria are clearly met here, since each patent dates back to the mid- 1990s, and each has about 400 forward non-self citations. To determine technical importance and market scope, we need to review the patents.

Consider the two independent claims for US 5,606,668:

> 1. [Preamble] A method of inspecting inbound and outbound data packets in a computer network, the inspection of said data packets occurring according to a security rule, the method comprising the steps of:
>
> a) generating a definition of each aspect or the computer network inspected by said security rule;
>
> b) generating said security rule in terms of said aspect definitions, said security rule controlling as least one of said aspects;
>
> c) converting said security rule into a set of packet filter language instructions for controlling the operation of a packet filtering module which inspects said data packets;
>
> d) providing a packet filter module coupled to said computer network for inspecting said data packets in accordance with said security rule, said packet filter module implementing a virtual packet filtering machine; and
>
> e) said packet filter module executing said packet filter language instructions for operating said virtual packet filtering machine to either accept or reject the passage of said data packets into and out of said computer network.

8. [Preamble] In a security system for inspecting inbound and outbound data packets in a computer network, said security system inspecting said data packets in said computer network according to a security rule, where each aspect of said computer network inspected by said security rule has been previously defined, said security rule previously defined in terms of said aspects and converted into packet filter language instructions, a method for operating said security system comprising the steps of:

a) providing a packet filter module coupled to said computer network in at least one entity of said computer network to be controlled by said security rule, said packet filter module emulating a virtual packet filtering machine inspecting said data packets passing into and out of said computer network;

b) said packet filter module reading and executing said packet filter language instructions for performing packet filtering operations;

c) storing the results obtained in said step of reading and executing said packet filter language instructions in a storage device; and

d) said packet filter module utilizing said stored results, from previous inspections, for operating said packet filter module to accept or reject the passage of said data packet into and out of said computer network.

The essence of the two independent claims in US 5,606,668 is this: (1) A security rule is defined for a computer network, (2) the rule is converted into packet filter instructions, (3) a packet filter module implements the rule by inspecting inbound and outbound aspects, and (4) the module then allows or prohibits passage of the packets based on the inspection. Based only on these two claims, we can determine that the general subject of US 5,606,668 is data security, and the specific subject is firewall protection.

The second Check Point patent, US 5,835,726, has independent claims which are in essence the same as those of the earlier patent, except they add the feature of "selectively modifying" data packets in accordance with the security rule.

The independent claims of these two patents cover critical features of a firewall, in particular, inspecting data packets to reject those that are harmful or threatening, and modifying some packets to make them acceptable for passage. The priority dates on these patents, going back to 1993 and 1995, respectively, are relatively early in the field of firewalls and network security. This is not a traditional VSD analysis, so we cannot yet determine that the claims are valid or broad in scope, but we can say that the patents have early priority dates, very strong forward non-self citations, and coverage of a very important technical area. The patents therefore meet at least the first three criteria of what I have called "a seminal patent".

*d. Are these two patents "valuable"?:*

We might rephrase this question as, "Do the patents meet the fourth criterion of seminal patents? Do they cover a large market of infringers?" The great thing about the independent claims in these two patents is the generality of the elements. The generality of the claim elements is a direct result of the patents having early priority dates in a ground-breaking technology area. If the technology area had been packed with prior art, these broad claim elements would not have been allowed.

Consider the following from claim #1 of 5,606,668:

1. The method applies to both "inbound" and "outbound" data. That would not have been required. It would have been possible to apply this invention only to inbound data, but the stated generality (both inbound and outbound) is much broader, and hence better.

2. The method relates to packets "in a computer network". There is no limitation on the kind of network, its size, speed, etc. In particular, both Internet and Intranets seem to be included, which is very good.

3. The security rule will be applied to "aspects", which is a key claim term that appears in elements (a) and (b) of claim #1. Absence of a definition of this term could reduce greatly the value of the entire patent. However, the term is clearly defined in the written description in column 4, lines 46–48, to include at least "network objects" and "services". Although there is no definition of "network object" in the written description, examples of such "objects" are listed in columns 3, line 49, including workstations, gateways, other computer hardware connected to the system. "Services" is similarly not defined, but examples are given in column 5, lines 7–8, such as "login" , "route", "syslog", and "telnet", all suggesting various kinds of communication connections. *A critical term may be defined with an explicit definition, which happened here with the term "aspects", or with multiple examples, which happened here with the word "network objects"*. Hence, the key claim term "aspects" is adequately defined.

4. Once "aspects" has been defined, there is no real problem, and very little limitation, to elements (a), (b), or (c), in claim #1 of US 5,606,668. However, an additional term appears in elements (d) and (e), which is, "virtual packet filtering machine". This is a key term in claim #1, but what is it?

A person reading this phrase might think the meaning is, "a machine that filters 'virtual packets'". However, the term "virtual packet" does not appear anywhere in the patent. In fact, the relevant concept, which does appear repeatedly, is "virtual machine", meaning a virtual machine that filters packets, not a machine that filters virtual packets. The term is defined in column 7, lines 57–61, as follows:

> The packet filter module is embodied in a "virtual machine" which, for purposes of this application, may be defined as an emulation of the machine shown in FIGS. 6–10 residing in the host computer, which is a computer on the network.

This definition of the term "virtual machine" is not clear, and the lack of clarity for the term "virtual machine" means that the term "virtual packet filtering machine" is also not clear. Generally, a "machine" is understood to be some kind of physical thing, and a "virtual machine" is a kind of structure that is "created", or perhaps we can say "emulated", by software.[197]

The definition given in the patent agrees with the general understanding in the industry of what is meant by "virtual machine". So far, so good. However, a problem arises because the definition quote from the patent, above, refers to emulation of "the machine shown in FIGS. 6–10 residing in the host computer..." *Figures 6–10 in this patent are NOT machines;*

---

197 See, for example, Robert C. Kahrl and Stuart B. Soffer, *Thesaurus of Claim Construction*, (Oxford University Press, New York, 2011), at p. 673, which says that a "virtual machine" is "*A representation of a computer architecture created by software.* [U.S. patent] 5,761,477 (7/18/1) *Filed:* 1995. VMWare, Inc. v. Connectix Corporation and Microsoft Corporation, Nos. 02–03705 and 03–0654 (N.D.Cal. March 25, 2005) *Stage:* Claim construction."

*they are not hardware, and they are not software emulations of hardware*. Each of these figures, as they appear in the patent and as defined in the "Brief Description of the Drawings", is a "flow diagram", in other words, a method. There are no machines or any structures, hardware or software, in any of Figures 6–10.

The intent of the patent applicant is not totally clear, but we may guess that the intent was, "the software that emulates a machine *carrying out the flows shown in Figures 6–10*". That was perhaps the intent, but unfortunately that is not what was written. Would a court recognize this error, and accept the applicant's true intent of this definition of "virtual machine"? If so, we would seem to have means-plus-function elements, which is to say, "means for implementing the method in Figure 6", "means for implementing the method in Figure 7", etc. Would the court find that there was enough structure defined in the patent to support these elements?

To the best to my knowledge, the two Check Point patents discussed here have had no reexamination, no certificate of correction for mistakes, and no litigation associated with them. The early priority dates of the patents means that their prosecution histories at the PTO are not available on-line. In any case, it is likely that the definition of "virtual machine" did not arise in prosecution. We are left only with the internal evidence of the patent itself. I believe that a court would say "Yes, we recognize the true intent of this definition", and "Yes, there is sufficient structure to support the term in the claims". However, the matter is not free of doubt. This patent would have been stronger had there been a clearer definition of "virtual packet filtering machine".

5. In this patent, Figures 1–2 and 4–15 are well discussed

in the written description. Conversely, each of Figures 3A, 3B, 3C, and 3D, has only one element, and the explanation of these Figures is both cursory and confusing. However, although Figures 3A — 3D are not well discussed, I do not think this deficiency harms the patent significantly, because all of these Figures relate only to the "computer screen of the administrator", whereas the core of the invention — the various firewall methods — is described in the "flow diagrams" of Figures 4–15.

The other independent claim in US 5,606,668, claim #8, is also a method claim, but it adds the additional feature of being a learning machine. That is to say, in addition to the general method of claim #1, in claim #8 the results of earlier filtering operations are stored in memory, and these stored results are used to improve the filtering process for future operations. Claim #8 is a very nice feature. It is certainly much narrower than the more general method in claim #1, but it is still a good feature to patent, and its inclusion increases the patent's value.

Let us now turn to the second patent, US 5,835,726. There are three independent claims in US 5,835,726: method claims 1 and 18, and system claim #24. Let's consider the method claims first.

Method claim #1 of US 5,835,726 is the counterpart of method claim #1 in US 5,606,668, and method claim #18 is the counterpart of method claim #8 in US 5,606,668. The significant difference between the two pairs of claims is that in US 5,835,726, the method claims add the limitation of "selectively modifying inbound and outbound data packets in a computer network", and this is done "in accordance with [the previously defined] said security rule". The key claim terms for these claims are "modify" and "modifying". The term "modify" is defined in the Summary of Invention, in these words:

> Yet another object of the invention is to provide the ability to modify the packet by any of [1] encrypting it, [2] modifying a destination address, [3] accepting external inputs as criteria for [a] accepting, [b] rejecting or [c] modifying the network communication." [Column 2, lines 57–61. Brackets [ ] added.]

Without this definition, the word "modify", which is in fact the key innovation in this patent, would be undefined and unclear. The fact that there is a definition in the written description is excellent. However, this definition is less than perfect, for the following reasons:

1. I understand [1] "encrypting the packet", and [2] "modifying the destination address of the packet". Is there a third possibility, which should read, [3] "or accepting external inputs..."? If this is a third possibility, then what happened to the word "or"? It was apparently left out by mistake. Could the omitted word be "and", so that "modify" would mean ALL THREE, that is, encrypt, change address, and accept external input? That would indeed be a possibility, except for the words "by any of", just before "encrypting it..." The fact is that an omission of the word "or" before "accepting external inputs" was an error, but no harm is likely to result because a judge is likely to understand the intent.

2. A third way to modify an inbound or outbound data packet is "accepting external inputs as criteria for" [a] "accepting...the network communication", or [b] "rejecting...the network communication", or [c] "modifying the network communication". I understand [a] and [c], but what is the

point of [b]? Let us assume we have a packet that is deficient in some way. Let's say an "external input" must be added to the packet so that the network communication will be "accepted" or "modified". These options make sense, but what would be the need to accept external input as a criterion for "rejecting" the network communication? There may be some resolution, but the lack of clarity for the term "modify" guarantees that if this patent ever went to trial, the defendant would attack this key claim term.

Is this discussion just technical nit-picking, arguing over insignificant details? Perhaps, but bear in mind that *all of the independent claims in US 5,835,726, and hence all of the claims in this patent, rely on the definition of the single term "selectively modifying a data packet"*. What is meant by the word "modifying" is not certain, although it does appear to include "encrypting" as one option and "modifying a destination address" as another option. There is also something related to "accepting external inputs", although that something is not entirely clear.

So much for the independent method claims in US 5,835,726. Let us look now at independent structure claim #24, and dependent structure claim #25. Here is claim #24:

> 24. [Preamble] In a security system for inspecting and selectively modifying inbound and outbound data packets in a computer network, said security system inspecting and selectively modifying said data packets passing through said computer network in accordance with a security rule, where each aspect of said computer network controlled by said security rule has been previously defined, said security rule being previously defined in terms of said aspects

and converted into packet filter language instructions, said security system comprising:
[1] a packet filter module coupled to said computer network, said packet filter module operating in accordance with said security rule, said packet filter module implementing a virtual packet filtering machine inspecting and selectively modifying said data packets passing into and out of said computer network; and
[2] processing means for reading and executing said packet filter language instruction integral with said packet filter module, said processing means operating said packet filtering module to either accept or reject the passage of said packets into and out of said computer network and to selectively modify said data packets so accepted.

There is much that could be said about claim #24, but let us focus specifically on the form of element [2] of the claim. Element [2] is a means-plus-function element, which is "processing means" for carrying out certain functions. Such an element must have some definition, or examples, of the "means" by which the function is implemented, and such definition or examples must appear in the written specification (as required for means-plus-function claims). In particular, I find nothing in the written description that defines, or gives examples for, "processing means", or "processing", or "processor". I see the word "processed" three times, but the meaning is not clear to me. Perhaps "packet filter module" is meant, but if so, why does element [1] say "packet filter module", while element [2] says "processing means"? There is probably some answer, but I am not sure what it is, and I am not sure whether a court would find sufficient structure to support the phrase "processing means" in means-plus-function element [2]. The term "processing means" should have been defined more clearly.

Claim #25 reads:

> The method according to claim 24, wherein said selective modification is chosen from the group consisting of encryption, decryption, signature generation and signature verification.

Dependent claim #25 is very weak. Its preamble makes reference to, "The method according to claim 24". However, claim #24 is a "security system", not a method. Therefore, claim #25 as written includes the structural elements [1] and [2] from claim #24, and the various methods of claim #25, which are "encryption", "decryption", "signature generation", and "signature verification". This mix of method and structural elements, by itself, makes claim #25 indefinite, and hence fatally defective, under 35 USC sec. 112(2). As explained in Chapter 1, section 112(2) requires that the claim "point out" and "distinctly claim" the subject matter of the invention. Mixing structural and method elements in one claim is on its face a violation of section 112(2), and hence invalid.

**Validity**: The claims in US 5,606,668 have at least two key claim terms. "Aspects" is well defined, but "virtual machine" is not, primarily because "virtual machine" must be some kind of structure, but the term is defined as being the method steps in Figures 6–10. The applicant meant to say, "The structure that implements the method steps in Figures 6–10". I think a court would agree that this is what the applicant meant, and save the claims on that basis, but I am not certain.

There is at least one key term in the independent method claims of US 5,835,726, which is the word "modify" (and its variant "modifying"). There is a definition for this term in the patent, which includes three alternative possibilities. The first two possibilities are clear, so these claims would be found by a court to be "definite", and hence valid. The unclarity of the third possibility might not invalidate the entire claim, but would likely restrict the scope of all the independent claims and hence of all the claims in the patent.

There are two structure claims in US 5,835,726. Claim #24 has some validity question, again with respect to whether the claim is "definite" under 35 USC sec. 112(2). There seem to be two different meanings of the term "modify". However, a court might interpret the word broadly, to include both meanings, so I would not conclude that claim #24 is invalid. Method claim #25, however, almost certainly would not survive in litigation.

**Scope**: The key patent here is the first one, US 5,606,668. The scope of claim #1 of this patent is extremely broad. Assuming this claim could survive validity challenges, it would likely be infringed by many or even most parties implementing Internet and intranet firewall security. This is a very broad claim indeed. Independent claim #8 adds a "learning feature" to the original method, improving the method based on the results of prior filters. That is a nice-to-have feature, albeit much narrower than the fundamental method of claim #1.

The claims of US 5,835,726 add to the earlier patent the limitation that the system will not only inspect a packet, then accept or reject passage of the packet, but also that the system may modify the packet, in some cases and for various purposes. That is a good feature, and does add value to the earlier patent. In the end, however, the scope of US 5,835,726 is narrower than that of US 5,606,668.

**Discoverability of Infringement**: Although infringement is not easily viewable, I see no particular problem in discovering infringement by review of relevant technical literature or by inference from the results generated by the system and methods of the claims.

**Summary**: These are two very early patents related to firewall protection. They are seminal patents, reflected in their early priority dates, their strong forward non-self citations, the significant technical problem addressed, and the broad scope of the market covered by the claims. 400 forward non-self citations reflect industry interest in the subject of the claims, but do not say necessarily that the patent claims are "good". In fact, there are some formal problems in the patent that may reduce the scope of or even invalidate some of the claims.

Nevertheless, notwithstanding some formal problems or defects in some of the claims, these patents have provided protection to the patentee in a highly competitive and rapidly changing technical field.[198] These two patents, the jewels of

198 In Chapter 1, in the discussion of "Relevant Parts of a Utility Patent", it was said that the "protection" afforded by a patent is the right to sue people who are threatening to sue you. That is especially the case in a very technical and rapidly changing field, such as Check Point's. Large and well-funded competitors could threaten Check Point with patent infringement lawsuits, but Check Point has enjoyed and continues to enjoy protection against such threats, as long as it has patent rights that it may threaten to use against its competitors. The doctrine of Mutually Assured Destruction ("MAD"), operates between competitive companies much as it does between heavily armed and competitive countries, with the obvious distinction that "war"

Check Point's patent portfolio, will expire in early 2014, and can no longer be used to obtain an injunction against anyone.[199] From the point of view of patents and patent protection, Check Point is currently standing at a crossroads, and will need to take action in the near future regarding its patent protection.

**Lessons Learned:** Here are some lesson we might learn about "good patents" from claims 1 and 8 of US 5,606,668, and claims 1, 24, and 25 from US 5,835,726, both patents issued to Check Point Software:

**Lessons for Individual Patents:**

7–1–1 (Individual). ***A "seminal patent" (1) has a relatively early priority date, (2) has strong forward non-self citations, (3) is a pillar on which rests an important technical innovation or even a whole technical industry, and (4) has broad market coverage.*** US 5,606,668 and US 5,835,726 are seminal patents in the firewall industry.

7–1–2 (Individual). ***The strength of seminal patents can overcome minor defects in the patent.*** In this case, what is the minor problem? There are two key claim terms in US 5,606,668, which are "aspects" and "virtual machine". "Aspects" is well defined. "Virtual machine" is defined in a defective manner, because it makes reference to "the machine shown

---

in the former case would bring heavy damage to the battling companies as opposed to annihilation of nations in the original MAD doctrine.

199 Infringement generally leads to an injunction, and that would certainly be expected if Check Point were to sue any of its competitors for patent infringement. However, any lawsuit Check Point might initiate in the second half of 2013 cannot advance far enough to generate an injunction by the time the patents expire. Therefore, the injunctive feature of these patents has already been lost, not by any error, but simply by the passage of time.

in Figures 6–10", but those figures are all method figures, not structure figures. The applicant apparently meant to say, "the structure which would be required to fulfill the methods of Figures 6–10". If this patent ever went to trial, would the court accept the applicant's true intent, correct the mistake, and rule that there is sufficient structure in the patent as a whole to define "virtual machine"? I cannot say that for sure. However, if I were Check Point Software Technologies, and someone were to offer to sell this patent to me, I would buy the patent for a significant sum, because I consider this problem to be a minor problem that would probably be overcome at trial (even though I cannot say for 100% certain that the problem would be overcome at trial). The patent's status as a seminal patent, and the value created by that status, overwhelm this minor deficiency.

7-1-3 (Individual). ***The strength of seminal patents cannot overcome major defects in the patent.*** What would be a "major defect" in patent claims? There are several examples here. In US 5,835,726, a key claim term is the word "modify", which appears in all the independent claims. The definition of that term in column 2 includes three possibilities, the first two of which are clear, but the third of which is not comprehensible. It is possible that this third possibility could be clarified or somehow reconstructed at trial, but I would not be willing to bet on that. The value of the patent must stand on the first two possibilities, and forget the third one. Even though the patent is seminal, it cannot overcome this deficiency in the definition of the word "modify".

Another major defect is the use of the phrase "processing means" in element [2] of claim #24 of US 5,835,726. This is a means-plus-function element. The means, in this case "processing means", must be defined somewhere in the written description, but it is not so defined. Again, an owner could argue, "processing means is implied to be the computer hardware and software required to operate the methods". Maybe a court would accept that argument, maybe not, but in my mind there is too much doubt, and I would consider this claim #24 to be simply of poor quality, hence of little or no financial value.

7–1–4 (Individual). ***There are some defects in patents, even major defects, which simply make no difference to the value of the patent.*** This may sound odd, but it is true. For example, the written description of US 5,606,668 cites and discusses "Figure 3". However, there is no "Figure 3" in the drawings, but rather Figures 3A, 3B, 3C, and 3D, which are never cited or discussed separately. This is simply not good practice. I would consider the discussion of fictitious Figure 3, and the lack of discussion of Figure 3A — 3D, to be a serious formal defect in the presentation of the written description. However, this defect makes no difference to the value of the patent, because the claims were not based on Figures 3, 3A, 3B, 3C, or 3D.

**Lessons for Patent Portfolios:** Here are some lesson we might learn about "good patent portfolios" from claims 1 and 8 of US 5,606,668, and claims 1, 24, and 25 from US 5,835,726, both patents issued to Check Point Software:

7–1–1 (Portfolio). ***A patent portfolio should be judged according to both the quantity and quality of its patents.***

In Chapter 5, we discussed the AOL portfolio sold to Microsoft. In the sale of a portfolio, both the quality of claims, and the quantity of patents, contributed to the price. In such a portfolio, the bulk of value is typically generated by a few high-quality patents.

Although in the AOL case the portfolio was sold, the same principle applies to a portfolio that is held by one company rather than sold to a second company. Check Point's total portfolio includes at least 103 patent items, and this quantity of portfolio items is one benchmark of portfolio value. However, although quantity of patents does contribute to portfolio value, the main driver of value will be a few high-quality items. Almost than 80% of Check Point's portfolio are U.S. items, which makes sense given the great importance of the U.S. market to Check Point. The critical component of the U.S. portfolio is the issued patents, not the pending applications. However, among all the issued patents, it is critical to find the main creators of value. For Check Point, US 5,606,668 and US 5,835,726, are two of the main drivers of value, for the following reasons:

(1) They have the earliest priority of the Check Point patents, with a 1993 priority date.[200]
(2) These patents are mentioned repeatedly in Check Point product literature, while other patents are not mentioned at all or are mentioned sparsely.
(3) They are the most heavily forward-cited of the patents filed and prosecuted by Check Point.
(4) They are the only patents filed in the name of the company's co-founder and CEO.

---

200 US 5,835,726 is a continuation-in-part of US 5,606,668, which means that some of the claims in 5,835,726 may have a 1993 priority date, while others have a 1996 priority date. In either case, US 5,606,668 remains Check Point's earliest patent, and US 5,835,726 remains Check Point's second earliest patent.

(5) I have reviewed briefly Check Point's early patents. Many seem to involve packet filtering, which is the same subject as US 5,606,668 and US 5,835,726, but US 5,606,668 and US 5,835,726, appear to be the broadest of the packet filtering patents.

Much of the value in the Check Point portfolio, and therefore much of the patent protection provided to Check Point, rests with these two patents, which terminate in February, 2014.[201]

7-1-2 (Portfolio). ***How can we know if a company is investing "the right amount" in patents?*** Unfortunately, there is no magic formula, but at least we can approximate some possibilities, or let's say a possible range of investment. Here are some rules of thumb:

a. ***For a standard technology company, one often-heard "rule" is that investment in patents should be 1% of the amount invested in R&D.*** For newer companies that rely on technology to enter a market, this probably should be substantially higher. For older companies in markets developing more slowly, particularly

201 I must make one exception to this general conclusion. Check Point also owns US 5,987,611, acquired when it took over the company Zone Labs. This patent, acquired rather than prosecuted by Check Point, also appears to be a key driver of value in this portfolio. The patent, entitled "System and methodology for managing internet access on a per application basis for client computers connected to the internet", appears to have very broad claims, and has a priority date of December 31, 1996, only a few months after the priority date for US 5,835,726. It will expire in 2017, which is coming up soon but which is still later than the US 5,606,668 and US 5,835,726. This patent has 519 non-self forward citations as of May 22, 2013, which is even more than either of the two patents discussed here. Acquiring this patent might have been one of Check Point's objectives in the acquisition of Zone Labs.

if the company relies more on backroom operations and components rather than on product or system integration, perhaps less than the standard would be acceptable. Check Point's position would seem to call for a higher than average investment in patents, but the company appears not to have reached that level, even in recent years.

b. ***Compare your patent portfolio with portfolios of other companies in your field***. A comparison of Check Point's U.S. portfolio to those of its competitors may suggest a need for the company to increase its investment in patents.

c. ***Compare patent costs to the likelihood of litigation, the possibility of losing, and costs either in damages or in being enjoined from selling products.*** An approach based on projected litigation costs may suggest a greater than standard investment. Ironically, perhaps, this risk is relatively higher for a market leader such as Check Point, specifically because it has more to lose in terms of market share, unit sales, sales revenue, and profitability than a smaller company in the same field.

7-1-3 (Portfolio). ***When the main drivers of value in a patent portfolio expire, the company has reached a decision point***. These two patents expire in February, 2014. They can still be used to sue for damages, but they will lose their power to obtain an injunction for Check Point against its competitors. In point of fact, they have already lost this power, since no patent lawsuit filed in 2013 could advance to the injunction stage before the patents expire.[202]

---

202 The acquired patent, US 5,987,611, expires in May, 2017. As a practical

Check Point seems to have increased investment in internal patenting activity in recent years, which is good, but might not be sufficient. What else might the company do? Here are some possible additional strategies:

(1) Buy early patents in this field, other "seminal patents", but with more years of life left. This would likely cost millions of dollars, but it is possible.
(2) Join commercial defensive patent aggregators, such as RPX, to access additional patents.
(3) Identify players who hold key patents in the industry, and license-in those patents, or acquire the companies.
(4) Create production and marketing alliances with other companies that can bear part, most, or even all of the risk and cost of patent litigation.
(5) Create an ownership alliance with another company that has a stronger patent position. This could be achieved by Check Point and the other company taking equity positions in one another, or more simply by Check Point selling a significant portion of its equity to the other company.

## *Scientific Atlanta and Silanis Technology, US 5,606,609*

### *a. Introduction to Scientific Atlanta:*

Scientific Atlanta, founded 1951 in Atlanta, Georgia, designs, manufactures, and sells products for broadband

matter, Check Point might be able to seek an injunction on US 5,987,611, perhaps as late as about mid-2016. Beyond that time, a lawsuit could not advance sufficiently to generate an injunction by May, 2017. In short, Check Point's ability to obtain an injunction on three key patents is essentially gone for US 5,606,608 and US 5,835,726, but will continue several more years for US 5,987,611.

communications, primarily for the cable television industry. It was a pioneer in supplying, and is still a leading supplier, of what are called "set top boxes" ("STBs") and "cable modems". In 2005, the last year it was an independent company, annual sales were about $1.9 billion. Scientific Atlanta was acquired by Cisco Systems (NASDAQ: CSCO) in early 2006 for about $7 billion.

Scientific Atlanta developed a very extensive patent portfolio over the years, which includes, as of May 22, 2013, about 719 U.S. patents, 106 U.S. patent applications, 650 European patents and applications, 223 German patents and applications, 34 Japanese patents and applications, and 616 PCT international applications. Even for a company the size of Scientific Atlanta when it was purchased, a portfolio of 2,317 items is a very significant size. Reported patent activity in recent years is very modest, with total U.S. items reported as 61 in 2009 (34 applications and 27 patents), 35 in 2010 (only 1 application and 34 patents), 3 in 2011 (2 applications and 1 patent), 1 in 2012 (1 application), and 2 in 2013 (two applications). (It is likely that after the Cisco purchase, many or perhaps most patent filings were assigned to Cisco rather than to Scientific Atlanta as the assignee.)

*b. Introduction to US 5,606,609:*

US 5,606,609 is entitled, "Electronic Document Verification System and Method". The patent was filed on September 19, 1994 and issued on February 25, 1997. As of May 22, 2013, it had 547 forward non-self citations.

Two things may be noted by way of introduction to US 5,606,609.

First, a patent may travel a long and winding road until

it arrives at an appropriate owner. In this case, US 5,606,609 began its life with a company operating in a totally different field than that of the patent. It was then transferred to a second owner, operating in a second field unrelated to the technology of the patent. Finally, it came into the hands of Silanis Technology, which specializes in the area of the patent, and which has now owned the patent for the past thirteen years. This patent has served and continues to serve as a cornerstone of Silanis' patent portfolio.

Second, the essence of the story discussed below is that there are three key claim terms, each of which is related to the term "select information". However, "select information" is not defined in the patent by any of the three traditional ways of explaining claim terms (i.e., by definition, examples, or appearance as an invention element in a figure). As explained in Chapter 5, when a key claim term is not defined in the patent by any of these three ways, the evaluator's only option to understand the claim is to see if any of the dependent claims clarify the term through the "doctrine of claim differentiation". This case is particularly complicated, because the doctrine does apply, but it requires *two differentiations* — one differentiation between claims 1 and 65 to clarify that "select information" includes "security information", and a second differentiation between claims 1 and 11 to clarify that "select information" also includes "non-security information such as 'objects' defined in the OLE technical standard". This is an extremely complicated, not to say tortuous, way to define the claim term "select information". This case illustrates (1) the doctrine of claim differentiation may indeed work to save claims that would otherwise be indefinite to the point of incomprehensibility, and (2) although an evaluator may rely on this doctrine as the method of last resort, the doctrine should *never* be relied on by a person writing a patent, because its application is simply too complicated to be certain how it will be applied by a court.

*c. US 5,606,609 — Ownership and Contribution to a Patent Portfolio:*

The patent has five independent claims. Here are their preambles:

- Claim #1: "An apparatus for embedding select information in an electronic document"
- Claim #14: "An embedded object interpreter for verification of an electronic document"
- Claim #32: "An electronic document verification system"
- Claim #43: "An electronic document verification method for verifying the integrity of an electronic document having an object embedded therein…"
- Claim #49: "An electronic document verification system"

The content of these claims may appear surprising. This patent is about verification of electronic signatures in a document, but the assignee, Scientific Atlanta, which is presumably the company that paid for the application, makes cable modems and set top boxes. What does this patent have to do with Scientific Atlanta? One could reason, "Well, electronic documents flow on the cable modem Internet system, so electronic signatures are relevant to the company." But if electronic documents are part of a cable modem company, then electronic movies, films, music, advertising, and every other kind of electronic information flowing on the system, might also be relevant to Scientific Atlanta's business. In other words, this argument, tying Scientific Atlanta to electronic signatures in documents, is too strong, because there is no natural limit to the argument.

A quick review of the titles of the Scientific Atlanta patents and applications shows that the vast majority are squarely within the company's business. However, US 5,606,609 falls outside the norm. This kind of thing actually happens quite a bit. Engineers come up with ideas only tangentially related to the company's business. The company might reject the idea, or simply let the inventor pursue it, or fund the idea (even if the invention is not really relevant to the company's business). I don't know what happened in this case but, for whatever reason, Scientific Atlanta was named as the assignee of the original patent application.

If a company owns a patent or application that is not really within the company's main business, what will it do with the item? The company could abandon the item, or sell it. When we check the "Patent Assignment Database" of the U.S. PTO, we find the following assignments recorded with the PTO:

1. October 31, 1994: The inventors assigned the application to Scientific Atlanta, shortly after the application was filed.

2. August 14, 1996: Scientific Atlanta assigned its interest to Global Associates, Ltd., a technology consulting firm based in Falls Church, Virginia, that appears to focus on consulting to the U.S. government. I do not know why this transfer was made. Global Associates might have been working on a specific project for which the patent was relevant. On the same date, Global Associates assigned a security interest (*not* ownership of the application) to Princeton Capital Finance Company, LLC, of Princeton Junction, New Jersey. Apparently Global Associates took a loan from Princeton

Capital Finance, and used this patent application as collateral against the loan. This is "collateralization", which is one way to obtain money on patents.

3. June 19, 1998: The application matured into US 5,606,609 on February 25, 1997. Global Associates, the owner of the application and now owner of the patent, assigned the patent to Smiths Industries Aerospace & Defense Systems, Inc., a San Diego, California subsidiary of Smiths Industries PLC, of London, England. The U.S. subsidiary focuses on avionic electronics.

4. January 18 and January 26, 2000: Smiths Industries transferred ownership to a New York law firm on January 18th, and the law firm then transferred ownership of the patent to Silanis Technology, Inc., of Montreal, Canada, a subsidiary of Silanis International, Ltd., of London, England.

5. July 30, 2003: Silanis Technology maintains control, but conveyed a security interest to GATX/MM Venture Finance Partnership of Toronto, Canada. GATX/MM specializes in equity and debt financing for start-up companies, preferably based in Canada, preferably within the fields of enterprise software, network, management, telecom, semiconductor, and biotech. Presumably GATX/MM provided venture financing for Silanis Technology, and received, in addition to other things, a security interest in the Silanis Technology patent portfolio.

That is the history of this patent's ownership, at least as recorded at the PTO. The patent has belonged to Silanis Technology since early 2000, and presumably will stay with Silanis Technology until the patent expires on September 19, 2014. The original owner of this patent, Scientific Atlanta, and the second owner, Smiths Industries Aerospace & Defense, did not appear to be good fits for this patent. What about the third, and presumably last, owner? Is US 5,606,609 a good fit for Silanis Technology?

Silanis Technology — founded in 1992 in Montreal, Quebec, Canada — provides electronic signature and electronic approval software for corporations, governments, and the military. It claims to allow the insertion of electronic signatures into MS-Word, MS-Excel, MS-Outlook, Adobe Acrobat, HMTL, XML, and other documents. It seems to focus on reducing paperwork and providing solutions secure enough to make electronic signatures legally binding. It is a private company with sales, according to estimates, in the range of about $5M-$10M per year.[203]

For a company of Silanis' size, its investments in patents are huge. It owns 6 U.S. patents, 3 U.S. patent applications, 3 Canadian patents, 12 Canadian applications, 5 European patents, 6 European applications, 5 German patents, and 10 International applications, for a total of 50 items.

---

203 A number of articles suggest revenues for the first half of 2012 of about $3M. For example, "Silanis Technology Inc. Reports Unaudited Consolidated Earnings Results for the Six Months Ended June 30, 2012", at investing.businessweek.com/research/stocks/private/snapshot.asp?privcapId=10454. Revenues may have been a bit higher in 2011, as reported by the Branham Group at www.branham300.com/details.php?year=2012&company_ID=181. For our purposes, only the general magnitude is important, not the specific number.

**Table 7–5: Silanis Technology's Patent Portfolio**[204]

| | US pats | US apps | CA pats | CA apps | EPO pats | EPO apps | DE grant | Int'l apps | Totals |
|---|---|---|---|---|---|---|---|---|---|
| **1992** | 0 | 0 | 0 | 0 | 0 | 0 | 0 | 0 | **0** |
| **1993** | 0 | 0 | 0 | 0 | 0 | 0 | 0 | 0 | **0** |
| **1994** | 0 | 0 | 0 | 0 | 0 | 0 | 0 | 0 | **0** |
| **1995** | 0 | 0 | 0 | 0 | 0 | 0 | 0 | 0 | **0** |
| **1996** | 0 | 0 | 0 | 0 | 0 | 0 | 0 | 0 | **0** |
| **1997** | 1 | 0 | 0 | 0 | 0 | 0 | 0 | 0 | **1** |
| **1998** | 0 | 0 | 0 | 0 | 0 | 0 | 0 | 0 | **0** |
| **1999** | 0 | 0 | 0 | 0 | 0 | 0 | 0 | 0 | **0** |
| **2000** | 0 | 0 | 0 | 3 | 0 | 0 | 0 | 6 | **9** |
| **2001** | 0 | 0 | 0 | 4 | 0 | 3 | 0 | 1 | **8** |
| **2002** | 0 | 3 | 0 | 2 | 0 | 1 | 0 | 3 | **9** |
| **2003** | 0 | 0 | 0 | 3 | 2 | 2 | 0 | 0 | **7** |
| **2004** | 1 | 0 | 0 | 0 | 0 | 0 | 2 | 0 | **3** |
| **2005** | 2 | 0 | 0 | 0 | 0 | 0 | 0 | 0 | **2** |
| **2006** | 0 | 0 | 1 | 0 | 0 | 0 | 0 | 0 | **1** |
| **2007** | 0 | 0 | 0 | 0 | 0 | 0 | 0 | 0 | **0** |

204 Information about U.S. patents and patent applications is from the U.S. PTO web site, www.uspto.gov. Information about Canadian patents and patent applications is from the Canadian Intellectual Property Office web site, www.cipo.ic.gc.ca/eic/site/cipointernet-internetopic.nsf/eng/Home. Information about European, German, Japanese, and International patents and patent applications is from the web site www.freepatentsonline.com. I have used dates of publication for applications and dates of issuance for patents, rather than dates of filing. I have removed duplications — if a particular application resulted in a patent, the patent will appear in Table 7–5 but not the application. Data in Table 7–5 was collected on May 22, 2013.

| | US pats | US apps | CA pats | CA apps | EPO pats | EPO apps | DE grant | Int'l apps | Totals |
|---|---|---|---|---|---|---|---|---|---|
| **2008** | 1 | 0 | 0 | 0 | 1 | 0 | 2 | 0 | **4** |
| **2009** | 0 | 0 | 0 | 0 | 2 | 0 | 1 | 0 | **3** |
| **2010** | 0 | 0 | 2 | 0 | 0 | 0 | 0 | 0 | **2** |
| **2011** | 0 | 0 | 0 | 0 | 0 | 0 | 0 | 0 | **0** |
| **2012** | 1 | 0 | 0 | 0 | 0 | 0 | 0 | 0 | **1** |
| **Totals** | **6** | **3** | **3** | **12** | **5** | **6** | **5** | **10** | **50** |

We can make some observations about this portfolio:

1. The company appears to have 19 patents, and 31 applications. For a portfolio like that charted above, cumulative costs over two decades might be in the range of \$1.0-\$1.5M, which is very large for a company with annual sales in the range of \$5M-\$10M.

2. The portfolio appears to be entirely self-generated, with the exception of US 5,606,609, which Silanis acquired for an unknown sum in the year 2000. The company did well to invest serious effort in pursuing its own inventions. It may have done even better when it acquired US 5,606,609, as we will see below.

3. Much of Silanis' patent activity occurred in the period 2000–2003,when the company acquired 66% of its patent portfolio, including US 5,606,609 in the year 2000. In its very early years, the company was not active in patents, but it became extremely active in subsequent years.

4. There seems to be a relatively heavy focus on international applications and European items (with 52% of the portfolio items), at the expense of Canada (30% of the portfolio items) and the U.S. (only 18% of the portfolio items). It is

possible that this portfolio is geographically misallocated. All high-tech markets may be interested in electronic security for documents, but the largest market is likely to be the U.S. Canada is also a reasonable focus of effort, given the company's location in Montreal. But why are more than 50% of the portfolio items outside of the U.S. and the home market of Canada?

5. US 5,606,609 is about to expire, and the other filings in the U.S. will need to be strengthened. Silanis Technology, like Check Point Software, is reaching a decision point regarding its patent portfolio.

*d. Why is this patent a "seminal patent"?:*

Bearing in mind the criteria we have set for a seminal patent, it appears that US 5,606,609 meets the requirements. First, the patent has an early priority date for this area of technology. Second, the patent has over 500 forward non-self citations. Third, the patent covers a technology of great importance to the patent owner, and to the electronic signature industry generally. Fourth, the claims appear to cover a broad market. Electronic signatures might not yet have become an important industry. With the growth of commerce on the Internet, and especially mobile devices, that market need may well grow. Commerce requires contractual commitment, which is going to require, increasingly, secure electronic signatures, particularly in the mobile market. This patent is very well placed for that industry.

Thus, the patent has an early priority, strong forward non-self citations, a technical area of importance to the owner and the industry, and claims that cover a potentially broad market. Therefore, this may be considered a seminal patent.[205]

*e. Why is this a good patent? — Claim Diversity and Claim Differentiation:*

The patent has excellent claim diversity. Here are the independent claims:

1. "An apparatus for embedding select information in an electronic document", followed by dependent claims 2–13 and 65. This is an *apparatus claim* to put information into a document.

14. "An embedded object interpreter for verification of an electronic document", followed by dependent claims 15–31 and 66. This is a *component claim* to take information out of the document.

32. "An electronic document verification system", followed by dependent claims 33–42 and 67. This is a *system claim* for putting information into a document, then taking it out.

43. "An electronic document verification method for verifying the integrity of an electronic document having an embedded object...", followed by dependent claims 44–48 and 68. This is a *method claim* for verifying the integrity of a document after information was put into the document.

205 The patent will expire in September, 2014. As a practical matter, it is highly dubious that a lawsuit could reach the stage of injunction before the patent expires. Is the patent therefore worthless? No, because by law, the patent can reach back in time for six years from the date of lawsuit, 35 U.S.C. sec. 286. Any action that occurs after patent expiration cannot be "current infringement", but depending on when a lawsuit is filed, the patent could cover the period from September, 2008 — September, 2014, and could generate legal damages for Silanis. None of this relates to the question of whether this patent is a "good patent" from the view of a fundamental analysis, but it does relate to the question of whether a patent about to expire can generate financial value.

49. "An electronic document verification system", followed by dependent claims #50–59. This is a *system claim* for verifying a document and displaying the verification.

60. "A verification system", followed by dependent claims #61–64. This is a *system claim* for creating and displaying an electronic "watermark".

The claims include apparatuses, components, systems, and methods, which is about as broad as claim diversity can be in a single patent. That is good.

Each of the six independent claims is relatively short, and has between only two and four claim elements. A paucity of elements and brevity generally are good for claim scope.

I will discuss only claim #1:

> 1. [Preamble] An apparatus for embedding select information in an electronic document, comprising:
> [1] an information assembler, responsive to a user's request, for assembling said select information into a predetermined format; and
> [2] an object embedder for embedding said select information and information for invoking a predetermined application for processing said select information in an electronic document.

The claim cannot get much shorter. Its purpose, as set forth in the preamble, is very clear. The elements are also clear — a device to assemble information, presumably an electronic signature or other information related to verification of the source or the contents, plus a device to place the information into the documents in the form of an object. The Point of Novelty seems to be the system itself, meaning the structure to assemble and insert information into a document. This PON supports a broad scope of claim coverage.

The potential problems relate to specific claim terms. What are the key claim terms in claim #1? Are they defined in the patent? I would suggest the following possibilities:

*Key claim term 1*: "Select information" appears in independent claim #1. This phrase appears about 60 times in the claims, including in the independent claims 1, 14, and 32, but not in independent claims 43, 49, or 60. Unfortunately, it is never defined in the patent, has no examples, does not appear in any of the figures, and in fact is never mentioned anywhere in the patent outside of the claims. Many other forms of "information" appear throughout the patent. The phrase "security information" appears very often in the written description, and may include information that "characterizes the electronic document", or that "characterizes the signator of the electronic documents", a "hash value", a "serial number", "public-key information", and more. Other kinds of "information" are mentioned, never as "select information" per se, but still as "information" such as "character information of a text", "watermark information" (which may or may not be part of "select information"), "control characteristics", and "text portions" such as "a font" or "pagination".

The phrase "select information" is clearly a key claim term in US 5,606,609, but what does it mean? For an evaluator, the only way to understand a key claim term that lacks definition, examples, and any appearance in a figure, is through the doctrine of claim differentiation, previously discussed in Chapter 5. In US 5,606,609, dependent claim #65 is "Claim 1, wherein said select information includes security information". By the doctrine of "claim differentiation" (which, as noted, means that every claim must have a separate meaning), claim #65 necessarily causes us to conclude that "select information" in claim #1 is "security information" *plus* something else that might be called "non-security information". The same doctrine of claim differentiation applies to dependent claims #66 ("selection information includes security information" in independent component claim #14), and #67 ("selection information includes security information" in independent system claim #32). It is clear, therefore, that "select information" includes "security information", which is discussed extensively in the patent, and also "non-security information", but there is no indication in the patent of the meaning of "non-security information".

Here is an important lesson. In this patent, the validity and scope of the independent claims are impacted negatively by an unclear definition of the key claim term, "select information". However, although this key term is not defined in the independent claim, it may be clarified, at least to some degree, in a dependent claim. In US 5,606,609, several dependent claims define the unclear term by using the well-known term "security information". The result is that the undefined key term (here "select information") has been defined to include both "security information" and "non-security information". In other words, the dependent claims provide meaning to the unclear term by operation of the doctrine of claim differentiation.

*Key claim term 2*: The term "information assembler" appears in element [1] of claim #1, and again in element [1] of independent claim #32. This term appears repeatedly in the written specification, but always with the word "security", as in "security information assembler", and never as just "information assembler". In fact, element 610 in Figure 6 is a "security information assembler" that is well-described in the text. The only difficulty is that, again, it is hard to know what "information assembler" means, apart from "assembler of security information". The term "non-security information" should have been described or defined in the text, but is not. It is not clear if the assembler assembles anything other than "security information".

*Key claim term 3*: "Object embedder" appears in element [2] of claim #1, and appears also in independent claims 14, 32, and 43. In the written description, this element is discussed in the context of a "security object embedder", not in relation to "non-security information". However, claim #11 mentions "OLE objects", and in fact, "OLE objects" are mentioned repeatedly in the written description, sometimes as a "security OLE object", but also as an "OLE object" without reference to "security". OLE, short for "Object Linking and Embedding", was introduced by Microsoft as OLE 1.0 in 1990, then as "OLE 2.0" in 1994, the year this patent was filed. OLE 2.0 is mentioned repeatedly in the text, sometimes in connection to security, as in the definition of element 5 as "OLE security object", but in many cases without specific reference to "security". According to the OLE technical standard, an OLE object can include objects such as a calendar, a video window, a sound player, a sound file, text, video, 3-D, updated news, controls, and other.

In short, although the term "object embedder" is often focused on "security information", it is not limited to such information. The definition of this key claim term is therefore broad, but also sufficiently clear. More important, since element [2] of claim #1 also applies to "select information", but element [2] includes an "object embedder" which may be an "OLE object embedder" independent of "security", a strong argument can be made that "select information" includes, at least, "security information" and also "non-security information *typical of OLE objects*". Element [2] saves claim #1.

*Conclusion as to key claim terms in claim #1*: The terms are adequately described for claim #1 to survive a validity challenge. The main difficulty is uncertainty as to whether the claim includes only "security information" or something else as well. We simply can not know, from the preamble or from element [1] of claim #1, if the claim includes only "security information" or something more. However, element [2] opens up the claims greatly to all kinds of non-security information in the form of OLE objects. Then claim #65, saying that "select information" includes "security information", makes sense according to the doctrine of claim differentiation.

The ultimate result is a very broad claim #1, but we arrived at this definition after a tortuous journey involving OLE objects and dependent claim #65. Whether a court would take the same journey, and apply a broad definition to "select information" in claim #1, is not clear. The original patent applicant would have done much better to define clearly key claim terms such as "selection information", "information assembler", and "object embedder". These definitions, or examples, or invention elements in figures, should be placed in either the Summary or in the Detailed Description. By failing to explain several key claim terms, the patent applicant left definition of these terms to the uncertain interpretation of the doctrine of claim differentiation, which is a thing that the patent writer should never do.

**Validity**: There is no serious problem with validity. The patent has an early priority date in this industry, and most of the key claim terms are well defined.

One key claim term, "select information" was not clearly defined, which might have put both the validity and scope of a number of claims in doubt. However, the discussion of "OLE objects", which were relatively new when the patent was filed in 1994, corrects the definition of "select information", and prevents these possible problems.

Further, although we have not analyzed the other independent claims, we should note that the patent includes independent claims for an apparatus, an "object interpreter" (which is a component), systems, and a method. This patent is an excellent example of the beneficial effects of having claim diversity. Some system claims may be invalidated, and other system claims may be limited in scope, but the patent includes also component, apparatus, and method claims, all of which appear valid and which serve to broaden the scope of the entire patent.

**Scope**: The diversity of claims maximizes scope of coverage.

The independent claims, including #1 and the others not reviewed in detail, are short and clear, with relatively few elements. Major aspects of electronic signatures are covered.

The doctrine of claim differentiation expands the scope of most of the independent claims. Specifically, a dependent claim that defines "select information" or "embedded object" as a term that "includes 'security information'", means each such independent claim must include both "security information" and "non-security information" such as OLE objects. Defining claim scope in this way is dangerous, and inferior to the standard approaches (definition, examples, or element in a figure), but in the absence of the standard approaches, it will have to do.[206]

**Discoverability of Infringement**: I see no particular problem for discoverability of infringement. The infringement may not be directly viewable, but would likely be easily inferable from the results of embedded and extracted information. Product literature would also likely confirm the infringement.

**Summary**: This is an early priority patent related to "signatures" in electronic documents. Scientific Atlanta, the original assignee and probably the party that paid for patent preparation and prosecution, may not have been a good fit for the subject of this patent. After a few rounds of assignment, the patent came to be owned by Silanis Technology, in Montreal, Quebec, Canada. This patent is a very good fit for Silanis, with excellent coverage of various aspects of electronic signatures. The scope of the claims may be broadened by application of the doctrine of claim differentiation.

Finally, in addition to the value of the patent in itself, the patent's placement in Silanis' patent portfolio teaches certain lessons about the value of a patent as part of a portfolio.

---

206 We reviewed claim #1, and observed that dependent claim #65 expands the scope of claim #1 by claim differentiation. In fact, the same thing happened with dependent claim #66 expanding the scope of independent claim #14, dependent claim #67 expanding the scope of independent claim #32, and dependent claim #68 expanding the scope of independent claim #43.

**Lessons Learned**: Here are lessons which may be learned about good patents from patent claims 1, 14, 32, 43, and 49 in US 5,606,668, issued to Scientific Atlanta, and later acquired by Silanis Technology. There are lessons to be learned both for individual patents and for the portfolio of a company. Let's look at each subject separately.

**Lessons for Individual Patents:**

7–2–1 (Individual). ***Claim diversity can save the day, even if some claims fail.*** In US 5,606,609, claim diversity protects against the risk and impact of claims being invalidated at trial. Here, all possible aspects, including components, apparatuses, systems, and methods, are covered, providing maximal scope to the claims.

7–2–2 (Individual). ***Dependent claims and claim differentiation broaden the scope of the independent claims.*** The key claim term, "select information", was not clearly defined, and might be taken to mean the rather narrow, "security information". Through claim differentiation, dependent claims may broaden the independent claims, although as previously noted, a patent writer should never rely on claim differentiation to determine the scope of the claims.

7–2–3 (Individual). ***Short, clear claims provide value.*** Of the six independent claims, four have 2 elements, one has 3, and one has 4, for a total of 15 elements in all six independent claims. With the exception of an element in claim #32, an element in claim #43, and an element in claim #49, all of the elements are short: four lines or less in the printed text. In other words, 80% of the claim elements in the independent claims of this patent are short, to a degree atypical of independent patent claims.

All the elements in the independent claims are "clear"

in the sense that (1) most of the words are commonly used, and (2) all of the key claim terms are explained in the patent. The explanations are by example only, which is acceptable, although examples plus broad definitions would have made the patent better. One of the 15 key claim terms, "select information", was not defined in a pretty way, but we can get there by importing "OLE objects" into element [2] of claim #1.

If a key claim term is not defined or otherwise explained in the patent, then both validity and scope of the entire independent claim, and all dependent claims that depend on that independent claim, are in severe doubt. In this case, claim #1 was saved by a dependent claims adding "security information" to the definition of "select information", and the definition of "non-select information" to include at least "OLE objects". (Whether something else should be included in the term "select information", apart from "security information" and "OLE objects", is simply not clear.) As we have seen before, claim differentiation helps expand the scope of the independent claims. However, as we have noted, this is a doctrine for an evaluator after patent issuance — the doctrine should never be relied upon by a patent writer to define the scope of the claims. The writer should use, instead, the traditional ways of explaining key claim terms.

7-2-4 (Individual). ***Incorporation by reference to a standard may expand the scope of a claim.*** In this case, the reference to an "OLE subject embedded" in claim #11, plus multiple references in the written description to OLE (including references such as "OLE version 2.0", "OLE feature", and "OLE controller") gave meaning to and expanded the scope of the key tem "select information" in claim #1. It is not entirely clear if this expansion was the intent of the patent writer, but that was the effect.

7–2–5 (Individual). ***A patent is properly placed with an owner who specializes in the technology of the patent.*** For whatever reason, the invention was made and the patent created at Scientific Atlanta, a manufacturer of cable television equipment. This may not have been not a good fit for a patent focused on securing information in electronic documents and verifying electronic signatures. Ownership passed to a defense avionics company, and that also appears to be a less than optimal placement. Finally, the patent came into the possession of Silanis Technology, an electronic signature company in Montreal, where it found a proper home.

The patent was not sued on, to the best of my knowledge, but from the time of acquisition and until patent expiration, meaning the period 2000 — 2014, the patent has given and will continue to give Silanis Technology significant patent protection in the U.S. After expiration, the patent may serve as the basis for Silanis Technology to seek monetary damages, but its deterrent value will be reduced significantly by expiration of the patent's ability to generate an injunction.

**Lessons for Patent Portfolios:**

7–2–1 (Portfolio). ***A good patent portfolio is balanced geographically.*** An entire essay could be written on what constitutes "geographic balance" in a patent portfolio. We won't do that, but let's look at some things Silanis has done well, or less well, in its portfolio, according to the information we have about the portfolio in Table 7–5.[207]

207 This review is based solely on the patent items reported in publicly available sites — it does not include applications filed but unpublished, nor

a. ***Protection in the U.S. is critical***: The U.S. is the main market for much ICT technology, a market where patent damages can run into the millions, tens of millions, or even hundreds of millions of dollars. Protection in the U.S. is critical, even if the company is a Canadian company. Silanis has 6 U.S. patents, and 3 U.S. applications, although the applications are from 2002 and may well be abandoned. For a company of this size, the U.S. patent protection appears reasonable, but US 5,606,609 will expire in 2014, and three of the remaining five U.S. patents will expire later this decade.

b. ***Protection in a home market is often appropriate***: There are 3 Canadian patents, and 12 Canadian applications, although it is likely that most or even all of the Canadian applications have been abandoned. Having protection in a home country often makes sense, and contributes to what makes a patent "good". Here, Canadian companies would be less likely to sue a holder of three Canadian patents.

c. ***One key to geographic balance is focus of efforts***: Unfortunately, geographic balance is not apparent in this case. Although Silanis is a Canadian company, and the primary market would seem to be the U.S, 52% of Silanis' patent items are European, German, or international.[208]

---

patents in specific European and Asian countries (with the exception of Germany and Japan, which are included).

208 Why is this portfolio so heavily weighted in this direction? Does the company have manufacturing or design in these places? Is the single major competitor located in these places, and if so, why not focus on that one place? Silanis International, a major investor in and possibly the parent company of Silanis Technology Montreal, is based in the UK (to be precise,

7-2-2 (Portfolio). ***A good patent portfolio is balanced in time.*** The company did not focus on patents in its early years, which is understandable, although it may be noted that high-tech companies often concentrate most of their patent activities at the very start. The company became very active in the period 2000–2003, creating about two-thirds of its portfolio in that period, and obtaining US 5,606,609 in the year 2000. For its size, the company's investment in patents, particularly in this period, is admirable. However, there has been little reported patent activity in recent years, particularly in the United States.

7-2-3 (Portfolio). ***If you lack patent protection, buy it.*** Silanis did this when it acquired US 5,606,609 in 2000. This patent has provided significant protection over the past 13 years. Also, according to the Assignments Database of the U.S. PTO, it appears that the patent was used as a security interest to help the company obtain debt or equity financing. The financial aspects of this patent appear to have been well executed. However, with US 5,606,609 to expire in 2014, what's next?

## *Qualcomm, US 5,414,796*

### *a. Introduction to Qualcomm and its technology:*

In Chapter 4, I discussed the settlement in which Qualcomm paid a significant sum to Broadcom. It is fair and

---

Jersey Island), which might help explain why the European focus developed. However, unless there are active sales, customers, facilities, or competitors in these markets, the reason for the portfolio's apparent focus on Europe would be unclear.

fitting to balance that discussion by focusing on a good patent by Qualcomm.

Qualcomm was founded in 1985 in San Diego, by Drs. Irwin Jacobs and Andrew Viterbi. From its beginning, it has been a pioneer in the development and application of CDMA technology for cellular communications. CDMA technology, discussed at length in Chapter 6, has the been the basis for a number of technical standards for mobile technology, including IS-95 (also known as "cdmaOne", which was the main 2G rival to GSM), and the main 3G technologies, W-CDMA, cdma2000, and TD-SCDMA (this last standard used only in the People's Republic of China). In addition to being a pioneer and developer of this fundamental technology, Qualcomm has been and continues to be a leader in the monetization of patents, generating over the years billions of dollars in revenue and profits from patent licensing. Although Qualcomm has always sold products, a significant percentage of its sales, and a higher percentage of its profits, have been generated by the licensing of its technology, including patents.

Qualcomm's monetization of patents is supported by its large portfolio.

**Table 7-6: Snapshot of Qualcomm's Patent Portfolio**[209]

| | |
|---|---|
| U.S. patents* | 6,878 |
| U.S. patent applications | 8,752 |
| European patents and applications | 12,347 |
| Japanese patents and applications | 1,687 |
| German patents and applications | 1,990 |
| International applications | 15,259 |
| TOTAL | 46,913 |

* Of the 6,878 issued U.S. patents, about 1,502 (about 22% of the total) were issued during the twelve-month period May 22, 2012–May 21, 2013. The intensity of current activity suggests strongly that Qualcomm is not relaxing its patenting efforts, and may be increasing the intensity of its patenting efforts.

The true number of patent items in the Qualcomm patent portfolio may be significantly higher than the total number listed in Table 7-6: 46,913. The number listed does not include U.S. applications not yet published, nor does it include patents in many countries where Qualcomm is active, including Canada, Australia, and individual countries in Asia (notably the Republic of Korea), Europe, and South America. Nevertheless, on the basis of only these 46,913 patent items, it

209 All the numbers for Qualcomm's U.S. patent portfolio are taken from the PTO web site, www.uspto.gov. All other numbers are taken from www.freepatentsonline.com. It is likely the case that there is some overlap between "U.S. patent applications" and "U.S. patents", with the former maturing into the latter. However, I have not made an effort to confirm this, nor to quantify the overlap. For present purposes, we want orders of magnitude for patent portfolio and patent investment — the exact numbers are simply unnecessary. All data were gathered on May 22, 2013.

is reasonable to estimate that Qualcomm has invested something like $1.41 billion in patents over its existence.[210]

In addition to this patent information, let's consider some basic financial information about Qualcomm, taken from its annual reports.

**Table 7-7: Financial Summary for Qualcomm[211]**

| | 2006 | 2007 | 2008 | 2009 | 2010 | 2011 | 2012 | CAGR |
|---|---|---|---|---|---|---|---|---|
| **Revenues ($B)** | 7.5 | 8.9 | 11.1 | 10.4 | 10.9 | 15.0 | 19.1 | 16.8% |
| **R&D ($B)** | 1.5 | 1.8 | 2.3 | 2.4 | 2.5 | 3.0 | 3.9 | 16.8% |
| **R&D/ Revenues (%)** | 20.4 | 20.6 | 20.5 | 22.6 | 22.3 | 20.0 | 20.5 | |
| **Pre-tax income from operations ($B)** | 2.8 | 3.4 | 3.7 | 2.5[212] | 3.7 | 5.0 | 5.7 | 12.51% |

210 The actual number might be $1 billion, or $2 billion, but these variations are irrelevant. We are looking for a general magnitude.

211 Financial numbers for Qualcomm were taken from its annual reports, available at http://investor.qualcomm.com/annuals.cfm. Due to adjustments and changes in accounting policy, there are minor some differences between annual reports with regards to numbers for revenue, R&D, and pre-tax income. These differences could impact slightly the percentage calculations for R&D/Revenue, PTI/Revenue, and CAGR, but any such impacts would simply not be relevant for present purposes.

212 Qualcomm's pre-tax income has shown a steady increase throughout the period 2005–2012, with the only exception being the year 2009. Qualcomm's annual reports demonstrate that a big part of the shortfall was a pre-tax charge in 2009 of $783 million, resulting from the Broadcom settlement, discussed in Chapter 4. See, for example, *Qualcomm 10-K Report for the Period Ending 09/26/10*, at p.F-27.

What might we conclude from the information in the table above?

1. *R&D Intensity*: Qualcomm invests very heavily in R&D. Its ratio for R&D/Revenue is in the range of 20–23% throughout the period 2006–2012, which is *way* above the average for technology companies, let alone for all companies. This is the kind of ratio one might see in a high-tech startup company, but rarely in an established company.

2. *Patent Activity Intensity*: Qualcomm invests very heavily in patents. In Table 7–7 above, we see R&D investments for the period listed of about $17.4B. Qualcomm claims that, since its founding in 1985, it has invested a total of $24.7B in R&D.[213] If we take my conservative estimate of $1.41B total investment in patents, the ratio of Patent Investments to R&D Investment is 5.70%. Again, this is *way* above the average of technology companies, which is probably closer to 1%. This ratio tends to be higher for high-tech startups, but Qualcomm is far from being a startup, and its patent activity intensity is well above average for established companies.

3. *Qualcomm's Corporate Strategy*: If we were to plot technology companies for R&D intensity and patent activity intensity, Qualcomm would be an extreme outlier on both measures. What does this mean? Qualcomm must have made a basic decision, years ago and probably from its inception in the 1980s, to develop technology and obtain revenues from such technology in the form of licensing fees. Qualcomm's annual report for 2012 states, at p.F-26, that Qualcomm's revenues from technology licensing in recent years have been

213 Between its founding in 1985, and March 31, 2013, Qualcomm has invested a total of $24.7B in R&D. Investor Fact Sheets, http://investor.qualcomm.com/factsheets.cfm.

$3.7B in 2010, $5.4B in 2011, and $6.3B in 2012, constituting about 33%, 36%, and 33% of Qualcomm's total revenues in these three years, respectively. Also in these three years, profits from technology licensing were $3.0B in 2010, $4.8B in 2011, and $5.6B in 2012, constituting about 64%, 73%, and 73% of Qualcomm's total profits in these three years respectively (based on the results of Qualcomm's four operating divisions and ignoring "reconciling items"). *Ibid.* All of these revenues, and all of these profits, are derived from licensing technology, and particularly from licensing of Qualcomm's patent portfolio.[214]

From a geographic view, the summary statistics of U.S., European, Japanese, German, and international patent items show numerical strength in all of these places, and hints at additional strength in Europe, Asia, Australia, South America, etc.

Qualcomm's efforts extend from at least the early 1990s until today, with continuing intensity. In Table 7–8 below, we see a summary of some of Qualcomm's early efforts, focusing on its ten patents with the heaviest forward citations. US 5,414,796, analyzed here, is on this list of the ten most heavily cited Qualcomm patents. I have distinguished between forward non-self citations and forward self-citations.

---

214 Licenses surely include other intellectual property and know-how, but the core of the licensing is tied to Qualcomm's patent portfolio.

**Table 7–8: Forward Citations for Qualcomm's 10 Most Cited Patents[215]**

| US Patent Number | Forward citations | Forward non-self citations | Forward self-citations | Forward Non-Self citations/ Total Forward citations | Year of Filing | Year of Grant |
|---|---|---|---|---|---|---|
| **5,103,459** | 1,482 | 942 | 540 | 63.56% | 1990 | 1992 |
| **4,901,307** | 1,324 | 752 | 572 | 56.80% | 1986 | 1990 |
| **5,056,109** | 809 | 519 | 290 | 64.15% | 1989 | 1991 |
| **5,101,501** | 772 | 480 | 292 | 62.18% | 1989 | 1992 |
| **5,109,390** | 730 | 562 | 168 | 76.99% | 1989 | 1992 |
| **5,267,261** | 610 | 387 | 223 | 63.44% | 1992 | 1993 |
| **5,267,262** | 417 | 317 | 100 | 76.02% | 1991 | 1993 |
| **5,414,796** | 393 | 249 | 144 | 63.36% | 1993 | 1995 |
| **5,265,119** | 383 | 299 | 84 | 78.07% | 1991 | 1993 |
| **5,280,472** | 382 | 349 | 33 | 91.36% | 1992 | 1994 |

Whether we look at all of the forward citations, or at only the forward non-self citations, each of the ten most heavily cited Qualcomm patents has significant forward citations. Most interesting, in addition, is that all of these patents were filed from the late 1980s to the early 1990s, and all were issued in the early 1990s. Of the ten most heavily cited patents, the last one filed is US 5,414,796, filed on January 14, 1993, about six months before the first CDMA standard, IS-95, was

215 Numbers for forward citations, forward non-self citations, and forward self-citations were taken from the website www.patentbuddy.com on May 22, 2013.

published for the first time.[216] The filing dates of the patents listed above reflect Qualcomm's investments in both the technology *and the related patents* shortly before the filing of the first CDMA standard.

As noted, large patent portfolios are judged in part by their numerical strength. In even the largest portfolios, however, a few patents account for a disproportionate share of the value. I have not reviewed all ten of the patents in Table 7–8 above, but they appear to be good candidates for high value. In addition to strong forward citations, they have early priority dates, and in particular, filing dates that pre-date issuance of the first CDMA technical standard. As a group, these ten patents cover some of the main characteristics of the technology, including signal waveforms, radio repeaters, transmission power control, soft handoff, antennas, and "vocoders".

### *b. Introduction to US 5,414,796:*

This patent, entitled, "Variable Rate Vocoder", was filed on January 14, 1993, and issued on May 9, 1995, It has 249 forward non-self citations as of May 22, 3013. Despite the filing date, the priority date is June 11, 1991, because the application in this patent is a continuation of an earlier application, later abandoned.

The technology discussed in the patent is called a "variable rate vocoder". Short for "voice coder", the vocoder performs two functions, namely, analysis and synthesis. In analysis, the vocoder analyzes speech, which is analog, and converts it into digital signals. The conversion allows the speech signal

---

216 US 5,414,796 is a continuation of an earlier application, so its priority date is June 11, 1991, but the specific claims in the patent were presented when the application was filed in January, 1993.

to be sent in smaller bandwidths, hence at a higher data rate. This process of analysis is called "encoding". In addition to analysis, the vocoder receives the digitized encoded speech and "decodes" it to recreate the original analog speech. This is called "synthesis" of the original speech. This process of analysis and synthesis is "vocoding". In a "variable rate" vocoder, such as the one discussed here, the vocoder analyzes the pattern of speech, detects period of heavy usage (such as rapid talking) to which a high data rate is applied, and periods of low usage (such as silence) to which a low data rate is applied. Different data rates for different types of speech or silence are applied by a "variable rate vocoder".

*c. Why is US 5,414,796 a "seminal patent"?:*

First, this patent has an early priority date relative to the development of CDMA technology and the CDMA standards. Second, it has 249 forward non-self citations, far above the citation rate for an average patent. Third, it addresses a technical problem of great importance to Qualcomm and to the cellular industry. Fourth, its solution applies to a large market, as we will discuss.

An important and ever present issue in cellular systems is maximization of system capacity. This becomes a problem as more people use a system, or as new services are introduced, or as people make more intensive usage of current services. One obvious way to increase system capacity is to add more cell sites and more base stations. That works, but it is very expensive. A second solution is to introduce a new and more efficient air protocol, which is what happens when systems move from 1G to 2G, or 2G to 3G, or, most recently, from 3G to 4G. This kind of shift to a new generation of technology has happened about once a decade. Although the new technology almost always delivers a huge benefit in additional capacity, the shift is also expensive and time-consuming. A third solution is to "compress" speech, so that more speech may be sent in the same bandwidth. The bandwidth has not increased, but the information throughput rate has increased due to "compression". Anything that speeds up or increases the effectiveness of compression is a useful innovation.[217]

The basic innovation in US 5,414,796 is *not* that bits of information are transmitted only when there is speech (and when there is no speech, no bits are transmitted). Although such a technique is indeed a form of "compression", it was well known in the art at the time this patent was filed. This well-known technique had severe quality problems, including (1) clipped speech when talk was resumed, (2) a total absence of sound during periods of silence (which human beings find strange), (3) annoying bursts of noise created by background noise, and (4) the general ineffectiveness of adding "comfort background noise" (which was not effective because it would be akin to adding elevator music — the noise does not faithfully mimic what people hear during supposed silences in a conversation). The innovation here was not to eliminate all data during silence (the technique already well-known in the art), but rather to compress the data rate by applying relatively higher or lower data rates, while *always maintaining some level of transmission*. In other words, this is not a patent

217 Speech is never really "compressed", since that is not a physical possibility. What is meant by "compression" is that speech is digitized, information not required to recreate the voice is discarded, and the system will then transmit only the minimum number of data bits per time required to recreate the speech on the receiver side.

that increases compression, but rather one that combines a moderate degree of compression with a significantly higher level of speech quality.

To state the essence of the invention is to explain why this patent is of importance to Qualcomm and to the cellular industry. It is no surprise that the patent has received hundreds of forward non-self citations, and continues to receive such citations even now. With an early priority date and usefulness for its assignee and the industry as a whole, this is a seminal patent, and a good one for Qualcomm in terms of its claims, although not nearly as good as it could have been if certain mistakes had been avoided.

### *d. Why is US 5414,796 a "good patent"?:*

The independent claims are #1, a "*method* of speech signal compression", #18, an "*apparatus* for compressing an acoustical signal", #29, a "*circuit* for compressing an acoustical signal", and #48, a "*method* of speech signal compression". Immediately we see that, even with only four independent claims, this patent has good claim diversity.

Now let's consider the two independent method claims, #1 and #48. The best way to understand these claims is to place them side by side:

**Table 7–9: In US 5,414,796, Claims 1 and 48 Compared**

| Method claim #1 | Method claim #48 |
|---|---|
| 1. [Preamble] A method of speech signal compression, by variable rate coding of frames of digitized speech samples, comprising the steps of: | 48. [Preamble] A method of speech signal compression by variable rate coding of frames of digitized speech samples comprising the steps of: |
| [1A] determining a level of speech activity for a frame of digitized speech samples; | [1A] multiplying one frame of digitized speech samples in a sequence of said frames of digitized speech samples by a windowing function to provide a windowed frame of speech data; [2A] calculating a set of autocorrelation coefficients from said windowed frame of speech; |
| [2B] selecting an encoding rate from a set of rates based upon said determined level of speech activity for said frame; | [3B] determining an encoding rate from said set of autocorrelation coefficients; |

| Method claim #1 | Method claim #48 |
|---|---|
| [3C] coding said frame according to a coding format of a set of coding formats for said selected rate wherein each rate has a corresponding different coding format and wherein each coding format provides for a different plurality of parameter signals representing said digitized speech samples in accordance with a speech model; and | [4C] calculating from said set of autocorrelation coefficients a set of linear predictive coding (LPC) coefficients;<br>[5C] converting said set of LPC coefficients to a set of line spectral pair values;<br>[6C] quantizing said set of line spectral pair (LSP) coefficients in accordance with said rate command and said encoding rate;<br>[7C] selecting a pitch value from a predetermined set of pitch values to provide a selected pitch value for each pitch subframe in each frame of digitized speech;<br>[8C] quantizing said selected pitch value in accordance with said encoding rate and said rate command;<br>[9C] selecting a codebook value from a predetermined set of pitch values to provide a selected pitch value for a pitch frame;<br>[10C] quantizing said selected codebook value in accordance with said encoding rate and said rate command; and |
| [4D] generating for said frame a data packet of said parameter signals. | [11D] generating an output data packet comprising said quantized line spectral pair values, quantized selected pitch value, and quantized selected codebook value. |

These two claims, #1 and #48, address the same problem and present the same method. In Table 7–9, I have added a number to each claim element, as in 1, 2, 3, etc. In addition, I have added a letter to make a direct comparison between claim #1 and claim #48. For example, element [1A] in claim #1 is the first element in claim #1, and corresponds to elements [1A] and [2A] in claim #48. Similarly, element [2B] is the second element in claim #1, and corresponds to the third element in claim #48, which is [3B]. Therefore, element [3C] in claim #1 corresponds to all of elements [4C] — [10C] in claim #48, and element [4D] in claim #1 corresponds to element [11D] in claim #48.

Although claims #1 and #48 are similar in problem and solution, claim #1 is a good claim, while claim #48 is not, at least not as the word "good" is used in this book. The claims may both be valid, but the elements of #1 are sufficiently clear and broad that there may be many infringers, while claim #48 is so long and complicated that it likely does not catch any infringers.

Here is the relatively simple method outlined in #1: determine speech level => determine the encoding rate for each frame based on its speech level => apply appropriate parameter signals for each frame => use the parameter signals to create a data packet for each frame. In short, claim #1 presents a very clean and simple method.

By contrast, claim #48 has almost three times as many elements as claim #1 (11 elements versus 4), almost twice as many words (220 words versus 117), and many more nuances and complications which could be used by a defendant to avoid a charge of infringement. There is nothing technically wrong with claim #48, but the claim is so narrow that it likely has no economic value. Indeed:

- Probably no one has ever infringed #48, nor will they be likely to do so in the future;
- Even if there were infringement of claim #48, discovery of the infringement would be extremely difficult due to the many aspects that would need to appear in an infringing method;
- Even if there were discoverable infringement, a design

> around could be effected by the infringer with a small change to a single aspect of the infringing product.

A claim with such characteristics is an example of "the ninety percent rule of patent claim prosecution". This rule says that a patent may be obtained for the great majority of patent applications, perhaps 90% or more, even if the basic innovation is already well covered by prior art. The way to achieve such an allowance from a patent examiner is to add limitation upon limitation, detail upon detail, concession in prosecution upon concession, until finally the scope of the patent claim is so narrow that the examiner says, "Yes, there is something here that is not in the prior art, so I will allow this claim". Not only is the claim allowed, but also the odds are extremely high that the claim would defeat any attack on its validity. However, the odds are also extremely low that anyone would ever infringe this claim, because it is simply too narrow.[218]

The innovation here is not in specific claim terms, but rather in applying a different rate for each frame of digitized speech. It is really all of the claim elements acting together,

---

218 The "ninety percent rule of patent claim prosecution" is a phrase coined by me to express the concept that the very strong majority of patent applications can result in at least one or more allowed claims, *but only if* the applicant is prepared to make enough narrowing amendments to the claims and/or statements conceding claim coverage, so that at least something eventually will appear in a claim that is not barred by prior art. The phrase summarizes two concepts, that is, (1) in the great majority of cases, a claim may be allowed, and (2) in some cases the concession of coverage becomes so severe that it makes no economic sense to pursue the application. I do not know if 90% is the correct percentage. I am not aware of any study indicating what the correct percentage might be and, given that any study would need to require at least some speculation as to whether abandoned applications might have been allowed, it may be impossible to determine the exact percentage.

but summarized in element [3] of claim #1. This patent is an innovation to the basic method by which the system operates. The claim scope is therefore relatively broad against any defendant trying to implement the basic innovation — that is, trying to apply different data rates to different frames based on the level of speech activity in that frame.

Of the four independent claims, we have discussed already method claims #1 and #48. For the remaining independent claims, let us compare them directly to method claim #1:

**Table 7–10: In US 5,414,796, Claims 1, 18, and 29 Compared**

| Independent Method Claim #1 | Independent Apparatus Claim #18 | Independent Circuit Claim #29 |
|---|---|---|
| 1. [Preamble] A method of speech signal compression, by variable rate coding of frames of digitized speech samples, comprising the steps of: | 18. [Preamble] An apparatus for compressing an acoustical signal into variable rate data comprising: | 29. [Preamble] A circuit for compressing an acoustical signal into variable rate data comprising: |
| [1] determining a level of speech activity for a frame of digitized speech samples; | [1] means for determining a level of audio activity for an input frame of digitized samples of said acoustical signal; | [1] a circuit for determining a level of audio activity for an input frame of digitized samples of said acoustical signal; |

| Independent Method Claim #1 | Independent Apparatus Claim #18 | Independent Circuit Claim #29 |
|---|---|---|
| [2] selecting an encoding rate from a set of rates based upon said determined level of speech activity for said frame; | [2] means for selecting an output data rate from a predetermined set of rates based upon said determined level of audio activity within said frame; | [2] a circuit for selecting an output data rate from a predetermined set of rates based upon said determined level of audio activity within said frame; |
| [3] coding said frame according to a coding format of a set of coding formats for said selected rate wherein each rate has a corresponding different coding format and wherein each coding format provides for a different plurality of parameter signals representing said digitized speech samples in accordance with a speech model; and | [3] means for coding said frame according to a coding format of a set of coding formats for said selected rate to provide a plurality of parameter signals wherein each rate has a corresponding different coding format with each coding format providing a different plurality of parameter signals representing said digitized speech samples in accordance with a speech model; and | [3] a circuit for coding said frame according to a coding format of a set of coding formats for said selected rate to provide a plurality of parameter signals wherein each rate has a corresponding different coding format with each coding format providing a different plurality of parameter signals representing said digitized speech samples in accordance with a speech model; and |
| [4] generating for said frame a data packet of said parameter signals. | [4] means for providing for said frame a corresponding data packet at a data rate corresponding to said selected rate. | [4] a circuit for providing for said frame a corresponding data packet at a data rate corresponding to said selected rate. |

Even a cursory glance at these three claims suggests that they are intended to be parallel forms protecting the same basic Point of Novelty, where #1 is the method, #18 is the apparatus, and #29 is the component in the form of a circuit. This approach — where similar preambles, elements, and terminology are used to protect multiple aspects of one PON — may be called "claim parallelism", and it is one excellent technique for generating maximal protection for a particularly important Point of Novelty. In the case of US 5,414,796, however, we will see some changes in terminology that destroy the parallelism and thereby weaken the protection for the PON. In particular, there are some differences in the terminology between #1 on the one hand, and numbers 18 and 29 on the other hand.

In the preambles, claim #1 uses the phrase "digitized speech samples", whereas #18 and #29 use the phrase "acoustical signal". This change between different claims is permitted, and will not invalidate any claims, but we see already that the patent is deviating from true claim parallelism by using different terminology in different kinds of claim.

In element [1] of claim #1, the phrase used is "digitized speech samples". The equivalent phrase in #18 and #29 is "digitized sample of said acoustic signal". Each claim is consistent within itself, but it is absolutely clear now that the claims are not parallel, since claim #1 is different from claims 18 and 29. If the patentee intended to achieve claim parallelism, that has now been lost due to shifting terminology among the various claims.

In element [2], claim #1 says, "determined level of speech activity", whereas in #18 and #29 the parallel phrase is, "determined level of audio activity". Although we cannot be sure why different phrases are used, at least we can say that the elements of each claim are consistent within the claim, even though claim #1 is different from claims 18 and 29. That is to say, to this point, the various parts of claim #1 are consistent among themselves, the parts of claim #18 are consistent among themselves, and the parts of claim #29 are consistent within themselves. Claim #1 is different from claim #18, and also from claim #29, but again, each claim is consistent within itself, even though claim parallelism with claim #1 has been lost.

In element [3], claim #1 refers to "a different plurality of parameter signals representing said digitized speech samples in accordance with a speech model". *Element [3] of claim #18 and element [3] of claim #29 use exactly the same phrase as element [3] of claim #1, word for word. The shifting terminology within the single claim #18, and also within the single claim #29, creates an enormous problem for this patent.* The problem is that up to this point, claim #18 and claim #29 have been different from claim #1, but each of the three claims (1, 18, and 29) has been consistent within itself. However, claims 18 and 29 shift over to the language of claim #1 and use the phrase "said digitized *speech samples*" instead of "said digitized *samples of acoustical signals*". The problem is that neither claim #18 nor claim #29 present, in a preamble or in any of the elements [1] — [3], the phrase "digitized speech" or the phrase "speech samples". Therefore, element [3] in each of claim #18 and claim #29 appears to be "indefinite", violating the requirement of 35 USC sec. 112(2). Indefinite claims are invalid, and therefore cannot be infringed. We now see, in claims 18 and 29, examples of what is called "shifting terminology within a single claim".

Here are the specific words that create the problem:

**Table 7–11: Definite and Indefinite Claims in US 5,414,796**

| | **Claim #1** | **Claim #18** | **Claim #29** |
|---|---|---|---|
| **Preamble** | "digitized speech samples" | "acoustical signal" | "acoustical signal" |
| **Element [1]** | "digitized speech samples" | "digitized samples of said acoustical signals" | "digitized samples of said acoustical signals" |
| **Element [2]** | "speech activity" | "audio activity" | "audio activity" |
| **Element [3]** | "said digi-tized speech samples" | "said digitized speech samples" | "said digitized speech samples" |
| **RESULT** | **This claim is fine.** | **This claim is indefinite due to shifting terminol-ogy in element [3]. It is therefore invalid.** | **This claim is indefinite due to shifting terminol-ogy in element [3]. It is therefore invalid.** |

What does all this really mean? The patent never went to litigation, to the best of my knowledge. Had it gone to litigation, there is a serious possibility that the judge would have invalidated independent claim #18, dependent claims 19–28 which depend on #18, independent claim #29, and dependent claims 30–47 which depend on #29. In other words, there would have been a serious possibility that a judge would invalidate 62.5% of the claims in US 5,414,796. Why? Because people reading the claims 18 and 29 cannot know what is meant by "acoustic signals" or "digitized speech", they cannot know why the claim language changed from one phrase to the other, and they therefore cannot know the true scope of claims 18 and 29. As a result of shifting terminology within claim #18, and also within claim #29, there has been created "vertical claim confusion", which occurs when different elements within a single claim use different terminology. Vertical claim confusion is a fatal defect in the infected claim.[219]

*Arguments by the patent owner Qualcomm:* How might the patentee Qualcomm argue to save claims 18–47? Here are some arguments it might have made to a judge to preserve the claims:

(1) It is clear that the patent equates "acoustical signal" with "digitized speech", and in fact digitized speech is a form of acoustical signal. Therefore, "said digitized speech" should be read as "said acoustical signal", and there is no problem of indefiniteness under 35 USC sec.112(2).

(2) Even if there were such a problem, the Court of Appeals for the Federal Circuit has clearly ruled in past decisions that lack of antecedent basis is *not* a reason to invalidate a claim, *if* there is no confusion as to what the claim means.[220]

---

219 If the patentee's intent was to create claim parallelism between different claims, then shifting terminology between claims will create "horizontal claim confusion", which destroys the parallelism and weakens protection for the Point of Novelty. However, "horizontal claim confusion" does not destroy an individual claim, since each claim may still be consistent within itself. By contrast, "vertical claim confusion" means that different elements *of the same claim* use different terms, and this is a fatal flaw, because a reader of the claim cannot know what the claim actually covers. A claim with vertical claim confusion should never be allowed by the PTO but, if allowed in error, will almost certainly not survive in litigation.

220 See *Energizer Holdings, Inc. v. International Trade Commission,* 435 F.3d 1366; 77 U.S.P.Q.2D 1625 (Fed. Cir. 2006). In *Energizer Holdings*, the problem with the patent claim related to the appearance of the modifying word "said" in the claim, where the object to which the modifier attached had

Moreover, it is the defendant's burden to show confusion. Since the intent is clear, and there is no real evidence of confusion, it would be inequitable to invalidate more than 60% of the claims simply because the word "said" appears incorrectly in claim #18 and claim #29.

*Counter-arguments by a defendant against Qualcomm:* Hearing these arguments from Qualcomm, a defendant might reply to the court as follows:

(1) There is no doubt that all of the claims 18–47 are indefinite under 35 USC sec.112(2). A definite phrase such as "said noun", requires that the "noun", whatever it be, appear earlier in the claim. This is not an optional rule, but rather a requirement. The phrase "digitized speech sample" or "speech samples" may appear in element [3] of claims 18 and 29, but it does not appear in the preambles, or in element [1] or element [2]. Because claims 18 and 29 are clearly indefinite, all of their dependent claims are also indefinite, with the result

---

not appeared in the claim. That seems to be similar to what happened here, with the Qualcomm patent. In *Energizer Holdings*, the phrase was "said zinc anode", and the antecedent object "zinc anode" had not appeared in the claim. In the current case, the phrase at issue is "said digitized speech samples", where "digitized speech samples" does not appear in claim #18 or claim #29. So Qualcomm might argue that on the basis of *Energizer Holdings*, incorrect use of "said" might make the claim inelegant, but should not invalidate the claim for indefiniteness. Note, however, one big difference between the two cases. In *Energizer Holdings*, the antecedent precedent was "anode gel comprised of zinc", later called, incorrectly, "*said zinc anode*" when the correct formulation should have been: "*said anode gel comprised of zinc*". This was bad claim drafting by Energizer Holdings. However, everyone, not only an expert in the technology, would know what the patent meant. That is not the case with US 5,414,796, in which the antecedent precedent was "acoustical signal" and the further refinement was "said digitized speech samples". The error in US 5,414,796 is one where a reader would have great trouble knowing what the patent really means. This is a potentially fatal error, and this kind of the confusion can kill most of the claims in Qualcomm's patent.

that claims 18–47 are all indefinite. Whether these claims may be rehabilitated is a separate question, but in the first instance they are all indefinite.

(2) The patentee, Qualcomm, has correctly stated the legal standard for "indefiniteness", but the question is whether there is confusion in this particular patent. The defendant points out:

a. At no point in the patent is "digitized speech" equated with "acoustical signals", nor is the phrase "speech samples" equated with "acoustical signals". This is confusing in itself. If the patent had intended to equate "acoustical signals" with "digitized speech samples", either (1) that definition would have appeared in the patent, or (2) examples would have been presented equating the two terms or, (3) most simply, the patent would not have used "acoustical signals" in claims 18 and 29 but instead would have used "digitized speech samples" or "digitized speech" in the preambles and in elements [1] of these two claims. None of these occurred. Therefore, there is confusion about the meaning of independent claims 18 and 29, so claims 18–47 should be invalidated by the court.

b. One of the problems in the prior art that this patent intends to solve, as stated in column 2, lines 31–38, is the problem of introducing "comfort noise" into speech information as part of the decoding process. Introducing comfort noise as done in the prior art works badly because, according to the patent, "the comfort noise does not model the actual background noise at the encoder". US 5,414,796 solves this problem by retaining the background noise, which it does by a "reduction in the data rate, as opposed to a complete halt in data transmission", col. 2, lines 46–47. *Therefore, the invention involves compressing both speech and background noise.*

*However, both of these, speech and background noise, are types of "acoustical signals".*

In short, both "speech" and "noise" are types of "acoustical signals". So when "acoustical signal" appears in both the preamble and element [1] of claims 18 and 29, but "said digitized speech samples" appears in element [3], there is confusion as to whether claims 18 and 29 are intended to cover only "speech", or both "speech" and "noise". This is specifically the kind of confusion that 35 USC sec.112(2) is intended to prevent. Hence, shifting terminology within claim #18 has created vertical claim confusion, which should invalidate both claim #18 and all of claims 19–28 dependent on claim #18. Similarly, shifting terminology within claim #29 creates vertical claim confusion that should invalidate both claim #29 and all of claims 30–47 dependent on claim #29. Thus, in US 5,414,796, all of claims 18–47 should be invalidated if the patent went to trial, and all this due to the shifting of terminology in claims 28 and 29.

Qualcomm could respond to a defendant's arguments, after which the defendant could respond to Qualcomm's response, and so on. One cannot know which way a court would rule ultimately. We can say only that a defendant would have a strong argument to invalidate all of these claims, primarily because "acoustical signal" seems to include both "noise" and "speech", with the result that it is very difficult for people reading claims 18 and 29 to understand the true scope of these claims.

In fact, the problem is not really the phrase "said digitized speech samples", but rather the appearance of the single word "said". Apart from that one word, element [3] in claims 18 and 29 could be interpreted without reference to the preamble or prior elements, and the claims would probably be interpreted in some way to maintain their validity. It is the fatal combination of the word "said" with the shifting terminology in element [3] of claims 18 and 29 which casts doubt on the validity of claims #18–47.

**Validity**: I see no validity problems with independent claim #1, dependent claims 2–17, or independent claim #48. However, the validity of claims 18–47 is doubtful.

**Scope**: The scope of the independent claims 1, 18, and 29, is broad, particularly claim #1. This patent does not cover all forms of speech compression. It does not cover, for example, compression techniques in which absence of speech is not transmitted, or where artificial "comfort noise" is inserted to mimic natural background noise. However, the patent does cover implementations of speech compression where each frame is transmitted at its own data rate. That is a broad scope in an important technology, which makes the patent valuable.

The claim mix is very good with #1 (method), #18 (apparatus), and #29 (component, specifically a circuit). Unfortunately, the dubious validity of claims 18 and 29 reduces very much the value that might have been derived from this claim mix.

Independent method claim #48 is so long and complicated as to be almost useless in terms of scope. It has eleven claim elements and over 200 words, which will mean that infringement probably has not occurred, if it did occur the infringement might not be discoverable, and if discoverable infringement occurred the infringer could still probably design around claim #48. As noted, validity and scope are natural enemies. In this case, claim #48 is almost certainly valid, but its claim scope is very narrow.

**Discoverability of Infringement**: I see no great problem in discovery of infringement for claims 1, 18, and 29. Discovering infringement of claim #48 is more difficult, as noted.

**Summary**: This patent has hundreds of forward non-self citations and covers technical implementations of speech compression of great interest both to Qualcomm and the cellular mobile industry. Except for claim #48, the independent claims have few elements, and the claim elements are clear, with key claim terms either well understood or defined in the patent.

Unfortunately, because of the addition of the word "said" into element [3] of claim #18 and claim #29, combined with shifting terminology within each claim, the validity of almost all the structure claims is in doubt. Nevertheless, even if claims 18–47 were invalidated, and even though claim #48 is essentially without any value in catching infringers, the validity of method claims 1–17 and their breadth of scope combine to create significant value to Qualcomm in US 5,414,796. Even if claims 18–47 were lost, this "seminal patent" would retain significant value.

**Lessons Learned**: Here are some lessons which may be learned about good patents from patent claims 1, 18, 29, and 48 in US 5,414,796, issued to Qualcomm. There are lessons to be learned both for individual patents, and for the portfolio of a company. Let's look at each subject separately.

**Lessons for Individual Patents:**

7–3–1 (Individual). ***A seminal patent may cover only some***

***implementations, but still be seminal.*** In this case the innovation, contrary to prior art and to what you might expect, is *not* increasing data compression to improve bandwidth and increase system capacity. In fact, the patent does the opposite, since it ensures that at all times, even during periods of speech silence, there is some rate of transmission, albeit slow. Rather, the innovation is to combine compression with good speech quality, which is achieved by transmitting background noise together with digitized and compressed speech. Although this patent does not cover all implementations of compression, it does cover enough important implementations to make this a seminal patent.

7–3–2 (Individual). ***"Normal claims" and "claims by the ninety percent rule" are significantly different.*** A "normal claim" is one that has passed through ordinary application preparation and prosecution. A "claim by the ninety percent rule" is a claim allowed only because it has added enough amendments and other limitations to finally distinguish its Point of Novelty from the prior art. A "ninety percent rule" claim is not only allowed but becomes highly resistant to validity challenges, because the PON is based on a clear and narrow distinction from prior art. However, a "ninety percent rule claim" has the three disadvantages of (1) being unlikely to be infringed due to its narrow scope, (2) having difficult discovery of infringement, and (3) being vulnerable to design around. In this case, #48 appears to be a classic example of a "claim by the ninety percent rule".

7–3–3 (Individual). ***Definitions of key claim terms are not required if all of the terms are very well known in the prior art.*** This is the case in the current patent. The innovation is not the change in one of the claim terms, but rather to reverse the general technical approach. The prior approach said, "Let's do as much data compression as we can". The approach in this patent says, "Let's have only a reasonable amount of compression, but continue transmitting at lower rates to maintain speech quality". With this approach, it was not necessary to use new and unique claim terms, or to change the standard meaning of claim terms well known in the prior art.

7-3-4 (Individual). ***Parallel claim structure between different claims requires exactly parallel claim language***. This requirement may seem obvious, but it is unfulfilled in many cases, as here. Method claim #1 uses the phrase "digitized speech samples", whereas the parallel claims, apparatus claim #18 and component claim #29, use the phrase "acoustical signal". The difference in phrasing destroys the parallelism among the claims, because the claims are referring to different things. If the patentee's intent was to use claim parallelism to maximize protection of a single Point of Novelty, the intent was frustrated and maximal protection unachieved, due to shifting terminology between different claims that creates horizontal claim confusion. The result is that what should have been excellent claim diversity in this patent is destroyed, because we have method claims talking about one thing ("digitized speech samples"), and structure claims, both for the apparatus and the component, talking about a different thing ("acoustical signals"). When you ask yourself, "How do I know if my patent's any good?", ask yourself, "Am I creating parallel claims for claim diversity?" If the answer is yes, then make sure that the language in your patent claims is in fact parallel. That is exactly what did not happen in claims 1, 18, and 29, of US 5,414,796.

7-3-5 (Individual). ***Shifting terms within a single claim can cause catastrophic consequences.*** The result of shifting terminology within a single claim is "vertical claim confusion". That is what happened here. Independent claims 18 and 29 use the term "acoustical signal" and then inexplicably shift to "digitized speech samples". This shift in terminology by itself creates confusion. Much worse, the phrase used is not merely "digitized speech samples", which might be interpreted in some way, but rather "*said* digitized speech samples" [emphasis in italics added]. The word "said" is a patent word that means, "in reference to the term already introduced *in the same claim*, there is an additional limitation". However, if there is no prior reference *in the same claim*, then a situation of "indefiniteness" is created, in violation of the requirement of 35 USC sec.112(2). If a court feels that everyone clearly knows what was intended, then the court might rehabilitate this otherwise "indefinite claim". Here, however, the problem is that the clash is between two terms, "acoustical signal" and "digitized speech samples", in which the former term seems to include both "digitized speech" and "background noise". The result is that it is very difficult to know what is covered in claim #18 and claim #29. If this patent went to litigation, there is a serious chance that both of these claims would be invalidated, together with all of their dependent claims. The catastrophic result would be invalidation of most of the claims due to shifting claim terminology combined with the indefiniteness caused by the single word "said".

7-3-6 (Individual). ***A patent that suffers catastrophic loss of claims may still be valuable.*** Even if claims 18–47 were invalidated, and claim #48 were too narrow to be of much value, method claims 1–17 would still survive, preserving much of the value inherent in US 5,414,796. *External events* (such as the late filing for US 5,774,670 discussed in Chapter 5) *can destroy an entire patent and all its claims. By contrast, events internal to the patent* (such as the shifting terminology in claims 18 and 19 here) *may destroy all the claims relying upon such terminology but will leaved untouched other claims.*

**Lessons for Patent Portfolios:**

7-3-1 (Portfolio). ***A technology company must determine its strategic focus with regard to patents***. Qualcomm is an aggressive developer and licensor of technology. We can judge this by the magnitude of its perennial investment in R&D, its investment in patents, its patent portfolio, its revenues derived from technology licensing, and its profits derived from technology licensing. We can judge this also by benchmark ratios such as R&D investment/Revenues, Patent investment/R&D investment, Technology licensing revenue/Total Revenues, and Licensing Profits/Total Profits. In all these benchmarks, Qualcomm's numbers are much higher than those of the average technology company. All of this information is consistent with the company's strategic focus on aggressively developing and licensing technology.

7-3-2 (Portfolio). ***A good patent portfolio matches the strategic focus of its owner***. Qualcomm's portfolio has at least 40,000 patent items, and probably more, geographically distributed among multiple countries of interest. In terms of timing, Qualcomm invested heavily in patents at the beginning of CDMA technology in the late 1980's and early 1990's, and the company continues to generate thousands of patents per year. By any of the three measures of patent portfolio, which are (1) absolute size of the portfolio, (2) geographic balance of the portfolio, and (3) balance of the portfolio over time, Qualcomm's portfolio supports its strategic focus.

The issues regarding Qualcomm's patent portfolio are the quality of its key patents and the scope of coverage by these patents. I have discussed here only one of Qualcomm's most heavily cited patents.[221] A full review of this portfolio would require, at a minimum, identification of the key patents in the portfolio, and then review of the claims in those key patents. Whatever the result of such a review, it is clear already that Qualcomm has aspired, with much effort, to create the kind of patent portfolio whose quality and coverage will support its licensing activities.[222]

7–3–3 (Portfolio). ***To maintain portfolio value, patenting activities must continue over time***. This may appear obvious, but many companies engage in bursts of patenting activity in a concentrated period of time, then stop their efforts. That may be true, for example, of Silanis Technology, discussed earlier. Although suspension of patenting activity is a possible

---

221 In fact, as of May 22, 2013, at least seven Qualcomm patents have more forward citations than US 5,414,796, and at least nine Qualcomm patents have more forward non-self citations than US 5,414,796.

222 Qualcomm has been one of premier developers and licensors of advanced technology. Like many companies involved in monetizing technology, Qualcomm finds that its licensing practices are challenged on occasion. A spirited defense of Qualcomm's activities with regard to FRAND licensing was written by Stéphane Tronchon (Director of IPR Policy at Qualcomm), and appears in the book by Claudia Tapia, *Industrial Property Rights, Technical Standards and Licensing Practices (FRAND) in the Telecommunications Industry*, Carl Heymanns Verlag, Cologne (2010), at pp.269–280. This is a fine book about the legal issues of FRAND licensing, with some excellent primary source material in the Annexes. The author is now known by the full name Claudia Tapia Garcia, and she is co-author of the article "Patent Application Prioritization and Resource Allocation Strategy", previously referenced.

strategic approach, it will lead inevitably to the decline over time in the scope and quality of the portfolio. Qualcomm has pursued persistently an aggressive strategy with regard to patents, and has continued to invest in patents. Not every company will follow Qualcomm's approach, but each company should review its strategic focus periodically and decide how best to engage in continuing patent activities. To do nothing is a legitimate choice, but that should be a decision and not merely a drift over time.

7–3–4 (Portfolio). ***Timing of patent activity in relation to technical standards may impact portfolio value.*** All ten of the Qualcomm patents most heavily cited by forward citations were filed in the period 1986–1993, and were issued in the period 1990–1995. The patent filings for these ten patents all occurred before the first publication of a CDMA technical standard in July, 1993. These patents were all issued before the first deployment of the first CDMA system, which occurred in September, 1995, in Hong Kong. It would seem that Qualcomm made a conscious decision to contribute to the CDMA standard, and to obtain patents relevant to the standard. To have patents relevant to a standard, which predate publication of the standard, can enhance the value of a portfolio.[223]

---

223 "Relevant" to the standard is one thing. "Essential" to the standard is another thing. I discuss patent "essentiality" in Chapter 6 above and in my prior book, *Technology Patent Licensing, op. cit.* in Chapter 3, pp.88–141.

# Part III

# Summary

# Chapter 8

# Summary

Chapter 8 summarizes key ideas presented in the preceding chapters. These key ideas include basic concepts about patents in Chapter 1, the process of patent evaluation in Chapter 2, and the "lessons learned" about patents and patent portfolios in Chapters 3–7. The key ideas in Chapter 8 are presented in Question & Answer format, grouped according to logical topics.

I: Basic Characteristics of a Good Patent (Q & A 1–6)
II: What are Valuable Claims? (Q & A 7–23)
III: What is Good Support for Claims? (Q & A 24–29)
IV: External Events that Destroy Patent Value (Q & A 30–31)
V: Evaluating a Portfolio of Patents (Q & A 32–45)
VI: Final Thoughts (Q & A 46–48)

## I: Basic Characteristics of a Good Patent

### *Q1: What is a "good patent"?*

Recall Preface Chart 1. A "good patent" has two basic characteristics:

- Good claims
- Good support for the claims in the written description

A patent that meets these two criteria is a well-drafted patent, with coverage as reasonably broad as possible given the subject matter of the patent. However, a "good patent" alone is not a "valuable patent".

A valuable patent is a good patent that, in addition, is infringed now or will be infringed in the very near future. Also, there has been no "external event that destroys patent value". A patent that meets all of these criteria — good claims, good support, infringed, and no external events destroying value — has "true value".

If a marketing and financial study shows that there is very significant infringement of the claims, then the patent is, in addition, a "very valuable patent".

That answer summarizes this book. The rest is commentary.

### *Q2: Is there any difference between "patent quality" and "patent value"? If so, what is it?*

When speaking about patents, many people use the terms "quality" and "value" interchangeably, as though they are synonymous. The terms are not the same, and a distinction should be made.

A "high-quality" patent is a "good patent", meaning it has good claims (that are likely to be valid, and whose scope is as broad as reasonably possible), with good support of the claims in the written description (particularly, clear explanation of the "key claim terms"). This means only that the patent was well written, not that it has value.

Value is quality enhanced by significant infringement, and an absence of any external events that destroy the value of the patent.

## *Q3: When I look at the patent, what should I focus on?*

"The name of the game is the claim". Understand the claims and determine if they are supported sufficiently in the written description and figures.

For the claims, you should perform a VSD analysis, at least for every independent claim. To do that, you need to:

(1) Define the Point of Novelty for each independent claim,
(2) Identify the key claim terms in each independent claim, and
(3) Determine if the key claim terms are supported with definitions, examples, elements in the figures, or other explanation in the written description.

## *Q4: If I want to figure out if my patent is any good, what must I look at?*

To evaluate claims and their support, you must review, at a minimum: (1) the patent itself, and (2) the history of prosecution at the PTO. Together, they give you a basis to determine whether or not the patent is "good". Although even these are not sufficient, because they do not deal with "external events", the patent and its history are necessary starting points.

## *Q5: When I look at a prosecution history, what should I look at?*

Look at all of the following:

(1) Any amendment to the claims,
(2) Every "Rejection," whether "Final" or "Non-Final,"

by the patent office. (These are known as "Office Actions"),
(3) Applicant arguments/remarks in response to a Rejection,
(4) Terminal Disclaimer, if any,
(5) Advisory Action if any,
(6) Notice of Allowance, and
(7) Prior art cited by the patent examiner.

In other words, review every part of the prosecution history that has, or might have, substantial impact on the claims.

When you look at this material, try to determine (1) if any of the claims were disallowed and why (where "disallowed" means a claim was "rejected" or "objected to" by the examiner), (2) if the claims were amended, and (3) if there is any waiver or other concession of the applicant that might limit the claims. Also, (4) in the Notice of Allowance, determine why the examiner chose to allow the claims.

My experience is that it is very difficult to review a prosecution history the first few times. After you review many histories, you will become much better at it. However, this is truly an area of great complexity, and you should consider consulting a patent attorney before reaching a final conclusion about the meaning and impact of a prosecution history. Nevertheless, your preliminary work may save you time and money as well as provide you with a better basis for evaluating and using expert guidance.

### *Q6: Can't I just apply some proxy factors, like number of claims, or number of forward citations, and use that to evaluate the patent, rather than actually going through it?*

This question is really asking about the difference between proxy fundamental analysis, "PFA", based on factors applied in an automated manner, and expert fundamental analysis, "EFA", which requires evaluation by a human evaluator. These differences are explained in Chapter 2.

EFA is a higher quality review than PFA, but EFA is expensive in terms of the time and money that must be invested by technical and legal experts. EFA makes sense when a patent, or a group of patents, are subject to imminent sale, licensing, or litigation, or when a valuation is being performed on a company in which the value of the company's intellectual property is considered a significant asset or potential asset. That may seem broadly inclusive, but the fact is that most analyses are not in-depth EFA analyses. Rather, most analyses are either automated PFA analyses or abbreviated EFA analyses (often lasting no more than 2–5 minutes per patent). Because of the high cost of in-depth EFA analyses, PFA plays an important role in the analysis of patents.

No PFA is perfect, and PFA can't approach the quality of in-depth EFA. However, certain factors, or "gateways", indicate that a patent *might be good,* and thus be *a candidate for an expert fundamental analysis.* I have suggested several possible gateways here which do not prove, but which may strongly suggest, patent value. Victory in litigation, sale for a significant sum, essentiality to an important technical standard, seminality for an important technology area and market need — all are criteria that may be applied in an automated manner. None of them prove patent value, but they suggest that value might be discovered by an EFA.

In cases where quality of review is critical, there is no substitute for an in-depth review by a skilled human evaluator. Helping you prepare for such a review, whether you do it yourself or work with others, is one purpose of this book.

## II: What Are Valuable Claims?

### *Q7: What are "good claims" and what are "valuable claims"?*

A "good claim" is a claim that is likely to be valid, and whose scope of coverage is as broad as reasonably possible for the subject matter. A "valuable claim" is a good claim that creates "value". Value requires three things:

(1) Importance of the technical problem addressed by the patent,
(2) Market size of the subject in the patent, and
(3) Simplicity and elegance of the solutions presented in the patent claims.

Market and technology are important in determining the value of a patent. However, do not forget that in patent law, patent claims are like the trump suit in a game of bridge — they take precedence over the size of the market and the technical problem addressed by the patent. A patent with an early priority date, a good market, and an important technical problem, will be "trumped", that is to say, its claim will be invalidated, by a serious problem in the definition of key claim terms. In essence, a poor quality patent, due to weak claims, cannot have significant value.

In determining whether the patent has value, market scope and technology importance might overcome minor problems in a claim, lesson 7–1–2, but they will not overcome major problems in a claim, lesson 7–1–3.

These three things — importance of technical problem addressed, market size, and solution in the claims — apply to every kind of patent, whether the innovation is breakthrough or incremental.

### *Q8: Why is the importance of the technical problem addressed by the patent a factor in patent value?*

This is a lesson that has come up several times in the cases. All of the seminal patents in Chapter 7 — including the patents of Check Point Software, Scientific Atlanta/Silanis Technology, and Qualcomm — are patents that appear to address large and pressing technical problems in their respective fields, such as, respectively, electronic firewalls, electronic signatures, and voice coding for cellular communication.

By contrast, all of the patents determined to be "essential" to either MPEG-2 or W-CDMA, discussed in Chapter 6, including the patents of Philips, Sharp, and Siemens, present incremental improvements only. The patents in Chapter 6 have value, but they are not "seminal" or breakthrough patents, either because the technical problem discussed was a problem that was declining in importance (in the case of Philips, related to compact discs) or because the technical problem addressed was important but the solution was incremental (in the cases of Sharp and Siemens, related to minor improvements of power control in cellular communication).

Patents with incremental technical improvements can be high-quality, and may add financial value as part of a large portfolio, but generally such patents do not take the lead in licensing and litigation programs.

### *Q9: Without even reading the patent, are there technology areas unlikely to be good?*

This book focuses on ICT patents, not BCP patents. BCP patents can be extremely valuable, but they are not the focus here. Within ICT, semiconductor and manufacturing patents tend to be relatively problematic, specifically because discoverability of infringement is often difficult. That does not mean the patents are not valuable, and in fact there have been some large court awards in the area of semiconductors.[224] Nevertheless, it is relatively difficult to establish value in such patents due to problems of discovering infringement. However, if difficulties of discoverability can be overcome, then there is nothing wrong or problematic with semiconductor or manufacturing patents.

### *Q10: Are there areas that are likely to be good for patent value?*

There is a discussion of "technology inflection points" in Chapter 2, Section 5. There are two kinds of technology inflection points. One is a point of current technology where system

---

224 In a recent semiconductor case, *Carnegie Mellon University v. Marvel Technology Group, Ltd., and Marvel Semiconductor, Inc.*, U.S. District Court, Western District of Pennsylvania, No. 09–00290 (decided December 26, 2012), a jury awarded the plaintiff $1.17 billion for the infringement of a patent claim in each of two patents. Despite the relative difficult in discovering infringement in semiconductor cases, such cases are brought and won.

performance can be improved dramatically by a change in the way things are done. The second is a point of technology that can be changed by a paradigm shift away from the current technology to a new type of technology. Examples are noted there in the areas of transportation, wireline communication, wireless communication, and the Internet.

New technology is not magic. It is planned work. In many cases, an analyst or evaluator can predict new technology inflection points. If you generate or buy early-priority patents with strong coverage for a technology inflection point, you may create great patent value.

### *Q11: Why is market size a factor in determining value?*

By "market size", I mean, "who is infringing at this moment?", and "who will infringe in the very near future?" There is no accepted definition of "very near future". Some people pick "three years" as the time limit, but it really depends on a person's time horizon and on the person's tolerance for risk. In whatever way "very near future" is defined in a specific case, you can be sure of two things: (1) If there is no infringement now, and no infringement is expected in the very near future, then there is no market, hence no market size, hence no financial value to the patent, whether or not the patent is high-quality. (2) If there is no infringement now, but infringement is expected "in the very near future", then the patent will have value, but the value will be discounted by the risk that the infringement may not actually happen.

When you are trying to determine whether there is, or will soon be, infringement, *do not forget that there is both direct and indirect infringement*. Remember that in the case of *Broadcom v. Qualcomm*, Broadcom patent 6,714,983 (lesson

4–1–7) won the day primarily because of the double threat of indirect infringement liability for Qualcomm and direct liability for Qualcomm's customers. Consider also the Ballantyne patent, US 5,133,079 (lesson 5–1–6), where there was a serious threat that cable television customers might be directly liable, which could create *indirect* liability for the suppliers of cable equipment and cable system operators.[225]

When you are determining value, try to think of all possible infringers, both direct and indirect, now and in the very near future.

### *Q12: What is meant by "simplicity and elegance of the solutions presented in the patent claims"?*

I mean that the claims do well in a VSD evaluation.

### *Q13: What is a VSD Evaluation?*

This is a way of evaluating the quality of claims in a patent. "VSD" is an acronym for "**V**alidity, **S**cope of coverage, and **D**iscoverability of infringement". Scores for each of V, S, and D, are typically the end result of an expert fundamental analysis ("EFA"), which is analysis of value by a human evaluator.

In performing a VSD analysis, remember that Validity and Scope are natural enemies. A patent with claims of extremely broad scope might seem to be a great patent, but unfortunately claims of such scope are often subject in litigation to

225 Further, the majority opinion in CAFC *Akamai* created an entirely new theory of legal liability, which is "indirect liability (specifically inducement) where there is no direct liability". This change in law increases the need to consider both possible direct infringement and possible indirect infringement, in order to determine the value of the patent.

challenges of invalidity. Correspondingly, patent claims can be written so narrowly that they are almost certainly valid, but in the end they may be subject to the "ninety percent rule of patent prosecution" that makes the claims virtually worthless for the purpose of finding and prosecuting infringement.

An excellent example of this tension between Validity and Scope appears in the case *Broadcom v. Qualcomm*, US 6,714,983, lesson 4-1-5, in which the plaintiff, the owner of the patent, argued for a narrow definition of the key claim term "different" whereas the defendant argued for a broader definition of the same key claim term. Why did they reverse the typical postures of a plaintiff and a defendant in a patent litigation? Both parties knew that if this key claim term were interpreted broadly, there was a good chance the claim would be invalidated as not being new. In other word, Broadcom argued for a narrower scope but a strong chance of validity, while Qualcomm argued for a broader scope and a good chance of invalidity. The court interpreted the word "different" narrowly, and in the resulting settlement, Qualcomm paid Broadcom $891 million. (Had the court interpreted "different" broadly, the claim might have been invalidated, and Qualcomm might have paid Broadcom nothing.)

### *Q14: What is the ninety percent rule of patent prosecution?*

This is a rule that says that it is possible to obtain a patent claim in 90% or so of prosecutions, but the resulting claim may be so narrowed by amendments or other limitations as to be useless for purposes of proving any infringement. Such a claim will probably be allowed, but it will have very narrow scope, because (1) probably no one infringes or will infringe the claim, (2) if they did infringe, you wouldn't know it, and (3) even if you did discover an infringement, the infringer would very likely be able to design around the infringement.

Method claim #48 in US 5,414,796, lesson 7–3–2 (Individual), is a possible example of a claim subject to this rule. It is instructive because its parallel claim, method claim #1, has a much greater scope than claim #48.

## *Q15: What are the important parts of a claim?*

A claim has three components, and they are all important.

*Claim Component (1): The Preamble.* A short preamble with little detail beyond a basic introduction of the topic is almost always good. For example, in AT&T's patent 6,478,200, lesson 3–1–1, the entire preamble is, "A telephone system". This preamble introduces the topic, but does not include details. The difficulty with details in the preamble is that sometimes they become part of the claim (if they introduce a claim term discussed in the elements) and sometimes they do not become part of the claim, *but you can never be 100% sure, before litigation, if the preamble details will be interpreted by a court to be part of the claim.* Confusion is avoided by omitting details from the preamble, and putting them instead into the body of the claim.

Here is an example which, on first glance, might seem to show the exact opposite of what I just said. In the case *Uniloc v. Microsoft*, lesson 3–2–1, US 5,490,216, claim #19, the entire preamble is, "A remote registration station". The elements of the claim seem to include both server-side elements (such as "remote" ID generating means) and client-side elements (such as "local" ID generating means). Microsoft's second argument, as noted in Chapter 3, is essentially a divided infringement argument. Microsoft said it did not control the local elements, hence such elements were not fulfilled, and hence there is no direct infringement. The CAFC held for the plaintiff Uniloc because, said the Court, the entire claim was for a "remote registration station" *as set out in the preamble*, and such a station was indeed supplied and used by Microsoft. Hence, the split in the elements between "client-side" ("local") and "server-side" ("remote"), was irrelevant because, *as the preamble stated*, this was a single station controlled by patentee Microsoft. The addition of the word "remote" *to the preamble* won this argument for Uniloc.

However, this example is *not* contrary to the general rule, because *Uniloc v. Microsoft* might easily have gone the other way, since the winning term was in the preamble (improperly) rather than in the body of the claim (where it should have been). If the winning claim term had been in the body of the claim, there would have been no doubt, and the plaintiff would have won this argument without a battle. (In fact, the argument almost certainly would never have been made by Microsoft). Again, you can never be certain in advance of litigation how a court will interpret a claim preamble. If you put details into the preamble, you can never be sure if the court will include those terms in the claim (as the court did in *Uniloc*) or not. Better to remove any doubt by placing all details of the claim in the elements, not the preamble.

*Claim Component (2): The Transition.* In an ICT patent, there is no advantage to deviate from the standard claim transition, "comprising". This is an "open-ended" transition, meaning it includes everything in the claim, but anything else added will not alter a judgment of infringement. By contrast, the "close-ended" transitions, "consisting", and "consisting essentially of", may be suitable for BCP patents but should never appear in an ICT application. Phrases like "having", which might or might not be interpreted as "comprising", should not be used, because they are ambiguous, unlike "comprising".

If I see an ICT patent with the transition "consisting" in an independent claim, I deeply discount the patent's value. If I see any transition in an independent claim that might be other than "comprising", such as "having", I will take a closer look, but I will be suspicious about claim scope.

*Claim Component (3): The Elements.* Everything after the "transition" is called the "body" of the claim. Everything in the body of the claim, every word and every punctuation mark, belongs to only one "element" of the claim. Any or all of the preamble, transition, and elements of the claim may determine the validity, scope, or discoverability of infringement of the claim. However, in a well-written claim, the validity, scope, and discoverability are each determined solely by what is written in the elements of the claim, not from the preamble or the transition.

## *Q16: How are claims categorized?*

There are several ways, of which I will mention two here. First, claims are either independent (meaning they do not rely on any prior claim) or dependent (meaning they do rely on one or more prior claims). Evaluations typically focus mainly, or even exclusively, on the independent claims, which determine validity, scope, and discoverability of the patent claims. A dependent claim only comes alive, meaning it becomes relevant, when the independent claim on which it is based becomes either invalid or unenforceable. It is sometimes said that independent claims create the "breadth" of a patent, whereas dependent claims create "depth" of a patent.

A second way to categorize claims is between method claims and structure claims, where the structure claims may be systems, products (i.e., apparatuses or machines), or components. A good patent with a "good mix" of method and structure claims, is said to have "good claim diversity."

## *Q17: What are characteristics of a good independent claim?*

There are several things we might note about a good independent claim.

1. *A good independent claim is typically short, with few elements and few words per element.* A good example is to compare method claim #1 with method claim #48 in Qualcomm vocoder patent 5,414,769. These two claims are similar in subject, but claim #1 has four elements and 116 words, whereas claim #48 has eleven elements and 221 words.

Another example is the "Jepson claim". Many U.S. practitioners do not like this claim, because it has the disadvantage of listing prior art. However, it has also the advantage of a single claim element focused specifically on a Point of Novelty that is an improvement to the prior art. Consider claim #1 in US 6,430,398, and claim #1 in US 6,549,758 (lesson 6–1–1). This kind of claim, though it generally does not appear in patents originating from a U.S. application, appears not infrequently in patents originating from a European application. The Jepson format makes clear the idea that it is desirable to have fewer elements in an independent claim.

Even a long claim, with many elements and/or many words, may be good, if the elements are very general (meaning both simple and clear), and if the elements describe functions or structure that you would always expect to see in the method or structure described in the claim. AT&T patent 6,478,200 (lessons 3–1–3 and 3–1–4), provides good examples.

2. *A good independent claim should have only one Point of Novelty.* If there are two or more PONs, then the claim is written too narrowly. The second PON was not required and should have a claim of its own. Moreover, the PON on which the claim is allowed may not be what the patentee thought initially, as we saw in Siemens patent US 6,888,875, claim #25 (lesson 6–2–2). When you write claims, include only one PON in each independent claim. When you analyze claims, expect to see only one PON in a well-drafted independent claim.

3. *A good independent claim does not mix method and structural elements.* This is disallowed as being "indefinite" under 35 USC sec. 112(2), and will invalidate the claim.[226] However:

a. Method claims run on some kind of structure, and that structure must be explained in the written description and figures, to support the method claims.

b. Structure claims produce some kind of effect to implement a technical solution. Although structure claims may not have method elements, they may have "structural tags", which

---

226 In fact, any claim that mixes method and structural elements is on its face indefinite, and hence invalid. This is true for both independent claims and dependent claims. For dependent claims, it happens, albeit very rarely, that the dependent claim impermissibly adds a method element to an independent structure claim, or a structural component to an independent method claim. That appears to be the case with US 5,606,668, in which dependent claim #25 refers to independent method claim #24, and adds a new method element. Claim #24 is a system claim, not a method claim, which means that the reference in claim #25 is wrong, and claim #25 is probably invalid due to its mixing of structural and method elements in the same claim. This kind of thing does not happen very often, but it does happen.

are state-of-being verbs such as "adapted to", "configured to", "set up to", "designed to", etc. In the *Broadcom v. Qualcomm* case, element [2b] of claim #1 of US 6,714,983, lesson 4–1–4, had the structural tag "adapted to", which was critical to saving that claim and winning the case for Broadcom.

If you use structural tags, stick to standard terminology and don't make up terms such as "ready to", "intended to", etc. Why risk your patent claim with non-standard terminology, when well-known and well-accepted alternatives are available?

## *Q18: Why do people write dependent claims at all?*

If the only thing that matters in a patent is the independent claims, why do people write dependent claims at all? Dependent claims seem to have no use. In fact, however, it happens frequently in litigation that an independent claim is invalidated, in which case a claim dependent on the invalidated independent claim becomes the new independent claim. For example, in the ITC case of *Trend Micro v. Fortinet*, (Chapter 4), claim #8 became an independent claim when claim #4 was invalidated. Also, in Netscape/AOL/Microsoft patent 5,774,670 (lesson 5–2–3), claim #1 was invalidated by a court, but dependent claims 2–8 survived, each becoming its own independent claim.[227]

*Don't forget — substitution of a dependent claim for an*

227 In regard to US 5,774,670, I said in Chapter 5 that validity of all of the claims is in doubt due to the disclosure that caused the court there to invalidate claim #1. That statement is true. However, the litigation about this patent ended before a final ruling on claims 2–8. Therefore, unless or until such a ruling is made, these claims survive, and become independent claims as a result of the invalidation of claim #1.

*independent claim occurs only if there is prior art that knocks out the independent claim without invalidating the dependent claim. If, however, the problem is not prior art, but rather a poorly defined key term in claim #1, then the defective definition in claim #1 flows through to all the claims dependent on the independent claim, and will invalidate the entire claim set rather than just the one independent claim.*

*This is one of several reasons why good definitions for key claim terms are critically important, and why the absence of such definitions is characteristic of a "bad" patent.*

### *Q19: What is a Point of Novelty? What problems may arise with a PON?*

A PON is the part of a patent claim that represents what is new, which means the essential point of innovation for which the patent examiner allowed the claim.

Every independent claim should have one and only one PON. Further, each dependent claim is its own PON. A dependant claim comes alive, and may catch an infringing defendant, only if the independent claim on which it is based has been invalidated by prior art as being not new or by being judged as obvious.

While there should be only one PON per independent claim, the opposite is not true. It is not true that there should be only one independent claim per PON. In fact, the more independent claims per PON, the greater the "claim diversity" for that PON, and the greater the chance that the PON will survive in some form. In TiVo patent US 6,1233,389 (lesson 3–4–2), there were four independent claims, but they all focused on the same PON related to the functionality of digital video recorders. In *TiVo v. EchoStar*, TiVo won $500 million because two of these four claims, the so-called "software claims", were infringed. Having claim diversity for one PON proved very valuable for TiVo.

When you are writing a good patent, you must define each PON, then write one or more independent claims for each PON, with one and only one PON per independent claim, but as many independent claims as you want per PON.

When you analyze a patent and ask, "How do I know if this patent's any good?", ask yourself: "What is the PON for each independent claim?", and also, "Based on what the patentee thinks is new, is there at least one independent claim for each PON?" If there is a PON described in the patent which does *not* appear in the claims, then by law that PON has been dedicated by the patentee to the public. That's good for the public, but bad for the patentee. *If you define a Point of Novelty in the patent, make sure you claim it as well!*

If you are writing a patent and having trouble coming up with a PON, one creative technique sometimes used is to reverse the standard technical approach, and evaluate the result. That was the case, for example, with Qualcomm patent US 5,414,796, which added value not by increasing compression, but by decreasing compression slightly in exchange for obtaining a significant increase in voice quality.

### *Q20: If the act of patent writing creates the Point of Novelty, which defines the invention, does that mean that a patent writer is doing the job of the inventor?*

This is a good question because it highlights a very important aspect of the patenting process. No, the inventor invents, not the patent writer, but a good drafter of patents will do more than simply document the described invention. An important part of the patent drafter's job is to challenge the inventor's assumptions and suggest alternative implementations of the invention — different ways the invention might work. The act of writing a patent is a type of inventive process in which the drafter must capture and present the invention in words and figures. This is achieved most particularly by the drafter's selection of the "key terms" to be used in the claims, and making sure those terms are explained well in the patent. The scope of the claims, which is to say the scope of the legal protection, rests heavily on the draft's selection and definition of key claim terms that support the inventor's Points of Novelty.

### *Q21: What is a key claim term? Where in a patent are key claim terms explained?*

A key claim term is an important term in a patent claim that helps define the claim. Although a key claim term may be a technical expression, often it is a common non-technical word that is important in the context of the patent.

Key claim terms are generally explained in the figures, or in the written description, or both, as discussed in Part III below. A key claim term in one claim may also be explained by the usage of that term in a different claim, in a process called "claim differentiation", which is also discussed in Part III below.

### *Q22: When claims fail, does the patent lose all value?*

Maybe, depending on the reason for the failure. Failure of claims due to external reasons are often catastrophic — entire sets of claims are invalidated, and often the entire patent becomes worthless. Netscape/AOL/Microsoft patent US 5,774,670 (lesson 5–2–1) is an excellent example. Although Judge Ellis invalidated only independent claim #1, leaving dependent claims 2–8 intact together with many other claims in the patent, the reason for invalidation was sale of a product, including the invention, more than one year before the application was filed. This reason endangered *every one* of the claims of that patent, and the case was settled shortly thereafter.[228]

Another example of catastrophic consequences from an external event is the audio alarm for divers, US 5,106,236 (Additional Lesson 4 in Chapter 4), in which the failure to convey prior art to the PTO might have rendered the entire patent unenforceable. Although the ruling did not go that way, it might have.

Compared to catastrophic external events, the effect of internal events generally is not as clear. If all claims are found invalid or not infringed, then of course the effect is sweeping. However, in many cases, significant claims survive despite the invalidation of other claims. Had it gone to trial, Qualcomm patent US 5,414,796 (lesson 7–3–6) might have seen most of its claims invalidated, but this patent would have retained much of its value from the surviving claims.

## *Q23: Are there errors that just don't matter?*

Perhaps surprisingly, yes, even serious problems in patent drafting sometimes do not impact patent value. In the case

---

228 Had there been another round of litigation, all the claims would have been at risk of invalidation. The plaintiff might have succeeded in saving some of the claims, but that is not certain.

*Uniloc v. Microsoft*, Uniloc patent US 5,490,216 (lesson 3–2–2), independent claim #19 uses once the non-standard word "incorporating" as the transition from the claim preamble to the claim elements, and uses twice the non-standard word "including" as a transition from one claim element to another claim element. These usages were erroneous because they invite questions from a court or from the ITC that would never be raised if the traditional term "comprising" had been used instead. Although in this case these non-traditional transitions words did not harm the patent in litigation, their use was ill-advised.

Another example is the Ballantyne patent, US 5,133,079 (lesson 5–1–1), in which the key claim term "receiver means" is not clearly explained, placing in doubt the validity of independent claim #8. Further, since the problem in claim #8 is unclear definition (that is, lack of supporting structure) for an element in the independent claim, the validity of all the claims dependent on the independent claim, here claims 9–16, is also in doubt. In other words, the validity of more than half of the claims in the patent is in doubt because of the lack of clear supporting structure for the means-plus-function claim term "receiver means". Nevertheless, this problem, which might have been serious, turned out not to matter when the patent was sold, for two reasons. First, the unclarity of "receiver means" did not impact any of the method claims, which were 1–7. Second, and probably more important, claims 8–16 were not invalidated but rather placed in some doubt, and the patent's early priority date, its coverage of a very large market, and the major technical problem it addressed, overcame the claim deficiency and justified a market price over $1 million.

## III: What is Good Support for Claims?

### *Q24: How do I know if the figures and written description support the claims?*

The figures and written description are supposed to support the claims, without creating confusion. That's all. If they achieve this objective, they provide "good support". If not, then they are not doing what they should be doing.

Each section of the patent fulfills an important role in achieving this objective, but some sections are more important than others. This book discussed in particular the sections of a patent entitled "Background Art" (or "Related Art"), "Abstract", "Summary of the Invention", and "Detailed Description" (together with the figures). Let's review these sections.

*Background*: The main thing about the Background, or Related Art section, is that it must not include any of the implementations of the invention, traditionally called the "invention embodiments". In addition, it must not include any definitions of elements or key claim terms. All such inclusions in the Background section are misplaced, since they create confusion as to whether the embodiment or definition belongs to the prior art or to the invention.

In the Background, you must discuss prior art in some way. Make the discussion as short as possible, and as directly tied to the field of the invention as you can. Broad discussions of prior art risk limiting claim scope.

You should not add unnecessary limitations to the Background section. One example discussed in Chapter 6 relates to references to standards. If you must make such references, as did Siemens and Sharp for the CDMA patents in

Chapter 6, try not to limit the references. For example, saying "This invention applies to all kinds of air protocols, but most particularly to CDMA protocols", is better than saying "This invention applies to CDMA protocols", and is much better than saying "This invention applies to W-CDMA" (which is one specific implementation of CDMA).[229]

The examples offered in the preceding paragraph, however, are marred by a major defect. They all use the phrase "this invention". It's a common mistake, needlessly limiting your patent — you are saying, in essence, "*this* is my invention, and nothing else". Less limiting would be to say instead: "In some embodiments of the invention" or, more simply, "In some embodiments".[230]

*Abstract*: In contrast to the Background section, the Abstract should be given over entirely to the invention, not to "background" or "related art" or "prior art". If you must mention prior art in the Abstract to explain why your invention is different, then be clear: "The prior art is X. Unlike prior art, embodiments of the current invention do Y."

*Summary* and *Detailed Description:* These two sections,

---

229 Consider, too, US 5,606,539, also discussed in Chapter 6, which appeared to tie the patent to the relatively narrow CD-i standard. The Philips patent was accepted by professional evaluators into the MPEG-2 patent pool. This meant that the patent was essential to implementation of MPEG-2, which would be the case only if it is *not limited* to CD-i but rather included also MPEG-2. Apparently the evaluators did not believe that the patent was limited to CD-i. They may well be right, and had the patent gone to litigation, a court might have agreed with this broader reading. There was no reason to create uncertainty, however, and the uncertainty could have been avoided easily by simply stating that the patent applied to all CD standards, not just to CD-i.

230 I cite Sharp patent US 6,430,398 (lesson 6–2–4) as violating this rule by saying, "this invention". Whenever I see "this invention" in a patent, especially if it comes up repeatedly, there is reason to doubt the patent's scope.

although separate, are linked in operation and effect. All material describing the various embodiments of the invention must be in one or both of these sections. All definitions and all examples must be in one or both sections. For purposes of patent value, these two sections, "Summary" and "Detailed Description", work together. So what are the differences between them?

(1) Each figure, and each element in each figure, must be explained in the patent, and that occurs only in the Detailed Description, not in the Summary.

(2) A patent can be understood as a communication device. You are trying to communicate to the reader what your invention is, and why it is valuable. If you want to highlight something, put it in the Summary. You may also put it in the Detailed Description, but this addition is optional.[231] Remember that, in many cases, professional evaluators will have no more than 2–5 minutes to review a patent. Such evaluators will often read the Summary, but skip the Detailed Description. If you are trying to give people a clear and quick view of what this patent is about, put it in the Summary.[232]

---

231 If the material is lengthy, it should be in the Detailed Description, not the Summary. The Summary is for highlighting the important points.

232 If a patent is on the verge of being licensed, litigated, or sold, patent attorneys or other professional evaluators will invest the time to read the whole patent, *assuming the patent is either standing alone, or is a lead patent in a portfolio.* However, if the patent is simply being evaluated, probably by a professional evaluator as part of a mass evaluation, or if a patent is part of a large portfolio but is not one of the leading patents, then only limited time will be allocated to the patent.

### *Q25: How are "key claim terms" related to the figures and written description?*

Explaining key claim terms is the *main thing* that the figures and written description must do. If they do this well, without confusion, they provide good support for the claims. If they do not help define key claim terms, they fail to fulfill their primary role.

### *Q26: What is the process of explaining key claim terms?*

First, identify what the key claim terms are. If you are writing an application, you should always know, before starting to write the claims, what are the Points of Novelty that you want to protect. You should always plan, by writing an outline, what will be the independent claims. From all this preliminary work, you will sometimes know, before you write the claims, what the key claim terms will be.

In other cases, after writing the claims, you need to re-read them with a critical eye. You need to exercise your imagination to answer the question, "If I were reading these claims for the first time, what are the terms that would cause me concern, or for which I really need a definition or other explanation to understand the claim?" Very often it is difficult for the patent writer to do this, because the writer has become so involved in the drafting that he or she sees what is desired and not what actually appears on the page. If that is the case, ask a friend or colleague to read the claims and try to identify what the key claim terms are (or what the key claim terms might be if the patent went to trial).

Although you cannot call everything a "key claim term", you must identify the terms that are important for a clear understanding of the patent or that can cause serious confusion if misunderstood.

Once you know what the key claim terms are, plan how you want to explain them.

The process described above is for writing a patent. If you are analyzing rather than writing a patent, the process is virtually identical. For each independent claim, identify the PON and the key claim terms, using the "critical eye" discussed above. Once the terms have been identified, check to see if these terms are adequately explained.

### *Q27: How are key claim terms best explained?*

There are several ways to explain key claim terms. With the exception of the last way, all of these ways occur in the figures and written description, not in the claims. Here are the ways that key claim terms might be explained in a patent:

(1) *By definition.* A key claim term may be explicitly defined in the written description, as in, "thing X means ________".

Having an explicit definition in the written description eliminates possible confusion as to that key claim term. If you are writing a definition, or you are reviewing a definition as part of an analysis, make sure the definition is not too narrow. For example, say "includes all transmission protocols" rather than "is the GSM protocol".[233]

---

233 Also, as explained, do *not* put such a definition in the section called Background (or "Related Art"), because a reader will not know if the definition applies only to the prior art, or to the invention, or to both the prior art and the invention. If you read many patents, you often will see this happen, but it is bad practice. To avoid confusion, put the definition in either the Summary of Invention or the Detailed Description of the Invention.

(2) *By example.* A key claim term may be explained by an example, or optimally by several examples.

It is possible to have one example only. The CAFC, which is the sole appellate court for patent cases in the United States, has ruled that a single example in the written description will not mean that the claims are limited to only that example, "unless the patentee's intent to limit is clear from the patent or from the prosecution history".[234] However, if you must rely on the doctrine that "a single example does not necessarily limit the claims to that one example", then you are putting yourself in a desperate situation, betting your entire bankroll on the turn of the last card. Why do that?

In litigation, the patentee will always say that the claims are not limited, but the defendant *will always say, "The patentee intended to limit the scope of the invention"*. Maybe the court will agree with the patentee and say, "The patentee did not mean to limit the patent by using just one example in all the embodiments", or perhaps the court will agree with the defendant and say, "Yes, the patentee's intent *was to limit the scope of the claims* to have them allowed". You don't know what the court will decide. Don't take this risk — you put yourself in jeopardy! If you wish to explain a key claim term by way of example, use several examples plus an explicit definition.

Similarly, if you are trying to determine if a particular patent is "good", the presence of only a single example for a key claim term is discouraging and should cause you to discount the claim for possible invalidity or narrow scope.

---

234 That was the holding of the CAFC in the case, *Liebel-Flarsheim Co. v. Medrad, Inc.*, 358 F.3d 898 (Fed. Cir., 2004), *cert. denied* by U.S. Supreme Court in 2004, discussed in the book by Irah H. Donner, *Constructing and Deconstructing Patents*, (BNA Books, Arlington, Virginia, 2010), at p.77–79.

Examples of explaining key claim terms appear in all the patents of Chapter 6. For example, Philips patent US 5,606,539 erred by referring to one technical standard, CDI. Perhaps the intent was to include multiple compact disc standards, but that intent was not clear.

Compare the Sharp and Siemens patents, also in Chapter 6, which refer to "CDMA" but which do not limit the patents solely to CDMA. For example, Siemens patent US 6,885,875 makes reference to "CDMA" standards in the sections "Field of Invention", "Background", and "Summary". The Field of Invention is particularly well considered, as it states, "The invention relates to a method and radio communication system for controlling power between a base station and a subscriber station, *especially for CDMA* transmission methods in broadband transmission channels". [Emphasis *in italics* added]. "Especially for" includes all CDMA systems, but leaves the door open, properly, for applying the patent to TDMA and FDMA systems.[235]

(3) *By figures.* A key claim term may appear as an element in a figure, with a corresponding explanation of the figure in the written description.

Explanation with figures is an excellent way to show both function and connection with structure. This approach, although not required, is desirable. Another effective treatment of claim terms was seen in Philips patent US 5,606,539, in Chapter 6. There was only one structural figure, but the key claim terms "encoder" and "decoder" were included as

235 Perhaps even better might have been, "especially for CDMA... methods, but including also TDMA and FDMA methods". Different phrasing is always possible, but the key is not to limit the claim unnecessarily.

elements in the figure, then explained well in the written description.

(4) *By claim differentiation.* A key claim term may be defined by the "doctrine of claim differentiation", which means that no claim may duplicate another claim.

The necessary result of this doctrine is that the independent claim in a claim set must be broader than each dependent claim in the same claim set. A great example is Silanis Technology patent US 5,606,609 (lesson 7–2–2). Each independent claim used the term "select information", without explanation, but each such claim had a dependent claim, which said "wherein said select information includes security information". The dependent claims, acting by the doctrine of claim differentiation, broadened the independent claims to include both "security information" and "non-security information".

The doctrine of claim differentiation is used by a court or other evaluator to understand what a key claim term means, when there is no other way to interpret the claim — that is, the patent does not define the term, or provide examples, or illustrate the term in a figure. In other words, this is the interpretation method of last resort. Although for lack of an alternative it must be used by evaluators, the doctrine of claim differentiation should never be used by the patent writer to define the scope of claim terms. That is not the purpose of the doctrine. Claim terms should be defined by the patent writer using one or more of methods (1) — (3) above. A patent writer may, in addition to methods (1) — (3), but not as a substitute for them, use claim differentiation to create claim breadth (that is, to have a dependent claim ready if the independent claim is invalidated) or to reinforce the meanings of key claim terms already established by definitions, examples, and elements in a figure. A patent writer must not rely on claim differentiation as the sole or primary way of defining claim terms, because knowing how a court will apply the doctrine is simply impossible in many cases.

### *Q28: Why does confusion arise in key claim terms?*

Confusion with key claim terms can arise in various ways.

*(1) The term is undefined, and there are no examples or invention elements in a figure:* With no definition or examples, it may be impossible to know what a term means. Although this can happen with any key claim term, it happens often with non-technical terms. Why would a patent writer simply not write a definition or examples for a claim term? The reason may be that the meaning of the term seemed so clear to the application writer that there appeared no need to provide a definition or examples. One instance of this appears in the case *Broadcom v. Qualcomm*, US 6,714,983, lesson 4–1–1, in which the key claim term in claim #1 was the word "different". This term was not defined or explained anywhere in the patent. Although multiple implementations were presented, it was impossible to be sure what this word meant.

Another example is the case of *Uniloc v. Microsoft*, US 5,490,216 (lesson 3–2–3), in which two key claim terms were "remote licensee unique ID generating means" and "local licensee unique ID generating means". The meaning of "generating" was not clear. Uniloc won the argument as to what the term meant, and therefore won $100 million in the case, but the decision might have gone the other way.

*In short, clarity of the "key claim terms" is critically important.*

*(2) Shifting terminology within the patent:* In a single claim in Qualcomm vocoder patent 5,414,796, (lesson 7–3–5) (Individual), independent claims #18 and #29 use the phrase "acoustic signal", but then inexplicably shift to "said digitized speech samples". This is a perfect example of shifting terminology that, in this particular case, would probably invalidate the majority of claims in the patent (although the patent would retain some value in the surviving claims). In Siemens patent US 6,888,875 (lesson 6–2–4), one concept appears variously as "interrupt", "interruption", and "interrupted", creating uncertainty as to whether the meaning was changed by these varying usages.

There are several different types of shifting terminology.

One kind of shifting terminology is a horizontal claim shift, in which claims of different types (such as method, system, or apparatus) are intended to provide maximal coverage of a Point of Novelty through the technique of "claim parallelism", but the parallelism is destroyed by the use of term key terms in different claims. That happened in US 5,414,796, where the independent claims appeared to be parallel, but the terminology shifted between the term "digitized speech samples" independent method claim #1 on the one hand and, on the other hand, the term "acoustical signal" independent apparatus claim #18 and independent circuit claim #29. This also happened in the Ballantyne patent in Chapter 5, US 5,133,079, in which the independent method claim #1 uses the term "receiver", whereas the independent apparatus claim #8 inexplicable shifts to "receiver means". The result of horizontal claim shift is to create horizontal claim confusion, and destroy the attempt at claim parallelism. Maximal protection of the Point of Novelty is not achieved. However, as long as each individual claim is consistent within itself, the claim will not be invalidated, even though it may not be parallel to other independent claims.

A second kind of shifting terminology is vertical claim shift, in which terminology shifts between one element and another element of the same claim. This should never happen. Such a claim should not be allowed by the PTO and, if allowed, would likely be invalidated in litigation. Nevertheless, it is does happen sometimes, as for example in claims 18 and 29 of US 5,414,796. Vertical claim shift creates vertical claim confusion — the reader cannot understand the claim and cannot know what the claim covers. The likely result is that the claim with the vertical confusion, *and all claims dependent on that claim*, would be invalidated in litigation. Here, the validity of all the claims 18–47 in US 5,414,796 would be in doubt.

A third kind of shifting terminology is where the written description discusses a key claim term in one way, and the claim itself discusses the key claim term in a different way. That happened in US 6,885,875, where the term discussed in the claim is "interrupt", whereas the written description discusses "interrupted" and "interruption". There is now confusion as to what the claim means. In litigation, the claim might survive, or might be invalidated. If the claim survives, it may be interpreted by a court or by the ITC in any number of ways. This kind of shifting terminology between the written description and the claim is not as bad as vertical shift within a single claim (which is almost always fatal to the claim), but tends to be worse than horizontal shift between multiple claims (since horizontal shift in itself does not destroy a claim as long as the claim remains internally consistent, whereas shifting terminology between the written description and a claim *might* invalidate the claim).

A fourth kind of shifting terminology is a shift solely within the written description. If the claim term relies on the terminology in the written description, then the shift within the written description itself creates confusion. That happened in US 6,885,875, where the written description variously refers to "interrupted" or "interruption", with no definition. This happened also in the Philips patent US 5,606,539, discussed in Chapter 6, in which the written description seems to discuss variously compact discs ("CD"), interactive compact discs where the "interactive" is merely descriptive, or a specific technical standard ("CD-i") created by Philips. The results of shifting terminology within the written description, where a key claim term relies on the written description, are essentially the same as discussed in the third kind of shifting terminology above, that is, a shift between a definition in the written description and the claim. In the fourth kind of shifting terminology, as in the third kind of shifting terminology, the claim may survive or be invalidated and, if it survives, then it may be interpreted in multiple ways.

A fifth kind of shifting terminology, called "term stretching", is a situation where a single term is used in a patent to cover two or more different concepts. To use one term to represent multiple concepts is bad practice, will result in claim confusion at least, and may cause invalidation of claims at worst. An example of term stretching appears in US 6,714,983, discussed in Chapter 4 in conjunction with the *Broadcom v. Qualcomm* litigation, where the key claim term "different" was applied to multiple protocols. "Term stretching" always creates confusion and should be avoided.

A sixth kind of shifting terminology is not really shifting within the patent. Rather, it occurs where an industry uses a term in a certain way, but the patent uses the term in a different way. This may be done in a patent, since it is commonly stated that a patentee may be its own lexicographer. However, this practice may create confusion *unless the term is very clearly defined.*

The use of an industry-defined word in a non-standard way occurred in the case of *i4i v. Microsoft*, US 5,787,449 (lesson 3–3–4), in which the key claim term "metacode" appears in claim #14, but the patentee apparently meant, "I want a word that is like 'metacode' but does not have all the elements that go with the industry definition of 'metacode'". If that is what the patentee meant, which seems to be the case, the patentee should have (1) written a specific non-industry definition to "metacode", or (2) even better, made up its own new term for this concept rather than using an existing word such as "metacode".[236]

*Using industry-standard terms in a non-standard way causes confusion. You must do everything you can to eliminate or reduce the confusion.*

## *Q29: What is special about key claim terms in a means-plus-function structure claim?*

By definition of the means-plus-function type of claim, this claim does *not* include specific structure, but rather states the "means for doing" something. This is a structure claim in

236 A patentee is entitled to be a lexicographer, and may invent terms in the patent, including new words and phrases to represent the intended ideas. However, if the patentee invents a term, then that term must be explicitly defined and clarified, something that did not happen in US 5,787,449.

which the structure does not appear in the claim, but rather in the written description. All the ways described above could be used to clarify the "means" — (1) definition of the "means" in the written description, (2) examples of "means", or (3) an element in the figure plus explanation of the element. The "means" *must be clarified in some way in the written description.* One example is Philips patent US 5,606,539 (lesson 6–1–3), in which claim #18 has a means-plus-function element "means for encoding". This structure then appears as an "encoder" in FIG. 2, with a corresponding explanation in the written description. This is a particularly good example because there was only one figure with structure, making the definition "means for encoding" very clear.

By contrast, Check Point Software patent US 5,835,726 (lesson 7–1–3), uses the term "processing means" in element [2] of claim #24, but never defines or explains the processing means. Had this patent gone to trial, claim #24 may not have survived.

The special challenge of means-plus-function claims is that they put a burden on the patentee to explain the structure in the written description and preferably also in the figures. If the structure is not adequately explained, the claim probably will be invalidated.

## IV: What Can Destroy Patent Value?

### *Q30: How can external events destroy patent value?*

No matter how good the patent appears to be, and no matter how perfect the prosecution history, external events unrelated to the patent itself may limit the scope of the claims or even invalidate all the claims.

In Chapter 5, we looked at Netscape patent US 5,774,670, which was part of the portfolio sold by AOL to Microsoft for $1.056 billion. That patent is an artistic emerald, and it should have been very valuable, since it has an early priority date and covers cookies in Web browsers. Unfortunately, Netscape had negotiated with a company called MCI fourteen months before the patent application was filed, and had completed a sale of a browser product to MCI twelve months and 28 days before the application was filed. In the U.S., there is a strict twelve-month grace period, which means you may sell a product including the invention and file the patent application up to twelve months after the sale but not one day later. For US 6,774,670, the extra 28 days beyond the sale date exceeded this limit and caused the judge to invalidate claim #1, sharply limiting the patent's value, even though the invalidating events happened more than 15 years previously. This external event is an example of what is called the "on-sale bar".

As another example, I was involved in a matter where a patent was about to be sold for about $1 million, a price based on the expectation that a license fee would be obtained from a large company. It was then discovered that the inventors had given a certain technology license to the same company five years before in exchange for the company's funding of research equipment worth about $5,000. As a result, the sale was cancelled due to the external event of a patent license granted to the largest potential infringer (which was therefore also the largest potential licensee). In other words, a cheap license granted at one point in time greatly reduced the patent's value later on.[237]

---

237 In one sense, licensing-out is good, because it captures value for the patentee. However, it also reduces the value of the patent to any subsequent

There are sometimes problems involving inventors, where it cannot be determined who actually invented the technology in the patent, or where the wrong inventors are listed on the patent.

There are situations where the chain of title ownership is defective and, as a result, the ownership of the patent is in doubt.

External events that may invalidate whole patents include failing to tell the PTO about an important piece of prior art during prosecution, or failing to pay patent renewal fees (either by forgetting to do so, or by deliberately deciding to save the money).

### *Q31: What can I do to discover "external events that destroy patent value"?*

If you are not employed by the patentee, and you are also not an inventor, your ability to discover external events is limited. Nevertheless, here are some actions you could take:

1. Verify that known and relevant prior art was pointed out to the PTO, and particularly that any prior art from a related Asian, European, or other case was brought to the PTO.
2. Check to make sure that the title is good, with all recorded assignments appearing to be correct.
3. Check to make sure all renewal fees have been paid.

---

owner. If licenses are granted for fair and reasonable value, fine. If licenses are granted cheaply, the patentee may have undermined the patent's value by licensing unwisely.

If you are employed by or otherwise associated with the patentee, you can do much more, including:

4. Check to see that you have the correct inventors listed on the patent. You can talk to the inventors or other involved people to find out what happened.
5. List every license granted to the patent. This will tell you if much of the potential value has already been realized.
6. Talk with people involved in the development of the technology, and the patent. Try to discover if there were any sales or disclosures of the technology and, if so, when.

This answer is preliminary only. Checking external events is part of the process known as "due diligence". A full and accurate description of due diligence is not within the scope of this book. If you are involved in a specific case, and you suspect that an external event may have destroyed or reduced value, or if for any other reason you must perform due diligence as part of a transaction, you should consult with professionals and not rely on the general information provided here.

## V: Evaluating a Portfolio of Patents

### *Q32: What is a "patent portfolio"?*

A patent portfolio is a collection of two or more "patent items" (issued patents or pending patent applications) owned by the same entity, and directed at the same technical subject or problem. In some cases, the patent items are what are called "family members", where later items are continuations, continuations-in-part ("CIP"), or divisionals of earlier items.

In other cases, the patent items are not family members, but simply individual patents and applications with a shared technical subject or problem.

"Patent portfolio" can also refer to all, or a substantial portion, of the patents and applications owned by a single entity. The sale of the AOL "patent portfolio" to Microsoft included about 800 patents. These patents were a "portfolio" only in the sense that they were owned by one company, and sold to another. To analyze the patents and determine their value on sale, it would be necessary to break the patents into specific technical areas and then evaluate each patent as part of a portfolio for that technical area.

### *Q33: What makes a patent portfolio valuable?*

The overwhelming advantage of a portfolio is claim mix to create broader scope of coverage. A second advantage is that having multiple patents will reduce significantly the chances that all the patent claims will be invalidated in litigation.

These advantages apply to all portfolios, particularly those where the patents are not family members.

### *Q34: What is claim mix?*

Also called "claim diversity", this is a combination, in one patent "package", of different kinds of claims owned by the same entity. When people use the term "claim mix" or "claim diversity", they usually mean the mix of claim types, including structure claims (systems, apparatuses, and components) and method claims. I use the term to include (1) this traditional meaning of structure and method claims, (2) a mix of hardware and software claims, (3) a combination of client-side and server-side claims, and (4) a good mix of independent claims with supporting dependent claims. These four kinds of claim mix are discussed further below.

A "claim mix" can be achieved by one or more of the following four kinds of claim mix:

1. *Claim mix by claim type:* This means a mix of structure claims (such as systems, apparatuses, and components) with method claims. There are several examples of such a mix in the book. In the case *Trend Micro, Incorporated v. Fortinet, Inc.*, US 5,623,600 (lesson 4–2–1), all of the structure claims were invalidated — that is, all of the system claims were invalidated in the ITC litigation and all of the apparatus claims were invalidated on reexamination at the PTO. However, the patent still retained value due to the survival of the method claims (lesson 4–2–5).

Similarly, Qualcomm's vocoder patent, US 5,414,796, had 18 method claims, 9 apparatus claims, and 19 component claims (called "circuit claims" in the patent). Due to shifting terminology in the independent claims, it is possible that all of the structure claims (including the 9 apparatus claims and the 19 component claims) would be invalidated if the patent went to trial, but the method claims would survive (lesson 7–3–5), preserving much of the patent's value.

2. *Claim mix by hardware and software:* An excellent example is the case *TiVo v. EchoStar*, TiVo patent US 6,233,389 (lessons 3–4–2, 3–4–3, and 3–4–4).

By the way in which the claims were constructed, it appears that the software claims were added as an afterthought. If so, the afterthought won the day, because the court found that none of the hardware claims were infringed, but the two software claims were infringed. The ultimate result was that

EchoStar paid TiVo $500 million. A mix of hardware and software claims can be valuable indeed.

*3. Claim mix of client-side and server-side:* There are two separate concepts that need to be clarified here. First, combining client-side and server-side elements in a single claim will probably kill that claim. Second, including within one patent claims that are entirely client-side and other claims that are entirely server-side will create claim mix and strengthen the patent.

*a. An Individual Claim:* Including elements from both the client-side and the server-side *in a single claim* invites invalidation of that claim under the doctrine of divided infringement. Prior to the CAFC *Akamai* case in August, 2012, a method claim that included both client-side elements and server-side elements would be invalid due to divided infringement. Therefore, prior to CAFC *Akamai*, it was vital that client-side and server-side elements not be mixed in any method claim, meaning that a claim had to be either wholly client-side or wholly server-side. After *Akamai*, under the new standard of divided infringement set forth by the majority opinion in *Akamai*, a plaintiff may seek to prove indirect induced infringement even in the absence of any direct infringement, although this is not a simple case to prove. Although post-CAFC *Akamai*, it is now possible to combine client-side and server-side elements in one claim, this is still poor practice, for two reasons:

First, *Akamai* applies only to method claims. Structure claims are still judged by the pre-*Akamai* standard, which means that structure claims may not combine client-side and server-side elements in the same claim.

Second, the final word has not yet been written on the

doctrine of divided infringement. A situation in which there are two radically different legal regimes, one for method claims and a different one for structure claims (specifically, for "system" structure claims), is, in my opinion, illogical and ultimately unsustainable. In the patent world, inventive concepts can often be captured as both systems and methods. We see this all the time. There are several examples in this book where the same inventive concept, or PON, is presented as both a structure and a method. How can a situation exist in which one legal regime applies to an inventive concept presented as a system, and a radically different legal regime applies to the same inventive concept presented as a method? Something must change — either system claims must be interpreted as method claims now are under *Akamai*, or the interpretation of method claims must return to what it was pre-*Akamai*, or both system and method claims must move to a completely different regime. The ultimate decision cannot yet be known. Therefore, even after *Akamai*, to combine client-side and server-side elements in one claim is dangerous for method claims and fatal for system claims. If you are writing patent claims, do not combine client-side and server-side elements in a single claim. If you are evaluating patent claims, and you see client-side and server-side elements in a single claim, discount the value of that claim.[238]

---

238 The CAFC said, in *Akamai*, "The problem of divided infringement in induced infringement cases typically arises only with respect to method patents. When claims are directed to a product or apparatus, direct infringement is always present, because the entity that installs the final part and thereby completes the claimed invention is a direct infringer." 692 F.3d at pp. 1305–6. Whether or not this statement is correct as to "products and apparatuses", the comment does not apply to "systems", which by their nature include multiple "products and apparatuses". Therefore, the "problem" indicated by the Court arises not only in method claims, but also in system claims. Since

You should think of the doctrine of divided infringement in the same way that you think of the doctrine of claim differentiation. In both cases, these doctrines are used by evaluators, including courts, to interpret claims that are otherwise unclear (but clarified by doctrine claim differentiation) or invalid (but revived by the doctrine of divided infringement). *These doctrines are for evaluators of existing patents where no other option is available. The doctrines are not for patent writers, who should never rely on them* but should rather define key terms clearly (eliminating the need to rely on claim differentiation) or make sure not to mix client-side and server-side elements in one claim (eliminating the need to rely on the new *Akamai* standard).

*b. Mix of Client-Side and Server-Side Claims in One Patent:* In patents related to communication systems and methods, always consider writing solely client-side claims and solely server-side claims, without mixing client-side and server-side elements in the same claim. (This suggestion does not apply to product or component claims which, by their nature, are not divided among two or more different infringers.) Including claims on both sides of a system will increase claim diversity, and potentially can boost the value of the patent. In a patent portfolio, the portfolio's value will be enhanced if some

---

the exact same inventive concept can often be claimed as both a method and a system, the application of different legal principles to these different kinds of claims seems to be illogical. In the end, the CAFC may say, "No, we meant *Akamai* to apply to both methods and systems, but not to products or apparatuses". Whether this will ultimately happen, and whether it is even a sensible solution, is not relevant. For our purposes, there has not yet been a final resolution to the problem of divided infringement, and no patent writer should rely on *Akamai* to write either a method or a structure claim to include both client-side and server-side elements within the same claim.

patents cover server-side embodiments and other patents cover client-side embodiments.

*4. Claim mix by independent claims and dependent claims:* As explained in the case of US 5,623,600, issued to Trend Micro (lesson 4–2–4), a good patent must have both good breadth of claims to create good coverage, and good depth of claims to protect against charges of invalidity. Good breadth is created by good independent claims. Good depth is created by good dependent claims backing up the independent claims.

## *Q35: What are examples of good "claim mix"?*

Look at Scientific Atlanta/Silanis patent US 5,606,609, lesson 7–2–1. There was an excellent mix of apparatus, component ("embedded object interpreter"), system, and method claims. Although some of the system claims could be invalidated during litigation, the patent probably would retain its value due to the presence of the other claims.

Look also at the patent portfolio of Fuji Photo Film, in Chapter 4, Additional Lesson 3. This portfolio, with 15 patents, created a dense "thicket" of claims for the packaging and appearance of film cartridges and cameras as well as methods of use. This kind of claim mix creates serious problems for an infringing defendant.

## *Q36: What are examples of advantages of a claim mix?*

The two great advantages of a portfolio are survivability of claims at trial and scope of coverage. Of the claim mix examples cited in Q&A 34 and 35 above, survivability of claims is illustrated in the cases of Trend Micro, Qualcomm, TiVo, and Scientific Atlanta/Silanis, whereas scope of coverage is illustrated in the cases of TiVo, Scientific Atlanta/Silanis, and Fuji Photo Film.

### *Q37: How can I achieve good claim mix?*

There are at least two general ways to do this. One way is to sit down, think about all the various structures and methods which may be embodied by the invention, and write an independent claim plus a claim set for each embodiment.

The second way is to identify one PON that you want to protect, write an independent claim for that PON, and then write one or more additional independent claims with language parallel to the first independent claim. In the TiVo patent US 6,233,389, discussed in Chapter 3, hardware method claim #1 and hardware apparatus claim #32 are almost mirror images, with the same number of elements, in the same order, many common words, and almost exactly the same number of words. The same similarity exists in this patent between software method claim #31 and software apparatus claim #61. These are two examples of using parallel language to create multiple independent claims, with a "claim mix" for the same Point of Novelty.

If you write claims using parallel language, make sure that the language is actually parallel. In the Qualcomm vocoder patent US 5,414,796, discussed in Chapter 7, three independent claims, #1, #18, and #29 covered, respectively, a method for data compression, an apparatus for data compression, and a circuit for compressing data. All three claims have four elements, listed in the same order, with similar words, covering similar concepts. Unfortunately, whereas claim #1 used the phrase "digitized speech" through the claim, claims 18 and

29 noted "acoustical signal" in the preamble and element [1]. This change of terminology between different independent claims is an example of shifting terminology that destroys claim parallelism. *If you decide to use parallel claim language to maximize claim coverage for one PON, make sure that the claim language is truly parallel.*

## *Q38: Why do you discuss individual patents in the portfolio section of the Q&A?*

The idea of a "portfolio" is to have multiple patent claims on the same technical subject, preferably with a claim mix within the "portfolio". In this sense, a single patent may act like a "portfolio", since it has multiple claims on the same technical subject, and may have a claim mix within that patent. Indeed, one very strong patent may have greater value than a group of weaker patents. Although that is true, there are nevertheless two advantages of a group of patents that tend to make it stronger than a single patent.

First, by law, a single patent must be limited to one invention. If there are two or more inventions, the patent examiner will require that only one invention be prosecuted to the end of the process. By contrast, a group of patents, by its nature, may include multiple inventions, and may therefore have a wider scope of claim coverage than a single patent.

Second, a single patent is vulnerable to all kinds of internal and external events that may invalidate entire claim sets, or even the whole patent. A group of patents is much less vulnerable to invalidation — some patents might be invalidated or restricted, but others would likely survive intact.

The best portfolio strategy is to have one or a small number of strong patents, plus many weaker patents, within a single portfolio. *Nevertheless, whether a patent is strong or weak, membership in a group of patents on the same technical subject is likely to increase the value of any patent, no matter how strong that patent may be individually.*

## *Q39: How can I create a patent portfolio?*

The portfolio created by Fuji Photo Film in ITC Case No. 337-TA-406, entitled, "In the Matter of Certain Lens-Fitted Film Packages", *Fuji Photo Film Co., Ltd., of Japan v. Achiever Industries of Hong Kong* (Additional Lesson 3 in Chapter 4), is an excellent example. There are 15 patents in the case — 11 standard utility patents, 1 a reexamination utility patent, and 3 design patents. Of the 15, four were members of one patent family, but the rest were independent filings. There were a total of 214 claims, including 50 independent claims and 164 dependent claims. All of the patents were related to diposable handheld cameras and camera film. The claims covered photographic "film units" (disposable cameras), photographic film packaging, methods for assembling photographic film packages, and the ornamental design of handheld cameras. It would be frightening for a defendant to face this thicket of patents and patent claims, covering all aspects of handheld cameras. In the end, the ITC found the defendants liable of infringing thirty-three of the independent claims, including all three design claims.

This portfolio was created by multiple patent filings on distinct but related subjects, which are cameras and camera film. The powerful impact of this portfolio could not have been achieved by a single patent, for two reasons. First, utility and design inventions, both of which are in the portfolio, cannot be captured in a single patent. Second, there are multiple utility inventions in this portfolio, and multiple inventions can be captured only in multiple patents.

## *Q40: What is the character of a patent portfolio?*

The character of a patent portfolio is determined by two kinds of patents — a "reasonably good patent" which adds some value to a portfolio, and a "very good" patent which produces very strong results in a VSD analysis and which adds major value to the portfolio.

A portfolio of patents will almost always have a relatively large number of patents, each with a small improvement to the existing technology. These are the "reasonably good patents" that contribute to portfolio value, but would not create much value standing on their own. This was true, for example, of the patents discussed in Chapter 6, belonging to Philips, Sharp, and Siemens.

A portfolio might also have a few very good patents that could either be licensed individually, or act as lead patents of the portfolio. Qualcomm has such patents, including the vocoder patent US 5,414,796, discussed in Chapter 7.

## *Q41: How could I monetize a patent portfolio?*

If the portfolio has a few "very good" lead patents and many "reasonably good" patents which protect small improvements, then it is an excellent portfolio, and it may be licensed by itself. If it has only patents with small improvements, then it may still be a valuable portfolio, probably *not* to be licensed by itself, but rather as part of a group package (perhaps in a patent pool, or by a patent aggregator). Another option is to sell the portfolio to another company which can merge the portfolio purchased into a larger portfolio.

### *Q42: What are the primary ways to judge a portfolio's value?*

A portfolio's value is judged by (1) its strategic coverage, (2) its geographic balance, and (3) its time balance.

### *Q43: How can I judge a portfolio's strategic coverage?*

A well-managed technology company goes through a strategic process with respect to its patents. First, the company determines its corporate strategy. Second, it determines a patent strategy that will support the corporate strategy. Third, it asks and answers the question, "What kind of patent portfolio does the company need to support this patent strategy? In particular, what do we need in terms of coverage, geographic balance, and time balance?" Fourth, it asks and answers the question: "What kind of resources of time and money must we invest, and when, to achieve the needed patent portfolio?"

Someone analyzing the company — whether an equity analyst, a competitor, a potential buyer, a potential investor, or any other analyst — goes through the same process, in roughly the reverse order. The analyst will review the portfolio, from which he or she will determine the level of resources that have been invested in patents, the probable patent strategy, and the probable corporate strategy (at least in regard to patents). The analyst will certainly look at the kinds of ratios presented in Chapter 7, such as (1) R&D investment/Total revenues, (2) Investment in patents/R&D investment, (3) Patent revenues/ Total revenues, and (4a) Patent profits/Total profits, or (4b) profit margin on patent revenues versus profit margin on all revenues.

The contrast between Qualcomm, in Chapter 7, and Silanis or Check Point, is striking. With R&D/sales of about 20%, patent investment/R&D of about 6%[239], patent revenues/total revenues of about 35%, and patent profits/total profits above 50%, Qualcomm is a prime example of an aggressive developer and monetizer of technology. Although this strategy has worked extremely well for Qualcomm, it puts powerful and continuing pressure on the company to advance technology, to invest heavily in patents, and to engage in licensing & litigation programs that will inevitably result in at least some litigation. This is an aggressive posture.

Silanis and Check Point have much lower profiles with regard to patents. Silanis' investment in patents is large for a company its size, but the portfolio appears not to have been sued on, and apparently very little seems to have been invested in recent years. This is definitely a defensive posture. Nevertheless, although Silanis may continue its defensive posture, the upcoming expiration of US 5,606,609 in 2014 may cause the company to rethink its posture and, in particular, may cause it to invest additional resources in its U.S. patent portfolio.

Check Point has been involved in some patent litigation as both a plaintiff and a defendant, but this litigation does not yet seem to have generated significant results. The company had some very good early patents, but overall appears to have invested relatively modest sums in its own patents.

---

239 Calculated as 5.70%. This number is based on my estimate of Qualcomm's costs to generate a portfolio of 46,913 items. My cost estimate does not include any costs of patent litigation.

Past internal investment has been supplemented by some significant acquisitions of patents in 2004 and 2009, plus what appears to be a significant increase in internal investment in the period 2006–2012. Although historically Check Point's patent strategy has been defensive, its most recent actions are difficult to interpret.

Of the at least 80 patent filings and prosecutions made by Check Point during its twenty-year history, over 55% have been since the start of 2009, including almost 30% of all its U.S. patents in 2012 alone. The company has strongly increased its internal patenting activity in the past few years. Is this a continuation of its defensive posture, or a new and more aggressive posture? The current strategy is not clear but, in any case, Check Point needs to deal with a situation in which two of its most important U.S. patents, 5,606,668 and 5,835,726, will expire in 2014.

## *Q44: How can I judge geographic balance in a portfolio?*

There tend to be at least three possible areas of geographic interest for a patent portfolio.

The first is the United States, because it is the largest market in the world for technologies and technological products, with a highly developed intellectual property system. Patent litigation involves extremely high stakes (with potentially huge damage awards and possible injunctions against the sale of products). Any company that is active in, or plans to be active in, the U.S., must at least consider strong U.S. patent protection as part of its portfolio. All of the companies discussed in Chapter 7 have or at least had reasonable-to-strong patent protection in the U.S. Check Point, in particular, appears to place the majority of its patenting effort in the U.S.

The second area of interest is the home country of the company. Protection here may make sense to prevent competitors from suing a company in the place of its main activity. That did seem to be a concern of Silanis Technology, which has significant patent activity in its home country of Canada.

The third area of interest includes places where the company does business, or where for some other reason (such as location of a competitor) the company has an interest. Qualcomm, for example, has strong U.S. protection, with over 15,000 patent items there. Nevertheless, Qualcomm's European patent filings are over 12,000, almost equaling its U.S. activity. Overall, about two-thirds of Qualcomm's filings have been outside the U.S.

Each individual company needs to decide priorities among these three areas of the U.S., home country, and other countries of interest. Each company needs to allocate patent resources in accordance with these priorities, and adjust the allocation as the geographic priorities change over time.

## *Q45: How can I judge time balance in a portfolio?*

A portfolio is balanced in time if its owner's objectives are achieved over the relevant time period. If key patents in a portfolio expire at a time and substitute patents do not replace them, then patent expiration marks the time when a portfolio becomes unbalanced. As expiration of key patents approaches, a company reaches a decision point.

To the best of my understanding, Qualcomm presents an example of a company whose portfolio has always been balanced in time. Starting with its initial patenting efforts in the late 1980's and early 1990's, the company continued to invest substantial resources in patenting activity to support its core strategy of obtaining a financial return on its R&D investment. The company has had over 40,000 patent items in its overall portfolio, including many patents allowed in recent years.

Silanis Technology, by contrast, has had a different pattern over time. It had relatively low patent activity in its early life, but this changed to a burst of activity in the early part of last decade, particularly with its acquisition of US 5,606,609 in January, 2000. Silanis Technology has had some, relatively modest, patenting activity in the past five years. The acquired patent, US 5,606,609, will expire soon, and four of Silanis' five remaining U.S. patents will expire before the end of this decade. Overall, we can say that Silanis Technology's pattern over time has been no-balance (since zero patent activities in the early years), followed by rebalance (with relatively strong activities in the period 2000–2004), followed by a gradual decline in recent years (2008–2012) as patents run out and there is little new activity. As a result of its history of activity, Silanis Technology has either reached a decision point for its patents, or will soon.

Check Point Software Technologies has also had its unique pattern over time. There was very little patent activity in the first decade of the company's existence (about 1994–2004), but in this period the company generated two high-quality and valuable patents (reviewed in Chapter 7) and acquired one heavily cited patent when it purchased Zone Labs in late 2003. The company's patenting activity then increased significantly and, in the past few years (2008–2013), the company generated more than 50% of its portfolio. Check Point's pattern over time is more complex than the pattern of either Qualcomm or Silanis Technology. Overall, we can say that the *quality* of

Check Point's portfolio was balanced in the early years, but is becoming unbalanced now as some of its best patents reach expiration. At the same time, the company's *quantity* of patent activity has been relatively modest throughout its history, but has picked up, particularly in the United States, in recent years (2010–2013).

## VI: Final Thoughts

### *Q46: Who should own a patent?*

Like other economic assets, intellectual property generally, and patents specifically, should be placed with an entity, usually a company, that can make the best use of it. What kind of "use"? The old Roman adage is, "*Si vis pacem, para bellum*", translated as, "*If you want peace, prepare for war*". Some companies want to generate a return on their investment in R&D, so they prepare for war by building significnat portfolios and pursuing campaigns of licensing & litigation. Some companis want peace in the sense that they do not want to be troubled by patent litigation, so they build portfolios to threaten counter-suit against potential plaintiffs. In either case, whether to generate money or to prevent others from taking your money, a patent is best owned by a party vitally interested in the technical field of the patent.

This principle is illustrated by ownership of US 5,606,609, discussed in Chapter 7. This patent, which is focused on electronic signatures, was created by a cable modem manufacturer, sold to a defense avionics company, and finally resold to a proper owner in the technical field, Silanis Technology.[240]

---

240 A company not expert in the technology field of the patent could simply license-out the patent, but even here, the company's lack of relevant expertise

To the best of my knowledge, this patent never went to litigation, but it has provided valuable defense to Silanis.

## *Q47: If you lack patents, what should you do?*

The answer is obvious, but for reasons not clear to me, companies sometimes do not take the appropriate action. If you are lacking patents, you need to first understand what you are lacking, and then go get the patents you need.

By "understanding what you are lacking", I mean that you must be clear on corporate strategy, and you must understand the role you want patents to play in supporting that strategy. You then assess what patents you need, compare that to what you currently have, and identify the gap that must be filled.

There are two ways to fill the gap. First, you may file and prosecute your own patent applications. This way has several advantages. It allows you to maintain great control of the process, and it is, in comparison to the second approach, relatively inexpensive. This way has disadvantages, however. It consumes your resources, particularly the time of R&D personnel. It takes a long time, measured in years, before you begin to obtain patents. It is uncertain, because when you can never know in advance which claims in an application will eventually be allowed by the patent office.

The second way to fill a strategic patent gap is to go to the market and buy the patents you need. This might not have been possible in the past, but the market for patents has expanded tremendously over the past 20 years. Today it is possible to buy patents in very many fields.

---

could inhibit its ability to make the licensing program as successful as it might be.

This second way has advantages which are approximately the opposite of the disadvantages of the first way. Buying patents is relatively fast and does not consume much of your R&D resources. You know exactly what patent claims and written support you are buying. In this sense, although you do not control the crafting of the claims, you do control selection of the claims you buy.

The prime disadvantage of buying patents is that it costs money, often considerable sums. Acquisition of key patents in important technical fields will likely cost millions of dollars. Is this investment worthwhile? Every company must decide for itself, balancing the purchase costs versus possible costs of losing patent litigation (i.e., damages for infringement, and possible injunction against selling one's products in the market). This is a balance each company must make, seeking to match the nature, size, and quality of its patent portfolio with its company's strategic objectives.

In this book, we have seen several examples of companies purchasing patent protection. I will cite three such examples now.

Silanis Technology acquired US 5,606,609, as discussed above and in Chapter 7.

In the *Broadcom v. Qualcomm* litigation, lesson 4–4–1 and Table 4–5, Broadcom sued Qualcomm at the ITC on five patents, three of which were filed and prosecuted by Broadcom, and two of which were acquired by Broadcom from other companies. Broadcom also sued Qualcomm in Federal District Court on three patents, one of which was filed and prosecuted by Broadcom, and two of which were acquired by Broadcom from other companies. In the ITC litigation, Broadcom won on US 6,714,983, which was a patent that it had filed and prosecuted. In the court litigation, Broadcom won on US 5,657,317 and US 6,389,010, both acquired, the former from Norand Corporation and the latter from Intermec IP Corporation. It was the mix of internally generated patents and externally acquired patents that proved so powerful for Broadcom in this litigation.

Finally, I cite Check Point, the first case presented in Chapter 7. I analyzed two patents, US 5,606,668 and US 5,835,726, both of which were internally generated and based on original inventions of the founder and CEO. A third patent, US 5,987,611, came to Check Point as part of its acquistion of Zone Labs in late 2003. I have not analyzed US 5,987,611, but it has more forward non-self citations than either US 5,606,668 or US 5,835,726, and might provide some protection after the expiration of these other patents.[241]

## *Q48: What can go wrong?*

You can never be 100% sure of the value of a patent, no matter how much time and money you invest in writing, prosecuting, or reviewing the patent. Uncertainty occurs in legal processes related directly to the patent, such as examination and reexamination at the patent office, and litigation at the ITC, federal district court, CAFC, and even the Supreme Court. Uncertainty occurs in legal change not related specifically to the patent, such as the evolving judicial doctrine of the law of divided infringement, new statutes (such as the changes to the U.S. patent statute in 2011), and new regulations by either the PTO or the ITC. Uncertainty occurs in

---

241 US 5,987,611 will itself expire in May, 2017, so the added protection will last only a few years, but those few years may be of use to Check Point.

external actions or failures to act by the patent applicant, actions which may impact greatly the financial value of the patent even though they are not related to the quality of the claims or the written description. These uncertainties generally relate to claim Validity and/or claim Scope, but generally not to Discoverability of infringement.

The uncertainties with patents are significant. In a patent war in only the United States, there may be litigation in multiple forums with multiple rounds of litigation in each forum, and a patent may be limited or invalidated in any round. The situation becomes much more complicated when two major companies are involved in multiple lawsuits in 5–10 countries across three or four continents. These multi-country patent wars are happening more and more these days, particularly in the ICT areas. In these circumstances, you can never be sure what the final result will be, no matter how much you invest in your patents. You can, of course, take action to increase your chance of victory by investing more, but you can never know for sure. I call this the Uncertainty Principle of Patent Valuation.

But uncertainty does not mean we are helpless. Let us do what we can. When you analyze an existing patent by asking, "How do I know if my patent's any good?", do the best job you can looking at the patent and prosecution history. Aim to reduce what is uncertain and to anticipate what can go wrong. Ask yourself the tough questions first, because if you do not prepare for them in advance, you are likely to face them later, under less advantageous conditions.

We have neither absolute knowledge nor absolute confidence in the knowledge we do have. Nevertheless, the lessons we have learned about patent quality should help us make reasonable estimates about the validity and scope of our patent claims. Therefore, although it is impossible to eliminate uncertainty about patent value and the outcome of patent litigation, still we can reduce the uncertainty, and that is a good thing.

# Afterword

Chart 1–1 suggests a radical reorientation of corporate value during the period 1975–2005. At the beginning of this period, the value of intellectual property was less than 20% of all corporate value. Last decade, according to the chart, intellectual property made up 80% of corporate value. Well, as the great American writer, Mark Twain, observed: "There are three kinds of lies — lies, damned lies, and statistics." Are these statistics lies, or real?

I suggest two things:

First, innovation has always been the driving force for economic advancement. That was true in 1975, it is true today, and it will be true in another 40 years. In that sense, the statistics in Chart 1–1 are a lie, because they suggest a change in the basis of economic value, and there was no such change. The basis of economic value is always innovation.

Second, Chart 1–1 suggests a great change in the measured value of corporate assets. That change is true, and in that sense, the statistics in Chart 1–1 are real. However, measured value is true only if you know what it is you are measuring. During the past 40 years, and especially in the past decade, we have witnessed rapid and jarring changes in the world economy. Most particularly, much of manufacturing has shifted to lower-cost locales which would never have been considered had it not been for the revolution in computers and communications. Also, we have witnessed rapid rises in value for companies that really do not manufacture much, but rather design, plan, and market products manufactured by others.

In this book, we've looked at patents belonging to about twenty technology companies. The value of these companies is based in large measure upon their ability to innovate and invent new products and services, and to figure out how to market these innovations to customers. The past 40 years have witnessed a revolution in value from manufacturing and physical assets to innovation based on new ideas. In that sense, the statistics in Chart 1–1 are real, because they tell us correctly that in major corporations, measured value has shifted strongly in the direction of new knowledge and innovation skills.

Peter Drucker, arguably the greatest management consultant of all time, said, in what may be his most famous quote:

> Because the purpose of business is to create a customer, the business enterprise has two — and only these two — basic functions: marketing and innovation. Marketing and innovation produce results; all the rest are costs. Marketing is the distinguishing, unique function of the business.[242]

Patents are neither innovation nor marketing, but they are tied to both. Patents define, describe, and focus innovation, documenting invention in a way that allows clear

---

242 Peter F. Drucker, Management (Taylor & Francis, London, 1999), p.57. This quote from Mr. Drucker is reported in many documents, although in some publications the phrase noted is "only these two" as above, and in other publications the phrase is "only two" without the word "these". I believe the former is the correct version, which I why I cite it above, but the difference between these two versions may not be substantial in any case.

communication, and protection of the invented progress. More than that, patents contribute to the ability of a company to differentiate itself from the competition by positing "unique selling points" that have the additional advantages of being protected by law and deterring imitation. Patents help companies to market and sell their innovations profitably, a prime motivator for the innovation. The enhanced role of intellectual property in the innovation and marketing of new goods and services is why patents are a hot topic today, and why patents will continue to shape the business and technology landscape for the foreseeable future.

# Glossary (Including Acronyms)

**Aggregator:** An entity that collects and administers multiple patents on the same subject. The most common examples are a Non-Practicing Entity, or "NPE", which aggregates patents to license or litigate, and a Defensive Patent Aggregator, or "DPA", which aggregates patents to keep them out of the hands of hostile parties. The administrator of a patent pool is not generally considered an aggregator, but in fact, a patent pool is an aggregation of patents. Similarly, when a single company or entity "aggregates" patents, for whatever purpose, that company is generally not considered an aggregator, although in reality the company is acting as one. See "Defensive Patent Aggregator", "DPA", "Non-Practicing Entity", "NPE", and "Patent Pool".

***Akamai***: See "Divided Infringement"

**Backward Citation:** When patent Y cites back in time to an earlier patent X, patent Y is said to make a "backward citation" to patent X. This is also called a "reverse citation". Compare with "Forward Citation".

**BCP:** Acronym for "biotechnology, chemical, and pharmaceutical", representing three technology areas based on applied chemistry and biology, which are fundamentally differ from

ICT. These areas are sometimes called "the unpredictable arts". Nanotechnology, to the extent it may be manipulated by chemical processes, may belong in this group, or it may be classed in the ICT group. Compare with "ICT".

**CAFC:** Short for "Court of Appeals for the Federal Circuit", this often appears in legal citations as "Fed.Cir." In the U.S., patent cases are federal, not state, cases, heard first in the federal district courts. An appeal from a federal district court decision goes to the CAFC. The CAFC also hears all appeals from a decision of the ITC. Each party has the right to appeal a district court opinion, or an ITC opinion, to the CAFC. If someone wants to appeal a decision of the CAFC, he or she must ask the U.S. Supreme Court to hear the case. The Supreme Court can either agree or (more likely) decline to hear the appeal.

**CAFC *Akamai*:** See "Divided Infringement".

**Certificate of Correction:** One of three procedures by which a patentee may change a patent after issuance is to obtain a "certificate of correction" from the patent office. If the patent has a purely formal error, such as an incorrect inventor name, or a misspelled word, or an absent word, the owner may ask the PTO to issue a "certificate of correction", which will be attached to the patent and show the correction or corrections made. See also "Reexamination" and "Reissue Patent".

**Claim Differentiation:** This is a doctrine that states that each claim in a single claim set must have is own meaning, or "scope", that differs from the scope of any other claim in the same claim set. (If the scopes were the same, then two claims would be saying exactly the same thing in the same claim set, and that is forbidden by law.) Since claim scope is determined by a court, the court will interpret the claims to give a different scope to each claim set. The practical effect is that the court will interpret the claims in a way to make the one independent claim in a claim set broader in scope than each of the dependent claims. Here is an example: Claim #1 is a device to guard the health of "household pets". Claim #23 is, "Claim 1, in which the household pet is a dog". By the doctrine of claim differentiation, claim #1 must include "dog" *and one or more additional animals*. Claim #1 *may not be restricted to only "dogs"*, because that would make claim #1 and claim #23 the exact same thing.

**Claim Mix:** One way of judging the quality of a patent is by seeing if there is a "claim mix," also called "claim diversity". When people use the term "claim mix", they are usually referring to the types of claims in the patent, meaning system claims, apparatus or product claims, component claims (which may be a circuit, or a sub-system, or some piece of a machine that performs a particular function), and method claims. This term can also be used in reference to a hardware and software mix of claims, and to a mix of "client-side" and "server-side" claims. The term is also used to refer to a mix of independent claims (which create breadth of claim coverage within a patent) and dependent claims (which create depth of claim coverage). A greater claim mix in a patent is often associated with higher quality and higher value because the same inventive concept can be captured in multiple ways. Good claim mix can mean broader scope of coverage and less chance that all the claims will be invalidated in litigation. See also "Claim Parallelism".

**Claim Parallelism**: This is a particular kind of claim mix in which a single Point of Novelty is protected by multiple types of claims, in which the mix is achieved by using the same claim structure and same claim terminology in method, apparatus, and component claims of the same patent. When done properly, claim parallelism provides very strong protection for a single Point of Novelty. However, claim parallelism requires the same terminology in the various kinds of claims. If different terminology is used, the parallelism is lost, and maximal protection is not obtained. We saw imperfect claim parallelism in US 5,414,796, and particularly in lesson 7-3-4 (Individual). See also "Claim Mix", "Horizontal Claim Confusion", and "Shifting Terminology".

**Claim Set:** There are independent claims, which do not rely on any other claim, and there are dependent claims, each of which relies on an independent claim. The dependent claim modifies, and thereby narrows, the independent claim. One independent claim, plus all the claims that depend on it, are called together a "claim set". Of logical necessity, all the claims in a set are of one type (e.g., method claims, or apparatus claims, or system claims), and their character is derived from the independent claim.

**Client-side:** Most communication systems have a client-side, sometimes called customer premises, consumer site, mobile station, the home, etc., and a server-side. For ICT system and method claims, it is important that you know whether *each element of a claim* is on the client-side or the server-side. If you have one claim that has both client elements and server elements, that claim is in danger of being invalidated by the doctrine of divided infringement. (Although this danger applies to system claims, it is generally not a concern for apparatus or component claims, which, by their nature, are not split between two or more entities.) Compare with "Server-side".

**Collateralization of a Patent:** If money is lent against a security interest in the patent or in revenues generated by the patent, the patent has been "collateralized". If money is lent or invested not against revenues, but to give a preference for obtaining the patent in case of insolvency, the patent has also been "collateralized".

**Critical Claim Term:** See "Key Claim Term".

**Defensive Patent Aggregator:** A company or other entity that aggregates patents primarily to keep them out of the hands of potentially hostile parties. See "Aggregator". Compare with "Non-Practicing Entity".

**Dependent Claim:** A "dependent claim" is a claim that depends on an earlier claim. Each dependent claim will refer to the earlier claim at the very start. For example, "2. Claim 1, further comprising...", is dependent claim #2, which depends on earlier claim #1. A dependent claim includes all of the elements in the claim depended on, plus the added element in the dependent claim. The scope of the dependent claim is necessarily narrower than the claim on which it depends. The dependent claim never comes to life, that is, it does not become operative as a practical matter, unless the claim on which it depends has been rendered invalid or unenforceable. See "Independent Claim".

**Description-Claim Mismatch:** When a key claim term is explained or used differently in the written description and in the claims, there is a mismatch. This can occur in two ways.

First, there may be one meaning in the written description, and a different meaning in the claims. This kind of mismatch may lead to invalidation of the claim, or to limitations on the scope of a valid claim, but the result cannot be predicted in advance. Second, a written description may present two or more different meanings for the same key claim term. In other words, there is shifting terminology in the written description rather than in the claim. When the key term then appears in a claim, the term may be interpreted to apply to only one of the meanings from the written description, or to multiple meanings from the written description. The situation is now chaotic — the claim might be invalidated as being unclear, or might be limited to some subset of possible meanings from the written description, or might be interpreted to include all of the meanings from the written description (assuming such meanings can be harmonized).

**Design Around:** If a certain product or method infringes a patent claim, it is sometimes possible for the infringer to modify the product or method in a way that makes it non-infringing. In such a case, there may be liability for past infringement, but there will not be an injunction prohibiting future sales of the re-designed non-infringing product or method. The process of modifying the product or method to be non-infringing is called "design around", sometimes called "work around".

**Design Patent:** A patent in which typically a single drawing is presented, with a single claim stating, simply, "The design shown in the figure".

**Divided Infringement:** Also known as "joint infringement," this is a controversial doctrine of patent law which says that all the elements of a claim must be practiced by one party, what is called the "single entity", for that party to be directly liable for patent infringement. If the elements are practiced by two or more parties, then neither party is directly liable for infringement, *unless* one party is the agent of the other, or one party controls the other, or the parties collude in some manner to conduct the infringement in a way to avoid liability. Under the doctrine in its original form, there can be no indirect liability (for contributory infringement or inducement to infringe) unless there is direct infringement.

Recently, the form of the doctrine changed. On August 31, 2012, the CAFC ruled in the consolidated case of *Akamai Technologies v. Limelight Networks* and *McKesson Technologies v. Epic Systems* (called in this book "*CAFC Akamai*") that for method claims it may be possible for the patentee to show indirect infringement even without direct infringement. The doctrine *in its original form* still applies to all structure claims, but the doctrine has now been modified for method claims by the *Akamai* case.

**Doctrine of Equivalents (DOE):** This is a legal rule in effect in the U.S. (and in other jurisdictions as well), which says that a defendant may be liable for infringement even if the defendant has not done exactly what is included in the structure or method claim. Two kinds of tests are applied in the U.S. Under one test, the defendant's actions will be considered "equivalent" to the claim if the differences between the defendant's actions and the claim elements are "insubstantial". Under a second test, the defendant will be found liable if its actions (1) perform "substantially the same function" as the claim elements, (2) in "substantially the same way" as the claim elements, and (3) produce "substantially the same result".

The scope of protection under the DOE is not always clear prior to litigation. Further, under the Supreme Court decision in *Festo v. Shoketsu Kogyo Kabushiki Co.* (2002), all DOE protection is lost for any claim element amended during patent prosecution (unless the amendment was merely a technical or insubstantial amendment). The *Festo* case adds another level to the degree of uncertainty regarding the scope of the DOE in a particular case. Nevertheless, the DOE can expand the scope of coverage for some patent claims.

**DOE:** Acronym for "doctrine of equivalents".

**DPA:** Acronym for "defensive patent aggregator".

**Drawings:** See "Figures".

**EFA:** Acronym for "expert fundamental analysis".

**Expert Fundamental Analysis ("EFA"):** Analysis of a patent's value conducted by a human evaluator reading the patent and determining its quality. The main topic of this book.

**External Events that Destroy Patent Value:** Value in patents is created by good claims, good support for the claims in the written description, and coverage of current infringement (or infringement in the very near future). However, the value of even the best patent can be destroyed by "external events" not related to the patent itself. A clear example is (1) what happened to the Netscape/AOL/Microsoft patent, described in Chapter 5, in which independent claim #1 was invalidated because the patent owner had sold a product including claim #1 one year and twenty-eight days before filing a patent application, thereby violating the one-year limit on such action. Many other external events may destroy patent value, such as (2) failing to tell the PTO about an important piece of prior art during prosecution, (3) having the wrong inventors listed on the patent, (4) forgetting to pay renewal fees, or deliberately deciding not to pay them, or (5) licensing-out the patent, which gathers value from the license fees but reduces the remaining value of the patent. All of these cases have nothing to do with the subject matter of the patent, the patent claims, or support for the claims in the written description. These are all "external events that destroy patent value". Such events may, depending on the circumstances, invalidate a single claim, or make the claim unenforceable against one party, or, in the worst case, invalidate *all of the claims* in the patent.

**Field of Invention:** Sometimes called "Field of Technology", or just "Field", this is a short statement of the general area of a patent. It appears just after the Title of Invention (or after the Cross-reference to related patent filings, if there are any such filings), and just before the Background section. The Field of Invention is optional, and does not appear in many patents. On the one hand, it is a good tool for communicating quickly and briefly the general subject matter. On the other hand, it presents a danger, because if it is too narrow it may limit the scope of the invention, and if it is too broad it may be used by an examiner or court to apply against the claims prior art that otherwise might not be cited. Some patent practitioners use the Field of Invention to try to direct the application to specific examination groups within the patent office.

**Figures:** Almost every patent illustrates aspects of the

invention, including both the structure of the invention and methods associated with its implementation. Statute 35 USC sec. 113, says the patent must include "a drawing where necessary for the understanding of the subject matter to be patented". However, in practice, *multiple* drawings are *always necessary* in utility patents. "Design patents", by contrast, generally have only one drawing. Drawings are commonly called "figures" in patent speech.

**Forward Citation:** When prior patent X is cited in later patent Y as being relevant art, patent X has received a "forward citation", because the citation is forward in time relative to the cited patent. If patent X and patent Y are owned by the same patentee, the forward citation is called a "forward self-citation". If patents X and Y have different owners, the forward citation is a "forward non-self citation". In theory, a "forward citation" may be made by either a patent or a technical paper, but when people say "forward citation", they typically mean only forward citations in later patents. Compare with "Backward Citation".

**Forward Non-Self Citation:** See "Forward Citation".

**Forward Self-Citation:** See "Forward Citation".

**Horizontal Claim Confusion:** This is the confusion about the interpretation or scope of one or more claims in a patent that results when the patent attempts but fails to achieve claim parallelism. Claim parallelism requires a consistency of key claim terms in the parallel independent claims. When there is inconsistency of term usage, parallelism fails, the interpretation of claims becomes more complicated, and there may be a gap in the scope of claim coverage for the Point of Novelty addressed by the claims. However, horizontal claim confusion will not invalidate a particular claim, as long as the claim uses key claims consistently *within itself* (despite the fact the terminology shifts *between* different independent claims). This claim confusion is called "horizontal" because when claim charts are made (whether the purpose is a comparison of claims as in Tables 7–10 and 7–11 for US 5,414,796, or a comparison between the elements of a particular claim and a piece of prior art, or a comparison between the elements of a particular claim and a possibly infringing product or method), the comparison typically places the claim and the compared item side by side, with comparisons between each claim element and each part of the compared item displayed horizontally on the screen or page. Therefore, if there is confusion, it is "horizontal". See "Claim Parallelism" and "Shifting Terminology". Contrast with "Vertical Claim Confusion".

**Horizontal shift:** Also called "horizontal shifting terminology", this is what happens when the usage of a key claim term shifts between different independent claims in one patent. When this happens, "horizontal claim confusion" occurs. The minimal result is that the possible protection of "claim parallelism" fails and the resulting protection is less than what the patentee wanted. In other words, claim scope is almost certain to be reduced. In addition, claims may be invalidated, but that is not an inevitable result. See also "Claim Parallelism", "Horizontal Claim Confusion", and "Shifting Terminology".

**ICT:** Acronym for "information & communication technologies", with patents typically featuring electronic or mechanical structures or methods, and which tend to be based on applied physics. The group includes computers, electronics, and communication systems, including hardware and software. This group also includes mechanical patents, and also medical device patents (e.g., implants, tools). Material science patents, particularly those in nanotechnology, are also sometimes grouped in ICT. Compare with "BCP".

**Independent Claim:** A claim that does not depend on any earlier claim is called "independent". An independent claim will not refer to an earlier claim. An independent claim includes only the elements in that claim itself and, when correctly drafted, includes a single Point of Novelty, although each PON may have multiple independent claims (for systems, methods, hardware, software, etc.). Compare with "Dependent Claim".

**ITC:** Acronym for "International Trade Commission", or "United States International Trade Commission", a forum for patent litigation which serves as an alternative to the federal district courts. Both the ITC and the courts deal with many of the same patent issues, but there are several key differences.

Procedures tend to be less formal at the ITC. For example, in ITC litigation there is usually nothing like a Markman hearing, and claims are often interpreted at the main hearing.

The deciders of the ultimate issues tend to be jury laymen in federal court litigation rather than the legal and sometimes technical experts known as "Administrative Law Judges" in ITC cases.

Although both the ITC and the Courts determine issues related to infringement, the ITC is restricted to issuing injunctions and cannot award damages.

As an administrative body, the ITC is bound by statutes,

but not by judicial doctrine created by the CAFC or the Supreme Court.

Litigation at the ITC tends to be much faster than court litigation (although there are a few federal district courts which are about as fast as or even faster than the ITC).

ITC litigation has become very popular in recent years, with many more lawsuits being filed, primarily because of the speed of ITC litigation, and also because of the very high likelihood of obtaining an injunction if the plaintiff wins the case.

**Joint Infringement:** Or the "doctrine of joint infringement", also known as the "doctrine of divided infringement". See "Divided Infringement".

**Key claim terms:** Also known as "critical claim terms", these are important words or phrases in a patent claim that help define the claim. Often these claim terms relate to a specific Point of Novelty in the claim, although a key term may appear in either a claim preamble or in a claim element that does not include a PON.

***Lear* challenge:** A rule established by the U.S. Supreme Court in *Lear, Inc. v. Adkins*, 305 U.S. 653 (1969), which says, in essence, that a licensee of a patent may challenge the validity of a patent or its claims, despite the fact that the licensee has taken a license to the patent. It is sometimes called a "challenge under the *Lear* doctrine".

**License-in:** When a party "takes" a license to a patent, paying money to receive a license to use the patent, that party is the "licensee", and is said to "license-in" use rights. Compare with "License-out".

**License-out:** When a patent owner "grants" a license to a patent, which is to say the owner receives money to give a license to use the patent, the owner is also said to be the patent "licensor", and is said to "license-out" the right to use the patent. Compare with "License-in".

**Markman hearing:** In the United States, patent trials occur only in federal district court, not in the courts of the 50 states. However, before the trial, the federal district court judge holds what is called a "Markman hearing", after which the judge writes an opinion stating how key claim terms will be interpreted in the trial. The judge may also invalidate claims entirely. After the parties know the results of the Markman hearing, expectations of the litigation tend to come closer, which may induce settlement of the litigation before trial. This type of hearing was initiated by the U.S. Supreme Court in the case of *Markman v. Westview Instruments, Inc.* (1996).

**Ninety percent rule of patent claim prosecution**: This rule says that it is possible to obtain a specific patent claim in the great majority of patent prosecutions. However, the resulting claim may be so narrowed by amendments or other limitations as to become useless for purposes of proving infringement. This rule is a phrase coined by me to express succinctly the ideas that

(1) in the great majority of applications a claim of some scope may be obtained,
(2) claims obtained by severe concessions of narrowing amendments and waiver of material may not be worth the cost of acquisition, and
(3) in a minority of applications, perhaps 10%, no claims

of any kind can be obtained due to the nature of the application or the existence of strong prior art.

I do not know if 90% is the correct percentage, but it is my best estimate and expresses the three ideas succinctly.

**Non-Practicing Entity**: A company or other entity that aggregates patents primarily to assert them in a licensing and litigation campaign against possible infringers. The entity is "non-practicing" in the sense that it does not actually implement the methods or produce the products which are the subjects of the aggregated patents. The term "Non-Practicing Entity" is neutral. A pejorative term for the same concept is "patent troll". See "Aggregator". Compare with "Defensive Patent Aggregator".

**Non-standard Usage:** When a patent presents a key claim term that appears commonly in the industry, *but the usage in the patent is different than what the industry understands the term to be,* confusion is certain to result. If the patent presents an explicit definition of the non-standard term, that definition will control the interpretation of the claim. If there is no definition, then both claim scope and claim validity will be uncertain. In Chapter 3, US 5,787,449 uses the term "metacode" in a way not typically used in the industry, and this non-standard usage created confusion as to scope of the claims. See "Shifting Terminology".

**NPE:** Acronym for "Non-Practicing Entity".

**Objective Patent Value:** Also known as "objective value", this is the value of a patent determined by the inherent quality of the claims, the quality of support to the claims provided by the written description and figures, and the scope of claim coverage. This is also called "true fundamental value". The only way to establish objective value is through an expert fundamental analysis performed by a technical and legal expert, or by some decisive and measurable event (such as a major litigation victory as in Chapters 3 and 4, sale for a large sum as in Chapter 5, placement in a patent pool as in Chapter 6, or meeting the requisites of a "seminal patent" as in Chapter 7). Compare with "Subjective Patent Value".

**Patent Activity Intensity:** A measure of the degree to which a company or entity invests in patents. One way to measure patent activity intensity is to compare the resources invested in patents over time to the total investment in R&D over the same period. Compare "R&D Intensity".

**Patent Family:** A patent may stand on its own, without any family members. Alternatively, it may be part of a group of other patents and applications that are related in some chain of priority. In the United States, a patent may be "continued" where the patent depends on, and specifically states its dependence on, an earlier patent or application. In the U.S., there are three forms for creating a chain of priority, which are the "continuation application", the "continuation in part application", and the "divisional application". There are differing opinions as to whether membership in a patent family has positive or negative value — some people hold that a family with many patents and applications is a sign of positive value, but others believe it is a sign of poor value.

**Patent Pool:** Multiple patents, owned by different parties and aggregated into a single group for joint licensing or litigation, are described as being in a patent pool. A patent pool typically is formed around a written technical standard, and patents admitted to the pool must be, by law, "essential" to implementation of the standard. Because entry into a patent pool follows evaluation by technical and legal experts who have determined that the patent is indeed "essential" to the standard, presence in a pool is one sign of potential value in the patent.

**Patent Quality:** The internal worth of a patent, considering the patent's claims, written description, and the figures supporting the claims. This is a basis of "patent value", but is not itself such value.

**Patent Thicket:** A group of patents working together to protect various aspects of the same general invention. Generally owned and administered by one company, but may also be administered (and not owned) by a single entity such as a patent pool administrator, an NPE, or a DPA. Patent pools, NPE aggregations, and DPA aggregations, are generally not thought of in the industry as "patent thickets", but in reality that is what they are. See "Aggregator", "Defensive Patent Aggregator", "Non-Practicing Entity", and "Patent Pool".

**Patent Value:** The worth of a patent determined by a fundamental analysis (which may be either an expert fundamental analysis or a proxy fundamental analysis). A patent that is both high-quality and covers current infringement (or infringement to occur in the very near future) is a "valuable patent". Some patents are extremely valuable, in the range of multiple millions to tens of millions of dollars, and these "very valuable" patents are a subset of all "valuable patents".

**PFA:** Acronym for "proxy fundamental analysis".

**Point of Novelty ("PON"):** This is the part of the claim that is new, for which a particular patent claim was allowed by an examiner. In every independent claim, there should be a single PON. Sometimes the examiner decides that the PON is not what the patentee believed it to be. We saw this in Chapter 6, in Siemens' US 6,885,875, where Siemens thought that the PON for claim #25 was element [2], but the examiner allowed the claim only because of element [4].

**PON:** Acronym for "Point of Novelty".

**Prior Art:** The structure and method of the way things were done before the invention described in the patent. No invention is created out of thin air — there is no magic in the world of innovation. Invention takes prior art and reorganizes it to create a new and useful thing. Just as invention involves both the innovation and the prior art on which the invention is based, a patent describes both the invention and the prior art that is changed or reorganized by the invention.

**Priority Date:** The date on which the patent is considered to have been filed. If the patent does not rely on an earlier filing, then the "priority date" is the date the patent was first filed. If the patent explicitly relies on an earlier patent, then the "priority date" is the filing date of the earlier patent. Assume a patent Y. If patent Y states that it relies on an earlier filed patent X, then the priority date of patent Y is the priority date of patent X, *not the later date* on which patent Y was filed.

For example, an earlier application may be a U.S. Provisional Patent Application ("PPA"), a U.S. Non-Provisional Application ("NPA"), or an international PCT application. If patent Y states specifically that it relies upon the earlier application, that it is a "continuation" of the earlier application, then the priority date will be the filing date of the earlier application. The priority date is critical for purposes of determining whether a patent application is "new" and "non-obvious" over prior art. Prior art is determined by the priority date, which may be earlier than the filing date — therefore, patent Y will not be rejected because of prior art that arose after the "priority date", even if the prior art arose before the filing date of patent Y.

**Proxy Fundamental Analysis ("PFA"):** Analysis of a patent's value using a pre-defined algorithm that focuses on one or more factors believed to be associated with patent value. PFA is often performed by a computer, but it may also be performed by a person acting in strict adherence to the algorithm.

**R&D Intensity:** A measure of the degree to which a company or entity invests in R&D. One way to measure R&D intensity is to compare the resources invested in R&D over time to the total revenues generated by the company over the same period. Compare "Patent Activity Intensity".

**Reexamination:** The PTO sometimes reexamines patents by considering prior art that was not considered in the original prosecution. The reexamination process may be launched by the patent owner, by a third party, or by the PTO itself. The PTO decides which claims to review, and each claim reviewed will be confirmed, cancelled, or amended. Reexamination is one of three procedures by which a patent owner may have the patent changed after issuance. Compare with "Certificate of Correction", and "Reissue Patent".

**Reissue Patent:** When a patent is considered by its owner to be inoperative or invalid in some way, the owner may ask the patent office to substitute a "reissue patent" in place of the original patent. This is different from a certificate of correction in that the mistake here is more than formal. The mistake may be, for example, a defect in either the written description, a defect in one of the figures, or a request to cancel claims that should not have been allowed. A reissue also may broaden the original patent, but only within two years of issuance. This is one of three procedures by which a patent owner may have the patent changed after issuance, and the only procedure by which the patent owner may have the patent broadened after issuance. Compare with "Certificate of Correction", and "Reexamination".

**Reverse Citation:** See "Backward Citation".

**Seminal Patent:** A patent that has certain characteristics that can make it "fundamental" or "a breakthrough" in a particular industry. These characteristics are: (1) early priority date, (2) hundreds of forward non-self citations, (3) addresses a major technical problem, or contributes significantly to its technology area, and (4) has sufficiently broad scope to cover a significantly sized market. The technical problem and breadth of coverage are determined as part of an expert fundamental analysis.

**Server-side:** Most communication systems tend to have a client side and a server side, the latter sometimes called head end, network operations center, or network control center. For ICT system and method claims, it is important that you know whether *each element of a claim* is on the client-side or the server-side. If you have one claim that has both client elements and server elements, that claim is in danger of being invalidated by the doctrine of divided infringement. Compare with "Client-side".

**Shifting Terminology:** Changes in the explanation of key claim terms can impact the validity and/or scope of the claims. Changes may occur in only the written description of the invention, or only in the claims, or in both the written description of the invention and the claims. Shifting terminology is never good. In certain cases, the results can be catastrophic. There are several types of shifting terminology, including the following:

1. When terminology shifts between different independent claims in one patent, horizontal claim confusion results. Claims may or may not be invalidated, but the scope of claim coverage will almost certainly be impacted negatively. See also "Horizontal Shift".

2. When there is shifting terminology between different elements *of the same claim,* the result is vertical claim confusion. Often the interpretation and scope of the claim become impossible to understand. The result of vertical claim confusion may be invalidation of both the confused claim and of all the claims depending on the confused claim. See also "Vertical Shift".

3. Shifting terminology occurs when the written description presents a key term in one way, and the claim presents it in a different way. This kind of shifting terminology happens frequently in patents that do not give explicit definitions of key claim terms, or (less frequently) where explicit definitions are given but the claims deviate from the definitions. The results of this kind of shifting terminology cannot be known in advance of litigation. Claims may be invalidated, or claim scope may be restricted by a court or by the ITC. The results, although they may be bad, are usually not as serious

as those for vertical claim confusion. See also "Description-Claim Mismatch".

4. Shifting terminology occurs where the written description refers to one concept in multiple forms, and the claim uses one of these multiple forms. The claim will probably be valid in accordance with the particular form used by the claim, but there will be substantial doubt if the scope of the claim includes implementations of the written description based on forms of the concept not used by the claim. This kind of confusion, resulting from shifting terminology within only the written description, appears with surprising frequency. See also "Description-Claim Mismatch".

5. Shifting terminology occurs where a single key term is expanded to include two or more different concepts. The stretching may occur only in the written description (where one term describes two concepts in the written description), or in the claims (where one term describes two concepts in a claim), or in a mismatch between the written description (using the term for one concept) and a claim (using the term for a second concept). In my experience, term stretching occurs less frequently than the previously mentioned types of shifting terminology. When it occurs, however, there may arise significant doubt about both the validity and scope of every claim infected by the stretched term. See also "Term Stretching".

6. Presenting a key term that is well-known in the relevant industry, but using that term in a way that is *not the common industry understanding*, is a kind of shifting terminology that is guaranteed to confuse the reader, whether a potential licensee, a competitor, a potential buyer, a judge, a jury, an administrative official, or any other kind of evaluator. Using

standard terms in a non-standard way is bad practice, and should be avoided. If you use an industry-standard term in a standard way, fine. If you wish to use the term in a non-standard way, then present in the patent an explicit and clear definition of the non-standard usage. Or, better yet, invent your own term, define it, and use the invented term, rather than using the industry-standard term in a non-standard way. See also "Non-standard Usage".

See "Claim Parallelism" "Description-Claim Mismatch", "Horizontal Claim Confusion", "Horizontal Shift", "Non-standard Usage", "Term Stretching", "Vertical Claim Confusion", and "Vertical Shift".

**Specification:** The "specification" is the part of the patent that describes both the invention and the prior art associated with the invention. A patent specification includes its written description, claims, and figures. It is essentially the entire patent application, but does not include official forms or correspondence with the patent office.

**Structural tag:** This term expresses a state of being for an element in a structure claim. It is useful for converting a method into a structure, without combining structural and method elements in the same claim (since such a combination is not allowed in patent law). Examples include phrases such as, "some structure ____ *adapted to* ___", or "some structure _____ *configured to* ______".

**Subjective Patent Value:** The value of a patent in the eyes of a certain party, usually the patent owner. Subjective patent value says only that the patentee (or some other party) thinks the patent has value, but such value has not been established by the market or by a technical and legal expert performing an expert fundamental analysis. Compare with "Objective Patent Value".

**Technology Inflection Point ("TIP"):** As technology changes, we may sometimes anticipate what the changes are likely to be. Major changes occur where (1) a change in approach can have great impact on the performance of existing technology, or (2) new technology supplants the old technology in a paradigm shift.

**Term Stretching:** The use of a single term to try to cover two or more different concepts is both misdirected and doomed to failure, because a single term cannot adequately cover multiple concepts. If the stretched term is a key term in one or more claims, both the validity and the scope of those claims will be unclear. See "Shifting Terminology".

**TIP:** Acronym for "technology inflection point".

**True Fundamental Value:** Also referenced as "True Patent Value", this is the value of a patent determined by either an expert fundamental analysis (EFA) or a proxy fundamental analysis (PFA). This is the inherent value of the patent based on the clarity and validity of the claims, the support provided to the claims by the written description of the invention, and the scope of claim coverage (covering current infringement or infringement in the very near future). This value is the basis of financial value, but it is not financial value itself.

**True Patent Value:** See "True Fundamental Value".

**Uncertainty Principle of Patent Value:** The concept that there are so many levels at which a patent may be challenged, so many possible avenues of attack, and so many possible influences of external events, that you can never be 100% sure of a patent's value or even of the patent's validity. Examples of levels of challenge include an ITC hearing, reexamination at the PTO, Markman hearing at federal district court, invalidity and non-infringement allegations to a jury or to a district court judge, appeal to the CAFC, and appeal to the Supreme Court. Avenues of attack include claim invalidity for a host of possible reasons (such as anticipation by prior art, or obviousness over prior art), patent invalidity (due to fraud in patent acquisition, or misuse after issuance), non-infringement, or non-infringement for design around products.

**Unique Selling Point**: Sometimes called "Unique Selling Proposition", this is something about a company that establishes an advantage for that company over its competitors. This is a well-known marketing term meant to reflect value in a company. Having a "good patent portfolio" may help a company establish a unique selling point.

**USP:** An acronym for "unique selling point", sometimes called "unique selling proposition". See "Unique Selling Point".

**Utility Patent**: A category of patent for a new and useful process, machine, manufacture, or composition of matter, under statute 35 USC sec. 101. Compare with "Design Patent".

**Vertical Claim Confusion**: This is the result when a single concept appears as different terms in different elements of the same claim. It is a type of shifting terminology that occurs entirely within a single claim. This kind of shift does not appear often in patents, but when it does appear, the resulting confusion is often catastrophic. If a court or the ITC cannot understand what the claim says, which is very possible, the likely result is that both the confused claim and all claims dependent on the confused claim will be invalidated. (This claim confusion is called "vertical" because when a claim is presented on either a screen or a page, it is generally presented such that the readers scans down from one claim element to the next. This vertical scan reveals the confusion, and hence the confusion is "vertical".) See "Shifting Terminology". Compare "Horizontal Claim Confusion".

**Vertical Shift:** Also called "vertical shifting terminology", this is what happens when the usage or meaning of a key claim term shift *between different elements of the same claim*. When this happens, "vertical claim confusion" occurs. The results of vertical shift are often catastrophic, invalidating both the infected claim and all claims dependent on the infected claim, because a reader of the patent cannot be certain what the infected claim means. In Chapter 7, there was vertical shift in independent apparatus claim #18 and independent circuit claim #29 of US 5,414,796. Although only a court or the ITC can render a final decision, the likely result of vertical shift in this case is that more than 50% of the patent's claim would be invalidated in litigation. See also "Shifting Terminology" and "Vertical Claim Confusion".

**Work Around**: See "Design Around".

**Written Description**: As described in 35 USC sec. 112(1), the written description includes all the sections of a patent that describe how to make and use the various implementations of the invention, including the invention's structure and method. Multiple structures, and/or multiple methods, may be described, in which case they are often called "alternative embodiments". The key sections of the patent included in the written description are the Title, Cross-Reference to Related Applications to establish an early priority date, Field of Invention (which is optional and which often does not appear), Background of the Invention (also called "Related Art"), Brief Summary of the Invention, Brief Description of the Drawings, Detailed Description of the Invention (or "Detailed Description of Preferred Embodiments", or simply "Detailed Description"), and Abstract.[243] The explanation of the patent is always called "the written description" and not merely "the description". The written description includes all parts of the patent except the figures and the claims. Compare with "Specification".

243 Technically, claims are part of the specification, not the written description. The specification therefore includes the written description, the figures, and the claims.

# Appendix, Bibliography, and Indexes

# APPENDIX:
# US 5,133,079

US005133079A


# United States Patent [19]

**Ballantyne et al.**

[11] **Patent Number: 5,133,079**

[45] **Date of Patent: Jul. 21, 1992**


[54] **METHOD AND APPARATUS FOR DISTRIBUTION OF MOVIES**


[76] Inventors: **Douglas J. Ballantyne**, 21 Horner Dr., Nepean, Ontario, K2H 5E6, Canada; **Michael Mulhall**, 28 Carlyle Ave., Ottawa, Ontario, K1S 4Y3, Canada



[21] Appl. No.: **573,707**

[22] Filed: **Aug. 28, 1990**

[30] **Foreign Application Priority Data**

Jul. 30, 1990 [CA] Canada ................................ 2022302

[51] **Int. Cl.**[5] ......................... **H04H 1/02**; H04N 7/10

[52] **U.S. Cl.** ....................................... **455/4.1**; 358/86; 358/335; 455/5.1; 455/72

[58] **Field of Search** ......................... 455/3, 5, 6, 72, 4; 358/86, 102, 142, 146, 133, 335; 381/34, 35, 30, 31; 370/110.1, 109; 360/8, 13, 15; 369/30



[56] **References Cited**

U.S. PATENT DOCUMENTS

| | | | |
|---|---|---|---|
| 4,787,085 | 11/1988 | Suto et al. | 370/110.1 |
| 4,920,432 | 4/1990 | Eggers et al. | 360/33.1 |
| 4,949,170 | 8/1990 | Yanagidaira et al. | 358/86 |
| 4,949,187 | 8/1990 | Cohen | 358/335 |
| 4,961,109 | 10/1990 | Tanaka | 358/84 |
| 4,963,995 | 10/1990 | Lang | 358/335 |
| 4,975,771 | 12/1990 | Kassatly | 358/146 |



*Primary Examiner*—Curtis Kuntz
*Assistant Examiner*—Chi H. Pham
*Attorney, Agent, or Firm*—Burke-Robertson



[57] **ABSTRACT**

A new and useful method and apparatus for distribution of movies for viewing on a customer's television set. Digitized compressed signals containing audio and visual components of the movie selected by the customer are sent to the customer's receiver. The digital signals are converted to corresponding electronic signals; which are decompressed and converted to audio and video signals. These converted signals are passed to a conventional television set for viewing by the customer.


**16 Claims, 6 Drawing Sheets**

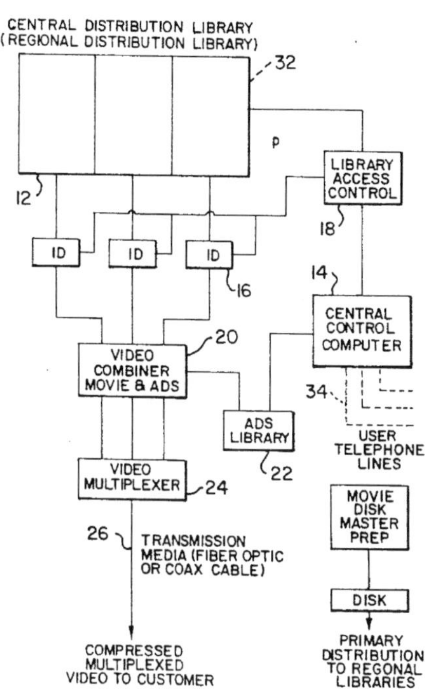

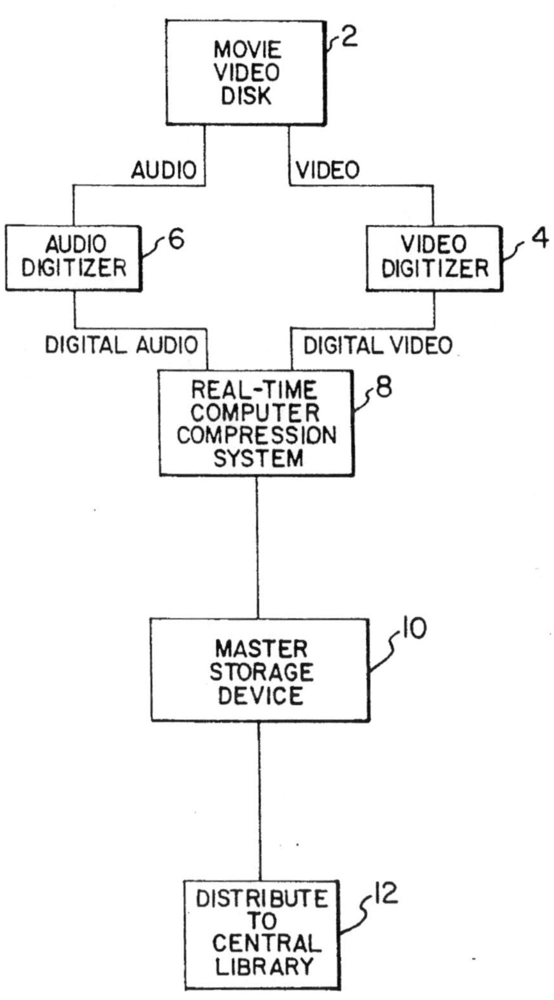
VIDEO MASTER COMPRESSION SYSTEM
MOVIE VIDEO DISK
2
AUDIO
VIDEO
AUDIO DIGITIZER
6
VIDEO DIGITIZER
4
DIGITAL AUDIO
DIGITAL VIDEO
REAL-TIME COMPUTER COMPRESSION SYSTEM
8
MASTER STORAGE DEVICE
10
DISTRIBUTE TO CENTRAL LIBRARY
12

FIG. 1A

U.S. Patent July 21, 1992 Sheet 2 of 6 5,133,079

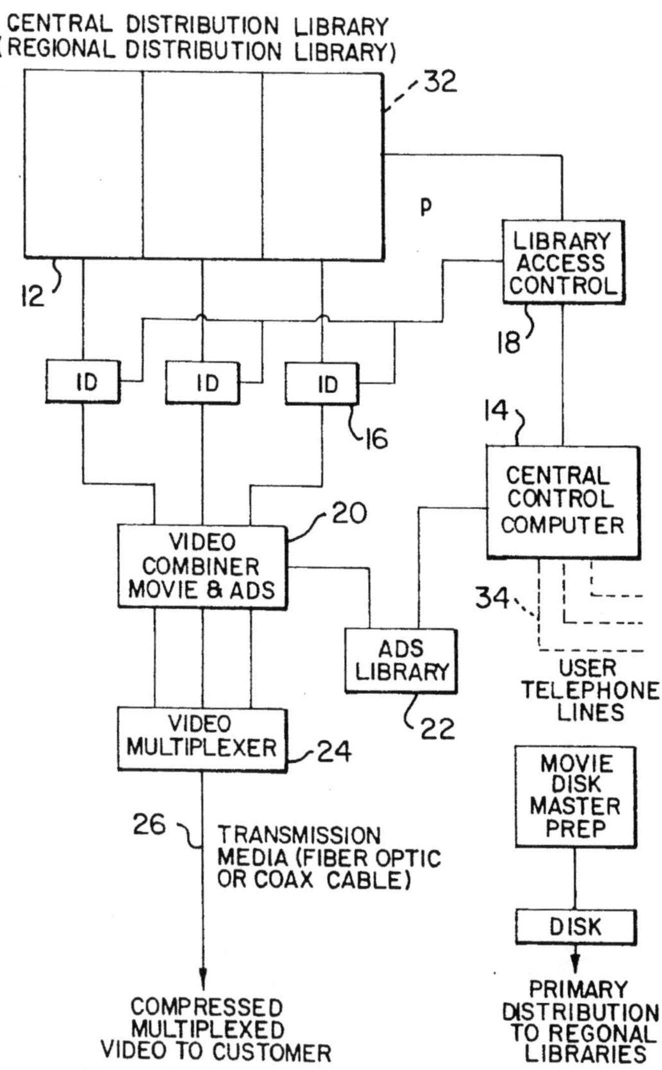


FIG. 1B

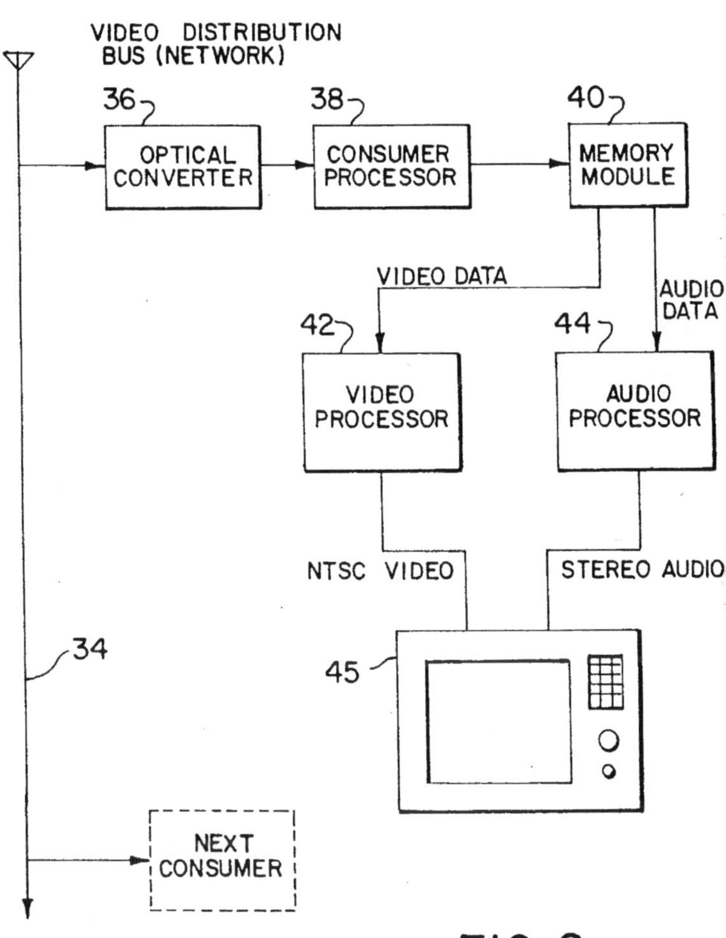
VIDEO DISTRIBUTION BUS (NETWORK)
36
OPTICAL CONVERTER
38
CONSUMER PROCESSOR
40
MEMORY MODULE
VIDEO DATA
AUDIO DATA
42
VIDEO PROCESSOR
44
AUDIO PROCESSOR
NTSC VIDEO
STEREO AUDIO
34
45
NEXT CONSUMER

FIG. 2

U.S. Patent July 21, 1992 Sheet 4 of 6 5,133,079

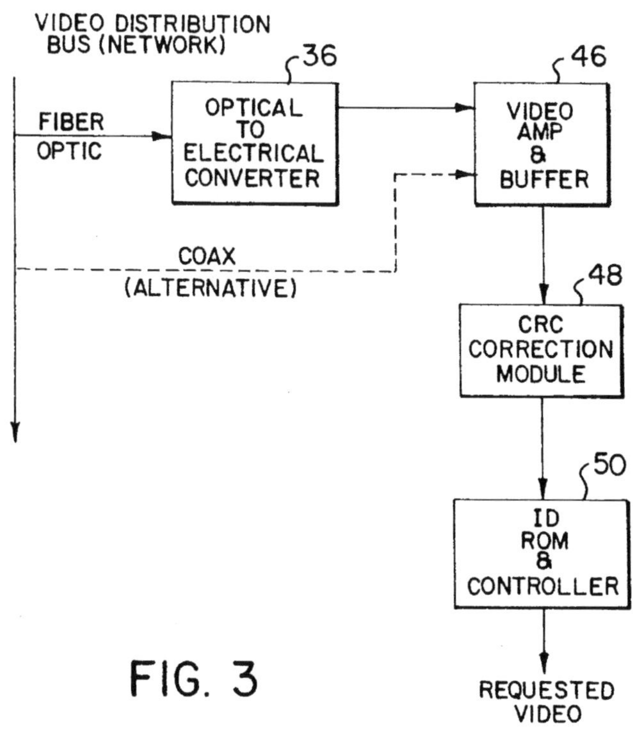


FIG. 3

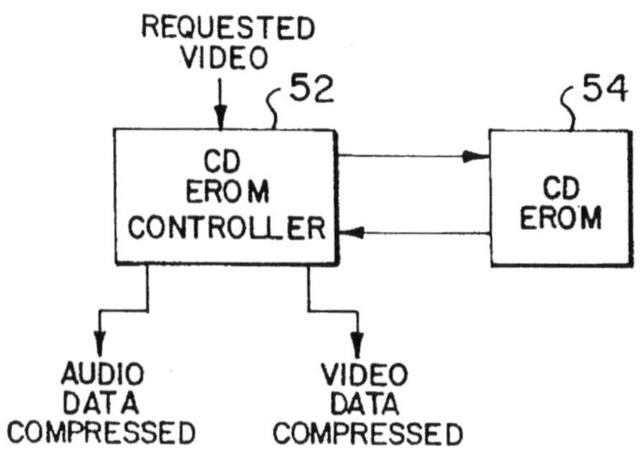


FIG. 4

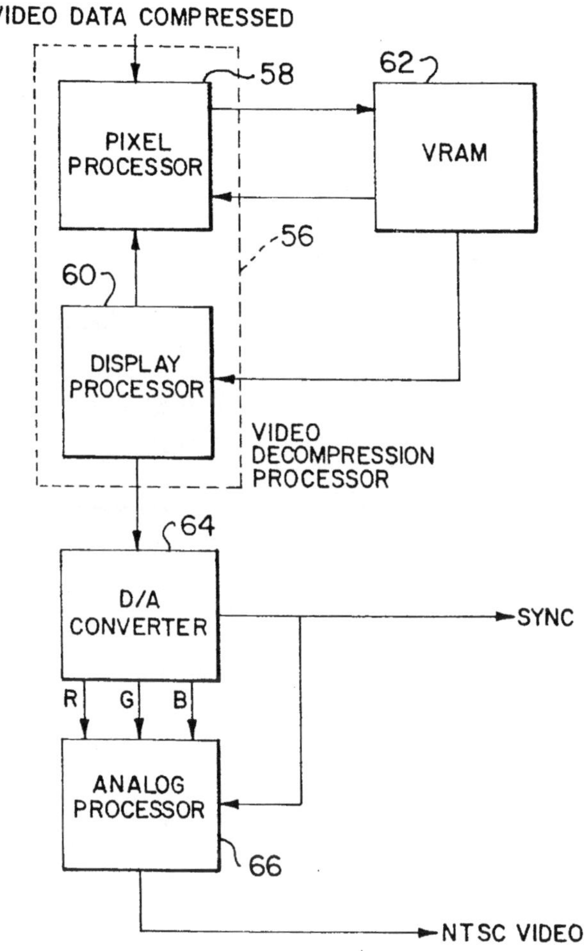
VIDEO DATA COMPRESSED
58
62
PIXEL PROCESSOR
VRAM
56
60
DISPLAY PROCESSOR
VIDEO DECOMPRESSION PROCESSOR
64
D/A CONVERTER
SYNC
R
G
B
ANALOG PROCESSOR
66
NTSC VIDEO

FIG. 5

U.S. Patent July 21, 1992 Sheet 6 of 6 5,133,079

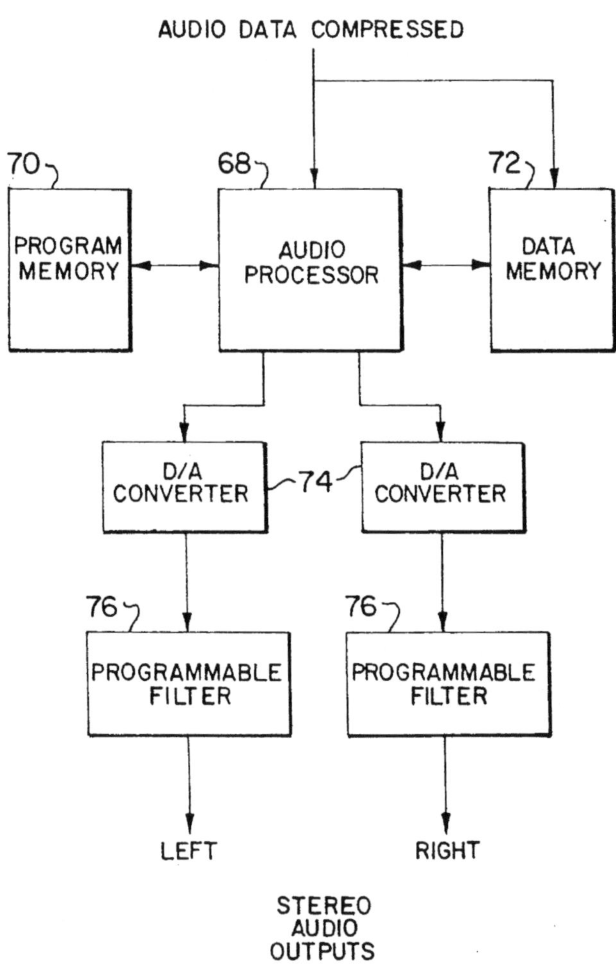


FIG. 6

# METHOD AND APPARATUS FOR DISTRIBUTION OF MOVIES

## BACKGROUND OF THE INVENTION

The present invention relates to a method and apparatus for distribution of movies to a customer's home, and more particularly to an electronic system whereby movies may be selected from a central library, from a customer's home and supplied electronically to that home for subsequent viewing at a time determined by the customer, on that customer's television set.

At the present time, commercial movies selected by a customer for home viewing are conventionally provided on cassette tapes in electromagnetic form. These tapes are often rented for a short period of time by the customer at a video cassette shop, taken to the customer's home and played there on a video cassette player electronically connected to the customer's television. This method of delivery of movies to a customer's home requires the customer to have a video cassette player and requires the customer actually to go to a video cassette rental shop to select the movie to be played.

It is an object of the present invention to provide a system which will avoid the need for a customer to leave home to select a movie, and as well avoid the need for a video cassette player at the customer's home to enable the viewing of a selected movie. It is a further object of the present invention to provide a novel method and apparatus to electronically distribute movies selected by a customer to the customer's home from a central location.

## SUMMARY OF THE INVENTION

In accordance with the present invention there is provided a method for distribution of movies for viewing on a customer's television set. The method comprises the steps of sending digitized compressed optical signals containing audio visual data corresponding to the movie selected by the customer from a source to the customer's receiver over a fibre optic network, passing the optical signal to an optical converter to convert the optical signal to corresponding electronic signals, passing the electronic signals to processors where they are decompressed and converted to audio and visual signals compatible with conventional television sets, and passing these converted signals to a conventional television set for viewing by the customer.

A preferred embodiment of the method according to the present invention additionally includes the step wherein the signals from the optical converter are stored in memory means for retrieval and passage to the signal processors for decompression and a single viewing on the television set at a time selected by the customer.

As well, in accordance with the present invention there is provided an apparatus for enabling a customer to electronically receive and play on a television set a pre-determined movie. The apparatus comprises a receiver to receive from a source, data in digitized compressed optical signal format containing audio visual data corresponding to the movie. An optical converter is electronically associated with the receiver to convert the optical signal data to corresponding electronic signals. A video processor is electronically associated with the optical converter to receive the video electronic signals, decompress them and convert them to electronic video signals compatible with the television set to



provide a video image of the movie on the television set. An audio processor is electronically associated with the optical converter to receive the audio electronic signals from the optical converter, decompress them and convert them to electronic audio signals compatible with the television set to provide an audible sound track of the movie through the television set with the video processor and audio processor electronically associated with the television set.

The present invention provides a novel method and apparatus to electronically distribute movies for viewing to a customer's home from a central or regional library. This may be achieved for example through existing coax cable or fibre optic networks. If coax cable is used, electrical to optical conversion, as described in the previous paragraphs, is not required. A customer may, from his or her own home, electronically access the central library, select a movie to be viewed and have the movie electronically sent to the customer's receiver in compressed form where it is then decompressed and played on the customer's television set or stored for subsequent viewing.

## BRIEF DESCRIPTION OF THE DRAWINGS

These and other objects and advantages of the invention will become apparent upon reading the following detailed description and upon referring to the drawings in which:

FIGS. **1A** and **1B** constitute a flow chart illustrating the manner in which movies are prepared for storage and stored in a distributor's library, and accessed there by a customer, in accordance with the present invention;

FIG. **2** is a schematic diagram of the method of and apparatus for retaining movies at a customer's location for viewing on the customer's television set, in accordance with the present invention;

FIG. **3** is a schematic diagram of apparatus to be used by a customer in receiving and converting electronic signals from a distributor's library, for subsequent viewing on a television set;

FIG. **4** is a schematic diagram of apparatus for use in storage of signals through the apparatus of FIG. **3**;

FIG. **5** is a schematic diagram of apparatus to be used to convert the compressed video signals received by a customer into signals to provide for the video display on the customer's television set; and

FIG. **6** is a schematic diagram of apparatus to be used to convert audio signals received by a customer into signals to produce the movie's audio tract on the customer's television set.

While the invention will be described in conjunction with an example embodiment, it will be understood that it is not intended to limit the invention to such an embodiment. On the contrary, it is intended to cover all alternatives, modifications and equivalents as may be included within the spirit and scope of the invention as defined by the appended claims.

## DETAILED DESCRIPTION OF THE INVENTION

The present invention relates to a commercial movie distribution system consisting of a central distribution centre comprised of a video master compression system and a digital movie data bank library, illustrated in more detail in FIGS. **1A** and **1B**. Located at the customer's site is a compatible digital video storage system (FIGS.

2 - 6) facilitating movie playback in real-time on the user's television unit.

### 1. Video Compression Mastering Process

Turning to FIGS. **1A** and **1B**, a complete motion picture movie is received on laser disks (**2**) either in conventional video analog or digital format. Typically, video output is in real-time at 30 frames per second portraying full motion effects with synchronized stereo audio. The video and audio signals are digitized with separate video and audio analog to digital converters (**4** and **6** respectively) and input to the computer compression system (**8**).

The computer compression system (**8**) consists of a typical P.C./A.T. computer with a CD-ROM drive and special purpose software. The system captures and compresses motion video in real-time and stores the compressed video on the CD-ROM at a reduced frame rate. A typical data compression factor of **150:1** will give the following level of data reduction:

Conventional video frame in digital form
  512 × 480 pixels = approximately 750 kbytes
Compressed video frame at **150:1** compression
  5 kbytes/frame
Compressed video storage requirements for a typical 2 hour movie
  5 kbytes/frame
  30 frames/sec.
  150 kbytes/sec.
  9000 kbytes/min.
  1.08 Gbytes/2 hrs.

The master storage device (**10**) must have the capacity to store the required amount of compressed data for the entire duration of the movie, as received from computer compression system (**8**). Various technologies can be utilized for this storage device. The following lists several such technologies as well as their present capacities.

| | | |
|---|---|---|
| CD-ROM | Mode 1 | 660 Mbytes |
| | Mode 2 | 750 Mbytes |
| WORM | | 200 Mbytes |
| Hard Disks | | 100 Mbytes |
| | | • |
| | | • |
| | | • |
| | | 1 Gbyte |
| Solid State Memory | | 2 Mbytes |

These technologies can be grouped individually to ensure sufficient storage capacity or a combination of different technologies can be utilized. However, the actual technological combination must be portable enough to allow distribution to the Central Distribution Library (**12**).

### 2. Central Distribution Library

Illustrated in FIG. **1B**, the Central Distribution Library (CDL) (**12**) is the central depository for the compressed movie data from the video master compression system. It is arranged such that each movie type has a unique identification code that is appended to the digital video data when it is initially entered into the library. The data is retrieved in digital format and at a very high rate such that the data from a 2 hour movie can be transmitted in a very short time duration. Because the data is compressed, it actually appears as if it is scrambled, thus allowing a secure transmission of proprietary movie information.

Central control computer (**14**) is responsible for the access control of the library and all interaction with the user. Initial user requests are taken either through CDL operator intervention or totally automatic by means of the digital telephone system. In either case, the movie is requested by using its unique identification number (ID) (**16**). After verification of the customer's credit and/or membership card number, confirmation is given to the user as to the movie to be transmitted and the actual time of transmission. User requests are queued as the demand increases. Confirmation of the transaction (i.e. movie title, time of transmittal, etcetera) may be provided on the screen of the user's television set. The central control computer (**14**) also automatically collects statistics (busy time periods, most frequently requested movie, etc.) and performs all accounting requirements.

The library access control (**18**) contains a record of where the relevant movies are located within the library and requests data transmission when a specific movie is requested. It is also responsible for appending the user identification number (UIN) to the requested movie to ensure the correct distribution of the movie is completed.

The video combiner (**20**) makes it possible to mix specific advertisements, previews of additional movies, etc. to each movie being transmitted. It also generates an error check code to enable the re-generation of lost data due to poor transmission interconnections.

As an option, an advertisement library (**22**) may be provided which contains a repository of digital video ads that have been authored by the master video compression system. These ads can be custom created and can be specifically transmitted on a daily basis, only during busy periods, only with respect to specific movies (environmentally conscious advertisements), etc.

The compressed digital video is then converted into light energy to facilitate the transmission over a fibre optic communication network. If standard coax cable is used, this optical conversion is not required. The data may also be multiplexed at multiplexer (**24**) with respect to light wavelength enabling the transmission of several movies at the same time. (This is not feasible if coax cable is the transmission media.)

The compressed multiplexed movie data is then broadcast over a wide area fibre optic network (**26**) for user distribution.

As illustrated in FIG. **1B**, a regional distribution library (**32**) of similar make-up to Central Distribution Library (**12**), but accessible through customer or user telephone lines (**34**) as illustrated, is preferably provided in each of the geographical areas to be provided with a commercial movie distribution system in accordance with the present invention.

Turning to FIG. **2**, there is illustrated in schematic form the digital video storage and movie playback system at the customer's location, where transferred movie data from the central or regional distribution library is transferred to be played back at a desired time. This system comprises an optical converter, if a fibre optic network is used (**36**), consumer processor (**38**), memory module (**40**), video processor (**42**), audio processor (**44**) and the customer's television set (**45**). The transmission system connecting the central or regional distribution library to the customer's facility is preferably a fibre optic communication network which will serve additionally as the user's telephone lines (**34**). The digital movie data is transmitted at a very high rate allowing a typical two hour movie to be transmitted in several minutes. Digital data bit error correction is performed, as will be described in more detail hereinafter, at the customer's facility to restore the integrity of the data after transmission.

As can be seen in more detail in FIG. **3**, a signal from transmission line (**34**) passes to optical converter (**36**) which is preferably an optical-to-electrical converter photo diode module (available, for example, from Optical Data Systems). There the optical data is converted to electrical data. The consumer processor (**38**) comprises a video amplifier and buffer (available, for example, from National Semi-Conductor) intended to enhance the video signal level and act as a temporary video frame buffer memory capable of storing at least two frames of video data (approximately 10 Kbytes). The Cyclic Redundancy Code (CRC) correction module (**48**) (available from Texas Instruments) receives the signal from the video amplifier and buffer (**46**) and detects and corrects the digital video data on a frame-by-frame basis. Identification read only memory (ID-ROM) (**50**) (also available from Texas Instruments) contains the customer identification number (UIN). This UIN value is checked against the UIN number tagged to the distributed video movie, and if a match occurs, the signal is passed for further processing to the compact disc erasable read only memory (CD-EROM) controller (**52**) (FIG. **4**). This controller (available from Sony Corp.) stores and retrieves the video digital data from the physical compact disk. Once the entire video data has been read from the disk it is erased, preventing further replay. There is no limitation as to the length of the time of storage, but the data can only be replayed once. The video data is still in compressed form rendering it unusable if copied, at this stage. Controller (**52**) outputs audio and video data as illustrated. Associated with controller (**52**) is a physical compact disk erasable read only memory (CD-EROM) (**54**) (available from Sony Corp.) which at the present state of technology development has the capacity of storing 600 Mbytes of digital data.

Video data form controller (**52**) is passed, when desired by a customer, to video decompression processor (**56**) which comprises two microprocessors, a pixel processor (**58**) and an output display processor (**60**) (both available from Intel Semiconductor), configured as illustrated in FIG. **5**. These are responsible for converting the compressed video data to conventional video signals. The special decompression algorithms are inherent in these microprocessors.

Video random access memory (VRAM) (**62**) (available, for example from Toshiba) is a type of digital memory that has two ports, one with random access for storing data at any memory location and the other, a serial port to output data at a high rate compatible with television scanning techniques. Activity at either port is independent of the other. VRAM (**62**) is electronically associated with pixel processor (**58**) and display processor (**60**) as illustrated.

The digital-to-analog (D/A) converter (**64**) receives the signal from video decompression processor (**56**) as illustrated, and converts the digital video data into analog data that can be used by, for example, colour RGB monitors. Analog processor (**66**) converts the RGB output from D/A converter (**64**) into contemporary or NTSC colour television format to be viewed on a conventional television set (**45**).

Compressed audio data from controller (**52**) is passed, as required, to audio processor (**68**) (available from Texas Instruments) which decompresses the retrieved audio data. Program memory module (**70**) (also available from Texas Instruments) stores the operations program of audio processor (**68**) to perform the decompression process. Data memory module (**72**) (also available from Texas Instruments) temporarily stores the audio data from controller (**52**) if required.

The digital-to-analog (D/A) converters (**74**) translate the digital decompressed audio data to analog and programmable filters (**76**) smooths out any D/A conversion anomalies that can distort the final output. Full stereo output is available as illustrated. While a conventional television (**45**) that requires NTSC video format for viewing is illustrated, it should be noted that the video processor will also support future digital television video formats.

3. Operation

In operation, a customer requests the delivery of a desired movie by phoning the central distribution centre or regional distribution centre (**12**) and identifying the movie with an identification code unique to the movie. Membership and credit card validation is then requested and if authorized, movie distribution is initiated. At the start of transmission, the customer's UIN is appended to the video being distributed. This UIN is embedded in the customer video storage system (at the customer's location) ensuring a one-to-one match between the customer and the requested movie. The customer's requests are either conveyed verbally over the phone system to a CDL operator or through an automated communication system using a touchtone key pad on a telephone handset (not illustrated).

It is a preferred aspect of the present invention that the customer's storage device allows only one replay, where upon the stored data is either erased or locked from further replay.

Thus it is apparent that there has been provided in accordance with the invention a method and apparatus for distribution of movies to a customer's home and the like that fully satisfies the objects, aims and advantages set forth above. While the invention has been described in conjunction with a specific embodiment thereof, it is evident that many alternatives, modifications and variations will be apparent to those skilled in the art in light of the foregoing description. Accordingly, it is intended to embrace all such alternatives, modifications and variations as fall within the spirit and broad scope of the invention.

What we claim as our invention:

**1**. A method for distribution of movies for viewing on a customer's television set, the method comprising the steps of:

(a) compressing and digitizing audio visual data corresponding to an entire movie and storing the compressed, digitized data at a remote source;

(b) sending digitized compressed signals containing audio visual data corresponding to the entire movie selected by the customer from a source to a receiver of the customer;

(c) passing the signals to a converter to convert the signals to corresponding electronic signals;

(d) passing the electronic signals to processors where they are decompressed and converted to signals compatible with conventional television sets; and

(e) passing these converted signals to a conventional television set for viewing by the customer.

2. A method according to claim 1 wherein the signals from the converter are temporarily stored in memory means for retrieval and passage to the signal processors for decompression and single viewing on the television set at a time selected by the customer.

3. A method according to claim 2 requiring the preliminary step of the customer providing a satisfactory identification electronically to the source and being cleared by the source before the digitized compressed signal is sent to the customer's receiver by the source.

4. A method according to claim 2 wherein a library of movies in digitized compressed form is maintained at the source, individual movies thereof to be selected by a customer for viewing.

5. A method according to claim 4 further comprising the preliminary step of digitizing and compressing audio visual data making up the films for storage at the source.

6. A method according to claim 1 wherein the digitized compressed signals are sent from the source in optical signal format.

7. A method according to claim 1 wherein the digitized compressed signals are sent from the source via coaxial cable.

8. An apparatus for enabling a customer to electronically receive and play on a television set a pre-determined movie, the apparatus comprising:

(a) receiver means to receive from a remote source data in digitized compressed signal format containing audio visual data corresponding to the movie;

(b) a converter to be electronically associated with the receiver means to convert the signal data to corresponding electronic signal data;

(c) a video processor to be electronically associated with the converter to receive the electronic video signals, decompress them and convert them to electronic video signals compatible with the television set to provide a video image of the movie on the television set; and

(d) an audio processor to be electronically associated with the converter to receive the audio electronic signals from the converter, decompress them and convert them to electronic audio signals compatible with the television set, the video processor and audio processor to be electronically associated with the television set to provide an audible sound tract of the movie through the television set.

9. Apparatus according to claim 8 further comprising a television set electronically associated with the video processor and audio processor to receive signals therefrom.

10. Apparatus according to claim 8 further comprising memory means to be electronically associated with the converter and with the video processor and audio processor, to store and retrieve electronic signals from the converter until desired by the customer for viewing the movie on the television set.

11. Apparatus according to claim 10 wherein the signals from the converter are placed on a compact disc and wherein the memory means comprises a compact disc erasable read only memory (CD-EROM) controller to store and retrieve the electronic signals from the compact disc.

12. Apparatus according to claim 10 wherein the video processor comprises a pixel processor provided with a decompression algorithm to convert the compressed electronic video signals to conventional decompressed video signals and a video random access memory (VRAM) to be electronically associated with the pixel processor for storing data and providing output data at a high rate compatible with the television set.

13. Apparatus for electronically distributing movies to a customer's television set in conjunction with the apparatus of claim 8, comprising a video library of movies stored in digitized compressed audio visual format and computer means electronically associated with said library to provide customer electronic access to individual movies in that library and to send to said receiver means in digital signal form the digitized compressed audio visual data for a selected movie in that library.

14. Apparatus according to claim 13 further comprising electronic customer access means electronically associated with said computer means to control and document customer access to the library.

15. Apparatus according to claim 8 wherein the receiver means is adapted to receive data from the source in optical signal format and the converter is an optical converter.

16. Apparatus according to claim 8 wherein the receiver means is adapted to receive data from the source from a coaxial cable.

* * * * *

# Bibliography

## *ARTICLES, BOOKS, AND QUOTATIONS*

Allison, John R., and Lemley, Mark A., "Empirical Evidence on the Validity of Litigated Patents", *AIPLA Quarterly Journal*, Vol. 26, Number 3, pp.185–275 (1998), available at *http://bayhdolecentral.com/3_DIV_SCAN/3068_001_OCR_DBL_ZIP_0.pdf.*

Allison, John R.; Lemley, Mark A.; and Walker, Joshua, "Extreme Value or Trolls on Top? The Characteristics of the Most-Litigated Patents", *University of Pennsylvania Law Review*, Vol. 158, No.1, pp.101–137 (December, 2009).

Allison, John R.; Lemley, Mark A.; and Walker, Joshua, "Patent Quality and Settlement Among Repeat Patent Litigants", *Georgetown Law Review*, Vol. 99, pp.677–712 (2011).

Bader, Martin A., and Ruether, Frauke, "Still a Long Way to Value-Based Patent Valuation: The Patent Valuation Practices of Europe's Top 500", printed in *les Nouvelles,* Journal of the Licensing Executives Society International, June, 2009, at pp.121–124. *http://www.wipo.int/edocs/mdocs/sme/en/wipo_insme_smes_ge_10/wipo_insme_smes_ge_10_ref_theme06_01.pdf*

BBC News, "Compact disc hits 25th birthday", August 17, 2007, available at *http://news.bbc.co.uk/2/hi/technology/6950845.stm.*

Bessen, James E., "The Value of U.S. Patents by Owner and Patent

Characteristics", *Boston University School of Law Working Paper no. 06–46*, pp.1–35 (2006).

Bible, Ecclesiastes 12:12. I have made the translation myself. The original Hebrew is
ויתר מהמה בני הזהר עשות ספרים הרבה אין קץ ולהג הרבה יגעת בשר.

Bloomberg Businessweek, "Silanis Technology Inc. Reports Unaudited Consolidated Earnings Results for the Six Months Ended June 30, 2012", (September 5, 2012).

Branham Group, "Silanis Technology", reporting 2011 and 2012 revenues, available at *http://www.branham300.com/details.php?year=2012&company_ID=181*. This article had no date of publication.

Brinckerhoff, Courtenay C., partner at Foley & Lardner, LLP, "USPTO considers best practices to improve patent application quality", published in *Lexology,* an on-line publication of ACC, the Association of Corporate Counsel, and available also at *http://www.foley.com/uspto-considers-best-practices-to-improve-patent-application-quality-02–14–2013/*.

Brookings Institution — the Metropolitan Policy Program, "Patenting Prosperity: Invention and Economic Performance in the United States and its Metropolitan Areas", Washington, D.C., February, 2013, available at URL *http://www.brookings.edu/~/media/Research/Files/Reports/2013/02/patenting%20prosperity%20rothwell/patenting%20prosperity%20rothwell.pdf.*

Chien, Colleen V., and Lemley, Mark A., "Patent Holdups, the ITC, and the Public Interest", *Cornell Law Review*, Vol. 98:1–46, 2012.

Chien, Colleen V., "Predicting Patent Litigation", *Texas Law Review*, vol. 90, pp.283–328 (2011).

CNET, "Patents: a necessary evil", January 5, 2002 (copyright by the *Wharton School of the University of Pennsylvania*, one of the leading business schools in the United States), at http://news.cnet.com/2009–1001–801896.html).

Donner, Irah H., *Constructing and Deconstructing Patents*, (BNA Books, Arlington, Virginia, 2010).

Drucker, Peter F., *Management* (Taylor & Francis, London, 1999).

Duhigg, Charles, and Lohr, Steve, "Innovation a casualty in tech patent wars", *International Herald Tribune*, October 9, 2012, page 14.

Ethics of the Fathers, also known as Pirkei Avot, a compilation of ethical teachings and moral principles of the Rabbis from the Talmudic period.

Federal Register / Vol. 78, No. 10 / Tuesday, January 15, 2013 / Notices, p.2960, United States PTO Docket No. PTO-P-2011–0046, "Request for Comments on Preparation of Patent Applications", available at *http://www.gpo.gov/fdsys/pkg/FR-2013–01–15/pdf/2013–00690.pdf.*

Fish, Robert D., *Strategic Patenting*, (Trafford Publishing, Victoria, British Colombia, Canada, 2007).

Gambardella, Alfonso; Harhoff, Dietmar; and Verspagen, Bart, "The Value of European Patents", *European Management Review*, Vol. 5, pp.69–84, (2008).

Gambardella, Alfonso; Giuri, Paola; Mariani, Myriam; Giovannoni, Serena; Luzzi, Alessandra; Magazzini, Laura; Martolini, Luisa; and Romanelli, Marzia, "The Value of European Patents: Evidence from a Survey of European Inventors: Final Report of the PatVal EU Project", European Commission (2005).

Gertner, Jon, *The Idea Factory: Bell Labs and the Great Age of American Innovation*, (Penguin Press, New York, 2012).

Gies, Erica, "Baby steps vs. giant leaps in motors", *International Herald Tribune*, June 21, 2012, page12.

Goldstein, Larry M., and Kearsey, Brian N., *Technology Patent Licensing: An International Reference on 21st Century Patent Licensing, Patent Pools and Patent Platforms*, (Aspatore Books, a division of Thomson Reuters, Boston, Massachusetts, 2004).

Greene Jay, and Shankland, Stephen, "Why Microsoft spent $1 billion on AOL's patents", CNET News, April 9, 2012, available at *http://news.cnet.com/8301-10805_3-57411434-75/why-microsoft-spent-$1-billion-on-aols-patents/*.

Horace, formal name Quintus Horatius Flaccus, Roman poet of the 1st century BCE, *Odes*, 1:11.

Hughes, Christopher, and Lutz, Regina, Cadwalader, Wickersham & Taft "Doctrine of equivalents: prosecution beyond the literal patent claims", printed in *Patents in the USA 2008*, Intellectual Asset Management Magazine (2008). *http://www.iam-magazine.com/issues/Article.ashx?g=c112a8a4-87b2-4875-ae38-8dfdb05b9827*

Intellectual Asset Management Magazine, *Patents in the USA 2008* (2008).

Kahrl, Robert C., and Soffer, Stuart B., *Thesaurus of Claim Construction*, (Oxford University Press, New York, 2011).

Kerstetter, Jim, "How much is that patent going to cost you?", CNET News, (April 5, 2012), available at *http://news.cnet.com/8301-32973_3-57409792-296/how-much-is-that-patent-lawsuit-going-to-cost-you/*).

Lemley, Mark A., "Inducing Patent Infringement", *University of California Davis Law Review*, Volume 35, pp.225–247 (2005).

Malackowski, James E., and Barney, Jonathan A., "What is Patent Quality? A Merchant Banc's Perspective", published in *les Nouvelles,* Journal of the Licensing Executives Society, June, 2008, at page 123.

Marvell, Andrew, English poet and politician (1621–1678), *To His Coy Mistress.*

McMillan, Robert, "Trend Micro: Barracuda Suit Not About Open Source", *PC World, PCW Business Center*, June 13, 2008, available at *http://www.pcworld.com/article/147085/article.html.*

Moore, Kimberly A., "Worthless Patents", Berkeley Law Journal, volume 20, pp.1521–1552, (2005), available at *http://btlj.org/data/articles/20_04_02.pdf.*

Mouawad, Jad, "Use of university's patents costs Marvel a big penalty", *International Herald Tribune*, December 28, 2012, p.15.

Paczkowski, John, "Google Says Some Apple Inventions Are So Great They Ought to Be Shared", in the on-line publication *AllThingsD.com*, wholly owned by Dow Jones & Company, member of the Wall Street Journal Digital Network, July 20, 2012, available at *http://allthingsd.com/20120720/google-claims-popularity-has-made-some-apple-patents-de-facto-essentials/.*

Parchomovsky, Gideon, and Wagner, R. Polk, "Patent Portfolios", *University of Pennsylvania Law Review*, Vol. 154, No. 1, pp.1–77 (2005).

Patently Obvious, "Intellectual Property Analysis of Intellectual Ventures' U.S. Patent No. 5,987,610", December 16, 2010, available at *http://www.m-cam.com/sites/www.m-cam.com/files/20101216_IntellectualVentures_v_McAfee.pdf.*

Plambeck, Joseph, "As CD Sales Wane, Music Retailers Diversify", New York Times, May 30, 2010, available at *http://www.nytimes.com/2010/05/31/business/media/31bestbuy.html.*

PwC, (formerly known as PriceWaterhouseCoopers, which to the best of my knowledge is also still the legal name), "2012 Patent Litigation Study: Litigation continues to rise amid growing awareness of patent value", (2012), freely available at *http://www.pwc.com/en_US/us/forensic-services/publications/assets/2012-patent-litigation-study.pdf.*

Qualcomm, Inc., "Accelerating Mobility: How Qualcomm's business model drives wireless innovation and growth", June 5, 2012, at p.8, available at *http://www.qualcomm.com/media/documents/files/qualcomm-business-model-white-paper-accelerating-mobility.pdf.*

Quinn, Gene, "Happy 5th Anniversary: The Impact of eBay v.

MercExchange", *IPWatchdog*, an intellectual property law blog, published May 15, 2011, available at *http://www.ipwatchdog.com/2011/05/15/happy-5th-anniversary-ebay-v-mercexchange/id=16894/*.

Rahnasto, Ilkka, *Intellectual Property Rights, External Effects and Anti-Trust Law: Leveraging IPRs in the Communications Industry*, (Oxford University Press, 2003).

Rich, Giles S., "The Extent of the Protection and Interpretation of Claims-American Perspectives", *21 Int'l Rev. Indus. Prop. & Copyright L., 497, 499* (1990). I have not found the original article by Judge Rich, but his statement about "the claim" is very famous in the patent world, and is quoted in literally dozens of articles, books, and judicial decisions. See, for example, Warren, Leigh M., "Term Interpretation in Patents and Trademarks Refining the Vicarious Inquiry in Claim Construction", *Columbia Science and Technology Law Review*, Volume 7, at p.5 (2006); and *In re Hiniker Co.*, 150 F3d 1362 (Fed. Cir. 1998).

Sreedharan, Sunita K., *An Introduction to Intellectual Asset Management*, (Kluwer Law International, London, 2010).

Tapia, Claudia (current name Claudia Tapia Garcia), *Industrial Property Rights, Technical Standards and Licensing Practices (FRAND) in the Telecommunications Industry*, Carl Heymanns Verlag, Cologne (2010).

Tu, Sean, "Luck/Unluck of the Draw: An Empirical Study of Examiner Allowance Rates", *2012 Stanford Technology Law Review 10* (2012).

Wilson, Kelce S., and Tapia Garcia, Claudia "Patent Application Prioritization and Resource Allocation Strategy", appearing in the June, 2011 edition of *les Nouvelles,* Journal of the Licensing Executives Society International, June, 2011, at p.87. *http://www.iam-magazine.com/issues/Article.ashx?g=c112a8a4-87b2-4875-ae38-8dfdb05b9827*.

## *LEGAL AUTHORITIES:*

### *Conventions and Statutes:*

#### *European Patent Convention:*

Rule 43(1)(b)

#### *United States Patent Statutes:*

19 United States Code Chapter 4, sections 1202–1683g, commonly known as the U.S. Tariff Act of 1930

35 United States Code, sections 1–376, commonly known as the U.S. Patent Act. (Note: The Leahy-Smith America Invents Act, which became law in September, 2011, amends the Patent Act and is included within the various sections of the Patent Act.) Sections of the Patent Act cited in this book include the following:

35 United States Code sec. 100

35 United States Code sec. 101

35 United States Code sec. 102

35 United States Code sec. 103(a)

35 United States Code sec. 112

35 United States Code sec. 112(1)

35 United States Code sec. 112(2)

35 United States Code sec. 112(3)

35 United States Code sec. 112(4)

35 United States Code sec. 112(5)

35 United States Code sec. 112(6)

35 United States Code sec. 113

35 United States Code sec. 271(a)

35 United States Code sec. 271(b)

35 United States Code sec. 271(c)

35 United States Code sec. 282

35 United States Code sec. 283

35 United States Code sec. 302–307

## *Judicial Decisions, Administrative Decisions, & Administrative Reports:*

*Akamai Technologies, Inc. v. Limelight Networks, Inc.*, consolidated with *McKesson Technologies, Inc. v. Epic Systems Corp.*, 692 F.3d 1301 (Fed. Cir. 2012)(en banc).

*Aro Mfg. Co. v. Convertible Top Replacement Co.*, 377 U.S. 476 (1964).

*AT&T Corp. v. Vonage Holdings Corp.*, Civil Docket 3:07-cv-00585-bbc, Federal District Court for the Western District of Wisconsin, 2007. This case settled before trial, and therefore, no decision is reported.

*Broadcom Corporation v. Qualcomm, Inc.*, 543 F.3d 683 (Fed. Cir. September 24, 2008).

*Broadcom Corporation v. Qualcomm Incorporated,* "In the Matter of Certain Baseband Processor Chips and Chipsets, Transmitter and Receiver (Radio) Chips, Power Control Chips, and Products Containing Same, Including Cellular Telephone Handsets", U.S. International Trade Commission ("ITC") Case No. 337-TA-543.

*Carnegie Mellon University v. Marvel Technology Group, Ltd., and Marvel Semiconductor, Inc.*, U.S. District Court, Western District of Pennsylvania, No. 09–00290 (decided December 26, 2012).

*DSU Medical Corp. v. JMS Co.*, 471 F.3d 1293 (Fed. Cir. 2006).

*eBay Inc. v. MercExchange, L.L.C.*, 547 U.S. 388 (2006).

*Energizer Holdings, Inc. v. International Trade Commission,* 435 F.3d 1366 (Fed. Cir. 2006).

*Festo Corp. v Shoketsu Kinzoku Kogyo Kabushiki Co.*, 535 U.S. 722 (2002).

*Fuji Photo Film Co., Ltd. v. Achiever Industries, Ltd.* (and twenty-six other defendants), "In the Matter of Certain Lens-Fitted Film Packages", U.S. International Trade Commission ("ITC") Case No. 337-TA-406.

*Funai Electric Corporation v. Vizio, Inc. (and 10 other defendants),* "In the Matter of Certain Digital Televisions and Certain Products Containing Same and Methods of Using Same", U.S. International Trade Commission ("ITC") Case No. 337-TA-617.

*Hancock, David A., and Ideations Designs v. Duton Industry of Taiwan and IKH International,* "In the Matter of Certain Audible Alarm Devices for Divers", .S. International Trade Commission ("ITC") Case No. 337-TA-365.

*i4i Limited Partnership v. Microsoft Corporation,* F.Supp.2d 568 (E.D.Tx. 2009), *affirmed* 589 F.3d 1246 (Fed. Cir. 2009), *withdrawn and superseded on rehearing,* 598 F.3d 831 (Fed. Cir. 2010), *affirmed* 564 U.S. ____, 131 S. Ct. 2238, Slip Opinion 10–290 (2011)/

*In re Hiniker Co.,* 150 F3d 1362 (Fed. Cir. 1998).

*In re Nuitjen,* 515 F.3d 1361 (Fed.Cir. 2008).

*Jazz Photo Corporation et al. v. ITC and Fuji Photo Film, Co., Ltd.,* 264 F.3d 1094 (Fed.Cir. 2001), *cert. denied* 122 S.Ct. 2644 (2002).

*Kyocera Wireless Corporation LG USA v. ITC,* No. 2007–1493 (Fed. Cir., Oct. 14, 2008).

*Lear, Inc. v. Adkins,* 395 U.S. 653 (1969).

*Liebel-Flarsheim Co. v. Medrad, Inc.*, 358 F.3d 898 (Fed. Cir. 2004), *cert. denied,* 543 U.S. 925 (2004).

*Magnequench International, Inc. of Indiana, USA (formerly a division of General Motors), and Sumitomo Special Metals Co., Ltd., of Japan v. Houghes International, Inc., of Great Neck, New York* (and nine other defendants from the United States, Republic of China — Taiwan, and People's Republic of China — PRC), "In the Matter of Certain Rare-Earth Magnetic Materials and Articles Containing the Same", U.S. International Trade Commission ("ITC") Case No. 337-TA-413.

*Markman v. Westview Instruments, Inc.*, 517 US 360 (1996).

*McKesson Technologies, Inc. v. Epic Systems Corp.*: See *Akamai Technologies, Inc. v. Limelight Networks, Inc.*, above.

*Netscape Communications Corp. v. ValueClick, Inc.*, 684 F.Supp.2d 678 (E.D.Va., October 22, 2009) (The "first Netscape opinion").

*Netscape Communications Corp. v. ValueClick, Inc.*, 684 F.Supp.2d 699 (E.D.Va., January 29, 2010) (The "second Netscape opinion").

*Netscape Communications Corp. v. ValueClick, Inc.*, 704 F.Supp.2d 554 (E.D.Va., April 2, 2010) (The "third Netscape opinion").

*Netscape Communications Corp. v. ValueClick, Inc.*, 707 F.Supp.2d 640 (E.D.Va., April 15, 2010) (The "fourth Netscape opinion").

*TiVo, Inc. v. EchoStar Communications Corporation*, 446 F.Supp.2d 664 (E.D.Tx. 2006), *affirmed in part, reversed in part, and remanded* in TiVo Federal Circuit I, 516 F.3d 1290 (Fed. Cir. 2008) (TiVo "District Court I").

*TiVo, Inc. v. EchoStar Communications Corporation*, 516 F.3d 1290 (Fed. Cir., 2008), *cert.denied,* 129 S.Ct. 306 (2008) (TiVo "Federal Circuit I").

*TiVo, Inc. v. Dish Network Corporation*, 640 F.Supp.2d 853 (E.D.Tx. 2009), *affirmed* in TiVo Federal Circuit II, 597 F.3d 1247 (Fed. Cir. 2010), *affirmed in part, vacated in part, and remanded* in TiVo "Federal Circuit III", 646 F.3d 869 (Fed.Cir. 2011)(en banc) (TiVo "District Court III").

*TiVo, Inc. v. Dish Network Corporation*, 655 F.Supp.2d 661 (E.D.Tx. 2009) (TiVo "District Court III").

*TiVo, Inc. v. EchoStar Communications Corporation*, 597 F.3d 1247 (Fed.Cir. 2010) (TiVo "Federal Circuit II").

*TiVo, Inc. v. EchoStar Communications Corporation*, 646 F.3d 869 (Fed. Cir. 2011) (en banc) (TiVo "Federal Circuit III").

*Trend Micro, Incorporated v. Fortinet, Inc.*, "In the Matter of Certain Systems for Detecting and Removing Viruses or Worms, Components Thereof, and Products Containing Same", U.S. International Trade Commission ("ITC") Case No. 337-TA-510.

Trend Micro: United States Patent and Trademark Office, *Ex Parte* Reexamination of US 5,623,600, Decision of the Board of Patent Appeals and Interferences ("BOPAI").

Trend Micro: United States Patent and Trademark Office, *Ex Parte* Reexamination of US 5,623,600, Examiner's Answer.

Trend Micro: United States Patent and Trademark Office, *Ex Parte* Reexamination of US 5,623,600, Final Initial and Recommended Decisions of Administrative Law Judge Paul J. Luckern.

Trend Micro: United States Patent and Trademark Office, Fortinet's Request for Reexamination of US 5,623,600 Under 35 USC Sections 302–307, *Ex Parte* Reexamination of US 5,623,600.

*Uniloc USA, Inc., and Uniloc Singapore Private Limited v. Microsoft Corporation*, 632 F.3rd 1292 (Fed. Cir., 2011).

United States Patent and Trademark Office, "AVERAGE MONTHLY ALLOWANCE RATE — PPH RATE VS USPTO OVERALL RATE", 2011, available at http://www.uspto.gov/about/stratplan/ar/2011/vl_mda02_03_fig6.html.

United States Patent and Trademark Office, "Ex Parte Reexamination Filing Data – September 30, 2012", available at http://www.uspto.gov/patents/stats/ex_parte_historical_stats_roll_up_EOY2012.pdf.

United States Patent and Trademark Office, "Inter Partes Reexamination Filing Data – September 30, 2012", available at http://www.uspto.gov/patents/stats/inter_parte_historical_stats_roll_up_EOY2012.pdf

*Vizio, Inc. v. International Trade Commission*, 604 F.3d 1330 (Fed. Cir. 2010).

*VMWare, Inc. v. Connectix Corporation and Microsoft Corporation*, Nos. C 02-3705 CW, C 03-0654 (N.D.Ca. 2005), cited in Kahrl, Robert C., and Soffer, Stuart B., *Thesaurus of Claim Construction*, (Oxford University Press, New York, 2011).

## *PATENTS:*

Des. 345,750, "Single use camera", original assignee is Fuji Photo Film Co. of Japan.

Des. 356,101, "Single use camera", original assignee is Fuji Photo Film Co. of Japan.

Des. 372,722, "Camera", original assignee is Fuji Photo Film Co. of Japan.

RE 34,168, "Lens-fitted photographic film package", original assignee is Fuji Photo Film Co., Ltd., of Japan.

US 4,496,395, "High coercivity rare earth-iron magnets", original assignee is General Motors Corporation".

US 4,833,495, "Lens-fitted photographic film package", original assignee is Fuji Photo Film Co., Ltd., of Japan.

US 4,855,774, "Lens-fitted photographic film package", original assignee is Fuji Photo Film Co., Ltd., of Japan.

US 4,884,087, "Photographic film package and method of making the same", original assignee is Fuji Photo Film Co., Ltd., of Japan.

US 4,901,307, "Spread spectrum multiple access communication system using satellite or terrestrial repeaters", original assignee is Qualcomm, Inc.

US 4,954,857, "Photographic film package and method of making the same", original assignee is Fuji Photo Film Co., Ltd., of Japan.

US 4,972,649, "Photographic film package and method of making the same", original assignee is Fuji Photo Film Co., Ltd., of Japan.

US 5,056,109, "Method and apparatus for controlling transmission power in a CDMA cellular mobile telephone system", original assignee is Qualcomm, Inc.

US 5,063,400, "Lens-fitted photographic film package", original assignee is Fuji Photo Film Co., Ltd., of Japan.

US 5,101,501, "Method and system for providing a soft handoff in communications in a CDMA cellular telephone system", original assignee is Qualcomm, Incorporated.

US 5,103,459, "System and method for generating signal waveforms in a CDMA cellular telephone system", original assignee is Qualcomm, Incorporated.

US 5,106,236, "Audible alarm device for divers and others", no original assignee listed, inventors are David A. Hancock and Barry A. Kornett.

US 5,109,390, "Diversity receiver in a CDMA cellular telephone system", original assignee is Qualcomm, Incorporated.

US 5,133,079, "Method and apparatus for distribution of movies", no original assignee, inventors are Douglas J. Ballantyne and Michael Mulhall.

US 5,235,364, "Lens-fitted photographic film package with flash unit", original assignee is Fuji Photo Film Co., Ltd., of Japan.

US 5,265,119, "Method and apparatus for controlling transmission power in a CDMA cellular mobile telephone system", original assignee is Qualcomm, Incorporated.

US 5,267,261, "Mobile station assisted soft handoff in a CDMA cellular communications system", original assignee is Qualcomm, Incorporated.

US 5,267,262, "Transmitter power control system", original assignee is Qualcomm, Incorporated.

US 5,280,472, "CDMA microcellular telephone system and distributed antenna system therefore", original assignee is Qualcomm, Incorporated.

US 5,361,111, "Lens-fitted photographic film unit with means preventing unintended actuation of pushbuttons", original assignee is Fuji Photo Film Co., Ltd., of Japan.

US 5,381,200, "Lens-fitted photographic film unit", original assigned is Fuji Photo Film Co., Ltd., of Japan.

US 5,408,288, "Photographic film cassette and lens-fitted photographic film unit using the same", original assigned is Fuji Photo Film Co., Ltd., of Japan.

US 5,414,796, "Variable rate vocoder", original assignee is Qualcomm, Incorporated.

US 5,436,685, "Lens-fitted photographic film unit whose parts can be recycled easily", original assignee is Fuji Photo Film Co., Ltd., of Japan.

US 5,490,216, "System for software registration", original assignee is Uniloc Private Limited (Singapore).

US 5,606,539, "Method and apparatus for encoding and decoding an audio and/or video signal, and a record carrier for use with such apparatus", original assignee is U.S. Philips Corporation.

US 5,606,609, "Electronic document verification system and method", original assignee is Scientific Atlanta, subsequently acquired by Smiths Industries Aerospace & Defense Systems, Inc.,, subsequently acquired by Silanis Technology, Inc. (Montreal, Canada).

US 5,606,668, "System for securing inbound and outbound data packet flow in a computer network", original assignee is Check Point Software Technologies, Ltd.

US 5,623,600, "Virus detection and removal apparatus for computer networks", original assignee is Trend Micro, Incorporated.

US 5,657,317, "Hierarchical communication system using premises, peripheral and vehicular local area networking, original assignee is Norand Corporation, subsequently acquired by Broadcom Corporation.

US 5,682,379, "Wireless personal local area network", original assignee is Norand Corporation, subsequently acquired by Broadcom Corporation.

US 5,761,477, "Methods for safe and efficient implementations of virtual machines", original assignee is Microsoft Corporation, cited in Kahrl, Robert C., and Soffer, Stuart B., *Thesaurus of Claim Construction*, (Oxford University Press, New York, 2011).

US 5,774,670, "Persistent client state in a hypertext transfer protocol based client-server system", original assignee is Netscape Communications Corporation, subsequently acquired by AOL, Inc., subsequently acquired by Microsoft Corporation.

US 5,787,449, "Method and system for manipulating the architecture and the content of a document separately from each other", original assignee is Infrastructures for Information, Inc. ("i4i", Toronto, Canada).

US 5,835,726, "System for securing the flow of and selectively modifying packets in a computer network", original assignee is Check Point Software Technologies, Ltd.

US 5,987,610, "Computer virus screening methods and systems", original assignee is Ameritech Corporation, subsequently acquired by Intellectual Ventures.

US 5,987,611, "System and methodology for managing internet access on a per application basis for client computers connected to the internet", original assignee is Zone Labs, Inc., subsequently acquired by Check Point Software Technologies, Ltd.

US 6,115,074, "System for forming and processing program map information suitable for terrestrial, cable or satellite broadcast", inventors are Ozkan, Mehmet; Teng, Chia-Yuan; and Heredia, Edwin Arturo; assigned first to Thomson Consumer Electronics, Inc., subsequently acquired by Funai Electric Co., Ltd., of Japan.

US 6,201,839, "Method and apparatus for correlation-sensitive adaptive sequence detection", original assignee is Carnegie Mellon University.

US 6,233,389, "Multimedia time warping system", original assignee is TiVo, Inc.

US 6,359,872, "Wireless personal local area network", original assignee is Intermec IP Corporation, subsequently acquired by Broadcom Corporation.

US 6,374,311, "Communication network having a plurality of bridging nodes which transmit a beacon to terminal nodes in power saving state that it has messages awaiting delivery", original assignee is Intermec IP Corporation, subsequently acquired by Broadcom Corporation.

US 6,389,010, "Hierarchical data collection network supporting packetized voice communications among wireless terminals and telephones", original assignee is Intermec IP Corporation, subsequently acquired by Broadcom Corporation.

US 6,430,398, "Method for improving performance of a mobile radiocommunication system using power control", original assignee is Alcatel (Paris, France), subsequently acquired by Sharp Corporation (Osaka, Japan), but the assignment from Alcatel to Sharp is not recorded in U.S. PTO Patent Assignment Database.

US 6,438,180, "Soft and hard sequence detection in ISI memory channels", original assignee is Carnegie Mellon University.

US 6,487,200, "Packet telephone system", original assignee is AT&T Corporation.

US 6,549,785, "Method for improving performances of a mobile radiocommunication system using a power control algorithm", original assignee is Alcatel (Paris, France), subsequently acquired by Sharp Corporation (Osaka, Japan), but the assignment from Alcatel to Sharp is not recorded in U.S. PTO Patent Assignment Database.

US 6,583,675, "Apparatus and method for phase lock loop gain control using unit current sources", original assignee is Broadcom Corporation.

US 6,714,983, "Modular, portable data processing terminal for use in a communication network", original assignee is Broadcom Corporation.

US 6,847,686, "Video encoding device", original assignee is Broadcom Corporation.

US 6,885,875, "Method and radio communication system for regulating power between a base station and a subscriber station", original assignee is Siemens Aktiengesellschaft (Munich, Germany).

US 7,536,312, "Method of appraising and insuring intellectual property", original assignee is Ocean Tomo, LLC.

## *WEB SITES:*

Avvika AB. This is a Swedish IPR consulting firm. *www.avvika.com*, and in particular *www.avvika.com/patentengineering4.html*, which discusses differences between what are called "Discrete Technologies" and "Complex Technologies".

Check Point Software Technologies, Ltd.
Annual Report for 2012 (Form 20-F) *http://www.checkpoint.com/corporate/investor-relations/index.html.*
Comparative financial information
*http://www.checkpoint.com/corporate/investor-relations/earnings-history/index.html.*

Freepatentsonline. Databases of the following:
(1) U.S. patents,
(2) Published U.S. patent applications,
(3) European patents and patent applications,
(4) Abstracts of Japanese patents,
(5) International patent applications filed with the World Intellectual Property Organization ("WIPO") under the Patent Cooperation Treaty ("PCT"),
(6) German patents, and
(7) some non-patent literature
*www.freepatentonline.com.*

Ocean Tomo. An intellectual capital merchant bank:
*http://www.oceantomo.com/.*
In particular, the chart comparing tangible and intangible assets is at *http://www.oceantomo.com/productsandservices/investments/intangible-market-value.*

Patentbuddy. Web site with patent citation statistics, including forward and reverse citations, self-citations and non-self citations, with detailed citation listings by year, and with comparisons

to other patents of the same filing year and same general subject:
*www.patentbuddy.com.*

PricewaterhouseCoopers. A world-wide accounting and business consulting firm. Publishes an annual review of patent litigation in the United States.
*www.pwc.com.*
For the 2012 patent litigation study:
*http://www.pwc.com/en_US/us/forensic-services/publications/assets/2012-patent-litigation-study.pdf.*

Qualcomm, Inc.
Annual financial statements:
*http://investor.qualcomm.com/annuals.cfm.*

TruePatentValue. The name of the Web site associated with this book, and with its author.
www.truepatentvalue.com

United States Patent and Trademark Office. Official Web site for both U.S. patents and published U.S. patent applications, including search capabilities, prosecution histories of many patents and applications, a Patent Assignment Database, fee schedules, a status of maintenance fees paid, and much more information:
*www.uspto.gov.*

## *NOTES TO BIBLIOGRAPHY:*

(1) All references to Web pages were last viewed, and were available, at May 22, 2013. These pages may have been changed or removed since that view date.

(2) For patents where no assignee is listed on the face of the patent, I have listed instead the named inventors.

(3) Some patents include an original assignee, and also one or more subsequent owners. I have included the subsequent owners for these patents because they were relevant to the cases and discussion in the text. However, I have made no effort to recite the full chain of title for any patent. Further, the absence of subsequent owners for most of the patents does *not* mean that these patents were not subsequently acquired from the original assignees — I have not checked the chain of legal title for all of the patents mentioned in this book, and as to these patents, no statement of ownership is made or implied.

# Index of Charts and Tables

# Index of Authorities



**BOOKS and POEMS**

**CASES (Judicial and ITC)**

**CONVENTIONS and STATUTES**

## REPORTS OF THE U.S. PATENT & TRADEMARK OFFICE



## U.S. PATENTS (by owner)

## WEB SITES

# Index of Names and Subjects

## A

## B

## C

## D

## E

## F

## G



## H

## I

## Q

## R



## S

# About the Author

Larry M. Goldstein is a U.S. patent attorney specializing in Information & Communication Technologies. He evaluates patent quality, manages patent portfolios, and creates patent harvesting programs for high-tech companies. He helped establish the patent pool for 3G W-CDMA technology, specifically in creating the methodology for determining the essentiality of patents to the W-CDMA technical standard, preparing licensing agreements to implement FRAND terms & conditions, and obtaining the approval of the Antitrust Division of the United States Department of Justice. He is a co-author of the book *Technology Patent Licensing: An International Reference on 21st Century Patent Licensing, Patent Pools and Patent Platforms*. Mr. Goldstein holds a B.A. from Harvard College, an MBA from the Kellogg School of Management at Northwestern University, and a J.D. from the University of Chicago Law School. His web site is www.truepatentvalue.com.

Made in the USA
Lexington, KY
26 September 2015